University of London Historical Studies

XXXIV

FRANCESCO VETTORI

This volume is published with the help of grants from the late Miss Isobel Thornley's Bequest to the University of London and from the Twenty-Seven Foundation

FRANCESCO VETTORI

Florentine Citizen and Medici Servant

by

ROSEMARY DEVONSHIRE JONES

UNIVERSITY OF LONDON
THE ATHLONE PRESS
1972

Published by
THE ATHLONE PRESS
UNIVERSITY OF LONDON
at 4 Gower Street London WC 1

*Distributed by Tiptree Book Services Ltd
Tiptree, Essex*

*USA and Canada
Humanities Press Inc
New York*

ISBN 0 485 13134 X

Printed in Great Britain by
WESTERN PRINTING SERVICES LTD
Bristol

To Susi

PREFACE

THE PRESENT WORK is based on a study of Francesco Vettori submitted as a thesis for the degree of Doctor of Philosophy in the University of London in 1958. An additional chapter on Vettori as historian has had to be excluded for reasons of length.

During the long period over which my researches have extended, I have incurred many debts of gratitude. I am grateful to Westfield College, London University, for a two-year Postgraduate Studentship, to the Institute of Historical Research for a grant which enabled me to work in the Florentine archives and to procure microfilms, and to the Italian Institute, London, for a *borsa di studio*.

Throughout my researches I have received constant help and kindness from a number of Italian archivists and librarians, but to the staff of the Archivio di Stato and the Biblioteca Nazionale, Florence, I owe a special debt of gratitude for their unfailingly generous assistance during my innumerable visits. In particular I should like to thank the Director of the Archives, Dr Guido Pampaloni, for his friendly encouragement and interest, Dr Gino Corti for his assistance in transcriptions, and Commendatore Roberto Abbondanza, now Director of the Archives in Perugia, who gave me such valuable help in my early years in Florence. My thanks go also to Dottoressa Eugenia Levi, for her kindness in the Sala dei Manoscritti of the Biblioteca Nazionale. I would express my gratitude similarly to the Director of the Archivio di Stato, Rome, Dr Marcello Del Piazzo.

At home, the staff of the British Museum Students' and Reading rooms have shown me constant courtesy, as also the staff of the London Library, St James's Square.

Fellow scholars have been extremely generous in giving me their time, encouragement and suggestions. My thesis supervisor and friend, Professor Nicolai Rubinstein, whose constructive criticism and unfailing encouragement have guided my work at every one of many laborious stages, has my deepest gratitude. Thanks are due also to Professor A. G. Dickens for his kind support and for reading my manuscript in its penulti-mate draft. Mrs Rosalyn Pesman (née Cooper) has most generously allowed me to make use of material from her thesis on Piero Soderini and Dr Gino Corti, Mr Edward Sanchez, Mr William Kent and Mr Humphrey Butters have all drawn my attention to source material, which I have acknowledged in the relevant footnotes.

To my husband who devoted many hours of convalescence to reading and commenting on my manuscript I owe a loving debt. But for Miss Swoboda's skilled and patient criticism, this book would be a still less fitting tribute to a long friendship.

R.D.J.

CONTENTS

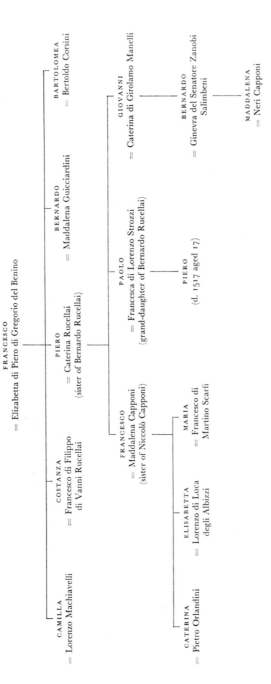

FRANCESCO VETTORI's family, showing marriage connections

CHAPTER I

The Vettori Family

FRANCESCO VETTORI was born in Florence in 1474; he died there in 1539.[1] Hence his eyes opened on what he and his contemporaries subsequently came to admire as the civic government of Lorenzo de' Medici the Magnificent,[2] and they closed on what many Florentines could only deplore as the loss of civic freedom under the city's second Medici duke, Cosimo I. In the wider context of Europe, from the French invasion twenty years after Francesco's birth until the peace of Cateau-Cambrésis twenty years after his death, Italy and his native city were sucked seemingly helpless into the vortex of Franco-Imperial diplomacy.

The Vettori were Florentine upper-class citizens, optimates (*ottimati*), and Francesco was thus one of those *uomini da bene* whose corporate wisdom and merits, in the opinion of the historian Francesco Guicciardini, made them most eligible for political and diplomatic office.[3] The humanist Ugolino Verino gives the family's place of origin as the district of Gangalandi in the Val d'Arno and points out that their name derived from early military victories,[4] a fact not lost on the wit of the Magnificent who used to say that victory would always be where Piero, Francesco's father, fought.[5] Antonio Benivieni, the sixteenth-century biographer of Piero, claims that the family belonged to 'that good merchant class' which began to establish

---

[1] Opera di Duomo Archivio, Florence, Libri di battesimo, maschi e femmine 1472–9.

[2] For the early 16th-century attitude to the rule of Lorenzo de' Medici, see F. Gilbert, 'Bernardo Rucellai and the Orti Oricellari' in *J.W.C.I.*, xii (1949), pp. 120–2.

[3] F. Guicciardini, *Dialogo del Reggimento di Firenze*, ed. R. Palmarocchi (Bari, 1932), p. 20.

[4] *De Illustratione Urbis Florentiae* (Paris, 1790), Lib. III, pp. 8, 9.

[5] 'Vita di Piero Vettori', B.N.F. Ms. Landau Finaly, 74, fo. 3r.

a position in about 1282.[6] Ugolino Verino couples them with the Capponi. In fact there was no blood relationship between the two families but they had become associates (*consorti*) for purposes of trade and mutual defence. In 1452 this association was virtually terminated. By then it must have proved a disadvantage owing to the proscription (*divieto*) limiting the number of families holding office at the same time.[7] Trade[8] and marriage connections continued, however. Francesco Vettori was to marry Maddalena, sister of Florence's noted gonfalonier, Niccolò Capponi.[9] The arms of the two families remained very similar, that of the Vettori being distinguished only by the three *fleurs-de-lis* added to the bend of the Capponi crest.

Marriage and trade linked the Vettori also with the Rucellai. Francesco's father married Caterina, a sister of Bernardo di Giovanni Rucellai, and his aunt Costanza on his father's side was the wife of Francesco di Filippo di Vanni Rucellai.[10] Piero Vettori and Francesco di Filippo's brother, Girolamo, had been business partners until the Pazzi war caused their firm to go into liquidation.[11] Piero Vettori's second son, Paolo, was to have a daughter of Bernardo Rucellai as his mother-in-law.[12]

Paolo's marriage connected him also to the Strozzi family, for he took to wife Francesca, daughter of Filippo Strozzi's brother Lorenzo.[13] The Strozzi connection was to be of importance in Francesco Vettori's career.

The Vettori had a house in the quarter of S. Spirito (Gonfalone Nicchio)[14] near the Ponte Trinita on the bank popular, it would appear, with sixteenth-century historians since Niccolò Machiavelli, Francesco Guicciardini, Bernardo Segni and

---

[6] A. Benivieni, *Vita di Piero Vettori, l'antico, gentil'huomo fiorentino* (Florence, 1583), p. 4.

[7] Balie, 27, fos. 25v–26v: 'Familiarum de Capponibus et Vettoris divisio'; cp. Tratte 1075, fo. 15v: 'Casati che si danno divieto' where Vettori and Capponi are thus listed, 'solo hanno divieto a sedere insieme a 3 maggiori ufici'. I am grateful to Mr William Kent for drawing my attention to this late 15th-century chancery compilation.

[8] Below, p. 4.

[9] P. Litta, *Famiglie Celebri Italiane*, vii (Milan, 1844), Vettori.

[10] *Ibid.*; Decima Republicana, 4, 1498, S. Spirito (Nicchio) I–Z, fo. 268r; L. Passerini, *Genealogia e Storia della Famiglia Rucellai* (Florence, 1861), plate vii.

[11] Catasto, S. Spirito (Nicchio), 1480, part II, No. 995, fo. 187r.

[12] L. Passerini, *Genealogia*, plate xvi.

[13] P. Litta, vii; below, p. 148.   [14] Catasto, *loc. cit.*, fo. 185r.

Filippo Nerli all owned property on this side of the Arno. The family also owned farms and villas in the communes of Cepparello and Barberino in the Val d'Elsa; between Poggibonsi and Castellina in Chianti, and in San Casciano in the Val di Pesa.[15] As the Machiavelli possessed a villa at S. Andrea in Percussina, near San Casciano, and a house in the quarter of S. Spirito,[16] the connection between Francesco Vettori and Niccolò Machiavelli could have been established in quite early years. A property of Niccolò's cousin, Filippo, adjoined the Vettori's in the commune of Cepparello.[17] In any case the famous letter of 10 December 1513, addressed to Vettori, in which Machiavelli described his life at S. Andrea in Percussina was written to a friend well familiar with that part of the country.[18] In 1481 Vettori's father retired from Florence for a while to live on his estates and repair the ravages of the Pazzi war which had caused him the loss of all his olive trees and live-stock.[19] In the previous year he had made an entry in the *catasto* (tax account) claiming that his possessions between Poggibonsi and Castellina in Chianti were 'all ruined'.[20]

The family fortunes were founded on the wool and cloth trades. Apart from those members registered in the wool guild,[21] thirty-seven were registered in the cloth guild between 1409 and 1526.[22] Like their father, Francesco,[23] Paolo and Giovanni were members of it and all three followed in his foot-steps in holding the office of Consul.[24] Once again the Pazzi war was disastrous; in the tax return of 1480 Piero states that

[15] *Ibid.*; Decima Republicana, *loc cit.*, fos. 267r–8r.

[16] P. Villari, *The Life and Times of Niccolò Machiavelli*, trans. L. Villari (London, s.d.), p. 219.

[17] Catasto, *loc. cit.*, fo. 185r; Decima Republicana, *loc. cit.*, fo. 267r.

[18] N. Machiavelli, *Lettere*, ed. F. Gaeta (Milan, 1961), pp. 302–4.

[19] 'Vita di Piero Vettori', fo. 2r.

[20] Catasto, *loc. cit.*, fo. 187r.

[21] Matricula of the Arte della Lana, vol. 20, fo. 1r; vol. 21, fos. 1r, 5v, 6r–v, 29v, 30v, 35v; vol. 22, fos. 4r, 10r, 18r, 19v.

[22] Mercanti di Calimala, 13, fo. 18v; G. Filippi, *L'Arte dei Mercanti di Calimala in Firenze* (Torino, 1889), p. 193.

[23] B.R.F., Ms. Riccardiana, 3239, fo. 304v.

[24] *Ibid.*, fo. 318r, 3 March 1500 for Paolo and Giovanni; Francesco's name does not occur in this register of which, however, the years 1483–1500 when he might have been registered are missing; but, see A.S.F., Mercanti di Calimara, 13, fo. 18v for names of all three brothers and a 'v' beside the names = 'sarà et è veduto al consolato'. Paolo's son, Piero and Giovanni's son, Bernardo are also listed.

the family warehouse in Via Maggio had to be closed down.[25]
Piero tried to recoup the family's losses by mining alum, a
mineral important in the processing of cloth, but with little
success.[26]

Part of the cloth trade was the production of fine brocade for
which the goldsmiths produced the metal thread.[27] No doubt
the Vettori goldsmith business situated in the Borgo SS.
Apostoli attended to this side of the trade.[28] An undated note of
Lorenzo Strozzi to the money changers' guild reveals that
Paolo Vettori had his own goldsmith's company.[29]

The goldsmiths were subordinate to the silk guild,[30] and
Paolo Vettori served an apprenticeship of two years from
December 1492 to November 1494 in Niccolò Capponi's company of silk merchants.[31] In November 1501 he matriculated in
the silk guild on his own account. Against this background of
the Vettori family's connection with the wool and silk guilds,
Machiavelli's regretful admission to Francesco that he was
unable to discuss the guilds but only affairs of state acquires a
personal note hitherto overlooked.[32]

In addition to their involvement in Florence's wool and cloth
business, Francesco's two brothers seem also to have operated a
furnace in which they smelted iron and probably also steel.[33] At
this period Italy's deposits of iron—confined to the island of
Elba off the coast of Tuscany—belonged to the lords of Piombino who sold the output of their mines to a group of merchants
forming 'a territorial cartel' known as the *Magona del Ferro*.[34]
The ore which each member of this group recovered from the
particular area of Elba allocated to him was resold to local

[25] Catasto, *loc. cit.*, fo. 187r.

[26] 'Vita di Piero Vettori', fo. 2v.

[27] G. Richards, *Florentine Merchants in the Age of the Medici* (Cambridge, Mass., 1932), p. 168, n. 3.

[28] N. Machiavelli, *Lettere*, ed. F. Gaeta, p. 327.

[29] M.A.P., 97, fo. 69r: 'una promessa a Paolo di Piero Vettori e Compagnia battiloro . . .'.

[30] G. Richards, p. 168, n. 3.

[31] Arte della Seta, 10 (Matricole, 1474–1512), fo. 130v.

[32] N. Machiavelli, *Lettere*, ed. F. Gaeta, p. 239.

[33] C. Strozz., Ser. I, 136, fo. 229r, F.V. to Paolo, Rome, 16 June 1513: 'Harei charo intendere che'l forno facessi buon ferro . . . se facessi acciaio sarebbe dav-antaggio, ma scrivimi se fa ferro.'

[34] R. de Roover, *The Rise and Decline of the Medici Bank* (1966), p. 165.

ironmasters who operated furnaces on the wooded slopes of the Apennines, since Elba itself has no fuel for the smelting of iron. A letter in which Paolo Vettori complains of the cutting down of some of the trees used in the operation of his factories indicates that it was in just such a wooded area at Buti, near Vicopisano, that he was working his furnace.[35] Here he and Giovanni appear to have produced arms[36] and ammunition;[37] also iron for the port of Palo near Rome.[38] Some of the arms being manufactured in 1513 were evidently destined for England,[39] probably for use in Henry VIII's war against France.

Francesco's father was an able soldier and governor under the Medici regime and during the Republic. He held office as military governor (*capitano*), as a rector (*podestà*) governing Florentine subject cities and territories, and as a commissary (*commissario*) conducting military operations or restoring order in rebellious towns. He was for about a year Florence's ambassador to Ferdinand, king of Naples.[40] At the time of Lorenzo the Magnificent's death (1492) he was sent to secure the Romagna in case the king of France should invade Italy,[41] and when Charles VIII crossed the Alps two years later and Lorenzo's successor, Piero de' Medici, was expelled from Florence, Piero Vettori became a member of the foreign committee, the Ten (*Dieci*), in the new republican regime.[42] He also served it as commissary in the rebel city of Pisa. In 1496 he died in office as *capitano* of Pistoia from a fever induced, according to

[35] B.N.F., Ginori Conti, 29, 68, Paolo Vettori to Niccolò Michelozzi, 7 July 1513, a Pontedera: 'Io venni iermattina qui a Buti per rivedere un pocho le fabriche et trovai che certe quantità di boschaglie . . . m'erono sute messe assecho et in gran parte tagliate chon danno grandissimo di queste opere delle fabriche . . .'; cp. O. Tommasini, *La vita e gli scritti di Niccolò Machiavelli*, ii (Rome, 1911), p. 1068.

[36] C. Strozz., Ser. I, 136, fo. 228r, F.V. to Paolo, Rome, 16 May 1513: 'L'arme di Giovanni doverrebbono essere pur giunte in Inghilterra . . .'.

[37] Otto, Delib., 6, fos. 43r, 53r: 'Giovan Vectori cittadino fiorentino il quale è obligato consegnare al magistrato loro numero di palle di ferro da artigliere . . .'.

[38] B.M. Add. Ms. 10279, fo. 22r, P. Ardinghelli to Paolo Vettori in Pisa, Rome, 3 Mar. 1521: '. . . circa al ferro per Palo Sua Santità ha hauto piacere intendere che lo mandiate . . .'.

[39] See note 36.

[40] 'Vita di Piero Vettori', *passim* and fo. 3r: '. . . fu mandato imbasciadore a Napoli nell'anno 1488 dove stette circa a uno anno . . .'.

[41] *Ibid.*, fo. 3r–v.

[42] F. Guicciardini, *Storie Fiorentine*, ed. R. Palmarocchi (Bari, 1931), p. 107. For foreign affairs committees, v. below, p. 12, n. 20.

his son, by the information that the castellan of Pisa had handed over the fortress to its rebel citizens.[43]

In his eldest son's estimation, Piero Vettori succeeded not only in active life but in the world of letters. Francesco relates that his father devoted himself to study in his early years, reaching a high standard in Latin, and would have excelled in Greek but for his business and family commitments. Even in his later years he wrote Latin verse and apparently attained considerable skill in Italian verse and in that favourite renaissance pastime of devising mottoes. Francesco's own history of his times may well have been stimulated by his father's uncompleted attempt.[44]

Francesco's biography of his father gives the impression of a sober and temperate household under a man who loved his wife and children, was just in his dealings with subordinates and generous to those in need. Continent, abstemious in food and drink, not given to anger, a peacemaker and a Christian whose religion was devoid of superstition and almost free of outward observance, Piero Vettori must, if we are to believe his son's portrayal,[45] have been in ascetic contrast to many of his contemporaries, but close in spirit to the followers of Savonarola (the *piagnoni*), an example of the moral climate preceding the reformation. Francesco's portrayal of his father's attitude to religion is indicative of his own practical piety, rejection of scholasticism, and interest in Erasmus.[46]

Of the education which Piero gave his sons we are told tantalizingly little. Francesco's biography merely mentions that his father took pains to have them learn 'good letters and good manners'.[47] Other sources indicate that Francesco studied together with Niccolò Capponi,[48] the son of his father's close

---

[43] 'Vita di Piero Vettori', fo. 3v.

[44] *Ibid.*, fo. 4r: 'Scrisse . . . una historia de tempi sua la quale lasciò imperfecta.'

[45] 'Vita di Piero Vettori', fo. 4v: 'Religioso era quanto bixogna ma non superstitioso, facendo una volta l'anno quello chomanda la chiesa et chosi udendo la messa e dì festivi e stimava che'l fare elemosine a chi ha bixogno e sobvenire l'uno huomo al'altro fussi quello dovessi fare un Christiano.'

[46] F. Vettori, *Viaggio in Alemagna* (Paris-Florence, 1837), p. 55 (cited in future as *Viaggio*); cp. below, p. 8, n. 57, and p. 209.

[47] 'Vita di Piero Vettori', fo. 4r: 'ingegnandosi imparassino buone lettere e buoni chostumi . . .'.

[48] B.R.F. Ms. Riccardiana, 1882, Alessandro Segni, 'Memorie della famiglia Segni' (17th cent.), fo. 110v.

friend Piero,[49] and with Lorenzo Segni, the father of the historian Bernardo, in the house of Lorenzo's parents. One of the 'excellent masters' employed by Lorenzo's father for a large salary was most likely the priest ser Paolo Sasso da Ronciglione, whom Bernardo Machiavelli records as the tutor of his sons Niccolò and Toto.[50] Ser Paolo is described by Niccolò Machiavelli's father as a grammarian. He taught the clerics of S. Maria del Fiore, and numbered also among his pupils Piero del Riccio, better known by his Latinized name of Pietro Crinito, and Michele Verino, the son of Ugo from whose *De Illustratione Urbis Florentiae* we derive our knowledge of the origins of the Vettori. A book of model letters dated 1486 belonging to Piero del Riccio and containing a letter exemplar supposedly written by Francesco Vettori to Niccolò Capponi is extant and we know that Piero was then still under the tuition of ser Paolo.[51] Thus already at the age of twelve Vettori was associating with some of the Florentines who would later meet for philosophical and political discussion in the gardens of Bernardo Rucellai.[52]

Certainly Francesco's later thought and writing betray the humanist education of the period. Like his father he enjoyed reading history and shared with Machiavelli a taste for Roman history. He read Livy, Sallust, Tacitus, Ammianus Marcellinus, Suetonius and Aelius Lampridius, but was also acquainted with the Greek writers Appian, Plutarch, Herodian and Procopius.[53] Vettori's reading was in line with current humanist interests. The first six books of Tacitus' *Annals*, for example, were brought to Rome in the first decade of the sixteenth century and were published under Leo X's patronage in 1515,[54] the year

---

[49] 'Vita de Piero Vettori', fo. 3v: 'Piero Chapponi e Chosimo Rucellai e' quali lui amava grandemente . . .'; cp. fo. 4r.

[50] F. Gilbert, *Machiavelli and Guicciardini* (Princeton, 1965), p. 321.

[51] B.R.F. Ms. Riccardiana, 2621, fo. 1r: 'Hic liber est mei petri bartolomei de Riccis anno 1486'; M. E. Cosenza, *Biographical and Bibliographical Dictionary of the Italian Humanists and of the World of Classical Scholarship in Italy, 1300–1800* (Boston, 1962), vol. 4, p. 3206 says Crinito was ser Paolo's pupil till after 22 May 1487. In Ms. Riccardiana, 2621, fo. 36v under Paulus Roncilionensis is the model letter beginning 'Francesco Vectorio a Nicholo Capponi'. I am indebted to Mr Edward H. Sanchez for drawing my attention to this Ms.

[52] For the members of this group, see F. Gilbert, 'Bernardo Rucellai', etc.

[53] N. Machiavelli, *Lettere*, ed. F. Gaeta, p. 299.

[54] H. Furneaux, ed., *The Annals of Tacitus*, i (Oxford, 1896), pp. 6–7.

Vettori left the papal court. His literary interests were not, however, confined to the ancient writers; they were cosmopolitan and up to date. Pontano's dialogue on fortune which Vettori was reading in 1514 had been printed in Naples only two years before.[55] By 1527 he had seen Sir Thomas More's *Utopia*,[56] and two years later he was wanting to read some of the works of Erasmus or other writings printed in Flanders or Germany.[57] He refers critically to Politian and Crinito.[58] He was even something of a literary patron since the Florentine printer Filippo Giunta dedicated to him his edition of the *Libri de re rustica* edited by Nicolaus Angellus Bucinensis which he published in July 1515,[59] and the humanist and politician, Giovanni Corsi, honoured him with the dedication of a translation of a dialogue by Plutarch.[60]

Besides the brief life of his father, Francesco's own writings consist of the *Viaggio in Alemagna*,[61] an anecdotal account of his diversions in Germany during his embassy to the court of Maximilian, a short life of Lorenzo, duke of Urbino,[62] a dialogue entitled *Il Sacco di Roma*[63] and a history of Italy from 1511 to 1527, the *Sommario della Storia d'Italia dal 1511 al 1527*.[64]

None of Piero's sons distinguished themselves in as many different fields of activity as he did, though each emulated him in at least one. Paolo inherited Piero's audacity and became a noted captain of the papal galleys.[65] He was also active in trade, diplomacy and politics. Giovanni held public office as a com-

---

[55] N. Machiavelli, *Lettere*, ed. F. Gaeta, p. 362.

[56] F. Vettori, 'Sommario della Storia d'Italia dal 1511 al 1527' in *A.S.I.*, Appendice vi (1848), p. 293 (cited in future as *Sommario*).

[57] C. Strozz., Ser. V, 1209, fo. 8or, F.V. to F. Strozzi, Florence, 1 June 1529.

[58] F. Vettori, *Viaggio*, p. 56.

[59] P. O. Kristeller, 'Un uomo di stato e umanista fiorentino, Giovanni Corsi', in *La Bibliofilia*, xxxviii (1936), p. 254.

[60] *Ibid.*, p. 249, below, pp. 59 and 107.

[61] Above, p. 6, n. 46; French trans. L. Passy, *Un ami de Machiavel, François Vettori, sa vie et ses œuvres*, ii (Paris, 1914), pp. 45–218.

[62] Pub. O. Tommasini, *La vita e gli scritti di Niccolò Machiavelli*, ii (Rome, 1911), Appendix VII, pp. 1055–63; for dating, v. below, p. 76, n. 120.

[63] Pub. C. Milanesi, *Il Sacco di Roma del MDXXVII. Narrazioni di Contemporanei* (Florence, 1867), pp. 411–61 (cited in future as *Sacco*).

[64] Above, n. 56.

[65] A. Guglielmotti, *La guerra dei pirati e la marina pontificia*, i (Florence, 1876), pp. 125–67, lib. III, 'Capitano Paolo Vettori, marchese della Gorgona'.

missary and in the city where he was elected several times to supreme office as one of the eight priors,[66] but there are fewer references to him in contemporary writings than to his brothers. Francesco alone inherited his father's literary ambition. Perhaps they also shared a taste for gambling. Francesco mentions that Piero turned a blind eye on gamesters, maintaining that in losing they had their punishment,[67] and he himself refused to condemn princes who gambled provided that they did not succumb to anger, fraud or avarice.[68] Certain traits in Francesco's character, however, do not correspond with the son's picture of his father, notably his delight in amorous adventures[69] and his lack of physical courage.[70] His correspondence also suggests a certain diffidence,[71] disregard for his appearance, and a dislike of court life.[72] This, however, did not debar him from a highly successful career as a diplomat and politician from 1504 to the end of his life.

[66] The most important governing body in Florence was the *Signoria*. This was composed of two priors from each quarter of the city and the gonfalonier. The *Signoria* was advised by two colleges, the *Dodici Buonuomini* and the Sixteen *Gonfalonieri*. A new *Signoria* was elected every two months. For detailed working of the constitution in the 15th century, v. N. Rubinstein, *The Government of Florence under the Medici* (Oxford, 1966). Giovanni was prior three times: Tratte, 94, fo. 10r, 1 Nov. 1514; fo. 12r, 1 Nov. 1526; fo. 12v, 1 Jan. 1532. Twice a member of the *Otto di Guardia*: Tratte, 84, fo. 86r, 1 Sept. 1516; fo. 87v, 1 May 1522. Commissario in Volterra, Aug. 1530, Balie, 51, fo. 3v, 'patente' for Giovanni Vettori; below, p. 228, n. 20.

[67] 'Vita di Piero Vettori', fo. 4v.

[68] *Sommario*, p. 316.

[69] See Vettori's *Viaggio*; his correspondence from Rome with Machiavelli, *Lettere*, ed. F. Gaeta; also, A. Moretti, *Corrispondenza di Niccolò Machiavelli con Francesco Vettori dal 1513 al 1515* (Florence, 1948).

[70] O. Tommasini, ii, Appendix IX, p. 1067; R. von Albertini, *Das Florentinische Staatsbewusstsein im Übergang von der Republik zum Prinzipat* (Bern, 1955), pp. 440, 447.

[71] N. Machiavelli, *Lettere*, ed. F. Gaeta, pp. 234, 344.

[72] *Ibid.*, pp. 245, 270, 300; O. Tommasini, ii, p. 1148, F. Vettori to F. del Nero, 5 Feb. 1523.

CHAPTER II

The Embassy to Maximilian (1507-9)

FOR the greater part of Vettori's career the Medici were in power in Florence. When he was born they had already been the leaders of the city for forty years; when he died they were its supreme masters. But for two brief periods from 1494 to 1512 and from 1527 to 1530 they were in exile. It was during the earlier of these that Francesco was given his first diplomatic assignment— the only one of his three principal missions which took place during a period of republican government. It was also the only one in which he was not an official ambassador. From the latter fact and from the Republic's uncertain situation at home and abroad stemmed most of the mission's difficulties apart from the secrecy of the court, problems of communication and the very great distances to be covered.

Florence's external relations during the Republic were conditioned by the city's diplomatic isolation.[1] An alliance concluded between Piero de' Medici and Charles VIII in 1494 when he invaded Italy and which had led to Piero's expulsion and the establishment of the republican government determined the city's foreign policy for the next eighteen years. One of the conditions of this alliance, which stipulated that the Florentine fortresses of Pisa, Sarzana, Pietrasanta and Livorno, handed over to the French king for the duration of the campaign in Naples, should be returned to the Republic after its conclusion, was violated.[2] The loss of these fortresses and in particular of Pisa bound Florence to France in expectation of military and financial help to recover them. The continued alliance with France prevented the Republic from joining the League between the pope, emperor, Spain, Venice and Milan which drove

[1] For this problem and the assumptions of Florentine foreign policy during the Republic see F. Gilbert, 'Florentine Political Assumptions in the period of Savonarola and Soderini' in J.W.C.I., xx (1957).

[2] F. Guicciardini, St. fior., pp. 95, 105.

Charles VIII back over the Alps,[3] and left her diplomatically isolated. On various occasions during the Republic one of the Italian states or a foreign power would try to win the allegiance of Florence but always there was the problem of the French alliance.[4]

Associated with the fact of isolation was the conviction among the city's advisers on foreign affairs that they had insufficient information about the intentions of the other (and especially the larger) powers at whose mercy Florence felt herself to be for the construction of a positive policy towards them. Consequently the city adopted the dangerous, difficult and negative line either of neutrality or of postponing decisions hoping that in the interval the situation would become clearer.[5]

The difficulty of Florence's foreign policy was further aggravated by the contemporary Italian diplomatic system: it was virtually impossible to establish contact with another power without the risk of offending an existing ally.[6] The official diplomatic agent of the Italian states was the ambassador, known as an *oratore* from the practice of making a formal oration, usually in Latin, in his first audience.[7] Ambassadors were either ceremonial, resident or *ad hoc*. Often several citizens would be appointed to join the resident ambassador to form a ceremonial embassy to congratulate a new ruler or to celebrate the birth of a son or a marriage.[8] Like the *ad hoc* ambassador these citizens were dispatched with a definite task on the completion of which they would return. But of whatever category, the arrival of ambassadors was attended by much ceremony,[9]

---

[3] N. Machiavelli, *Il Principe*, ed. A. Burd (Oxford, 1891), Historical Abstract, p. 96: 'Desiderarono i confederati che tutta Italia fosse unita in una medesima volontà' but Florence ['per aspettare la restituzione delle fortezze'] . . . refused to join.'

[4] Below, p. 13.

[5] For the policy 'godere il beneficio del tempo' referred to by Machiavelli and his contemporaries see A. Burd, *Il Principe*, Ch. 3, p. 192, n. 18.

[6] F. Gilbert, 'Florentine political assumptions', p. 196.

[7] A. von Reumont, *La diplomazia italiana dal secolo xiii al xvi* (Firenze, 1857); M. de Maulde-La-Clavière, *La diplomatie au temps de Machiavel*, i (Paris, 1892), pp. 294 ff.; E. Dupré Theseider, *Niccolò Machiavelli diplomatico* (Como, 1945), p. 92; G. Mattingly, *Renaissance Diplomacy* (London, 1955).

[8] Maulde-La-Clavière, i, pp. 401–28.

[9] See description by the Venetian ambassador, A. Giustinian, of the procession provided to welcome him to Rome in 1502, P. Villari, *Dispacci di Antonio Giustinian*, (Florence, 1876), pp. 11–12.

the object of their visit by much speculation and their dispatch interpreted as an indication of co-operation with the receiving power, the more so as even under the mask of a ceremonial embassy secret diplomatic or political discussions often took place.[10]

Such circumstances furthered the adoption of a variety of diplomatic agents, ranging from the *mandatario*, usually a man of lesser social status than an ambassador with either a limited or full mandate,[11] to a friend at court (*amico*)[12] or merchants[13] who would be merely spies. All of these men could be employed with greater secrecy than an ambassador and with less risk of offence to a susceptible ally. However, as the desired information could, in the main, only be obtained either direct from the ruler,[14] from his officials[15] or from other ambassadors,[16] an unofficial agent was obviously at a disadvantage compared with an official one. Whether to send an ambassador or some other variety of diplomatic agent to a particular power became in consequence a major issue of policy.

The main function of all Italian resident ambassadors and agents was to find out and to report.[17] Requests 'to expound and report what occurs from day to day'[18] and to write daily or frequently occur time and again in diplomatic correspondence. Negotiation usually offered little scope as the powers of an Italian ambassador of the period were generally limited and strictly defined.[19] In Florence he was elected, between 1480 and 1494 of the Medici regime and again after the restoration in 1512, by the Council of Seventy, and during the republican period, 1494–1512, by that of the Eighty.[20] If sent by a prince,

[10] Below, pp. 77ff., 163ff.
[11] It was as *mandatario* that N. Machiavelli was often employed (as on his second legation in 1499).
[12] Maulde-La-Clavière, ii, Ch. xii; E. Dupré Theseider, pp. 160–3.
[13] Below, pp. 31–2. [14] Below, pp. 21–3, 123, 130.
[15] Below, pp. 20, 130.
[16] Vettori records in the *Viaggio* how the ambassadors would meet in the church at Constance to exchange news, *Viaggio*, p. 86; L. Passy, ii (Paris, 1914), p. 107.
[17] E. Dupré Theseider, p. 99; G. Mattingly, ch. xi.
[18] Instruction to Florentine ambassador, G. B. Ridolfi, 1494, *ibid.*, p. 100; cp. instruction to Venetian, A. Giustinian, P. Villari, *Dispacci*, i, p. 6.
[19] Maulde-La-Clavière, ii, p. 151.
[20] The committee for foreign affairs during the Medici period were the Eight (*Otto di Pratica*), during the republican period, the Ten (*Dieci*).

he tended to represent the ruler rather than the state.[21] He took with him his *commissione*, or instructions, and he would carry them out almost to the letter, writing back to the foreign office for orders on any new developments which might occur. Such a *commissione* would contain a detailed exposition of the ceremonial speech to be made in the first audience and point by point instructions for subsequent interviews. An ambassador could not follow any course not indicated in his instructions and he could not use his own initiative unless given permission to do so. In the case of Florence 'La clause de confiance est rare'.[22] Lack of instructions could therefore be used as a tactical means of delaying negotiations.[23] Ambassadors or agents could be dispatched without a *mandato* empowering them to conclude an agreement. They could in fact be sent merely with 'good hopes and good promises' expressly designed to avoid a decision.[24] Given the contemporary conditions of travel, valuable time could be gained while they wrote home for the necessary powers or instructions.

The diplomatic isolation of the Republic and her chosen policy of playing for time would have presented problems even for the ablest of her diplomats; how much more so then for one with little or no experience, chosen as a result of political disagreement and accorded only minor diplomatic status. This was the position of Francesco Vettori.

The embassy to Maximilian with which Vettori was entrusted in July 1507 resulted from one of those occasions during the republican period—most notably also in the winter of 1495/6,[25] in 1502, 1509[26] and 1512[27]—when the city was approached either by other Italian or by external powers antagonistic to France in the hope of winning her allegiance or financial and military support. In February 1502, for example, two ambassadors had arrived in Florence on behalf of the Emperor Maximilian, announced their master's intention of

---

[21] The instructions given to G. B. Ridolfi (see above, p. 12, n. 18) speak not of the state of Milan but of 'la loro illustrissima casa'. They express, too, the representative function of an ambassador.

[22] Maulde-La-Clavière, ii, p. 151.

[23] E. Dupré Theseider, p. 139.

[24] F. Gilbert, 'Florentine political assumptions', pp. 197–8.

[25] *Ibid.*, p. 196.   [26] Below, p. 38.   [27] Below, p. 49.

coming to Italy to be crowned king of the Romans and requested 100 men-at-arms and 40,000 ducats.[28] In view of her
relations with France, the city had 'made general offers, not
binding herself to particulars, nor committing herself to anything'.[29] But though no agreement had been concluded, the
proposals of Maximilian's ambassadors had had an important
political effect: some Florentines had begun to favour a German
alliance and the city had become divided between pro-German
and pro-French sympathizers.[30]

Francesco Vettori's appointment to the German court is the
reflection of just this political division among the citizens. It was
also linked with the opposition to the gonfalonier, Piero
Soderini, whose leadership had allegedly become increasingly
autocratic since the extension of the office five years before from
a two months' to a life appointment.[31] Those who disliked his
domestic policy saw in the new diplomatic situation a chance to
demonstrate their disapproval.

In the summer of 1507 news reached Florence that the
emperor again intended to invade Italy. At Constance an
imperial diet was in session and the estates of the empire were
being asked for financial and military help for the expedition.
It was said that Maximilian's intention was not only to have
himself crowned emperor, but also to restore to the Church those
lands which had been taken from her, to make Italy effectively
part of the empire, and to frustrate the ambition of the king of
France and the designs of his chancellor, Georges d'Amboise,
cardinal of Rouen, on the papacy.[32] In short, a conflict might
ensue between Maximilian and Louis XII in which the states
of Italy would become involved; many of them, of which Venice
and the Papacy were the two most important, had ambassadors
at Constance; it seemed expedient for Florence also to be
represented. Prolonged discussions on the subject showed
opinions as divided as they had been in 1502.

Piero Soderini favoured an alliance with France;[33] his

---

[28] Parenti, Istorie, B.N.F. II, II, 132, fo. 174r–v; B. Cerretani, Istoria, B.N.F.,
II, III, 76, fos. 267v, 268r.
[29] Parenti, Istorie, fo. 176v: 'offerse in genere, non si ristringendo a' particolari,
ni obligandosi a cosa alcuna.'   [30] Ibid., fo. 177v.   [31] Below, p. 34.
[32] Parenti, Istorie, II, II, 134, fo. 148v; F. Guicciardini, St. fior., p. 297.
[33] F. Guicciardini, St. fior., p. 299.

opponents one with the emperor, but to send ambassadors to find out the likelihood and chances of success of an imperial invasion—the two criteria for a diplomatic reorientation— might risk the existing French alliance. Their dispatch to Constance, implying a possible change of allegiance, would signify the triumph of those who disliked the gonfalonier's policy; not to send them, however, could mean, if the emperor were to come to Italy, that Florence would be in a very vulnerable position and Soderini would be blamed for not having acted in time. Whether to send ambassadors to the Emperor Maximilian was thus a major political and diplomatic issue in Florence still provoking fierce controversy during the latter half of the year 1507.

The appointment of Francesco Vettori is recorded by Guicciardini as a victory for the opponents of Soderini.[34] Certainly Soderini had wanted to appoint Machiavelli and this election had been quashed because the *uomini da bene* had objected that there were many of their class who should be given experience and Vettori was chosen from among them.[35] But was this the triumph that Guicciardini would seem to suggest? Might Vettori not have been a compromise choice? Vettori's political career to this date would seem to suggest this.

Although the year 1507 probably brought Francesco his first taste of foreign diplomacy and travel abroad, he was not without political and military experience within his native city and its dominions. He was nearly twenty years of age when Charles VIII invaded Italy and the Medici were expelled from Florence. Though he was in the city at the time, there is no evidence of his views on the revolution; he may well have approved his father's opinion that since the French came 'for the common destruction of Italy' their arrival would spell the ruin of Florence.[36] Piero Vettori would most probably have shared the dissatisfaction of a number of the optimates, including his brother-in-law

[34] *Ibid.*, p. 297.

[35] Signori, Missive, Legaz. e Comm., 26, fo. 159v, entry 19 June 1507 appointing Machiavelli to Maximilian 'in nuntium et mandatarium reipublice florentine', cp. A. Nasi's reference to the cancelled election in his letter of 30 July 1507, N. Machiavelli, *Lettere*, ed. F. Gaeta, p. 182.

[36] 'Vita di Piero Vettori', fo. 3v: 'affermando che vedeva la rovina della città che franciosi venivano per chomune distructione d'italia.'

Bernardo Rucellai, with the rule of Piero de' Medici.[37] His attitude to the alliance with the French was evidently the same as that of Piero Capponi, a close friend,[38] whose audacious reaction to Charles VIII's terms of agreement with Florence is commented on by Guicciardini and Nardi.[39] After the expulsion of the Medici, Piero Vettori, in common with Savonarola and Paolantonio Soderini, stood for clemency and the preservation of liberty in Florence.[40] In the first of the constitutional reforms instituting the new regime he accepted office as one of the Ten to administer the foreign affairs of the Republic.[41] In one who had also held office in the Medici government this may be a sign, as in the case of a more famous Piero,[42] of political moderation, but it is also an indication of Piero Vettori's political position, it being well known that the first reform of 2 December 1494 introduced a predominantly aristocratic type of government which was followed three weeks later by a second in which the government was established on the popular base of the Great Council.[43] Francesco, too, must have been acceptable to the optimates for on his father's death in office in February 1495 the Ten elected him to complete the remaining four months of Piero's term as *capitano* in Pistoia.[44]

It is, however, significant that his earliest political experience in his own right was gained in Soderini's administration and, moreover, in one of the three highest offices—that of the College of the *Dodici Buonuomini*[45]—in the very year (1504) when, according to Guicciardini, the gonfalonier was beginning to

---

[37] N. Rubinstein, *The Government of Florence under the Medici*, p. 231; cp. below, n. 40 for Piero Vettori and Paolantonio Soderini.

[38] 'Vita di Piero Vettori', fo. 3v; above, p. 7, no 49.

[39] Guicciardini says Piero Capponi tore up the draft of the terms in Charles VIII's presence, *St. fior.*, p. 105; cp. J. Nardi, *Istorie di Firenze*, ed. A. Gelli, i, (Florence, 1858), p. 39.

[40] 'Vita di Piero Vettori', fo. 3v: 'nella mutazione dello stato sempre consigliò si perdonassi e che gli'uomini sanissino a mantenere la libertà:' cp. F. Guicciardini, *St. fior.*, p. 107 for Savonarola's clemency and for the association of Piero Vettori and Paolantonio Soderini in the Ten.

[41] 'Vita di Piero Vettori', fo. 3v.

[42] Viz. Piero Guicciardini, F. Guicciardini, 'Ricordanze', in *Scritti Autobiografici e Rari*, ed. R. Palmarocchi (Bari, 1936), p. 72.

[43] F. Guicciardini, *St. fior.*, pp. 106, 110.

[44] Tratte 70, fo. 3r.

[45] Tratte 94, fo. 100v, 15 March 1504; for the *Dodici Buonuomini*, above, p. 9, no. 66.

appoint lesser men whom he thought more likely than the
uomini da bene to be amenable to his will.[46] Six months later he
was elected one of the two representatives of his quarter to the
important police office of the *Otto di Guardia*,[47] and in the following year to the office of *podestà* of Castiglione Aretino, one of the
subject towns of the Florentine dominion.[48] Although his uncle
Bernardo Rucellai was a noted opponent of Soderini[49] and
Vettori himself might therefore have sympathized with the
views of one of his mother's side of the family, it is interesting to
note that he was in no way biased against Niccolò Machiavelli,
who was one of Soderini's most trusted supporters. In passing
through the Florentine dominion on his way out to Germany
Vettori was anxious to get a first-hand opinion on the success of
Machiavelli's scheme, sponsored by Soderini, for the raising of
the militia in the *contado*. While not refuting arguments against
it, he personally presents those in its favour.[50]

Even from the point of view of Soderini's opponents, Vettori's
appointment was not a complete triumph. He was not elected
an ambassador but to the less honourable position of *mandatario*
which Machiavelli also would have held.[51] The Ten and the
pratica, or advisory commission, assembled to discuss the diplomatic situation, agreed on an expedient already adopted in the
previous year when Bernardo Ricci had been sent to Germany
as *mandatario*.[52]

Vettori was appointed on 25 June 1507 'in nuntium et
mandatarium' to Maximilian and during the mission letters
were addressed to him as 'Mandatario apud Imperatore'.[53] In
his election it was stated that his *mandato*, or terms of reference,
were to be those given to Bernardo.[54] They are typical of the
Republic's cautious and hesitant attitude to foreign policy.
Bernardo had been sent to offer the emperor the Florentines'
good will. He had been instructed to keep a close watch on

---

[46] F. Giuicciardini, *St. fior.*, pp. 270–1; below, p. 34.
[47] Tratte 83, fo. 191r, 1 Sept. 1504.   [48] Tratte 70, fo. 3r.
[49] F. Guicciardini, *St. fior.*, p. 246.   [50] L. Passy, ii, pp. 46–7.
[51] Above, p. 12.
[52] Signori, Missive, Legaz. e. Comm., 26, fo. 157r, 9 Sept. 1506: 'Mandata
Bernardi Filii Bernardi de Ricciis electi in mandatarium ad Caesarem Maestem
per x viros.'
[53] Signori, Missive, Legaz. e Comm., 26, fo. 160r.   [54] *Ibid.*, fo. 157r.

events in order to find out if and when Maximilian was coming, in what strength and by what route, but to all requests he was to reply only in general terms. His principal task was to provide the government and the ambassadors who would be sent later with the fullest possible information. Francesco Vettori was, like Bernardo before him, to be an efficient observer and informant and a forerunner of the ambassadors to come.[55]

If Vettori was sent to Germany by those who desired to explore the need for a re-alignment of Florentine foreign policy, one might expect him to reflect their wishes by sending back reports which stressed the likelihood of Maximilian's invasion and the necessity for an alliance with him. Certainly Vettori's early reports do this but not, it would seem, on account of sensitivity to a section of opinion at home. For Maximilian to be able to invade Italy and to be successful, he needed to be certain that he had the political and military support of the German estates, and it is precisely on the unity of the German lands behind Maximilian and on the willingness of the princes and towns to supply troops or money that Vettori reports most favourably. A letter dated 14 July, three days after his arrival, while the Diet was in session at Constance, reported that all the German princes were united and 'everyone' was agreed that the emperor would at all events come to Italy;[56] Vettori's views were unchanged at the end of July and the beginning of August: all the princes and towns seemed to him united, and orders had been given for the amount of money, infantry and cavalry which each must supply. He thought it would be 'easy' for the greatness and power of Germany to provide for an army estimated at 25,000 infantry and 25,000 horse.[57] Although already during the Diet disruptive forces were at work[58] and the apparent unity hid underlying dissensions,[59] nevertheless nearly five months after its closure Vettori wrote to Florence that the emperor was

---

[55] Cp. F. Guicciardini, *St. fior.*, p. 297.

[56] L. Passy, ii, p. 223. Vol. 2 has translations of Vettori's letters.

[57] *Ibid.*, pp. 226–7; cp. N. Rubinstein, 'Firenze e il problema della politica imperiale al tempo di Massimiliano I' in *A.S.I.*, cxvi (1958), Disp. I and II.

[58] J. Janssen, *Frankfurts Reichscorrespondenz*, ii (Frankfort, 1872), n. 906, p. 710: Letter of Johann von Lunen and Johann Frosch to the Frankfort *Rat*, 23 May 1507, an agent for the French was 'sowing weeds' among the members of the emperor's Diet.   [59] *Ibid.*, nn. 907, 916, pp. 712–13 and 723–5.

quite 'beside himself' for joy that he had united the whole of Germany as no ruler had done for a long time.[60]

It was decided at the Diet that the troops for the proposed invasion should assemble at Constance between the feasts of St Michael (29 September) and St Gall (16 October).[61] A little less than a month before the final assembly date Vettori was sceptical about the punctual arrival of the troops, as was the Venetian ambassador.[62] Yet even after the feast of St Gall had passed without any obvious activity, Vettori wrote on 30 November in answer to doubts expressed in Florence, 'I know only this that the troops are in order and from Augsburg, Ulm and Nuremberg, . . . he [the emperor] has been advanced money on security and that although the invasion has been delayed a little, it has not been cancelled and on account of it France is involved in heavy expenditure.'[63] Vettori, who had earlier doubted the wisdom of a winter campaign (a view then shared in fact by the emperor but repudiated by his chancellor, Mathias Lang, bishop of Gurk[64]), reported on 29 October that the emperor believed himself to be in a position both to make war and to win.[65] On 30 November, in the dispatch mentioned above, he advised the Ten that a payment to Maximilian of 50,000 florins might not be misplaced. He had already recommended the dispatch of ambassadors to undertake the negotiations with the emperor.[66]

In spite of these recommendations, Vettori did not, however, want the invasion to take place. Of Pigello Portinari, the emperor's Florentine secretary, he remarked that being in favour of it, Pigello wrote more warmly than he would himself,[67] and even when advocating a monetary agreement with Maximilian, Vettori explained that he was 'not one of those who would like the barbarians in Italy' and he grieved when he saw signs that they were coming.[68]

[60] L. Passy, ii, p. 319; the Diet ended on 27 July, ibid., p. 268.
[61] Ibid., p. 237.
[62] Ibid., pp. 224, 252, cp. M. Sanuto, Diarii, vii (Venice, 1882), 154, dispatch read in Senate, 27 Sept.: 'non si vede novità alcuna'.
[63] L. Passy, ii, p. 308.
[64] Ibid., pp. 268, 270; cp. J. Janssen, ii, n. 917, p. 725.
[65] Ibid., p. 288.
[66] Ibid., p. 309; he had asked for ambassadors on 29 Oct., ibid., p. 292.
[67] Ibid., p. 242.   [68] Ibid., p. 308.

In urging an agreement with the emperor Vettori does not appear to be affected by the views of a particular section at home, but rather to be reacting to the bias of those around him. A redeeming feature of his otherwise rather misleading early reports on Maximilian's political and military strength is his critical awareness, constantly expressed, that 'my opinion and judgment are founded upon the conversations and reports of those who intensely desire it' [the expedition].[69] The papal ambassador, the Greek Constantine Comnenus, much in favour with the emperor, wanted him to come to Italy;[70] so, too, did the papal legate, the Spaniard Bernardo Carvajal, cardinal of S. Croce, whom Vettori at first thought 'very affectionate towards the city',[71] and even the Florentine secretary Pigello favoured the expedition.[72] Mathias Lang, one of the most important of Maximilian's courtiers,[73] and another of Vettori's sources of information, was only perhaps to be expected to present the imperial point of view.[74]

Another important influence on Vettori and an indication of his city's isolation was her unpopularity with many of the other Italian powers. The Florentines were accused by fellow Italians at the imperial court of being pro-French.[75] The Venetian ambassador told Maximilian that the king of France maintained himself in Italy thanks to Florentine money.[76] The Pisans, too, were anxious to make what use they could of the emperor.[77] The imperialists were fully aware of the weakness of Florence's position. When Vettori presented to them the disadvantage of 'being in the centre of Italy and exposed to the slightest movement there' and referred to the enmity of Florence's neighbours, especially Pisa, as the reason for her delay in coming to terms with Maximilian,[78] and of her need for an understanding with the emperor, Lang, for example, gave a menacing twist to Vettori's observation on the hostility of the city's neighbours by pointing out that all Florence's subject territories desired liberty, that the exiled Medici were making considerable offers to the emperor, that the Venetians

[69] Ibid., p. 256; cp. p. 250.   [70] Ibid., pp. 241, 249.
[71] Ibid., pp. 250, 269, 298.   [72] Ibid., p. 242.
[73] Ibid., p. 253.   [74] Ibid., p. 296.
[75] Ibid., pp. 235, 237.   [76] Ibid., p. 225.
[77] Ibid., pp. 244, 245.   [78] Ibid., p. 277.

had no other thought than the destruction of the Republic and that even the pope did not support her. Vettori's critical comment that he himself had not heard that the Medici had sent anyone to the court indicates that he was not entirely a victim of this pressure; nevertheless it must have played a part in his recommendation of a payment to Maximilian.[79]

Vettori's advice to send ambassadors, on the other hand, probably stemmed not only from the anxiety caused him by the information gleaned but from the limitations of his mandate and a sense of frustration.[80] His commission had instructed him to remain within generalities, to reply non-committally to any specific proposals and on no account to negotiate or to conclude an agreement with the emperor. The mission, however, developed in such a way that it became impossible to remain within these bounds and in fact before a year had passed Vettori had power not only to find out and to write but also 'to negotiate and to conclude'.

A tendency in this direction can already be detected in the meeting of the *pratica* of 30 July and the Ten's letter of 31 July based upon it.[81] Unless he had something to discuss, it was difficult for an ambassador, let alone a *mandatario*, to get an interview with a ruler. Probably for this reason, and also as a means of winning time, one of the chief speakers, Francesco Gualterotti, suggested giving Vettori 'something more than a general commission' and proposed as a talking point the 1502 negotiations.[82] The Ten's subsequent letter makes it clear that Vettori was not to come to an agreement but merely to construe the emperor's intentions from his reactions. But once the matter had been raised, the emperor determined to take it up and commissioned the cardinal of Brixen, who had been one of the ambassadors to Florence at that time, to go to Rome and to undertake negotiations with the city's representatives.[83] Vettori seems to have judged correctly that Maximilian's interest in Florence was largely financial.[84] The amount demanded was in-

[79] *Ibid.*, pp. 286–7.
[80] *Ibid.*, p. 292.
[81] Cons. e Prat., 68, fos. 81v–90v; Dieci, Missive, Legaz. e Comm., 32, fo. 19r.
[82] Cons. e Prat., 68, fo. 84r: 'qualche commissione fuora del generale'.
[83] L. Passy, ii, p. 264.
[84] *Ibid.*, p. 288.

creased from 40,000 to 50,000 ducats.[85] On 26 November a *pratica* was summoned in Florence to sound the members' opinions on this demand[86] and these views were incorporated in the Ten's letter of the following day.[87] The new sum was considered too high and some benefit was demanded from the emperor in return. On 16 December Vettori was instructed to ascertain the lowest sum of money under 50,000 ducats which the emperor would accept and to ask for a guarantee of all Florence's interests in the event of his coming to Italy.[88] Thus he was already carrying out instructions which could well form the basis of an agreement with Maximilian.

Since the city's aim was to avoid breaking off negotiations with the emperor while nevertheless withholding a money payment until such time as it was clear that the expedition would both take place and succeed, considerable ability was required to keep 'the thread' of them unbroken and Vettori expressed the opinion that he was 'not very skilled in this art'.[89] His own accounts to the Ten of his interviews with Maximilian do not, however, give this impression. He shrewdly kept to his brief and replied only in general terms to the imperial proposals even while recommending a financial settlement to Florence, as for example on 29 October.[90] Nor could he be drawn into detailed discussions on the question of Pisa.[91] In fact he tells the Ten he can only be blamed for having adhered too closely to his instructions.[92] A distant observer would judge that he fulfilled his diplomatic mission astutely, providing the Ten with his views and adhering at the same time to their instructions, and in the event of a disaster he could neither be blamed for not having warned his government nor for having exceeded his powers.

In accordance with his instructions of 31 July,[93] Vettori resorted also to another device used in contemporary interviews, that of interpreting the ruler's reactions from his facial expression and gestures.[94] 'In the interview which I had with

[85] *Ibid.*, p. 273.
[86] Cons. e Prat., 68, fos. 92v–97v, 26 Nov. 1507.
[87] Dieci, Missive, Legaz. e Comm., 32, fos. 66r–68v.
[88] *Ibid.*, fos. 84v–87v.   [89] L. Passy, ii, pp. 313–14.
[90] *Ibid.*, p. 292.   [91] *Ibid.*, p. 304.
[92] *Ibid.*, p. 309.   [93] Above, p. 21.
[94] F. Gilbert, 'Florentine political assumptions', p. 200.

His Majesty', Vettori wrote on 18 September, 'I did not see any indication of what your lordships wrote', and on another occasion, 'he in no way let me see his displeasure at my communications'.[95]

Vettori felt frustrated. He had no knowledge of German to facilitate communication[96] and although Latin was still the common language among the educated and a courtier like Lang knew it well, here was an excuse for Lang to say little.[97] The city's delaying tactics, too, were exasperating: Lang knew that the Florentines were only playing for time[98] and Vettori himself feared that the policy might be wrong: 'to gain time is sometimes useful and sometimes it may produce the opposite effect', he commented on 30 November.[99] He was vilified as a spy[100] and although he was not much worried by the lack of honour accorded to him, he resented being disbelieved and also the unprofitable expenditure of public money.[101] He felt that what he was doing could be done as well by Pigello Portinari who knew the court and the language,[102] and that neither at Constance, Überlingen, Innsbruck, Memmingen nor Trent did he have much official business to occupy him.[103] Even the weather was against him: he was dejected by the intense cold of the German winter.[104] There were thus personal as well as political considerations to account for his insistence on sending out ambassadors to replace him.

The advantages and disadvantages of official representation had been discussed in Florence ever since Vettori left. Already on 30 July most members of the *pratica* agreed that ambassadors should be created and on 8 November, by which time two had been appointed, their dispatch was under consideration.[105]

[95] L. Passy, ii, p. 249. Lang observed Vettori equally closely: if Vettori but spat, Lang took note of it, *ibid.*, p. 304.

[96] *Ibid.*, p. 219.

[97] *Ibid.*, p. 278.   [98] *Ibid.*, p. 286.

[99] *Ibid.*, p. 306.   [100] *Ibid.*, pp. 228, 277.

[101] Francesco to Paolo, Bolzano, 9 Jan. 1508 (copy). Dieci, Responsive, 88, fo. 30r.

[102] L. Passy, ii, pp. 228–9.

[103] *Ibid.*, pp. 112, 114, 134, 156. N. Machiavelli, *Lettere*, ed. F. Gaeta, p. 264, F. Vettori to N. Machiavelli, Rome, 27 June 1513.

[104] Above, n. 101.

[105] The two elected were Piero Guicciardini and Alamanno Salviati, F. Guicciardini, *St. fior.*, p. 298.

Although by mid-December, as a result of Vettori's dispatches, most citizens considered the emperor's arrival likely, the *pratica* held on the 15th was divided in its views on the dispatch of ambassadors.[106] Many held that the dignity and interests of the city would be better served by them; the majority, however, believed that the danger of alienating France outweighed these considerations. Two days earlier Lorenzo Morelli had made the suggestion welcomed by several members of employing Vettori to negotiate with the emperor[107] and on the 15th this idea was again favoured, mention being made of the ability he had shown so far and of his sound judgment.[108] By 17 December the idea of sending ambassadors had been abandoned for the time being and Morelli's suggestion accepted. There was opposition to sending Vettori a *mandato* granting him power to conclude an agreement but it was considered necessary to let him have new and full instructions.[109] In this way Vettori's pressing requests to send out ambassadors were overruled and instead his own responsibility was increased.

It is well known that the delivery of the new instructions was entrusted to Niccolò Machiavelli and that this was regarded by Guicciardini as a political triumph for Soderini. Though obviously Soderini was anxious to send Machiavelli to Germany neither the remarks of the speakers in the *pratica* nor a letter to Vettori from Soderini himself, nor letters from the Ten suggest that Francesco was unacceptable to the gonfalonier and his followers. It is to be noted, for example, that both Francesco Gualterotti who had recommended giving Vettori 'something more than a general commission'[110] and Antonio Canigiani, who had spoken most approvingly in the *pratica* of Vettori's performance in Germany were supporters of Soderini.[111] More-

---

[106] Cons. e Prat., 68, fos. 118r–125v. [107] *Ibid.*, fo. 115v.

[108] *Ibid.*, fo. 122r Antonio Canigiani: 'Veduto quanto Francesco discorre bene questa cosa' he could be entrusted to conclude what the Emperor wanted. Niccolò Zati commended Vettori (fo. 123r): 'iudicando Francesco Vettori prudente volentieri darebbe la commissione a lui . . .' cp. (fo. 119r) Antonio Strozzi who maintained that '. . . l'usare el mezo di Francesco era in parte a satisfactione della Città et in parte no per non essere in vero tanto pratico quanto bisognerebbe a si grave cosa et però li oratori electi migliorerebbono le condictioni della Città.'

[109] *Pratica*, 17 Dec. 1507, O. Tommasini, I, Appendix VI, pp. 676–81.

[110] F. Guicciardini, *St. fior.*, p. 271 and above, p. 21.

[111] *Ibid.*, p. 272.

over, on 2 October the gonfalonier himself had written to Vettori, 'Your writing and work give much satisfaction to everyone'.[112] The Ten, too, by no means all of whom were supporters of Soderini, on 22 November congratulated Vettori on his negotiations with the emperor.[113] Praise of his work at the court was also expressed in an unsigned letter from Germany written at the end of November and may have influenced the decision of the members of the *pratica* to continue to make use of his services rather than to send out the elected ambassadors.[114] The writer proposed that if no ambassadors were sent to the emperor for the time being, Vettori should be given this rank both for his 'good qualities' and because he was useful and 'considered by everyone extremely prudent'. He represented 'the favourable disposition of the Florentine Republic and government towards the emperor'.

Machiavelli arrived in Bolzano on 11 January where he joined his compatriot.[115] Despite the contention of Cerretani, there seems no reason to believe that Machiavelli's relationship to Vettori was that of a minion of Soderini's who interfered with dispatches in order to promote the gonfalonier's policy.[116] Paleographical analysis of the dispatches written from January to June 1508 provides evidence of scribal collaboration, eight out of a total of seventeen original dispatches containing passages penned by Machiavelli and Vettori respectively.[117] In three of these joint dispatches some items of news given in one hand are repeated in the passage penned by the second which suggests also joint redaction.[118] Occasionally a divergence of opinion is expressed in passages written by the two hands.[119] But Machiavelli seems no less convinced about the likelihood of the invasion than Vettori. In early February, for example, a passage written by the former reads 'the least enthusiastic no

[112] B.M. Add. Mss. 10, 278, fo. 79r.

[113] L. Passy, ii, p. 302, n.

[114] B.N.F. Ms. Ginori Conti, 29, 64, fo. 44r. S. Bertelli, 'Carteggi Machiavelliani', *Clio*, April–Sept. 1966, identifies the writer as Pigello Portinari.

[115] N. Machiavelli, *Legazioni e commissarie*, ed. S. Bertelli, ii (Milan, 1964), p. 1062 (cited in future as S. Bertelli).

[116] B. Cerretani, Istoria, B.N.F. II, III, 76, fo. 316r.

[117] For this analysis, R. Devonshire Jones, 'Francesco Vettori and Niccolò Machiavelli' in *Italian Studies*, xxiii (1968), pp. 93–113.

[118] *Ibid.*, p. 106.   [119] *Ibid.*, p. 107.

longer have doubts about the invasion'. Although Machiavelli perceived the financial weakness of Maximilian's military command he saw in the disunity of Italy and in her 'wretched arms' a chance of imperial success.[120]

The emperor did eventually invade northern Italy in February but the estates did not send the troops which they had promised at Constance, and Maximilian had to rely almost entirely on the forces of his hereditary domains.[121] His expedition was crushed by the Venetians. By mid-April Vettori had become sceptical while Machiavelli adhered to his previous assessment. The view expressed in Machiavelli's hand on the 16th that 'Germany can do much and she can have what she wants for the asking' is taken up again in his handwriting in a dispatch a fortnight later but apparently questioned in the same dispatch by Vettori who writes: 'And if someone says to me, "Germany is powerful and from one hour to the next she can do great things", I reply "this German power Your Lordships know as well as I do" '.[122] Furthermore the passages reporting lack of support for Maximilian from the empire are written in Vettori's hand.[123] The failure to support Maximilian in 1508 is compared in a dispatch of 8 June, for example, with the promises made by the estates at the Diet of Constance the year before, and the writer says since he (together with everyone else) was deceived on that occasion, he will now judge only by what he can actually see to be taking effect. Unlike Machiavelli, Vettori had been present at the Diet of Constance and these words reflect his experience. Even if one argues that Vettori's more sceptical attitude had been influenced by Machiavelli (and of this there is no proof), Vettori adopted it as his own for we find it expressed again immediately after his compatriot's departure. They say, he writes, that the treaty (with Venice) will not last and that 'Germany will do something' but 'I, as I wrote in my last letter, now believe here what I see and nothing else'.

There is no indication that Machiavelli himself supposed his mission to go beyond delivery of his instructions. On his arrival he asks the Ten about his return, 'because having expounded

[120] *Ibid.*
[121] S. Bertelli, pp. 1143, 1112.
[122] R. Devonshire Jones, p. 107.
[123] *Ibid.*, pp. 107–8.

your intention to Francesco, there is nothing more for me to do'.[124] It was not unusual to send an agent with fresh instructions rather than to entrust them to the vagaries of the post; once the messenger had delivered his orders he would either return immediately or stay to help carry them out and Machiavelli evidently expected to follow the former course.[125] The Ten in their reply did not give Machiavelli leave to return in case he could be of use to Vettori, leaving Vettori to decide whether he should stay or not.[126] Niccolò's position bears comparison with that of the Florentine secretary, Giovanni da Poppi, who had to contact Vettori during the latter's subsequent mission to the Council of Pisa in 1511. On this occasion the Ten instructed Vettori to 'arrange for him to stay or to return, as you see fit to make use of him'.[127] In the case of Machiavelli, Vettori replies that he does not wish him to be recalled because 'his stay . . . is necessary'.[128] Had Vettori found Machiavelli's presence constricting he would presumably have taken this opportunity to be rid of him.

Vettori employed Machiavelli in a two-fold capacity: as his secretary and co-editor of dispatches, and as an agent to gather information; two tasks which seemed so important that Vettori chose the word 'necessary' rather than 'useful' as one might have expected. Although it was not unusual for an ambassador to have a secretary,[129] since all the letters dispatched by Vettori before Machiavelli's arrival are in his own hand, presumably none of the four servants he took with him was one.[130] What could therefore be more natural at that moment when the mission had increased in importance than to enlist Machiavelli's service in writing the dispatches and in making several copies which were sent by different routes for security reasons? In fact, as demonstrated elsewhere,[131] the dispatches written while Machiavelli was in Germany provide ample evidence of scribal co-operation.

[124] S. Bertelli, p. 1068.
[125] For tasks of *ad hoc* agents and ambassadors, see Maulde-La-Clavière, i, p. 314; E. Dupré Theseider, pp. 104–8.
[126] S. Bertelli, p. 1087.   [127] O. Tommasini, i, p. 551, n.
[128] S. Bertelli, p. 1101.
[129] Vettori had one in Rome and France; cp. E. Dupré Theseider, p. 156.
[130] L. Passy, ii, p. 46.   [131] R. Devonshire Jones, p. 101.

Machiavelli was invaluable also as a collector of information. It would be nearly impossible, for example, in surveying the military situation, for one man to report on troop movements over a large area or on military strength with any degree of accuracy. The Ten had already dispatched Tommaso Benci to Germany for greater coverage.[132] Machiavelli was similarly employed. Vettori sent him to join the court at Trent when he himself was confined by imperial orders to Bolzano and, when he had hurt his arm and was unable to ride, Machiavelli was commissioned to go and observe the proceedings of the Diet in Swabia while he remained at Innsbruck.[133] In addition he employed the courier Bacino, and one realizes the great distances to be covered from Vettori's remark to the Ten that he had paid this man to travel some 600 miles to the imperial court at Cologne.[134] Vettori himself covered a distance of 500 miles in the course of twenty-four days travelling before and after Christmas.[135]

Machiavelli's rôle as collector of information is confirmed by the paleographical fact that in several of the joint dispatches the news items are in his hand.[136] Also certain views expressed in these passages can be attributed to him, as we find their like expressed elsewhere in his work. Others such as the reporting on the emperor's ceremonial procession in Trent bear the marks of an eyewitness account.[137] Nor could certain repetitions and divergences of opinion, to which reference has already been made, be otherwise explained.[138] But it was Vettori who was ultimately responsible for the dispatches which went out under his name and to visualize the co-operation as one of equal partnership would be to go too far. Vettori must have read, and possibly edited, the passages in question and could no doubt have refused to send anything of which he did not approve.

Analysis of the handwriting of the dispatches can offer only tentative suggestions as to how much Vettori was helped by Machiavelli in the conduct and report of negotiations.[139] On

[132] L. Passy, ii, pp. 267, 270, 280.   [133] S. Bertelli, p. 1124.
[134] Ibid., pp. 1124, 1148, 1150; Dieci, Responsive, 92, fo. 345v.
[135] S. Bertelli, p. 1068.   [136] R. Devonshire Jones, p. 104.
[137] Ibid., p. 105.   [138] Above, p. 26.
[139] For this analysis, R. Devonshire Jones, pp. 96–101, Plates I–III and Appendix I.

the evidence of several important letters Vettori was responsible for the negotiations with Maximilian or his courtiers with Machiavelli being present on certain occasions. Thus in the dispatch of 17 January, the first after Machiavelli's arrival, the part of the interview in which the new instructions were made known to Maximilian is reported in Machiavelli's hand (not unnaturally, perhaps, since he had delivered the instructions) but the emperor's reaction to the proposals and the development of negotiations is penned by Vettori.[140] Again in the joint dispatch of 24 January describing the next audience it is Vettori's writing which takes over where the report of the interview starts: 'and in the presence of the emperor . . . Lang told me how the emperor was aware of the offer I had made him in your name'.[141] Unfortunately the original of the dispatch 14-19-23 February in which the next interview is reported—again with Lang—does not appear to be extant so that it is impossible to say who penned it; that for 29 March detailing the subsequent interview however exists. Here again it is Vettori's hand which reports it and appends in code at the end the imperial terms proposed.[142] There followed a lengthy interim while Vettori waited for the Ten's reply and observed the current negotiations for a treaty between the emperor and the Venetians. The circumstances of the interview in which Vettori was informed of the conclusion of the truce illustrate Vettori's rôle as chief of the mission and primary negotiator and Machiavelli's subordinate position in the eyes of the imperial courtiers. When Machiavelli called on Cyprian von Sarnthein, one of Maximilian's chief ministers, to get his 'pass' to leave Germany on 10 June, the day before his departure, he was informed that the minister wished to see Vettori. Both men were present at the interview on the following morning but it was Vettori whom von Sarnthein questioned about the Florentine attitude towards the concluded treaty with the Venetians.[143] Vettori was undoubtedly primarily responsible for the conduct of negotiations; it was he who sought interviews and in many cases wrote out the accounts of them to the Ten. In the preparation for interviews however Machiavelli may

[140] *Ibid.*, pp. 108–9.   [141] *Ibid.*, p. 109.
[142] *Ibid.*   [143] *Ibid.*, p. 110.

have played a more important part. It would have been un-
natural if Vettori had not consulted his older and more experienced compatriot about the interpretation of the Ten's
instructions especially as by now these tended to leave to their
executant an alarming degree of responsibility. The instructions
brought by Machiavelli for example specified only the broad
limits of the offer to be made to Maximilian.[144] The place of
payment was a point of disagreement between the Ten and
Maximilian. The latter had suggested Trent as a city just within
Italy but since the emperor's arrival in a town so near the
frontier was no guarantee of his successful further advance and
resulting aid to Florence if she had allied with him the Ten
viewed it unfavourably. Only in case of 'absolute necessity', of
which Vettori was to be judge, was this city to be chosen. Vettori
and Machiavelli discussed the interpretation of these instructions[145] and the reply, although written in Machiavelli's
hand,[146] probably expressed the feeling of both men: the responsibility of the instructions was too onerous not only 'for the
wisest and most resolute citizen of your city but for an entire
senate if it were here'.[147] As before Machiavelli's arrival,
Vettori's policy was still to adhere strictly to his brief, and he
wanted instructions which would meet every contingency, as
the letter shows which he personally wrote on 29 March: the
Ten must tell him what to do in each case, if the situation
remained as it was, if it improved, or if it deteriorated, and then
he could act accordingly.[148] By 4 March the Ten had decided
to send Vettori a *mandato* with power to conclude an agreement
with Maximilian. Fullest confidence was thus expressed in his
judgment, but so anxious was Vettori to get precise instructions
that he even asked for commas to be put under the words which
were on no account to be altered.[149] On 1 April this *mandato*
arrived and thus legally completed the extension of Vettori's
power.[150] He now had full authority to commit his city to an
agreement which would cost her thousands of ducats. In May he
advised against one though not, he is careful to point out, 'on
the basis of my own opinion, but on that of Your Lordships'.[151]

---

[144] S. Bertelli, pp. 1069, 1084–5.   [145] *Ibid.*, p. 1095.
[146] R. Devonshire Jones, p. 98.   [147] S. Bertelli, p. 1095.   [148] *Ibid.*, p. 1129.
[149] *Ibid.*   [150] *Ibid.*, p. 1136.   [151] *Ibid.*, p. 1144.

By now, however, Vettori had no real cause to distrust his own judgment for with Maximilian's defeat by the Venetians and the subsequent truce between the two powers it was clear that the immediate threat of an invasion was removed.

By the same token there was little further need for Florence to be represented at the imperial court and indeed even Vettori's biographer Louis Passy has assumed this to be the end of the mission.[152] Machiavelli was in fact on his way back to Florence when he wrote from Bologna the letter of 14 June which is the last for his German embassy which the editors of his dispatches publish. But Vettori did not return in June 1508 as the evidence of the election register and that of several letters in his hand prove conclusively. The register has in the margin beside the note of the appointment 'Recursus est die 13 martii 1508' which is March 1509 according to modern computation.[153]

The letters hitherto overlooked enable us to reconstruct what Vettori did after Machiavelli's departure. During the early summer he remained 'unwillingly' at Trent, unable to leave on account of the dangers on the road, though anxious to return to Florence, as he considered his sojourn at the imperial court 'entirely unnecessary'.[154] Later he travelled to Antwerp, presumably at the emperor's command, where on 1 August he was awaiting Maximilian's arrival.[155] Again he asked the Ten's permission to return home for his presence at the court could only worsen Florence's relations with the emperor. Lang knew that he had power to conclude an agreement and as long as he remained in the imperial lands the imperialists would continue to seek one and the city's likely refusal could only give annoyance. On the 12th Vettori was still in Antwerp not knowing what his compatriots wanted him to do. It was three months since he had heard from them.[156] He pointed out that there were plenty of merchants who could provide Florence with information as long as the emperor remained in the Low Countries. There would still be time to send a new representative after Maximilian had returned to Germany. Vettori himself

---

[152] L. Passy, i, p. 27.   [153] Signori, Missive, Legaz. e. Comm., 26, fo. 16or.
[154] Dieci, Responsive, 92, fo. 345r, Trent, 17 June 1508: 'tutta fuori di proposito'.
[155] Dieci, Responsive, 93, fo. 31r.   [156] *Ibid.*, fo. 19r.

was far from the court and he could not report any news except what he picked up at his inn. This time he asked to come home before the winter and before the emperor returned to Germany. He begged the Ten to reply quickly as it was easy at the moment to send letters through France. On 17 August the tale (still from Antwerp) was much the same: Vettori was now twenty days' journey away from the court and was not sufficiently in the emperor's good graces to be allowed to travel there.[157] At last by 1 September the Ten decided upon his recall.[158] Their instructions illuminate Florence's devious relations with the emperor. Vettori was ordered not to take official leave of Maximilian but rather to let it appear that private business necessitated his departure. He was to leave the best possible impression of the city with the emperor, recommending to him her interests with all customary ceremony. As regards his journey the instructions were detailed and precise. He was to return immediately by way of France disguised as a merchant, 'making your presence little known' and shunning the court as much as he could in order not to remind the French of his stay in Germany. An interesting link with contemporary security precautions is the instruction to take good note of the contents of any documents he possessed 'because *mandati* and instructions are not things to carry about with you'. He should endeavour to return well informed on the affairs of the countries through which he passed. As the Ten were anxious for Vettori's departure to appear unofficial and also no doubt to preserve greater secrecy, they sent their letter care of the Rustichi, merchants at Bruges, to be forwarded. A copy was given to Francesco's brother, Paolo, to be sent by another route. Vettori did not receive the letter in Antwerp until the 23rd.[159] He regretted that, as a result of the delay, he had been unable to take such leave of the emperor as the occasion warranted because on 1 September he had fallen ill of a fever which had become progressively worse. If the letter had arrived at the proper time he would not have been so weak and he could have gone to the court and carried out the necessary duties but now

---

[157] *Ibid.*, fo. 46r (deciphered), fo. 48r (code).
[158] Dieci, Missive, Legaz. e Comm., 33, fos. 34v.
[159] Dieci, Responsive, 93, fo. 134r.

he could not go in person and would have to rely on the services of others. If the emperor would give him leave, he would try to set off, sick as he was, and if he returned safely he would be as well informed as anyone could be who had been ill for a month and had not been out of doors. He did not know whether he would return via France or take advantage of the legate's company and travel through Germany. If he should come through France, he promised to do what he considered best with his documents. Evidently Vettori did take a route through France since a letter from Florence of 21 January reveals that he was by then in Paris and so ill that his brother Paolo was going to fetch him home.[160] He was again instructed to return with the fullest possible information on German affairs and especially on the recent League of Cambrai formed between the king of France and the emperor. He arrived in Florence, as already mentioned, on 13 March 1509.

Vettori's almost immediate appointment to the priorate is evidence of the official approval of his work in Germany.[161] Mention of the praise it received is to be found in the unknown recorder of his *Azioni*.[162] The mission had considerably furthered his public career and had provided him with valuable experience of the empire which proved an advantage in the *pratiche* of 1512 and in his history of contemporary affairs (the *Sommario*).[163] He had met important ecclesiastics such as Mathias Lang, bishop of Gurk and Bernardo Carvajal, cardinal of S. Croce with whom he was again to have diplomatic dealings at a later date. It is possible that his admiration for the despot Pandolfo Petrucci which is reflected in his political memoranda of the early thirties was aroused by his friendship with the Sienese ambassador, Antonio Venafro, whom he met on the embassy,[164] and most likely that his later concern for the sound economy of a state owed something to this early experience of Maximilian's need for money and its effects on his relations with Florence.[165]

[160] Signori, Missive, Ia Cancelleria, 56, fo. 112r.
[161] Tratte 94, fo. 9r.
[162] *Raccolto delle Azioni di Francesco e di Pagolo Vettori*, ed. A. von Reumont in *A.S.I.*, Appendix vi (1848), p. 273 (cited in future as *Raccolto delle Azioni*).
[163] Below, pp. 49, 50.
[164] L. Passy, ii, p. 134; below, pp. 243, 245.   [165] Below, pp. 178, 231.

CHAPTER III

Francesco Vettori and the external policy of the Republic (1509–1512)

OWING TO the failure of the imperial invasion of Italy and the ability and caution of Vettori's negotiations with the emperor, the embassy to Maximilian had not resulted in political defeat for Soderini. But it was to be otherwise in the case of the foreign policy of the Republic during the remaining years of its existence after Vettori's return from Germany. Two major external problems caused grave public concern in this period: the city's war against Pisa, and her relations with France and the papacy. Soderini's policy was vigorously opposed and his refusal to reorientate his city's diplomacy was the external cause of his downfall in the summer of 1512.

Constitutionally the optimates' main complaint was that Soderini was becoming increasingly independent of them so that they were unable to fulfil their ambition to play a dominant rôle in their city's affairs. In their view the gonfalonier was governing more in collaboration with the *Signoria*, the colleges and the Council of Eighty than with the members of their own class who had become accustomed to being called to give their opinions in the *pratiche*. Since the members of the *Signoria* continued to be elected every two months, they tended to be men of less political experience than the now permanent gonfalonier. In the event of a divergence of opinion between the optimates and the gonfalonier, Soderini could circumvent the policy advised in the *pratiche* and rely for support on the *Signoria*, the colleges and the councils. Soderini's policy towards the confederates of the Holy League under the leadership of Pope Julius II in particular was vigorously opposed in some of the *pratiche*.

Through the offices to which he was elected and in the *pratiche* to which he was summoned we shall see Francesco Vettori continuing to be associated with the government of Soderini and with Soderini's trusted confidant Niccolò Machiavelli, but the problem for us to determine is his attitude towards that government. In this chapter Vettori's attitude to the gonfalonier's external policy will come under review and in the next the part which he played in the revolt against Soderini's leadership.

As soon as Maximilian had concluded with Venice the treaty reported by Vettori and Machiavelli on 8 June 1508,[1] the Florentines freed for the time being from their fear of imperial invasion had turned their attention to the long-standing problem of the reacquisition of Pisa.[2] Hardly had Machiavelli returned from Germany than he was sent to raise the troops of his militia[3] for use in the war against the rebellious city, and began to devastate the country round about it.[3] The League of Cambrai (about which Vettori had been instructed to return fully informed) which had been created by the king of France and the emperor as well as the pope and the king of Aragon against Venice had committed France to military intervention in northern Italy. This placed her in great financial need which she was already determined to meet at the expense of Florence:[4] her Florentine ally would not be allowed to bring the war against Pisa to an end without paying heavily for it.

On the day on which Vettori arrived back in his native city, Alessandro Nasi and Giovanni Ridolfi, the city's ambassadors in France, wrote that promises had been obtained from both France and Spain—at a cost to the Republic of 50,000 ducats to each power—that they would give no further help to the Pisans. In addition Florence had been forced to sign a second treaty with France alone (in great secrecy so that Spain would not attempt to do the same) promising her a further 50,000 ducats.[5]

---

[1] S. Bertelli, p. 1151.

[2] P. Villari, i, p. 449.

[3] *Ibid.*, p. 450; R. Ridolfi, *The Life of Niccolò Machiavelli* (London, 1963), p. 105.

[4] League of Cambrai in J. Dumont, *Corps universel diplomatique du droit des gens*, iv, part i (Amsterdam, 1726), pp. 111–13.

[5] A. Desjardins, *Négociations diplomatiques de la France avec la Toscane*, ii (Paris, 1861), p. 293.

In short, to secure her rights to conduct her own war against Pisa free from outside interference the Republic was relieved by her so-called ally of 100,000 ducats. Thereafter the struggle against Pisa was carried on in grim earnest, and no small part in the city's eventual capitulation on 4 June 1509 was due to the military enterprise of Machiavelli.

With this ultimate victory Vettori, too, was associated. By his election two months after his return from Germany as one of the two priors for his quarter of S. Spirito[6] he became one of the eight men who together with the gonfalonier, Piero Soderini, made up the *Signoria*, the magistracy which shared with the two colleges the highest rank in the Florentine constitution. Although the Ten who instructed Machiavelli and the commissioners on the spot were the men directly responsible for the war against Pisa, Vettori as a member of the *Signoria* helped to shape the government's policy and his signature like Machiavelli's appears on the act of capitulation signed during his second month of office.[7] It seems fitting that Francesco should have been associated with the end of the fifteen years' struggle on whose initial revolt he had blamed his father's death.[8]

On 8 June when the Florentine commissioners and Machiavelli with his battalions victoriously entered Pisa,[9] German ambassadors arrived in Florence seeking the alliance which was to be one of the strands in the diplomatic web of Soderini's downfall.[10] The League of Cambrai had resulted in a new diplomatic situation: Maximilian's alliance with Louis XII meant that he could now count on the political and military support of France,[11] and Florence, no longer worried as in 1507 by the fear of offending her ally France, could also seriously entertain the prospect of an alliance with the emperor and the dispatch of ambassadors. In response to the overture made by the emperor, Piero Guicciardini was dispatched to Maximilian together with the gonfalonier's brother Giovan Vittorio

---

[6] Above, p. 33.

[7] 'Submissio Civitatis Pisarum', pub. O. Tommasini, i, p. 685. Vettori's name, p. 700.

[8] Above, pp. 5–6.

[9] R. Ridolfi, *Machiavelli*, p. 108.

[10] N. Rubinstein, 'Firenze e il problema' (Disp. II), p. 162.

[11] *Ibid.*, p. 161.

Soderini.[12] Since Piero Guicciardini's election must have had
the support of the optimates and Giovan Vittorio Soderini's
that of the gonfalonier, the political balance of the mission was
the same as in December 1507 when Machiavelli was sent to
join Vettori.

Following an official request Machiavelli gave the new
ambassadors the benefit of his experience in his *Discourse on
German affairs and on the Emperor*,[13] but Vettori was not favoured
with any official commission. On 1 September he had been
elected one of the captains of the Guelf party.[14] Since one of the
duties of the captains was to administer and dispose of the
estates of rebel Pisans,[15] the Vettori family's previous connections with that city probably made Francesco a desirable
candidate. Again, matters concerning fortifications and munitions were referred to this office,[16] so that Vettori's earlier
military experiences as captain in Pistoia would have been useful to him. The knowledge thus gained must have stood him in
good stead in 1512 when he came to be appointed *commissario
generale* over the Florentine men-at-arms.[17] But also his experience gained in Germany was not wasted: evidently his opinions
on imperial affairs were valued for he was called to the *pratica* on
16 October to discuss the letters received from the Florentine
ambassadors to Maximilian and to decide whether or not to
come to an agreement with him.[18] The emperor had abandoned
his siege against Padua (2 October) and a fresh imperial offensive potentially dangerous to Florence seemed imminent.[19]
Vettori favoured an agreement with the emperor and approved
the sum of 40,000 ducats to be paid by Florence as the financial
basis of it; he was, however, anxious to defer the proposed
second instalment of 20,000 as long as possible—at least until
March 1510. In effect this is approximately what occurred. By

---

[12] *Ibid.*, p. 162.

[13] O. Tommasini, i, p. 417, n. 1. N. Rubinstein, 'Firenze e il problema', p. 162,
n. 205.

[14] Tratte 84, fo. 7r.

[15] M. Mallett, 'Pisa and Florence in the Fifteenth Century: Aspects of the Period
of the First Florentine Domination' in *Florentine Studies*, ed. N. Rubinstein (London
1968), pp. 432–3.

[16] Otto, Legaz. e Comm., Missive, 11, fo. 132r.   [17] Below, p. 64.

[18] Cons. e Prat., 68, fo. 162v; *ibid.*, 69, fo. 363v.

[19] N. Rubinstein, 'Firenze e il problema', p. 162.

the agreement reached on 24 October 1509 the Florentines bound themselves to pay the sum of 40,000 ducats but in four instalments instead of two, the last of which was to be handed over in February 1510. In fact the text of the 24 October agreement followed almost literally the draft of the terms sent by the Ten to Vettori in April 1508.[20] Both the draft and the terms as finally accepted contained an obligation which assumed some importance during the diplomatic negotiations in the summer of 1512: the emperor bound himself in 1509 to confirm and protect the existing regime. The protection which the government expected at this stage from Maximilian reflects the Republic's ever-present fear of a Medici attempt to return to power.[21]

Protection was indeed soon to be sorely needed for the following year saw the initial phases of the war directed by the pope against France and subsequently Florence. Julius II, who had been the driving force in forming the League of Cambrai against Venice, had waged war against her to regain the territories in the Romagna which she had annexed at the beginning of his pontificate. This completed, he turned against his former ally, France.[22] Once more the Florentines were in a dilemma: their treaty of 13 March 1509 bound them to Louis XII, yet they had no desire to antagonize the pope. Again Soderini called upon the services of Machiavelli: as Alessandro Nasi was on the point of returning, the gonfalonier sent Machiavelli temporarily to the French court to spy, to justify Florentine dealings with the papacy and to assure Louis of his city's, his own and his brother Cardinal Soderini's loyalty to France.[23]

When Machiavelli left Florence on 24 June 1510, Vettori was gravely ill,[24] but in August he had sufficiently recovered to send him a message by the new ambassador to France, Roberto Acciaiuoli, telling him to hurry back to Florence as he and Filippo Casavecchia daily desired his company. By now Machiavelli and Vettori were firm friends as appears from

[20] *Ibid.*, p. 164.
[21] *Ibid.*, p. 166.
[22] February 1510 Julius II signed peace treaty with Venice, F. Guicciardini, *St. d'It.*, ii (Bari, 1967), pp. 334–5.
[23] N. Ridolfi, *Machiavelli*, p. 114.
[24] F. Vettori to N. Machiavelli, 3 Aug. 1510, N. Machiavelli, *Lettere*, ed. F. Gaeta, p. 211.

Vettori's letter of 3 August which is signed simply 'Francesco'.[25] Here for the first time is written evidence of Vettori's personal interest in foreign policy and of his desire (which becomes more obvious in 1513 when he is ambassador in Rome) to discuss with his friend the aims and policies of the princes of the day. Although he held no office in Florence at this time which gave him access to foreign news, Vettori had obviously followed events in Italy carefully and had formed his own opinions on the diplomatic situation. In his letter to Machiavelli he wrote that he was amazed at Julius' audacity in challenging the strongest military power in Europe and that he could not understand how the pope could afford to take up the provocative attitude towards France implied in his attack on Louis' protégé, the duke of Ferrara, and in his imprisonment of the French Cardinal François de Clermont. This could only indicate that he desired war yet he had no allies but the weak and vanquished Venetians. Vettori betrayed sympathy for France in wishing that Louis would capture Bologna and chase Julius out of Rome so that Florence could emerge from her ambiguous situation, come what might. It remained to be seen, he went on, whether the pope could count on the emperor and Spain. Many thought he could; Vettori held the opposite view.

Vettori's letter is of interest in that it reveals what he knew of the diplomatic situation and his preference for the French. He either underestimated or did not know the importance of the Swiss in Julius' calculations; the pope's agreement with them is not mentioned.[26] He was correct in the view that neither the emperor nor Spain had yet sided with Julius.[27] The pro-French bias suggested by Vettori's desire to see Louis triumph over Julius is confirmed by his later admission to Machiavelli that he was at this stage in favour of the French.[28] It indicates a sympathy at this time with Soderini's policy.

From France Machiavelli warned the Ten that war between Louis XII and Julius was certain. On his way home to Florence he informed them of another fact: the king, he wrote from

[25] *Ibid.*, p. 213; N. Ridolfi, *Machiavelli*, p. 117.
[26] N. Machiavelli, *Lettere*, ed. F. Gaeta, p. 211; L. Pastor, *History of the Popes*, vi (London, 1898), pp. 324–6.
[27] L. Pastor, vi, pp. 323–4.   [28] Below, p. 53.

Tours on 10 September, was making efforts to assemble a council of his prelates.[29] This desire of the French king to gain the moral support of his clergy for a military attack on the pope also marks the first stage in an attempt to undermine the spiritual power of Julius II by calling into being that nightmare of renaissance popes—a general council of the Church. A core of ecclesiastical opposition to the pope already existed in the persons of five dissident cardinals who in the course of the papal warfare against Ferrara (referred to by Vettori as an instance of Julius' provocation of France) had left the papal court.[30] With these cardinals Louis opened negotiations in the winter of 1510 and in mid-May 1511 on their concurrence and that of the emperor (but not of course of the pope) a formal summons to a general council was issued.[31] On 18 July Julius issued a counter summons to a council to meet in the Vatican on 19 April 1512.[32]

Already in January 1511 Louis had announced to Florence that a council for the reform of the Church would take place and had asked for the city's agreement to his plan to hold it on Florentine territory at Pisa.[33] The Republic thus had the cruel choice of offending Julius if she agreed to the request or of forfeiting the friendship of France if she did not. *Pratiche* and a meeting of the Council of Eighty were summoned to consider the situation and considerable discussion ensued. There are no records of the *pratiche* extant for this period but it is possible to reconstruct the main views held at this time from the accounts given by the historians Cerretani, Guicciardini, Parenti and Nerli.[34] As before, political loyalties affected diplomatic alignments. According to Nerli,[35] three main groups emerged: the gonfalonier and his party who supported the council and France; the Salviati and others who sided with the pope and did not want the projected council to be held at Pisa; and a body of citizens, acting in the spirit of Savonarola and desiring the

[29] S. Bertelli, iii, p. 1347.

[30] J. Bridge, *A History of France*, iv (Oxford, 1929), p. 94.

[31] *Ibid.*, p. 95.   [32] *Ibid.*, p. 98.

[33] A. Desjardins, ii, p. 526, Louis XII to *Signoria*, 27 Jan. 1511.

[34] For this section of the chapter on Florence's relations with Pisa I am much indebted to the unpublished thesis submitted for a Ph.D. at the University of London, 1965, by R. Cooper: 'Piero Soderini', pp. 344ff.

[35] F. Nerli, *Commentari de' fatti civili occorsi dentro la città di Firenze dall'anno 1215 a 1537* (Augsburg, 1728), p. 103.

reform of the Church, who gave their allegiance to the gonfalonier thus causing his policy to prevail and permission to be
granted for the council to take place at Pisa. It should be added
that those who supported the pope were largely friends of the
Medici and desired a change of government.[36]

Given Vettori's diplomatic experience, he was likely to have
been called to give his views in the *pratiche* and it would be
interesting to know to which of the three groups he gave his
support. One may conjecture that he favoured the gonfalonier's
group as he was pro-French and anti-pope and as he had not
hitherto opposed Soderini's line of policy.

Even before the answer of the Republic was given, on 1
September three procurators attended in Pisa to the formal
preliminaries of the council.[37] In Florence the Ten still hoped to
suspend further proceedings or to secure the council's removal
elsewhere. To achieve one or other of these objectives, they sent
Machiavelli in the second week of September to persuade three
of the cardinals (Guillaume Briçonnet of Narbonne, Francesco
Borgia of Cosenza and Bernardo Carvajal of S. Croce), who had
set out for Pisa, to postpone their journey.[38] He conveyed the
same message to the viceroy of Milan and the king of France.
His mission failed with all concerned: the prelates continued on
their journey and the French king insisted on holding the
council in Pisa. Florentine relations with Rome deteriorated
and on 23 September the city came under papal interdict.[39]
Florence's resistance to French demands now stiffened: a request
for adequate military protection for the dissident cardinals on
their journey and also for the council itself at its meeting place
was firmly rejected.

Francesco Vettori's activities in connection with the Council
of Pisa show once again his perseverance and ability as a
negotiator. The commission given to Vettori on 29 September
instructed him to set off immediately to meet the rebel cardinals who were at that time expected to be leaving Borgo San

[36] B. Cerretani, Istoria, II, III, 74, fos. 403r–403v; R. Cooper, p. 346.
[37] P. Villari, i, p. 489; F. Guicciardini, *St. d'It.*, iii, p. 124; B. Buonaccorsi,
Diario (Florence, 1568), p. 163; R. Cooper, p. 350.
[38] S. Bertelli, iii, pp. 1379–85.
[39] L. Landucci, *A Florentine Diary*, trans. A. de Rosen Jervis (London, 1927),
p. 247.

Donnino *en route* for Pisa. The object of Vettori's mission was to make quite clear to the cardinals that they might not under any circumstances come, as they proposed, with an armed escort of 300 or 400 French lances. He was also to express the Ten's dissatisfaction with the answer previously given in this connection to their secretary ser Giovanni da Poppi. Vettori was to 'protest vigorously' against any advance of French troops across the Apennines which as the Ten had already pointed out to them, would constitute an intolerable threat to Pisa and its territory.[40]

Two of the five cardinals whom Vettori was instructed to meet, the Spaniard Bernardo Carvajal and the French Guillaume Briçonnet, he already knew from his embassy to Maximilian. Vettori first contacted Guillaume Briçonnet, cardinal of Narbonne.[41] He informed him that his government had heard from ser Giovanni da Poppi that the cardinals would be content to come to Pisa unarmed except for a small guard and that the troops intended for Pisa would be sent to the area between Pontremoli and Sarzana to guard the council from there. This, Vettori made clear, was the crux of the matter: his government had decided that no French troops must cross the Apennines; they would not be able to remain quartered there on account of the poverty of the region; to retire north would be a dishonour to the king and there would in consequence be no alternative but to advance on Pisa; this in turn would bring the papal troops into Tuscany and the war into Florentine territory. If Briçonnet and his fellow cardinals were to come to Pisa without troops, they would be most graciously received, but should they bring French troops over the Apennines they would, Vettori emphasized, be refused entry to Pisa and indeed to all Florentine dominions. Briçonnet was clearly dismayed and a vigorous discussion ensued in which the cardinal expressed his determination to carry on as planned, if need be in Lucca. Vettori, protesting that the devotion of his government to France merited greater consideration, laid stress on the sufferings of the city from the papal interdict and the confiscations of

[40] Commission to ser Giovanni da Poppi, Signori, Missive, Legaz. e. Comm., 26, fo. 174v, pub. O. Tommasini, i, pp. 547–8; A. Renaudet, *Le Concile Gallican de Pise-Milan* (Paris, 1922), p. 275; Vettori's commission, Signori, *cit.*, 26, fo. 176r pub. O Tommasini, i, pp. 550–1; A. Renaudet, p. 293.

[41] F. Vettori to the Ten, A. Renaudet, p. 312.

the goods of her merchants. Briçonnet finally told Vettori that the other cardinals should be brought into the discussion.

The meeting with Briçonnet occurred at a place some twenty-five miles from Borgo San Donnino where the other four ecclesiastics were staying and Vettori could not therefore interview them until the following morning. An hour before dawn (since he had learned of their imminent departure) Vettori set off to find Amanieu d'Albret, cardinal of S. Niccolò in Carcere and René de Prie, cardinal of Bayeux. René de Prie was already on the point of leaving, but he was prepared to be accommodating as he believed the cardinals to be safe on Florentine territory and an armed escort to be unnecessary. He took Vettori with him to Cardinal d'Albret's lodgings where he repeated his communication. Both cardinals then accompanied the Florentine ambassador on his visit to Bernardo Carvajal, cardinal of S. Croce. Carvajal was not in the best of humours, the hour being early and he still in bed having taken a dose: 'Then your government does not wish us to bring Monsieur de Lautrec to guard the Council with 150 to 200 light cavalry; and they object to our keeping men-at-arms in Sarzana or in the Lucca area to protect us against a naval landing at Piombino or a papal attack from inland', he said. 'Is it your wish that persons of our rank should entrust ourselves to your word when you have even made difficulties in granting us a safe conduct and I myself have not yet received one? You know that the pope would give 50,000 ducats to capture any one of us.'

Vettori repeated the reasons why Florence could not consent to the passage of troops over the Apennines and he added that if the cardinals wanted their troops to defend them, they should be sent to Bologna. The pope's attention would then be diverted from the council to the Romagna. Carvajal's reaction was to ask Vettori what Briçonnet had had to say about the matter. Evidently these two cardinals worked closely together and Vettori reported that everything depended upon them. Unfortunately for Florence, he found Briçonnet ill disposed towards the city and Carvajal very ambitious. Carvajal decided to consult the other cardinals, having first asked Vettori to leave the room. René de Prie and d'Albret expressed their willingness to satisfy the *Signoria* and Francesco Borgia was even more conciliatory. Eventually in a second interview Carvajal, too, conceded the point that the French troops would remain on the other side of the Apennines but he insisted on a guard of 150 archers. Vettori advised his government that the cardinals would probably stand firm on this point and asked for the *Signoria*'s opinion on it.

Vettori's resolution[42] and diplomacy allayed the Ten's anxiety, and they warmly commended their envoy on his execution of their instructions.[43] Since no French troops were to pass the Apennines, the *Signoria* would not deny the cardinals' demand for a guard of 150 archers, but Vettori was asked to do his utmost to get the number reduced and to have them quartered at Lucca on account of the extreme indigence of Pisa and the difficulty of provisioning so many there. As Vettori had proposed, those French troops not now to accompany the cardinals should be drafted to Bologna and the Romagna to create a diversion. Vettori's work was consolidated by Rosso Ridolfi, sent by the Ten to the cardinals to bring matters to a definite conclusion.[44] Rosso met them at Sarzana and on 13 October reported that they had decided to send back the companies which had crossed the Apennines and to put themselves under the protection of the Florentine *Signoria*.[45]

At the end of October the cardinals eventually reached Pisa.[46] Their reception was cold and the council was in no way representative: only four cardinals, sixteen prelates and a few doctors and abbots attended.[47] The local clergy refused them the use of the cathedral vestments and when the cardinals arrived to celebrate the inaugural mass on 1 November, the doors of the cathedral were locked against them and they had to go elsewhere.[48] The Florentine government was obliged to intervene before the council could hold its first session in the cathedral on 5 November.[49]

[42] *Raccolto delle Azioni*, p. 273.
[43] Ten to F. Vettori, A. Renaudet, p. 328.   [44] A. Renaudet, p. 337.
[45] Rosso Ridolfi to the Ten, A. Renaudet, p. 371.
[46] Piero del Nero and Niccolò Zati to the Ten, A. Renaudet, p. 432.
[47] J. Bridge, iv, p. 113.
[48] Piero del Nero and Niccolò Zati to the Ten, A. Renaudet, p. 436.
[49] The Ten to Piero del Nero and Niccolò Zati, A. Renaudet, p. 447; the Ten to Rosso Ridolfi, *ibid.*, p. 448; Rosso Ridolfi and Antonio Portinari to the Ten, *ibid.*, pp. 464ff.

Meanwhile, on 3 November, the day after he had returned to Florence from France, Machiavelli was dispatched to Pisa with orders to raise 300 troops to be in the town alongside the French armed guard and to persuade the prelates to hold the council elsewhere.[50] On 9 November (two days after a second session of the council had been held) an incident occurred which made the prelates more willing to listen to the persuasions of Machiavelli and the Ten anxious to call once more upon the services of Francesco Vettori.[51]

A quarrel over a courtesan had broken out between two soldiers, a Spaniard and a Pisan; what had begun as a minor street incident soon assumed the proportions of a serious riot as bystanders joined in, the Pisans and Florentines on one side and the French and Spanish servants of the cardinals on the other. After about half an hour the brawl was brought to an end, not however without scandal, some loss of life on both sides and injury to the French nobleman, Monsieur de Chastillon, a member of the cardinals' armed guard.[52]

The Ten fearing that the incident would activate French suspicions against Florence and that it would lose the city the favour of the king bought at the cost of antagonizing the pope, hastily sent two ambassadors to the cardinals at Pisa.[53] The choice of men throws light on the personnel of Soderini's government at this period. Francesco Vettori was now employed for the second time. His fellow ambassador, Neri Capponi, was a member of the Ten and a known enemy of the gonfalonier.[54]

The two men arrived in Pisa early in the morning of 13 November and went immediately to Carvajal, presenting their letter of credence and expressing the regret of the Florentine government at the incident.[55] The dispatch which the ambassadors sent back to Florence is a joint one, the greater part

[50] R. Ridolfi, *Machiavelli*, p. 125; S. Bertelli, iii, p. 1456.
[51] Piero del Nero and Niccolò Zati to the Ten, A. Renaudet, p. 494; Rosso Ridolfi and Antonio Portinari to the Ten, *ibid.*, p. 497.
[52] For the identity of M. de Chastillon, S. Bertelli, iii, p. 1460.
[53] *Commissione* for F. Vettori and N. Capponi, Florence 11 Nov. 1511, A. Renaudet, p. 507.
[54] A. Renaudet, p. 506, n. 109.
[55] N. Capponi and F. Vettori to the Ten, A. Renaudet, pp. 525ff.

being in the hand of Neri Capponi, Vettori penning the final paragraph, a postscript and both their signatures; it was he, too, who addressed it on the outside to the Ten in Florence. From this evidence it would seem as if Capponi, who was the older, was the more important of the two ambassadors. It was he who was responsible for the accounts of interviews. The final paragraph in Vettori's hand merely gives a few figures of those killed and wounded which the Ten would probably already have received from the captain and the *podestà*, as Vettori himself appreciated. These details are followed by the routine information on the correct amount of money to be paid to the courier which is common form at the end of dispatches.

Opening the dispatch Neri Capponi informed the Ten that in accordance with their instructions he and Vettori had communicated to Carvajal the Florentine government's regret for the incident, its desire to be absolved from any responsibility for it and its intention to investigate the causes of the disturbance as well as to punish the offenders. They had also besought him to stress the innocence of the Florentine government in his report of the matter to the king, and Carvajal had reassured them that the recent events would not damage Florence's reputation. Monsieur de Lautrec on whom they also called, received them well. Briçonnet, however, was markedly hostile: in 'bitter and abusive words' he deplored the lack of respect which the *Signoria* had paid Carvajal as he passed through their territory and also the ungracious treatment they had received which illbefitted cardinals and representatives of the king. Neri Capponi and Francesco Vettori did their best to excuse Florence but Briçonnet was not placated and left in high dudgeon, having in particular addressed some haughty words to Vettori which unfortunately for the historical record the ambassadors reserved for verbal report. The other French cardinal, René de Prie, the ambassadors were unable to contact as he had departed while they were talking to Guillaume Briçonnet.

By now the council was already in process of transfer from Pisa to Milan. On 13 November Vettori and Capponi reported that all the prelates with the exception of the four cardinals had gone; the third session of the council (fixed for the next day) had in fact been held the morning before they wrote and it had been decided to hold the fourth session in Milan in December. The rebel cardinals, the Florentine envoys went on, had nominated four ambassadors to request Julius II to select a place of meeting wherever he thought fit, provided that it was a neutral one. Carvajal was most anxious for Florentine support in the matter.[56]

Having discharged their duties with the cardinals, Vettori and Capponi turned their attention to the authorities responsible for public order in the city and learned what punitive measures had been taken. They visited in turn, Piero del Nero, the captain, and Niccolò Zati, the *podestà*.[57] On 14 November the Ten commended the work of the two envoys and instructed them to return home as all the members of the council had now departed.[58]

The Council of Pisa had failed as an oecumenical council of the Church and hence as a weapon in France's struggle with the pope. Its transfer to Milan was symbolic of the failure of Florentine diplomacy: Machiavelli had achieved what the *Signoria* had demanded of him but the transfer was too late; the whole episode of the council, ending as it did in earning for Florence the displeasure of both Louis XII and Julius II demonstrated the failure of the city's system of alliances and her isolation in the peninsula. This isolation, already the main preoccupation at the time of Vettori's embassy to Maximilian, assumed threatening dimensions with the publication on 5 October of the Holy League between the pope, the king of Spain and the Republic of Venice which Julius orientated against Florence and her ally France.[59] The pope attributed the responsibility for the city's pro-French policy and the concession of Pisa as the seat of the council to her gonfalonier and took the view that no change of direction in the foreign policy of the Florentine Republic could be expected while Piero Soderini was at the helm.[60] To remove him and to restore the Medici was to be one of Julius' aims: the other, which he tackled first, was to 'chase the French out of Italy'.

[56] Dieci, Responsive, 107, fo. 164v, A. Renaudet, p. 526.
[57] Tratte 71, fo. 2r, appointed *podestà* 1 Oct. 1511.
[58] The Ten to N. Capponi and F. Vettori, A. Renaudet, p. 528.
[59] L. Pastor, vi, p. 373.   [60] R. Cooper, p. 420.

In the early months of 1512 the expulsion of the French looked a difficult task for they had consolidated their position: in February the forces of the Holy League besieging Bologna had been forced to withdraw and the French military governor of Milan, Gaston de Foix, had recaptured Brescia.[61] By April French troops were at Ravenna and on the 11th of that month they defeated the confederate forces there, thus apparently making Julius' hated 'barbarians' masters of northern Italy.[62] Yet within five months of this victory not only was the greater part of the French army driven back over the Alps but Florence's pro-French gonfalonier was deposed and Julius' protégés, the Medici, re-entered the city whose government was soon to be more securely in their hands than ever before.

It is comparatively easy to account for the collapse of French power in Italy; the truth about the capitulation of the Florentine Republic and the fall of Soderini is far harder to establish. The French had won their victory at the cost of the death of Gaston de Foix. Without its ablest commander the army soon became disorganized and demoralized. Moreover, without actually joining the Holy League, from the spring of 1512 the emperor assumed an increasingly favourable attitude towards it and he withdrew the German mercenaries from the French army at a time when confederate strength was augmented by the Swiss entering the war in the service of Julius. England too was sending men to Spain to attack France from there.[63] Such a combination of circumstances explains why the pope was able so soon to turn the tables on the French, and chase them out of Italy, 'flying', as Vettori wrote, 'like mist before the wind'.[64] The collapse of French power in Italy did not, however, lead automatically to the capitulation of the Florentine Republic and the fall of Soderini; these consequences could probably have been averted if the gonfalonier had adapted his foreign policy to the changed diplomatic situation and if he had had behind him the wholehearted support of all the citizens.[65]

The analysis made by Vettori in his history of Italy (*Sommario*) of Florence's foreign policy after the departure of the

[61] P. Villari, ii, p. 3.   [62] *Ibid.*, pp. 5–6.
[63] *Ibid.*   [64] *Sommario*, p. 287, cit. P. Villari, ii, p. 7.
[65] R. Cooper, p. 378.

French army enables us to see the alternative to dependence on France advocated by certain of the citizens.

Vettori maintained that since Florence could neither get help from France nor defend herself with her own forces some other diplomatic alliance was imperative. With the hindsight of events, he wrote of the summer of 1512 that it was useless for the city to have sent, as she did in January of that year, an ambassador (Francesco Guicciardini) to Ferdinand of Aragon, because before proposals could be made and an answer received from Spain the game was certain to be over; nor was it any more worth while to have dispatched, as she also did, an ambassador (Giovan Vittorio Soderini) to the Emperor Maximilian because he 'hadn't a horse in Italy'. To have tried to divert the pope from his intentions would have been equally futile for he was an enemy of Soderini's government. The only hope for Florence, Vettori thought, would have been for her to have come to an agreement with the Spanish viceroy in Italy, Ramon de Cardona.[66]

This statement is of considerable importance for our knowledge of Vettori's diplomatic views, as it represents the opinion of those citizens who favoured some form of compromise with the Holy League led by Julius II and who expressed their opinions in the *pratiche* summoned during July and August 1512.[67]

On 15 July the papal datary, Lorenzo Pucci, and the Spanish ambassador in Rome, Cecco della Freda, arrived in Florence to request the city's adherence to the League. Their request was the subject of much argument among those citizens called to give their views in the *pratiche strette*, the more selective advisory committees, and in the *pratiche larghe*, the fuller committees which included representatives of the Great Council. On 17 July, two days after the arrival of the envoys, a large advisory committee made up of the magistrates, the Council of Eighty and approximately 500 additional citizens was called to discuss the answer which should be given the envoys.[68] The majority

[66] *Sommario*, p. 289. For the date of the *Sommario* see n. 75 below.

[67] For this analysis of the *pratiche* and for the view that there was a difference between the opinions expressed respectively in the smaller and larger *pratiche*, I am again indebted to the thesis of R. Cooper, pp. 424ff.

[68] R. Cooper, p. 424.

considered neutrality to be the best policy and refused to countenance any declaration against the king of France. On the following day the Ten summoned a small advisory committee of the leading citizens and here the majority of those who spoke were critical of the pro-French attitude adopted at the previous day's meeting and considered that Florence should enter the Holy League if reasonable terms were offered. The actual answer given to the two envoys was more in line with the majority view in the large committee than with that of the smaller.[69]

In view of the treaty which they had made with the emperor in October 1509 the Florentines had a right to expect that he would at least remain neutral. But, as mentioned, Maximilian had inclined towards the League since April 1512 and in July, far from helping his ally, he had made a fresh demand for money for the 'preservation' of the city through his lieutenant, Mathias Lang, an obligation to which he had already committed himself in the October treaty, as the Florentines were not slow to point out.[70] Nevertheless the Florentines had to consider whether the power of the emperor was sufficient to help them and to make the offer of another subsidy worth while. In contrast to earlier years, the *pratiche* called to discuss the imperial demands show a sceptical attitude to imperial power which is also adopted in Vettori's history.[71] The general tenor of the small *pratica* summoned on 22 July was that Florence would gain little by responding to the demand made by Maximilian's representative. Though negotiations with the emperor should not be broken off, the door should be left open for an agreement with the Holy League. In the larger *pratica* held on 27 July greater stress was laid on keeping faith with France.[72] Francesco Vettori attended this meeting and his views reflect those of the leading citizens in the small *pratica*. Money should not, he thought, be given to the emperor at this juncture because there was the likelihood of an agreement with the League and if this did not take place there was always France.[73]

[69] *Ibid.*, pp. 425–6.

[70] N. Rubinstein, 'Firenze e il problema', p. 168.

[71] *Sommario*, p. 289: 'lo Imperadore non avea in Italia uno cavallo' cit. N. Rubinstein, 'Firenze e il problema', p. 169.

[72] R. Cooper, pp. 427–8.   [73] O. Tommasini, i, p. 730.

By the end of July an opportunity of salvation was offered by the Spanish viceroy. By the 28th news of a mutiny on the part of Cardona's men who had not received their pay had reached Florence[74] and it was obvious, as Vettori also reported in his history later on,[75] that the viceroy urgently needed money. But in the *pratiche* held on the two subsequent days to discuss the question of a subsidy, members were divided as to whether this was the right moment to make a bid for entering the League or whether Cardona's difficulties did not provide an opportunity for avoiding any commitment. In the event a subsidy of 30,000 ducats was proposed; this was insufficient for the viceroy's needs and provided, as we shall see, an opportunity for the Medici to buy his support at the meeting of the confederates at Mantua in August. When the matter was discussed in two large *pratiche* on 29 and 30 July a number of members still advised against any commitment and the majority counselled that an agreement with the League should only be concluded when it was clear that the alliance with France would not be repudiated.[76]

The alliance problem was still under discussion in the *pratiche* as late as 12 and 15 August. On 12 August an alliance with the pope was advocated on the ground that, as Giovanbattista Ridolfi said, the League was dependent on Julius and to come to an agreement with him would therefore suffice. Vettori was one of the majority of this small *pratica* who supported this view.[77]

That one policy was being advocated in the small *pratiche* and another in the larger is suggested by Giovan Battista Ridolfi's remark in the small *pratica* assembled on 15 August that authority should be given to the person responsible for handling negotiations with the pope 'so that one thing is not decided upon here and then something else is done elsewhere'.[78] This hint in Ridolfi's speech is substantiated in Vettori's history where he

[74] R. Cooper, pp. 428–9.
[75] *Sommario*, p. 289; the *Sommario* was probably written in spring 1528; see R. Hughes, 'Francesco Vettori', thesis submitted for Ph.D., University of London, 1958, pp. 301–2.
[76] R. Cooper, pp. 429–30.
[77] Cons. e Prat., 68, fo. 169v; R. Cooper, p. 433.
[78] Cons. e Prat., 68, fo. 172r: 'Vorrebbe ne fussi dato auctorità a chi ha ad tractare adciò non si deliberassi una cosa et poi sene facessi un'altra altrove.' R. Cooper, p. 432.

explains Florence's failure to negotiate with the viceroy after he had advanced with his army as far as Bologna. A proposition for a subsidy to be paid to the viceroy was, Vettori says, put forward in the Great Council but not passed. In a small *pratica* called by the Ten to discuss whether an agreement should be made with the viceroy 'all present' declared that this was the only policy for the safety of the city; the same view was expressed in the Council of Eighty, but when the proposition came before the larger *pratica*, the additional citizens called to it would not hear of any agreement. Vettori went on to explain that the larger *pratiche* were necessary because no agreement could be reached without the offer of a subsidy and since the money for this had to be voted by the members of the Great Council some of their number were bound to be called.[79]

As always in periods of crisis and changes of government in Florence external and internal affairs interacted and it is clear that these differences of opinion on diplomatic policy represented also political differences. The smaller *pratiche* consisted mainly of optimates like Vettori whom we know from the summaries of his speeches to have been called twice to give his views although he may have been present also on other occasions when he did not speak.[80] Many of these citizens were opposed to Soderini's government and were even pro-Medici. Of the thirty-three men whose names constantly occur in the records of the small *pratiche* for July and August, ten became members of the Twenty who discussed the reform introduced on 7 September after the return of the Medici. With one exception, they also became members of the Medicean *Balìa* constituted after the *parlamento* of 17 September and of the Council of Seventy, re-elected January 1514. Of the rest of those who regularly attended the *pratiche strette*, a further seven became members both of the *Balìa* and of the Seventy and another two of the Council of Seventy.[81]

In advocating an alliance with the viceroy and even with the pope, Vettori was thus associating himself in foreign affairs with those optimates who had little sympathy for the political regime

[79] *Sommario*, p. 290.
[80] On 22 July, Secret Archives of the Vatican, Ottobon. 2759, fos. 130–3; on 25 July, O. Tommasini, i, p. 730.   [81] R. Cooper, pp. 434–5.

of Soderini and who were opposed to his diplomatic policy. Why had he changed his views on foreign affairs from those held in the summer of 1510 when he hoped for a French victory over Julius?

The answer is given by Vettori himself. In August 1513 he wrote to Machiavelli: 'Before the question of holding a council at Pisa was discussed, I always supported the French because I believed this was the best for Italy and our city would have peace . . . But when I saw how we mismanaged the council episode and how dissatisfied the French departed, I began to doubt whether their victory would not result in our ruin and that they would not treat us as they did Brescia, and Monsieur de Foix, young and cruel, made me fear even more, and so I turned from them. Nevertheless whenever there was any discussion of an agreement with them, I was in favour of it and advocated it because I hoped it would safeguard us against that danger.'[82] At the time of the *pratiche* in the summer of 1512 Vettori must have come to the conclusion that the only way to save his city was to accept the best possible terms from the members of the League before it was too late. For Vettori's political and diplomatic decisions the all-important consideration was the good of his city.[83]

Did the alternative to Soderini's pro-French alignment proposed by Vettori and like-minded optimates have any chance of success with the confederates or were they all too committed to the papal plan of action against Florence seriously to entertain the idea of an agreement with her? After the collapse of French power in Italy the confederates met at Mantua in mid-August to discuss their future policy. Although each member of the Holy League (albeit for different reasons) had desired the expulsion of the French, once this common aim had been achieved, their plans for future action were by no means concordant.[84] Neither the emperor's representative, Mathias Lang, nor the viceroy of the king of Aragon came to Mantua committed to Julius' aims to remove Soderini and to restore the

---

[82] N. Machiavelli, *Lettere*, ed. F. Gaeta, p. 285.
[83] For Vettori's patriotism, see letter to N. Machiavelli, 20 Aug. 1513. N. Machiavelli, *Lettere*, ed. F. Gaeta, p. 285. See, also, below, pp. 275, 281, 290.
[84] F. Guicciardini, *St. d'It.*, iii, p. 216, cp. *Sommario*, p. 288.

Medici; both were impecunious and prepared to treat with the Florentine government.[85] Mathias Lang had suggested to the Florentine ambassador at Trent, Giovan Vittorio Soderini, that if his government paid the emperor 40,000 ducats the city would win a protector against the pope, but after their previous experiences, the Florentines were sceptical of the effectiveness of imperial power in Italy[86] and by the time Lang reached Mantua he had received no satisfactory answer from them. While the confederates were assembling, the viceroy, too, had approached Florence and Cardona had received the offer which was too small to help him. Hence when the meeting at Mantua took place neither the emperor nor the viceroy was satisfied with the results of their respective negotiations. The Medici made both of them their adherents by a financial offer which was sufficient to meet their needs.[87] Thus Vettori and those optimates were quite right who maintained that the support of Cardona could be won by granting him the money he needed and some trifle in addition for himself, as this was the price at which the Medici won his support for the papal plan of action against Florence.[88]

Clearly in their refusal to reassess the foreign situation realistically and to consider a change of alliance Soderini and those of his supporters who adhered with such tragic faith to France enabled Julius and his Medici dependants to win at Mantua the diplomatic victory which was decisive for the fall of the Republic.

---

[85] R. Cooper, p. 419.
[86] Above, p. 50, n. 71, cp. F. Guicciardini, *St. d'It.*, iii, p. 219.
[87] R. Cooper, pp. 420–1.   [88] *Sommario*, p. 289.

CHAPTER IV

The Revolution of 1512

IF THE external cause of the revolution of 1512 was the failure of Florence's system of alliances after the collapse of French power in Italy, the growth within the city of opposition to Soderini and of sympathy with the Medici on the part of certain optimates may be said to be the internal one. In attempting to illuminate the rôle of Francesco Vettori in the fall of Soderini and in the return of the Medici some light will be shed on the motives which prompted the thought and action of others of his class during the gonfalonier's administration. Some idea can be formed, too, of the relation between the Medici and their supporters.

Many of Florence's leading citizens were not committed adherents either of the Medici or of the republican form of government; they supported a patron or regime as long as their personal motives of profit, power, honour or protection were satisfied. Frustrated, they became a dangerous element as much to the Medici as to a Republic. The selfish and private motives which led a Florentine citizen to support one particular patron or party rather than another were appreciated and commented on by historians and men of affairs: 'In all the revolutions which have taken place in this our city, it may be observed that the reforms of government, be they popular or oligarchic, are never made for the convenience or benefit of the people as a whole, but always for the security, convenience and greatness of the ruling group', wrote Filippo Nerli.[1] Lorenzo de' Medici admitted that 'in public affairs men are motivated only by their own advantage',[2] and Francesco Guicciardini maintained that it was not liberty that men wanted but command.[3]

[1] F. Nerli, p. 119.

[2] Letter to Cardinal de' Medici, 14 Feb. 1513. A. Giorgetti, 'Lorenzo de' Medici Duca d'Urbino e Jacopo V d'Appiano' in *A.S.I.*, Ser. iv, viii (1881), p. 319.

[3] F. Guicciardini, *Dialogo del Reggimento di Firenze*, ed. R. Palmarocchi (Bari, 1932), p. 37.

The desire on the part of the optimates to control the political affairs of their city is well illustrated by their hopes of and their disillusionment with the life gonfalonierate. In 1502 the leading citizens had been among the foremost advocates of political reform hoping thereby to recover what they regarded as their rightful position in the government.[4] They themselves abandoned the establishment (on the Venetian model) of an aristocratic senate of from twenty to a hundred upper class citizens appointed for life as they knew that it would be unacceptable to the populace. With the notable exception of Bernardo Rucellai, who was an arch enemy of Piero Soderini, and the notable assistance of Alamanno and Jacopo Salviati, who supported him warmly, most of the optimates were favourably disposed towards the principle of the life gonfalonierate.[5]

It was not long, however, before the gonfalonier's independence of the optimates,[6] began to arouse their opposition. It became manifest two years after Soderini's appointment[7] and by 1505 Nerli was able to discern three groups of upper class citizens whose attitudes and activities illustrate the diverse motives which made men of this social stratum desire a change of government. 'A certain type of young men' who began vigorously to speak against the gonfalonier are distinguished from those who opposed him 'in the magistracies, in the *pratiche* and in the councils' and from yet others who 'desired the return of the Medici'.[8]

Let us first consider the activities and membership of the group of 'young men' and other Florentines whom Nerli associates with them, who together frequented the gardens of Bernardo Rucellai. This reference to a group of citizens known to have met for the purpose of political and philosophical discussion in the Orti Oricellari belonging to the Rucellai family is of special interest since members of the Vettori family belonged to it. As early as 1502 Bernardo Rucellai and 'some other citizens' such as Luca Antonio degli Albizzi (whose son Antonfrancesco will be mentioned later) had begun to withdraw their support

---

[4] F. Guicciardini, *St. fior.*, p. 241.
[5] *Ibid.*, pp. 245, 246, 247.
[6] Above, p. 34.
[7] F. Guicciardini, *St. fior.*, p. 272.   [8] F. Nerli, p. 98.

from Soderini.[9] Bernardo Rucellai had gone into voluntary exile from which he returned in 1505 when Nerli mentions in connection with this group that certain masques were performed in which the gonfalonier was attacked.[10]

Associated with these citizens was what one might call the 'constitutional' opposition to the gonfalonier—that group of Florentines who according to Nerli acted against Soderini 'in the magistracies, in the *pratiche* and in the councils'. Chief among these were Jacopo Salviati and his cousin Alamanno who had gone out of their way to support the gonfalonier's election. Guicciardini attributed their estrangement to a grudge Jacopo bore the gonfalonier for removing from the chancellorship of the commercial tribunal known as the *Mercanzia* his close friend ser Jacopo di Martino.[11] From the line which Jacopo was to follow in September 1512 and in 1519 and from his activities during the period of Savonarola, one can surmise that his group was republican in principle but came to disapprove of the particular policies of Soderini. Both Alamanno and Jacopo Salviati (together with Lanfredo Lanfredini, who will be mentioned later in connection with the events of September 1512 and during the rule of Lorenzo, duke of Urbino)[12] formed part of the 'tail' of the Savonarola party,[13] and Jacopo Salviati favoured the enlargement of the Medici party after 1512 to include those who had a reputation and standing 'during the Republic'.[14] With the vigour of Alamanno's opposition to the gonfalonier, however, even a more exclusive aristocrat like Francesco Guicciardini desired to be associated by marrying his daughter against his own father's wishes.[15]

Among those who frequented the meetings in the gardens of Bernardo Rucellai was Paolo Vettori. Paolo is specifically mentioned as one of the 'certain type of young men' who had begun in 1505 to speak against the gonfalonier and to criticize his actions.[16] He seems to have been particularly wily: 'with great astuteness and very artfully he observed the gonfalonier',

[9] *Ibid.*, p. 93. See F. Gilbert, 'Bernardo Rucellai'.
[10] *Ibid.*, p. 99.   [11] F. Guicciardini, *St. fior.*, p. 272.
[12] Below, pp. 70, 137.   [13] F. Guicciardini, *St. fior.*, p. 123.
[14] F. Nerli, p. 120.
[15] R. Ridolfi, *The Life of Francesco Guicciardini* (London, 1967), p. 19. Guicciardini married Maria Salviati in November 1508.   [16] F. Nerli, p. 98.

says Nerli. Lorenzo Strozzi elucidates this statement by his remark that Paolo entered into an intimate friendship with Soderini so that he might the more easily carry out his designs in favour of the Medici,[17] and his brother recalls that Paolo was constantly at the gonfalonier's elbow.[18] Paolo's personal motives for revolution seem to have been those of a daring, spendthrift young man who has nothing to lose and perhaps something to gain by a change of regime. Segni describes him as 'bold and wary' and either on account of poverty or for some other reason discontent with the regime and 'desirous of something new'.[19] Guicciardini maintains that he was 'implicated' by overspending and debts.[20] Even his own brother implies that Paolo's main reason for taking part in the revolution was the precarious state of his financial affairs.[21] He had evidently lost a considerable amount of money, perhaps in connection with the iron foundry. After the revolution Francesco was anxious for Paolo to justify himself by saying that Soderini had tried to ruin him by involving him in this business in which he had staked his possessions and his reputation.[22] A commercial motive for Paolo's participation in the revolution seems more than likely.

The positively pro-Medici element in the revolution must now claim our attention. Nerli distinguishes it from mere dislike of Soderini's government, and Guicciardini speaks of citizens supporting Filippo Strozzi when he wished to marry Clarice de' Medici as doing so either on account of their affection for the Medici or their hatred for the gonfalonier.[23]

Until 1503 the pro-Medici faction in Florence had been small, comprising such convinced partisans as Piero di Filippo Tornabuoni, Jacopo di Buongianni Gianfigliazzi, Pandolfo di

---

[17] G.-B. Niccolini, *Filippo Strozzi, tragedia* (Firenze, 1847), p. xxx.

[18] C. Strozz., Ser. I, 136, fo. 219r, Francesco to Paolo, Rome, 5 Aug. 1513.

[19] B. Segni, *Vita di Niccolò Capponi*, ed. in Classici Italiani, iii (Milano, 1805), p. 282.

[20] F. Guicciardini, *St. d'It.*, iii, p. 231; cp. S. Ammirato, *Istorie Fiorentine*, ed. F. Ranalli, v (Florence, 1848), p. 529.

[21] C. Strozz., Ser. I, 136, fo. 219r, Francesco to Paolo, Rome, 5 Aug. 1513.

[22] *Ibid.*, 'a te bixogna monstrare havere havuto iuste cause d'inimicizia con Giovanbattista, . . . et che Piero Soderini t'haveva messo in questa materia del ferro, dove havevi messo lo stato tuo e la persona . . . et che cercava ogni via per farti rovinare . . .'; and below, p. 79.

[23] F. Guicciardini, *St. fior.*, p. 327.

Bernardo Corbinelli, Andrea di Tommaso Minerbetti, Francesco di Giovanni, Alessandro di Antonio Pucci and Piero di Niccolò Ridolfi. These had all been involved in Piero de' Medici's attempted *coup* against Florence in 1497 and were given office by the Medici after their restoration in 1512.[24] After Piero's death the Medici policy changed from one of military force to one of fifth column activities. By helping and befriending those citizens who had commercial or ecclesiastical business to transact in Rome, the Medici gradually began to build up a party in Florence which was in due course augmented by the citizens who were dissatisfied with Soderini's increasing independence.[25]

Once more the Orti Oricellari are a focal point. As Guicciardini's reference to the composition and activities of the pro-Medici group shows, it is impossible to make a clear-cut distinction between them and the anti-Soderini group; but one can outline certain trends. He mentions certain 'young upper class citizens' many of whose names appear among the 'certain type of young men' in Nerli's history. Their fathers had been enemies of the Medici in 1494 but now the sons appeared to be friendly with them, perhaps, Guicciardini says, with the idea of restoring the Medici, but maybe also because 'they wanted something else besides' or 'to spite the gonfalonier'.[26] Among these were Bartolomeo Valori, Gino Capponi, Antonfrancesco degli Albizzi, Piero Martelli, Giovanni Corsi, Giovanni Rucellai and Filippo Buondelmonti. The first three names will occur again in connection with the removal of Soderini from the palace.[27] Piero Martelli and Giovanni Corsi are two of the citizens specifically mentioned by Giovanni Battista Gelli as frequenting the gardens of the Rucellai.[28] To these may be added Paolo Vettori (also to be involved in the seizure of Soderini) because Filippo Strozzi discussed with him and Gino Capponi his marriage to Clarice de' Medici which was in flagrant defiance of the laws prohibiting any kind of association with the Medici.[29]

[24] R. Cooper, pp. 225–6.
[25] F. Guicciardini, *St. fior.*, pp. 323–4.
[26] *Ibid.*, p. 324.
[27] Below, p. 61.   [28] F. Gilbert, 'Bernardo Rucellai', p. 117.
[29] B. Segni, *Vita di Niccolò Capponi*, p. 282.

Let us consider some of their pro-Medici activities. Guicciardini states that these young men on going to Rome consorted openly with the Medici and were entertained by them. He does not give a date but it seems likely that the change in Medici policy was bearing fruit already a year after Piero's death. In October 1504 a *pratica* was summoned in Florence to discuss the news supplied by the city's ambassador in Rome that his compatriots had attended the Medici celebration in honour of the feast of Saint Cosmas and Saint Damian.[30] According to Parenti 'many of our young men of good family' went to Rome at Easter 1505 and held discussions with Cardinal de' Medici.[31] Parenti indicates too that there was support from within Florence for the plan in August 1505 of the *condottiere* captain Bartolommeo d'Alviano to take Florence by force and to restore the Medici.[32] Although there seems to be no conclusive proof that the young men who attended the meetings in the Rucellai gardens and who were already visiting the Medici in Rome were involved in Alviano's activities, it is at least likely that they were. Since Soderini was to be taken from the palace by three of the young men who are known to have gone to Rome, it is most probable that 'the fundamental elements' of the plot to remove Soderini and to restore the Medici were already present in 1505.[33]

Discussions were held outside Florence to consider ways and means of restoring the Medici. 'Trusting in certain discussions that the Medici had held with the Rucellai, Paolo Vettori, Bartolomeo Valori, Antonfrancesco degli Albizzi and the entire school of the gardens of Bernardo Rucellai', the confederate army pitched camp in the plain of Prato in August 1512.[34] In speaking of the actions of the young men in the palace Nardi says that they went there 'in conformity, however, with the other plotters of long standing of all these evils'.[35] Also Antonfrancesco and 'other friends' conducted a regular correspondence with Giuliano de' Medici by means of a peasant who hid Giuliano's letters on his person and deposited them in a hole in the wall of the cemetery of S. Maria Novella on the side near the

---

[30] R. Cooper, p. 228.
[31] Parenti, Istorie, B.N.F., II, II, 134, fo. 59r; cit. R. Cooper, p. 228.
[32] R. Cooper, p. 231.   [33] *Ibid.*   [34] F. Nerli, p. 107.   [35] J. Nardi, i, p. 427.

old piazza. Here too the replies were placed and the peasant transported them to his employer. Such letters had no saluta-tion and no signature but 'the conspirators were those who expelled Piero Soderini'.[36] Pitti provides evidence of Vettori complicity. He relates how their villa of Paneretta on Florentine territory close to the Sienese border was used by Paolo Vettori and Antonfrancesco degli Albizzi, 'noble, seditious young men avid for novelty' who already 'many months' before the down-fall of Soderini were 'secretly plotting with some others in favour of the Medici . . . to agree with them about the way of restoring them', talking secretly in the Vettori villa.[37] Corroboration of Pitti's statement comes from Filippo Strozzi's brother Lorenzo who speaks of conversations between the Medici, Paolo Vettori, Antonfrancesco degli Albizzi and Bernardo Rucellai's sons, Giovanni and Palla. He gives the greatest responsibility to Paolo Vettori who, albeit with Antonfrancesco's and the Rucellai's knowledge, 'alone and secretly' received Giulio de' Medici at the Vettori villa. Here the two men discussed how the Medici should govern and which people were to be trusted. Eventually, on 31 August, taking advantage of the fear en-gendered in the supporters of the republican regime by the sack of Prato by the Spaniards under the leadership of Ramon de Cardona and of the palpable desire among the leading citizens for a change of government, Paolo Vettori, Antonfrancesco degli Albizzi, Bartolomeo Valori and Gino Capponi entered the Palazzo della Signoria and seized Soderini.[38] He was then escorted to the Vettori house on the Lungarno.[39]

If active opposition to Soderini and complicity with the Medici in a plot to remove the gonfalonier from office describes Paolo Vettori's part in the preliminary stages of the revolution, what then can be said of Francesco's role?

Francesco's relationship with some of the principal members of the opposition to Soderini leads one to expect a much greater

[36] B.N.F., II, I, 394, fo. 71r, 'Modo di Giuliano de' Medici che usava quando era a Roma a mandare lettere a Firenze': 'e congiurati furno quelli che poi chacciorno Piero Soderini'.

[37] I. Pitti, 'Apologia de' Cappuci', *A.S.I.*, Ser. i, iv, pt. 2 (Florence, 1853), p. 311.

[38] G.-B. Niccolini, pp. xxix–xxx; but cp. J. Nardi, ii, p. 10.

[39] *Sommario*, p. 292; J. Nardi, i, p. 428.

participation in the various manifestations of hostility to the gonfalonier than the facts seem to warrant. Besides being Paolo's elder brother, he was as we know the nephew of Bernardo Rucellai[40] and the brother-in-law of Gino Capponi.[41] In 1515 he married his daughter Elisabetta to Lorenzo degli Albizzi, the brother of Antonfrancesco, and this link seems already to have been projected in 1513.[42] Of the four young men, Gino Capponi, Antonfrancesco degli Albizzi, Paolo Vettori and Bartolomeo Valori whose names are always given in the accounts of the seizure of Soderini, Francesco Vettori was therefore closely connected with at least three.

The fact that none of the historians mentions Vettori's name in connection with the activities against Soderini does not prove that he did not participate in them. Indeed, as we have seen,[43] he did share in one aspect of the antagonism to the gonfalonier, but there is also ground for believing that, while critical of his external policy, Vettori was personally friendly towards Soderini. The accounts of the closing phase of the gonfalonier's rule by Vettori's contemporaries are written in a very different vein from his. Nerli, who thought Soderini 'dismayed' and rendered helpless by the sack of Prato, maintained that the Medici would not have been successful if the gonfalonier had resolutely taken the decisions he ought to have and if he had 'wished to turn his face to fortune'. He sums up Soderini's policy saying that he 'neither knew how to be a good ruler nor a bad one' and that he thought he could overcome all the difficulties by patience and trust in 'the advantages of time' instead of forestalling them 'as wise princes and rulers of republics should do'.[44] Guicciardini is even more critical saying that 'the gonfalonier, repenting of the vanity of his counsel, terrified and devoid of standing and authority, irresolute, saved rather than saving, let himself be ruled by the will of others, making provision for nothing, neither for his own preservation nor for the common safety'.[45] But Vettori's assess-

---

[40] Above, p. 2.

[41] Gino was Niccolò Capponi's brother. For Vettori's marriage, above, p. 2.

[42] P. Litta, xi, plate xix (Albizzi); C. Strozz., Ser. I, 136, fo. 229r, Francesco to Paolo, Rome, 16 June 1513; ibid., fo. 225r.

[43] Above, pp. 52–3.

[44] F. Nerli, p. 110.   [45] F. Guicciardini, St. d'It., iii, p. 231.

ment, written admittedly during the next republican period,
betrays sympathy for his compatriot. He gives him a good
character saying that Soderini was 'certainly good and prudent
and rendered the city service; nor was he ever deflected from
the course of justice or swayed by ambition or avarice', and he
refrains from condemning his diplomatic policy, merely remark-
ing that 'the bad luck (I will not say his but of the wretched city)
did not allow either him or anyone else to see the way to avoid
the affronts of the confederates'. [46]

Although Vettori here glosses over Soderini's mistaken
external policy, in fact, as we have seen from the *pratiche* he was
not averse from criticizing it, and he may, therefore, be associated with that 'constitutional' opposition to Soderini led by
Jacopo Salviati which Nerli registers. [47]

Vettori's history contains several more passages showing a
generous attitude towards the gonfalonier. In his account of the
seizure of Soderini by the young men he relates that the gonfalonier replied to them in 'gracious and kindly words' and
eventually agreed to their demands 'being cautious and anxious
not to harm anyone'. [48] Vettori also emphasizes that he himself
did not wish 'in any way whatsoever' to oppose Soderini and the
government, and he told the gonfalonier that he considered 'he
had governed so well during his time in office that he did not
wish to be in the company of those who removed him' from it.
The recorder of Francesco's *Azioni*, who confirms this remark,
reveals Vettori's dilemma. He considered it inexpedient to
oppose his brother and 'having firmly resolved not to be against
the gonfalonier' had even considered fleeing. [49] In April of the
following year Vettori himself commented to Machiavelli on his
rôle in the events of 1512, 'it is sufficient for me to have satisfied
the city, my friendship with him [Soderini] and myself'. [50]

It would be interesting to know the reasons for Vettori's
sympathy with the man whom his brother and many of his
fellow optimates were so determined to remove. Probably
Machiavelli brought the two men together. As a result of the

[46] *Sommario*, p. 289, cp. 291.
[47] Above, pp. 56, 57.   [48] *Sommario*, p. 292.
[49] *Raccolto delle Azioni*, p. 273; *Sommario*, p. 292.
[50] N. Machiavelli, *Lettere*, ed. F. Gaeta, p. 241.

embassy to Germany when Machiavelli had been Soderini's choice, Machiavelli and Vettori had become close friends; both had subsequently been involved in their respective capacities in the reconquest of Pisa and in the crisis over the council in that city. On these occasions and on many others Vettori had been active in Soderini's government. In 1512 the three shared the responsibility for the defence of Florence and its territory, as Vettori was in charge of the mercenaries for the city's internal defence, as *commissario generale*, and Machiavelli's militia was responsible for her external protection. When Soderini was in danger of his life he sent Machiavelli to appeal to Francesco and it was Vettori (according to his own account) who took an oath from the young men that they would not harm him.[51]

Vettori's behaviour betrays the same humanitarian feeling as he ascribes to Soderini himself in his confrontation with the four young men. In June 1513, for example, he wrote to Machiavelli 'for me it would be impossible to do anyone harm, come what may',[52] and two months earlier, 'I have not offended anyone either in words or deeds, neither in public nor in private'.[53] Vettori's action in saving Soderini's life earned him unpopularity with both republicans and the Medici: 'in this preservation of Piero Soderini, it seems to me that I have acquired the ill will of one side and little esteem with the other', he was to write in April 1513.[54] A few days later he complained of tax discrimination against him saying that he had come to the conclusion that Paolo's part in taking the gonfalonier from the palace and his own in saving his life had greatly harmed both of them since the friends of the past regime wished Paolo ill and those of the present felt the same about him, as the death of Soderini would have removed a potential source of danger.[55]

After the young men had removed the gonfalonier from the palace and had taken him to the Vettori house, they returned.

[51] *Raccolto delle Azioni*, p. 273; *Sommario*, p. 292.

[52] N. Machiavelli, *Lettere*, ed. F. Gaeta, p. 264; cp. identical sentiment expressed by Soderini to his wife, 9 Sept. 1512: 'io mai fece male a nessuno'. B.N.F. Ginori Conti 29, 113, 3, cit. R. Cooper, p. 397; the caution which Vettori thought characteristic of Soderini, Clement VII apparently thought characteristic of Vettori, cp. '*rispettivo*' used of both, *Sommario*, pp. 292, 370.

[53] N. Machiavelli, *Lettere*, ed. F. Gaeta, p. 245.

[54] *Ibid.*, p. 241.   [55] *Ibid.*, pp. 245-6.

'Many of the young Rucellai, Tornabuoni, Pitti and some of the
Bartoli, together with Tommasino Corbinelli and one of the
sons of Filippo Buondelmonti and other relations and followers
of the Medici' had assembled in the palace to force the retiring
Signoria to deprive the gonfalonier of his office which the priors
were empowered to do on the strength of a law passed in
August 1502.[56] Ammirato's reference to the Rucellai indicates
the complicity of this family and their associates. So, too, does
Nardi's account. He refers to Bernardo Rucellai with his
following, the Tornabuoni and Guidantonio Vespucci, whose
name was not included by Ammirato.[57] In a letter which
Jacopo Guicciardini wrote to his brother Francesco on 3 September, he names the sons of Bernardo Rucellai 'with their
following', Benedetto Buondelmonti, Simone Tornabuoni and
Antonfrancesco degli Albizzi as the leaders of the 'many other
armed men' who had occupied the palace and were still guarding it when he wrote.[58]

Nardi reports Francesco Vettori as persuading the *Signoria* to
legalize the deposition of the gonfalonier. He states that those
who had removed Soderini, sent for Francesco to convince the
Signoria that the gonfalonier should be deposed and legally
deprived of office. As according to the law a valid reason had to
be given and none could be found, Francesco at first met with
no success and withdrew. Later he returned to the chamber and
'with outstretched arms' appealed to the *Signoria* to effect the
deposition, arguing that otherwise he feared for the life of 'that
innocent man'.[59] Cambi[60] and Ammirato[61] assign this rôle to
Paolo. Cambi recounts that Paolo exclaimed 'you wish to do
good by him in not depriving him but you do him ill because I
cannot restrain the populace who want to tear him to pieces'.
Francesco himself does not mention names and simply dis-
misses the proceedings with the clause, 'the gonfalonier having
first been deprived by those magistrates responsible for the said

[56] S. Ammirato, v, p. 530.

[57] J. Nardi, i, p. 428.

[58] R. Palmarocchi, *Carteggi di Francesco Guicciardini* in 'Fonti per la Storia d'Italia',
iii, i (Bologna, 1938), p. 96, cited in future as F. Guicciardini, *Carteggi*.

[59] J. Nardi, i, p. 429. 'facendo croce delle braccia'.

[60] G. Cambi, *Istorie fiorentine*, ed. I. di San Luigi in *Delizie degli eruditi toscani*, xxi
(Florence, 1785), p. 309.   [61] S. Ammirato, v, p. 530.

deposition according to the ordinances of the city'.[62] Since he had not hesitated to mention his part in the physical removal of Soderini from the palace, the omission here of any reference to his own or his brother's concern in winning over the *Signoria* is unlikely to be due to modesty. Either he had no part in it or he wished not to be implicated, or he wished to shield his brother. Whatever the answer there can be no doubt that the two Vettori had been deeply involved in the ultimate fate of Florence's first and last life gonfalonier.

We now turn to the establishment of the Medici regime. Three stages can be distinguished in the process: the period between Giuliano de' Medici's entry into Florence on 1 September and the new constitution which came into force on the 7th; the subsequent period of discussions which preceded the calling of a general assembly of the citizens (*parlamento*) and the establishment of a special council of Medici supporters with full powers (*Balìa*) both on 16 September; and finally the re-organization of the government and the creation of the Councils of the Seventy and the Hundred which was not completed until January 1514. An investigation into the fortunes of the Vettori in this process of Medici re-establishment will also throw light on Medici methods of rule.

After the defeat of the Republic two of the major factions behind the change of government, the more republican under Jacopo Salviati and the pro-Medici, again make their appearance.[63] Nerli describes the political situation prior to the legislation of 7 September. As soon as the new *Signoria* (without a gonfalonier) had been elected, it met together with Giuliano and the principal citizens to set about reforming the government and twenty men were commissioned by the *Signoria* to consider the measures to be taken.[64] The list of their names recorded by Cambi includes citizens of such divergent views as Lorenzo Morelli, a convinced supporter of the Medici, and Jacopo Salviati, Soderini's opponent and champion of the

---

[62] *Sommario*, p. 292.

[63] B. Cerretani, Dialogo della Mutatione, B.N.F. Magliab, II, I, 106, fo. 14v: 'Qui ci dividemo noi capi della mutatione, perchè una parte non volevano altro che levar' Piero Soderini, un'altra parte fra quali ero io, volevamo fare nuovo stato e capo e' Medici.'

[64] F. Nerli, p. 111; S. Ammirato, vi (Florence, 1849), p. 6.

Great Council.[65] The Medici partisans, consisting of older men like Morelli who remembered the government of Lorenzo the Magnificent,[66] and of the young men who had plotted to restore the Medici,[67] wanted to introduce a new regime with the Medici at its head. On the other hand, those optimates whose primary concern had been the overthrow of Soderini, did not want to exchange his rule for that of the Medici; they aimed to retain the republican form of government with the optimates in control.[68] They realized that it was impossible to take the Great Council from the populace which had grown accustomed to participation in it, but they could reinforce and increase the power of the smaller Council of Eighty, transforming it into the type of aristocratic senate which they had hoped to establish in 1502.[69] To the Council, whose members were elected every six months, they proposed to add a new body of councillors chosen for life and drawn from those among the citizens who had either held or been suggested for the office of gonfalonier, or had served as one of the Ten or an ambassador.[70] In order to satisfy some who had not held any of these offices, the Eighty were empowered to elect an additional fifty life members (*arroti*). Moreover, to include Giuliano and others who had not reached the qualifying age of forty, eight members were permitted to be younger.[71]

Although the committed Medici supporters felt that their safety depended upon a carefully selected and narrowly based Medicean government, Giuliano nevertheless accepted the more republican view of the majority who wanted to retain the Great Council and introduce the reform of the government.[72] Accordingly on 7 September a provision was passed decreeing that the Great Council be maintained, the Eighty together with its additional members instituted, and the gonfalonierate limited to one year. On the following day the republican Giovan

[65] G. Cambi, xxi, p. 310.

[66] *Sommario*, p. 293.

[67] F. Guicciardini, *St. d'It.*, iii, pp. 233, 234.

[68] F. Nerli, pp. 111–12; F. Guicciardini, *St. d'It.*, iii, p. 233.

[69] A. Anzilotti, *La crisi costituzionale della Repubblica Fiorentina* (Florence, 1912), p. 52; F. Gilbert, 'The Venetian Constitution' etc. in *Florentine Studies*, ed. N. Rubinstein, pp. 482–6.

[70] G. Cambi, xxi, p. 312; S. Ammirato, vi, p. 6.

[71] G. Cambi, p. 313; F. Nerli, pp. 112–13.   [72] F. Nerli, p. 112.

Battista Ridolfi was elected gonfalonier on the grounds that he was the only man who could defend the Great Council and see the reform through.[73] The first constitutional stage of the revolution had been concluded.

Francesco Vettori was not one of the twenty citizens whose discussions with Giuliano had led to the passing of the provision of 7 September, but was appointed one of the *Otto di Guardia* on 1 September, though he was later to be deprived of this office.[74] Owing to his qualifications as a former ambassador, his name was among those put forward to become life members of the reformed and enlarged Council of Eighty;[75] his uncle Bernardo qualified as a citizen who had in the past been considered for the office of gonfalonier,[76] and it was intended to bring Paolo in as one of the eight junior members for whom special provision had been made.[77] In the event, however, the calling of the *parlamento* and the establishment of the *Balìa* did away with this short-lived scheme.

As Vettori accepted office immediately after the revolution and allowed himself to be proposed for the enlarged Council of Eighty, he cannot have been opposed to the revolution in principle. We may assume from much of the evidence offered so far and from his disapproval in the *Sommario* of the tyrannical way in which the Medici eventually assumed supreme power that he favoured the republican type of government legislated for in the provision of 7 September.[78]

The second stage in the revolution, which was marked by the calling of the *parlamento* and the institution of the *Balìa*, was preceded by a series of discussions which show the rôle of the Medici supporters, the so-called 'friends' (*amici*). They pleaded for the Medici to consolidate their position in order to avoid the danger to themselves of a possible counter revolution, which could mean exile, or reprisals such as commercial or fiscal discrimination. What this could mean can be gauged from the fate which was to befall Francesco Vettori in the years of republican government from 1527 to 1530.

[73] F. Nerli, p. 114; B. Cerretani, Dialogo, fo. 15r–v; G. Cambi, xxi, p. 314. G. Cambi, p. 314 and S. Ammirato, vi, p. 6 say 8 Sept.; F. Nerli says 7 Sept.

[74] Tratte 84, fo. 85r; below, p. 72.

[75] G. Cambi, xxi, p. 317.

[76] *Ibid.*, p. 316.

[77] *Ibid.*, p. 322.

[78] *Sommario*, pp. 291, 293.

Already two or three days after the election of the new *Signoria* it was evident that those who desired the Medici as absolute rulers were in a precarious minority. On 3 September, for instance, Jacopo Guicciardini, observing and approving the intention of Giovan Battista Ridolfi to maintain the Great Council also noted that not one of the members elected to the College of the Sixteen *Gonfalonieri* belonged to the group of Medici partisans. The antagonism of the populace towards these partisans expressed in this election was only held in check by the presence on Florentine soil of the army of the League.[79] When consulted by Cardinal Giovanni de' Medici, Filippo Strozzi too opposed the return of the family except as ordinary citizens.[80]

It was the passing of the provision of 7 September and the election of Giovan Battista Ridolfi, considered by the pro-Medici citizens as 'the ambassadors of our ruin' which had increased their fears for their joint security and caused them to seek discussions with the Medici.[81] Conversations were held in three places: at Prato where Cardinal Giovanni had joined the army of the League as papal legate; at Campi to which he journeyed for the greater convenience of the Florentines coming to meet him, and ultimately at Sant'Antonio del Vescovo.

At Campi the pro-Medici citizens informed Cardinal Giovanni of the 'errors' which in their view his brother Giuliano had allowed to occur.[82] Giuliano, they said, was kindly and tranquil and by nature not suited to the trials of government; he had allowed the enemies of the Medici to establish themselves in the palace with their own head and they were only awaiting the departure of the Spanish troops before undertaking further action.[83] It was not difficult for these citizens to bring Cardinal Giovanni round to their point of view as neither he nor Giulio de' Medici, his cousin, thought their family could remain secure in Florence if the government was so broadly based.[84] Another meeting was arranged at Saint'Antonio del Vescovo four days later on Thursday 9 September where many relatives and

[79] F. Guicciardini, *Carteggi*, i, p. 97.

[80] G.-B. Niccolini, pp. xxxi–xxxii; Filippo to Lorenzo Strozzi, Florence, 18 Sept. 1512, in *A.S.I.*, xiv (1894), p. 37.

[81] B. Cerretani, Dialogo, fo. 15v.   [82] F. Nerli, p. 115.

[83] B. Cerretani, Dialogo, fo. 15v.   [84] F. Nerli, p. 115.

citizens had assembled for further discussions.[85] The pro-Medici citizens wanted to call a *parlamento* but Lanfredo Lanfredini, Jacopo Salviati and Piero Alamanni, whom the other two had won over to their way of thinking, took the view that the Great Council should be retained. More meetings followed at the same place, and it took several days to resolve the deadlock.[86] Back at Prato Filippo Strozzi was among those whose opinion was sought by the legate.[87] On the instigation of the pro-Medici citizens the Florentines were intimidated by some Spanish cavalry ostensibly inspecting the fortifications. The *amici* attempted, too, to win over the gonfalonier.

Evidence of the division of opinion in the city is provided both by the discussion in the *pratica* called by Ridolfi in the morning of Saturday 11 September and by the inconclusive results of the evening's meeting of twenty-four citizens to elect the *arroti* who were to be added to the Council of Eighty in accordance with the provision of 7 September.[88] In the morning meeting some of the citizens were in favour of calling their troops into the city and offering resistance to 'those who did not want what was right'. Others felt that such resistance was impracticable as the city was under the control of the Spaniards, but that ambassadors should be sent to find out the Spanish viceroy's true intentions. This was in fact the policy adopted but with the reservation that the ambassadors chosen, Ormannozzo Deti, Lorenzo Morelli, Guglielmo de' Pazzi and Pandolfo Corbinelli, should not leave the city until after the evening's meeting. Here Medicean and republican disagreement was such that only twenty-four of the fifty *arroti* could be elected.

Three days later Cardinal Giovanni entered Florence[89] and thereafter the discussions were continued with the pro-Medici group reiterating their view that there was no alternative to a *parlamento* and Jacopo Salviati, Lanfredo Lanfredini and Piero Alamanni holding the contrary opinion. The turning point in these discussions seems to have been the arrival of information from the viceroy that he was about to leave for Lombardy and if the Medici needed his help they should not delay. While the

[85] B. Cerretani, Dialogo, fo. 16r.   [86] *Ibid.*, fo. 17v.   [87] G.-B. Niccolini, p. xxxi.
[88] B. Cerretani, Dialogo, fo. 17v; G. Cambi, xxi, p. 314.
[89] G. Cambi, xxi, p. 323.

Signoria were still trying to elect the remainder of the *arroti*, the Medici supporters occupied the palace. With the help of the Spanish troops a *parlamento* was called and supreme power was given to a council (known with reference to its special powers as a *Balìa*) consisting of fifty-five citizens, including the priors already in office.[90] Their first act was to co-opt eleven citizens, thus bringing the total up to sixty-six.[91] The second stage in the revolution had been accomplished.

It is not easy to establish Francesco Vettori's rôle in this stage of the revolution. His sympathy, as already indicated,[92] was probably with the type of government introduced in the provision of 7 September and in which he already held office. Since he refers to Paolo's unpopularity with one section of citizens on account of his support for the *parlamento* and of his own with the other for his help to Soderini, it looks as if he himself took no active part in the seizure of the palace which would have ingratiated him with the partisans of the Medici.[93] He was one of the *Otto di Guardia* and as one of those proposed for the enlarged Council of Eighty he would probably have been inside the palace at the time of the armed onslaught.

A tantalizing document without address, signature or date in the Archivio di Stato, Florence, contains a list of Medici *amici* and three desiderata, presumably for the re-establishment of the Medici regime: first, to arm the *amici* (whose names are listed); second, to make eligible for office (*'imborsare'*) everyone who has merited it, reserving however for 'the true friends' membership of the *Signoria*, Colleges, Ten, Eight, and the captaincies of the Guelf party; and third, to impose an arbitrary tax for two years.[94] The document, drawn up in the first person singular, recalls that the writer has already discussed these three points verbally and at length with the recipients (*'voi'*). Certain

[90] Signori, Missive Legaz. e Comm., 27, fo. 8r: 'fu dato pienissima auctorita et balia a 46 cittadini et 9 priori che in tutto furono 55 di potere riformare tutta la citta et dominio in ogni sua parte . . .'.

[91] F. Nerli, p. 116.

[92] Above, p. 68.

[93] C. Strozz., Ser. I, 136, fo. 219v, Francesco to Paolo, Rome, 5 Aug. 1513, 'tu restavi chon non molti parenti, et quelli male disposti et male contenti di te, chi rispecto a Piero Soderini et chi al parlamento, perchè li altri dua dal parlamento furono alieni et che io non li volevo nominare nessuno.' N. Machiavelli, *Lettere*, ed. F. Gaeta, p. 241.   [94] M.A.P., 99, No. 45.

parallels with a letter written on 15 December 1512 by Cardinal
Giovanni in Bologna to Giulio and Giuliano de' Medici in
Florence[95] incline me to propose the Cardinal as sender and at
least two members of the Medici family as recipients. If factual
evidence is taken at its face value, the date would have to be
between 18 September 1512 and 22 April 1513. Instead of
Giuliano Salviati, son of Jacopo Salviati, who died on 18 September 1512[96] and who was still listed together with his father
on the 16th among the members of the *Balìa*, a Francesco
Salviati is coupled with Jacopo. Galeazzo Sassetti, another
member included in the list of *amici*, died on 22 April 1513.[97]

Francesco and Paolo are among the *amici* listed. As regards
Francesco this is in contrast with our findings so far. A possible
reason for the inclusion of Francesco's name in the document is
the fact that his father Piero had been a friend of the Medici at
the time of Lorenzo the Magnificent[98] and that Paolo had
played such an important part in the preliminary stages of the
revolution, although as Francesco was to write to Paolo in
August 1513, even his father's and his brother's friendship with
the Medici was not such as to lead Paolo to expect to influence
them.[99] Since even in this private letter Francesco does not
mention his own relationship with the Medici, he probably did
not consider it of much political significance. Yet he was included in the all-powerful *Balìa* which came into existence after
the summoning of the *parlamento*.[100] The fact that Paolo[101] and
their uncle Bernardo[102] were added to it in two subsequent
extensions, suggests that Francesco had additional advantages of
valued experience and efficiency. One of the *Balìa*'s first acts in
office was to cancel the appointments to the *Otto di Guardia* and
make new ones. Francesco was one of the five who were offered
a captaincy of the Guelf party in compensation. This office he

[95] C. Strozz., Ser. II, 86, Insert 22, fo. 225r, 'the *Signoria*, the Eight and the
Sixteen *Gonfalonieri* should be *amicissimi*'; in the document these offices are to be
reserved for '*i veri amici*'.

[96] G. Cambi, xxi, p. 326; B.N.F. Necr. Cirri, xvi, p. 370.

[97] B.N.F. Necr. Cirri, xvi, p. 491.

[98] Above, p. 5.

[99] C. Strozz., Ser. I, 136, fo. 219r: 'non havevi . . . tale amicitia con questi
Medici, nè nostro padre . . . l'haveva da potere credere d'haverli a governare.'

[100] Balie, 43, fo. 2v; F. Nerli, p. 116.

[101] C. Strozz., Ser. II, 145, fo. 130r.   [102] Balie, 43, 25v.

refused, suggesting Gherardo Paganelli instead.[103] One would like to know his reasons. Did he not wish to become further involved in the new regime than he was already as a member of the *Balìa*, or did he consider his work in the *Balìa* so important that he lacked time for another post?

Francesco's brief comment in the *Sommario* on the events leading up to the *parlamento* is interesting in that he is at pains to defend the part played by Cardinal Giovanni, the future Pope Leo X, as he does in a later passage in the same history when reporting on Leo's adjudication between Florence and Lucca.[104] He recounts that the citizens who were old enough to remember the government of Lorenzo the Magnificent—he omits to mention the rôle played by the young men—considering the reform (as instituted on 7 September) lacking the security they deemed necessary, persuaded Cardinal Giovanni, Giuliano and Giulio de' Medici that a *parlamento* must be called and the government be taken over as otherwise the *amici* would be in danger. So far this account is substantially in agreement with those given by Nerli and Cerretani but an important divergence now occurs as Nerli and Cerretani go on to show Cardinal Giovanni appreciating the force of the *amici*'s arguments and his willingness to act upon them, whereas Vettori at this point suggests that owing to the *amici*'s persuasions, the Cardinal did 'what he, perhaps, would not otherwise have done'. In this case, as in the later instance of the arbitration, the *amici* are blamed for the Medici's apparently despotic or arbitrary use of power.

We now turn to the final stage in the establishment of the Medici covering the period from the autumn of 1512 to the winter of 1513/14. This stage is particularly interesting, for it not only provides further evidence of the activity of Francesco Vettori and others who now supported the Medici but it also provides some clues to the characters of Cardinal Giovanni, Giuliano, Giulio and Lorenzo de' Medici and shows how power was allocated between them.

Already during the first stage of the re-establishment of the

---

[103] G. Cambi, xxi, pp. 327–8; S. Ammirato, vi, p. 8; cancellation of Otto di Guardia: Balie, 43, fo. 4v; appointment of captains of Parte Guelfa, incl. Gherardo Paganelli: *ibid.*, fo. 5r.

[104] *Sommario*, p. 293; below, pp. 93–4.

Medici in Florence it is clear that Cardinal Giovanni was becoming the leading member of the family as far as the re-
organization of the government was concerned. It was Cardinal
Giovanni who had corrected the 'errors' which the good-
natured Giuliano had allowed to occur and it was he who had
listened to, and eventually acted upon the remedy of calling a
parlamento suggested by the pro-Medici citizens. When Julius II
died on 20 February 1513, Cardinal Giovanni was elected Pope
Leo X and Giuliano and Giulio de' Medici were left to govern
Florence. Cerretani gives an illuminating description of the
character of the two men and the political position which arose
as a result of their different personalities. Giuliano, it seems, was
little suited to the art of government. He quickly tired of the
hard work of listening to the *pratiche* and his good nature made
him incline to all requests so that disorder soon set in.[105] It was
Giulio with his patience, his caution and sense of justice who
counterbalanced the inadequacy of Giuliano and checked
Jacopo Salviati's ambition to re-establish the Savonarolan, that
is more republican type of government.[106] But Giuliano cannot
have been without political ambition for the government of the
city since Cerretani also provides the interesting indication that
political rivalry between him and Lorenzo lay behind the
ostensibly pleasure-making carnival groups of the *Diamante* and
Broncone.[107] When Giuliano's group, the *Diamante*, was created
during the second half of November 1512,[108] a list of thirty-six
citizens which was drawn up contained almost exclusively the
names of sons whose fathers had been associated with Lorenzo
the Magnificent. The intention was that this company should
eventually rule the city, and Cerretani states that there was not
a magistracy without one of these young men in it. Lorenzo's
group, the *Broncone*, followed the tradition of his father, Piero,
and seems to have been inspired by his followers who sought to
convince him that lordship over Florence belonged not to

---

[105] B. Cerretani, Sommario, B.N.F., II, IV, 19, fo. 18v.

[106] *Ibid.*, 'Et se non fusse stato l'occhio suo l'havemo fatto male perchè Jacopo
Salviati . . . non attese mai ad altro che introdurre et tener via la parte del frate. . .'

[107] *Ibid.*, fos. 17v–18v. H. Reinhard, *Lorenzo von Medici, Herzog von Urbino*
(Freiburg, 1935), pp. 26–7.

[108] F. Guicciardini, *Carteggi*, i, p. 136. Iacopo to Francesco Guicciardini,
Florence, 8 Jan. 1513.

Giuliano but to him as Piero's heir.[109] Cerretani himself must have been a supporter of Giuliano,[110] and Paolo Vettori became majordomo of his household,[111] but Francesco was to become one of the influential intimates of Lorenzo, an indication that members of the same family did not necessarily support the same patron.

Clearly some division of power between the three members of the Medici house was necessary and the most urgent question to settle was whether Giuliano or Lorenzo was to govern Florence. Rome was the place where plans for future Florentine policy were thrashed out during the spring and summer of 1513. Eleven Florentine ambassadors arrived there on 24 May to pay their ceremonial visit,[112] and left on 14 June.[113] Francesco Vettori and other resident ambassadors were already at the papal court.[114] Lorenzo had been there since soon after Leo's election. Giuliano with a large number of his followers arrived on 4 May.[115] The prolonged discussions which took place between the Florentines present and Leo X revolved round two main topics: who was to be the ruler and what was to be the size and composition of the main organs of government.

Eventually, Lorenzo emerged as head of the government.[116] In compensation Giuliano received the captaincy of the ecclesiastical forces and was made patrician of Rome. The pope sent Lorenzo to Florence accompanied by Giulio de' Medici who had been made archbishop of the city and promised a cardinal's hat.[117] In this way power was divided between the three members of the Medici family.

Vettori in his writings portrays an ambitious Giuliano and a submissive Lorenzo. According to him, the advantages to be

---

[109] B. Cerretani, Sommario, fo. 18r.

[110] Ibid., fo. 17v.: 'Giuliano suo fratello, il quale creò per nostro ordine una compagnia' (my italics).

[111] Below, p. 103.

[112] Dieci, Responsive, 115, fo. 389r.

[113] Ibid., 116, fo. 78v.

[114] Below, p. 85.

[115] Dieci, Responsive, 115, fo. 222r; B. Cerretani, Sommario, fo. 23v.

[116] Accounts of the division of power between members of the Medici family in B. Cerretani, Sommario, fo. 24r; P. Parenti, Istorie, B.N.F. II, IV, 171, fo. 98r; F. Nerli, p. 125; F. Vettori, Sommario, p. 300.

[117] C. Strozz., Ser. I, 136, fo. 225r, Francesco to Paolo, Rome, 14 Aug. 1513; B. Cerretani, Sommario, fo. 24r; F. Nerli, p. 125.

gained in Rome from a Medici pope made neither Giuliano nor Lorenzo anxious to leave the papal court and govern Florence. In his biography of the young Medici Vettori says that on hearing of his uncle's election, Lorenzo rushed to Rome to beg Leo to let him stay with him because he knew how suitable Giuliano was to govern Florence. Having first granted his request, the pope changed his mind when Giuliano asked for the same favour. Thereupon Lorenzo consented to the wishes of his uncle, returned to Florence and began to lay the foundations of a just and constitutional government.[118] In the *Sommario* Vettori also gives reasons why the two men wanted to stay in Rome: Giuliano was thinking of 'excessive grandeur' and Lorenzo too had seen what position a relative of the pope enjoyed in Rome 'although he set little store by it'.[119] The pope, Vettori says, wanted Giuliano to govern the city since he was the older man and would undoubtedly be acceptable to the Florentines, but, as Giuliano refused to leave Rome and Leo did not want to take Giulio de' Medici from the Church, he was obliged to send Lorenzo to govern Florence. These accounts with their contrasts between the grandeur of Giuliano on the one hand and the reasonableness of Lorenzo and the favourable view taken of his early rule on the other present the latter to advantage. But the two sources, the biography written for the sister of Lorenzo, and the *Sommario* written during a republican period when Vettori's association with Lorenzo was damning to him could account for a biased view point.[120] Parenti takes a different view. He writes of a 'long dispute' between Lorenzo and Giuliano 'about the government of Florence from which Lorenzo ultimately emerged victorious as the permanent leader having determined from the beginning not to be liable to have to relinquish his position to Giuliano.[121]

The second topic of discussion with Leo concerned the crea-

[118] *Vita di Lorenzo*, in O. Tommasini, ii, p. 1056.   [119] *Sommario*, p. 300.

[120] The *Vita di Lorenzo* was sent to Clarice Strozzi. It was written between 1519 (when Lorenzo died) and 1523 (when Cardinal Giulio left his administration of Florence to become Pope Clement VII); see p. 1063 of the work.

[121] Istorie, II, IV, 171, fo. 98r: 'Lungha disputa fu a Roma tra lui e Giuliano circa el governo di Firenze ... Lorenzo ... benchè giovane fussi non voleva piglare quello che in brieve tempo dovessi alle tornate di Giuliano lasciare: così alquanto si dibatterono. Finalmente fu concluso che Giuliano restassi e Lorenzo venissi, e lui capo del nostro stato si facessi.'

tion of the various organs of government for Florence. Lorenzo left Rome on 4 August in company with the archbishop to be followed the next morning by Jacopo Salviati.[122] On the 13th he was officially recognized as Giuliano's successor,[123] and thereafter he began to put into operation the plans which had been discussed in Rome.

The Medici considered it important at least to keep up an appearance of co-operation with the leading citizens. Even during the 1530–2 discussions for the reform of the government they were led to believe that they were taking their own decisions.[124] In 1513 (as in 1524) the occasion of a ceremonial embassy to Rome was used to consult them.[125]

Both Francesco and Paolo Vettori were involved in the final stage of the Medici re-establishment. As ambassador, Francesco took part in the discussions in Rome and Paolo entertained Lorenzo and the archbishop at the Vettori villa of Paneretta on their way back to Florence.[126] Francesco does not appear to have participated enthusiastically in this interesting stage in Florentine politics. On one occasion he confessed to his brother that he would gladly go back to Florence if he were given leave as he understood nothing of governments.[127] On another he wrote that he was not sure whether he wanted any of the offices under consideration in the important discussions for which Pandolfo Corbinelli, one of the *accoppiatori*, or selectors for offices, had come to Rome.[128] Fear for the stability of the regime which he had now come to see as the only safeguard of his city's —and his own—safety can be deduced from many of his critical observations in his letters from Rome. In February 1513, during the last illness of Julius II, Francesco wondered what would

[122] C. Strozz., Ser. I. 136, fo. 219r, Francesco to Paolo, 5 Aug. 1513.

[123] Balie, 43, fo. 131r, 13 Aug. 1513.   [124] Below, p. 239.   [125] Below, p. 163.

[126] C. Strozz., Ser. I, 136, fo. 225r. Francesco to Paolo, Rome, 14 Aug. 1513.

[127] *Ibid.*, fo. 218v, Rome, 13 May 1513: 'perchè questi governi io non li intendo'.

[128] *Ibid.*, fo. 228r, Rome, 16 May 1513: 'Pandolfo è venuto . . . anchora che s'intendesse venissi per chose molte importante, le quale io non so nè le voglo cercare, perchè . . . a me pare che lli stati habbino grande dificultà a mantenersi quando si governino chon diligentia grande, sollecitudine e prudentia.' Cp. *ibid.*, fo. 221r and Parenti, Istorie, B.N.F. II, IV, 171, fo. 88v, May 1513: 'Di questi dello stato e con intelligentia di pochi si mandò a Roma Pandolfo Corbinelli per significare al pontefice chose segrete quali per altri non vollono che si sapessino.' Under this May entry Parenti speaks of the drawing up of the new *squittino*. I therefore assume that Vettori is concerned about office holding.

happen if the pope were to die. He knew that Cardinal Giovanni would leave Florence for the conclave in Rome and he feared that if this were a long one, his native city would be in grave danger, even perhaps from the French.[129] Some months earlier, Paolo had recommended to the cardinal the provision of a military force for the protection of the regime, considering the large number of enemies which the Medici had in Florence.[130] Francesco apparently supported Paolo in this.[131] Like him he realized that very many citizens were hostile to the Medici and he questioned Leo's wisdom in allowing such a large number of ambassadors and leading citizens to come to Rome, thus leaving Florence 'empty of friends and full of enemies'.[132] Francesco considered that the party had enough difficulty to remain in power even when it exercised extreme care, diligence and prudence,[133] and in common with Lanfredo Lanfredini he thought the Medici overconfident about their security.[134] In a letter of 13 May to his brother he mentioned having annoyed Giuliano by some advice on the composition of the colleges.[135] A month later he criticizes the nomination of Giovanni Berardi to the *Dodici Buonuomini* and his possible election as gonfalonier. Vettori was also critical of Medici expenditure in Rome,[136] and of their administration in Florence: 'there

[129] C. Strozz., Ser. I, 136, fo. 221r, Francesco to Paolo, Rome, 17 Feb. 1513; cp. n. 132, Parenti, Istorie.

[130] R. von Albertini, Appendix I, p. 345. Paolo had been *capitano* of the *guardia*, F. Guicciardini, *Carteggi*, i, p. 119.

[131] C. Strozz., Ser. I, 136, fo. 221r, Francesco to Paolo, Rome, 17 Feb. 1513: 'E battagloni mi piacciono ma fateli sollecitare e la guardia bene ordinata.'

[132] *Ibid.*, fo. 218v, Francesco to Paolo, Rome, 13 May 1513: 'nè si cura che venghino imbasciadori e principali e lasciare la città vota d'amici e piena di nimici', cp. Parenti, Istorie, B.N.F. II, IV, 171, fo. 88v, May 1513: 'La città malcontenta universalmente si mostrava. Aspectavasi da seguire fresca revolutione venendo di nuovo e franzesi in Italia.'

[133] See p. 77, n. 128.

[134] B.N.F. Ms. Ginori Conti, 29, 92, 3, fo. 13v, Lanfredo Lanfredini to Niccolò Michelozzi, Rome, 2 June 1513: 'chostoro sono molto ghagliardi, non anno sospetto nè temono di chosa alchuna'.

[135] C. Strozz., Ser. I, 136, fo. 218v. Francesco to Paolo, Rome, 13 May 1513: 'E ieri pure fui con Giuliano sopra e collegi, e conobbi non hebbe caro certe parole li dixi, e par loro essere troppo sicuri.'

[136] C. Strozz., Ser. I, 136, fo. 229r. Francesco to Paolo, Rome, 18 [June 1513]; *ibid.*, fo. 217b, 26 [June 1513]; *ibid.*, fo. 226r, 14 Aug 1513: 'lui [Giuliano] è uno spenditore tanto grande che sempre ha haver bixogno per sè'; cp. *ibid.*, fo. 228r, 16 May 1513.

government is bad and here not good'. His fear was that fortune would soon tear them to shreds.[137]

Critical of the Medici and reluctant to participate in politics as he was, Francesco does not hesitate to offer his brother some very calculating advice on ingratiating himself with the two members of the family about to establish themselves in Florence. In doing so he reveals not only his character but also the attitude of supporters towards the Medici and the type of government Lorenzo was hoping to institute. Paolo is recommended to bear in mind that Giulio de' Medici, a future cardinal and likely legate of Bologna, is a 'very important man'; he should observe him closely and get what he can from him.[138] The lease of some church lands in Pisan territory is suggested as something worthwhile obtaining.[139] His brother should commend himself also to Lorenzo who, being the son of Piero, will be surrounded by the members of 'the old regime' who will advise him to keep down the young supporters.[140] Nevertheless, Francesco went on, Lorenzo 'has great faith in Pandolfo (Corbinelli), Jacopo (Salviati), Giovanni (Rucellai) and Antonio Serristori and you. Keep in with him, and especially with Jacopo who is a man to be trusted.' More than once Vettori advised his brother to concentrate on his own needs and not to bother his patrons with petitions on behalf of others.[141] He should seek, too, to present the part which he had played in a favourable light, varying his story according to the political affiliations of his listeners: to the supporters of Piero Soderini one version; to those of the Medici another: 'Words vindicate men but you must judge to whom you address them';[142] 'words

[137] *Ibid.*, fo. 217b, Rome [June], 1513: 'io intendo chostì si governa male, e qui non bene, e la fortuna una volta, quando harà facto quello che la potrà, si stracherà, chome è suo chostume'.

[138] *Ibid.*, fo. 219v, Rome, 5 Aug. 1513: 'huomo grandissimo'.

[139] *Ibid.*, fo. 225r, Rome, 14 Aug. 1513: 'qualche ficto di chiese, o in quel di Pisa o altrove, che fussi a linea, che non c'è poi meglio che le possessione'. For Vettori connections with Pisa, above, pp. 36, 37 and below, p. 94, n. 61.

[140] *Ibid.*, fo. 226r: 'e harà intorno sempre quelli dello stato vechio che li persuaderanno a tenere sotto li altri'.

[141] *Ibid.*, fo. 225r, Rome, 14 Aug. 1513: 'e chiedi per te e non per altri'; *ibid.*, fo. 219v, Rome, 5 Aug. 1513: 'Observalo assai e pensa trarne per te e non lo infastidire cholle faccende delli amici.'

[142] *Ibid.*, fo. 219r, Rome, 5 Aug. 1513: 'le parole iustificano assai li huomini, ma bixogna havere electione chon chi si dicano'.

true or false cause many things to be believed'.[143] It is debatable whether to date Vettori had acted on the advice he gave, with the exception of not petitioning patrons on the part of others.[144] But here is the wary and calculating attitude to politics which could explain why Vettori succeeded in holding office both under the Republic and under the Medici, appearing as a friend of Soderini and an *amico* of the Medici. Certainly after 1530 Benedetto Buondelmonti was to speak of him as 'doppione'.[145]

Part of Francesco's advice to his brother contains the comment that Lorenzo as the son of Piero would be less tolerant of those who had been anti-Medici than the pope, Giuliano, or messer Giulio.[146] This hint of a difference in policy between the young Medici and the members of his family in Rome becomes more explicit in the discussions leading to the re-establishment of the Council of Seventy. To understand this complicated matter we must trace our steps back to the *Balìa* whose members had been given full powers to govern Florence after the *parlamento* on 16 September. From a letter written by Francesco Vettori to Paolo in June 1513 it emerges that an enlargement of the *Balìa*, already desired by the pope when he was cardinal, was again under discussion. Cardinal Giovanni's plan had apparently been to broaden the basis of the Medici government by adding about eighty more citizens to the *Balìa*.[147] The original number of the *Balìa* was in fact increased in stages. In the summer of 1513 the Medici, including Giovanni, now Leo X,[148] discussed with the ambassadors the transformation of the *Balìa* into the so-called Council of Seventy. They came to

---

[143] *Ibid.*, fo. 225v, Rome, 14 Aug. 1513: 'le parole o vere o false fanno credere di molte choxe'.

[144] Below, pp. 101–2.

[145] Buondelmonti to Giovan Francesco Negrini, 12 April 1531, *A.S.I.*, Ser. i, i (1842), p. 447; cp. G. Busini, *Lettere di Giovanni Batista Busini a Benedetto Varchi sugli avvenimenti dell' Assedio di Firenze* (Pisa, 1822), p. 7, Lettera Seconda.

[146] C. Strozz., Ser. I, 136, fo. 225v, Rome, 14 Aug. 1513: 'bixogna ti rachomandi a Lorenzo, perchè hai a pensare che lui è figliuolo di Piero, e vorrà peggio a chi gli fece male che il papa o Juliano o messer Julio'. Cp. pp.74–5.

[147] *Ibid.*, fo. 229 bis: 'il papa alhora Cardinale, disegnava allargare un poco lo stato in Firenze e per questo arrogere alla balia circa 80, che fussino poi insieme un Consiglio'.

[148] Below, p. 85.

the conclusion that it should be made up of one hundred and forty.[149] Cerretani, however, reveals that Lorenzo defied the views of those in Rome and that his advisers passed a law that, apart from the members of the *Balìa*, only those should be eligible for Lorenzo's Council of Seventy who had either belonged to the former Council of Seventy in the time of Lorenzo the Magnificent or who had held the office of gonfalonier or had been proposed for it. Furthermore only two from each of the great Florentine families would be admitted.[150] Lorenzo's Council of Seventy does not deviate from Leo's proposals as regards the *Balìa* but it differs by curtailing the number of additional members through all the conditions imposed. Lorenzo in fact wanted a more narrowly-based government than the pope. Lorenzo Strozzi mentions the Seventy as the creation of the young Lorenzo and that it was to carry out the functions previously executed by the *Balìa*.[151]

From a letter of Lorenzo to Cardinal Giulio de' Medici we learn how the choice of members for his Council of Seventy was made.[152] Towards the end of November 1513 Lorenzo had discussions with 'those eight citizens that Your Reverence knows' about the formation of the Seventy. These citizens were asked to draw up a list 'as they think best for putting this matter into effect'. This was done and Lorenzo found that the names on their list differed in only one or two cases from those on a note left him by Giulio de' Medici, the recipient of this letter who had meanwhile become cardinal.

There is in the State Archives, Florence, a document which seems to be connected with the formation of the Council of Seventy.[153] It is headed 'Men of the *Balìa*' but goes much further than this. According to Lorenzo's law, members of the *Balìa*, except for the priors who had been included by the *parlamento* in September 1512, were to form part of the Council of Seventy.[154] In the document 'Men of the *Balìa*' two of three names deemed ineligible are described as having been priors at

[149] B. Cerretani, Sommario, fos. 26r–v.
[150] *Ibid.*; provision of 22 Nov. 1513 in Balie 43, fo. 149r.
[151] G.-B Niccolini, p. xxxiv.
[152] 21 Nov. 1513, in O. Tommasini, ii, p. 986.
[153] Carte Torrigiani, Busta 5, xxv.
[154] G. Cambi, xxii, p. 34.

the time of the gonfalonier Giovan Battista Ridolfi.[155] Among those eligible from the quarter of S. Spirito, with the significant recommendation that they could not be omitted 'without great scandal', is Francesco Vettori. The document reiterates some of the conditions for membership of the Seventy: there must not be more than two per 'house'; former gonfaloniers and gonfaloniers-designate are eligible and so are sons and brothers of past members of Lorenzo the Magnificent's Seventy. It also contains a significant sentence, a key to Lorenzo's policy: 'my intention is not so much to carry on Lorenzo the Magnificent's work but to preserve it'.[156] It was drawn up after consultation with 'messer Piero' and 'Jacopo' and sent to a person who is referred to as 'la S.V.' Bearing in mind the part played in earlier discussions with the Medici by messer Piero Alamanni and Jacopo Salviati[157] and also the fact that Nerli lists them among the intimate counsellors of Lorenzo,[158] it seems likely that these are the two citizens whose opinions the author received. Piero Alamanni was not an ambassador in Rome and Jacopo Salviati who had been one had returned to Florence in August.[159] For the recipient to be Cardinal Giulio de' Medici, the document with its reference to 'la S.V.' would have to date from before September 1513 when he was made cardinal and was subsequently addressed by Lorenzo as 'la S.V.R.'[160] This, however, is not possible as the law relating to the Seventy was not passed until 22 November. The deferential tone of the admission that 'it is not our intention to do anything except as you shall order us' suggests the relationship of the young Lorenzo to one of the members of the Medici family in Rome from whom he was accustomed to receive directions.[161] Since it refers to the

---

[155] '*erono* de Signori con Giovanbatista Ridolphi' (my italics); and also, 'Et di questi della balia non ne resta fuori se non 3 che due ne sono di quelli Signori che sono Antonio Redditi e Giovanni Federighi.' For these priors, v. F. Nerli, p. 116.

[156] 'e non ci pare ne possi cadere alcuno de prenominati senza grande scandolo . . . l'animo mio è non tanto di seguitare le cose facte da la buona Magnificenza di Lorenzo ma mantenerle'. Carte Torrigiani, Busta 5, xxv.

[157] Above, p. 70.

[158] F. Nerli, p. 128.   [159] Below, p. 87.

[160] O. Tommasini, ii, pp. 973–4, Lorenzo addresses Cardinal Giulio as 'la S.V.R.'; on pp. 974, 975, Giuliano as 'S.V.'.

[161] 'Et se nessuno di questi paresse ala S.V. da doverci entrare, quella ne advisi che tutto si farà . . . non siamo per fare se non quanto di costì ci sarà ordinato.' Cp. O. Tommasini, ii, pp. 975 and 977.

recipient's greater knowledge of the Florentines, the document could have been addressed to Giuliano who had spent more time among them than Lorenzo who had arrived only in August. Perhaps we have here the result of Lorenzo's discussions with the eight citizens on the subject of the Seventy to which he refers in his letter to Cardinal Giulio, sent possibly to inform Giuliano in Rome of the nature and composition of the Council of Seventy which he was planning.

But whatever its origin, this document which recommends Francesco Vettori as one of those whose omission from the Council would be a 'great scandal' proves that he was regarded by Lorenzo and his friends as a loyal supporter. In the election which took place on 1 January 1514 he became a member of the Council of Seventy.[162]

The Council of Hundred was elected on 31 December 1513. Many faithful supporters felt that their services merited the reward of office and Lorenzo took pains to appease those who could not be included. On 21 November he explained to Cardinal Giulio that he knew how large the number of citizens was who hoped to become members of the council and who would have to be disappointed and he asked him to excuse him as politely as possible, pointing out that as many old men were among those elected the turn of those not included would soon come. Lorenzo specifically mentioned that Francesco Vettori was to be told why his name had not been put forward: there were so many candidates and he was too young. If he were to be elected, this would be in the nature of an exception and Lorenzo was loath to create such a precedent. He would be remembered next time.[163] As expected, Vettori was not elected in December; his name was however drawn at the next election but he was debarred from taking office (*divieto*) owing to his membership of the Seventy.[164]

With the establishment in January 1514 and December 1513 of the Councils of the Seventy and Hundred the last stage of the revolution of 1512 was concluded. The rôle of Francesco

[162] Tratte, 84, fo. 66r.

[163] Lorenzo de' Medici to Cardinal Giulio de' Medici, 21 Nov. 1513. O. Tommasini, ii, p. 986.

[164] Tratte, 338, fo. 20r (31 Dec. 1513); fo. 22r (21 June 1514).

Vettori in this episode of Florentine politics can most favourably be described as cautious and unenthusiastic. Unlike Francesco Guicciardini he was not expressly dissatisfied with the internal government of Soderini, nor, like Filippo Strozzi, did he openly criticize the Medici's intention to return as the supreme rulers of Florence. He was neither a declared republican like Jacopo Salviati nor an openly active participant in revolutionary activities like his brother Paolo. Finding himself involved in a crisis he did his best to save his city from disaster. Following his principle not to hurt or blame anyone, and probably even in the name of friendship, he saved the life of the gonfalonier. Whether or not he accepted office with the Medici from conviction or from expediency, as an ambassador in Rome he played his part in the political discussions for the restoration of the Medici government in Florence. He was not committed to the Medici cause in the beginning but hoped nonetheless for some reward for the service he considered he had rendered them. What were his expectations of a Medici pope and what his other activities as ambassador in Rome will be our next concern.

CHAPTER V

At the Court of Leo X (1513–15)

ON 30 December 1512, when Francesco Vettori was elected Florentine ambassador to Pope Julius II,[1] the *parlamento* had already been called and the Medicean *Balìa* of which he was a member had been given full power; in short the first of the three stages by which the Medici gained control over the city had been completed.[2] Within a short time however their power was to extend to Rome. Nineteen days after the death of Julius II on 20 February 1513[3] and two weeks after Vettori's arrival in Rome,[4] Cardinal Giovanni de' Medici succeeded to the papacy as Leo X. Investigation into Vettori's status and activities in Rome provides valuable evidence of the effects on Florence and her citizens of this extended Medicean dominion.

Vettori should have found the court of Leo X more agreeable than that of the Emperor Maximilian: his status was that of resident ambassador at the court of a ruler whose accession fulfilled the highest of Medici and Florentine ambitions. Within a few weeks of Leo's accession, however, he was asking leave to depart. His reasons were both personal and political.

From the beginning of his mission Vettori felt thwarted. His letters between 7 February, when he first wrote to the Ten from Rome, and 20 February, when his two predecessors reported the death of Julius II, contain a series of complaints at his enforced inactivity and apologies for his inability to get information.[5] But this frustration was merely temporary. According to the diplomatic custom of the time an ambassador might not be in

---

[1] Signori, Missive, Legaz. e. Comm., 27, fo. 14v–15r. [2] Above, p. 66.
[3] Dieci, Responsive, 108, fo. 292r; Julius II died 'during the night of 20–1 February. L. Pastor, *History of the Popes*, vi (London, 1898), p. 436.
[4] Dieci, Responsive, 108, fo. 210v, 5 Feb. 1513, J. Salviati and M. Strozzi announce that Vettori will enter Rome on the following day; fo. 216r, 7 Feb. 1513, Vettori reports his arrival on the previous day.
[5] *Ibid.*, fos. 216r, 246r, 256v.

circulation until he had had an audience.[6] Owing to the pope's illness, Vettori could not be received and was therefore unable to do any work. His mission may in consequence be said to have begun only with the accession of Leo X.

The diffidence which was apparent in his letters from Maximilian's court recurs in those from Leo X's. In Germany Vettori's self-distrust could be explained by his youth, inexperience and apprehension at the first important mission of his career, as well as by his ignorance of German and by the difficult political situation in Florence. By the time of his Roman mission however Vettori was a man of thirty-eight with valuable diplomatic experience behind him. Yet we find him writing to the Ten that he was not 'of so little judgment' that he had not realized as soon as Leo was made pope that the new situation demanded an ambassador of different calibre from him. Since the city would in future share the papacy's fortune, it was essential that matters in Rome should be most carefully examined and assessed.[7] Doubts as to his own worth expressed in an official letter need not necessarily be taken at their face value, but a private letter to Machiavelli, written about five weeks after Vettori's arrival, shows the same preoccupation. He would write, he informed his friend, when he knew whether he would be remaining in Rome, which he doubted, 'because I think there will be men of different standing who will want to be here'.[8]

More important than the psychological reasons were considerations connected with the embassy itself. On Vettori's arrival in Rome the two resident ambassadors, Matteo Strozzi and Jacopo Salviati, who had been appointed on 3 October 1512,[9] expected to be recalled, but only Strozzi was granted permission by the pope to depart.[10] On 24 May the ceremonial

[6] C. Strozz., Ser. I, 136, fo. 221r, Francesco to Paolo, Rome, 17 Feb. 1513; Dieci, Responsive, 116, fo. 2v, Rome, Francesco to the Ten 1 June 1513.

[7] Dieci, Responsive, 115, fo. 226r: 'Io non sono di tanto poco iudicio che subito che fu creato papa Leone non conoscessi che qui era chonveniente stessi huomo per oratore che havessi altre qualità che quelle sono in me, perchè havendo la città a correre la medesima fortuna che il pontefice è necessario che le cose sieno qui examinate e ponderate molto bene.'

[8] N. Machiavelli, Lettere, ed. F. Gaeta, p. 234.

[9] Signori, Missive, Legaz. e Comm., 27, fo. 11r.

[10] Dieci, Responsive, 115, fo. 130v, 21 April 1513. He left on 25 April, fo. 166r.

embassy of a further eleven Florentines entered the city.[11] The letters of 7 and 9 June were signed 'oratores tredecim'[12] and that of 13 June 'oratores duodecim',[13] Neri Capponi one of the newcomers having by then left. On 14 June all the members of the ceremonial embassy except Filippo Buondelmonti returned to Florence.[14] For a time there were thus three Florentine ambassadors in Rome and the dispatches are signed by Buondelmonti, Salviati and Vettori, Vettori appearing in the third place.[15] The first letter written by the Ten to Francesco Vettori alone is dated 11 August,[16] Buondelmonti having departed on 11 July[17] and Salviati on 5 August.[18]

Vettori undoubtedly felt concern at the number of ambassadors in Rome and considered himself redundant. In May he had informed the Ten that his sojourn there was a 'fruitless expense' and that he was accustomed to be more sparing with public money than with his own.[19] A private letter written in June corroborates his official correspondence. After informing Paolo of the number of ambassadors, Francesco confessed himself bewildered at this state of affairs, and not for personal reasons for, as his brother knew, he disliked work and the more ambassadors there were, the less there would be for him to do. His concern was for the city which 'acting in this haphazard way only God can bring into port'.[20]

Vettori's complaint does not concern only the number of ambassadors but his relation to them: in a letter to Machiavelli in July 1513 he writes that as the youngest his business was 'to look on'.[21] He seems to have felt superfluous mainly because Jacopo Salviati did most of the work.[22] Jacopo had been the senior of the three ambassadors in Rome during Leo's election;

[11] *Ibid.*, fo. 389r.   [12] Dieci, Responsive, 116, fos. 38v, 52v.
[13] *Ibid.*, fo. 79r.   [14] *Ibid.*, fo. 78v.
[15] *Ibid.*, fos. 103r, 129r, 138v, 145r, 154v, 169r, 170v, 178v, 200v, 202v, 233r.
[16] Dieci, Missive, Legaz. e Comm., 40, fos. 120v–21v.
[17] Dieci, Responsive, 116, fo. 263r.
[18] Dieci, Responsive, 117, fo. 2v. Below, p. 97 n. 76.
[19] Dieci, Responsive, 115, fo. 226r, Rome, 7 May, in Vettori's hand.
[20] C. Strozz., Ser. I, 136, fos. 229v, 229r (owing to faulty binding the folios run from tergo to recto): 'che governandosi in questo modo a caso altri che iddio farebbe si conduca in porto'.
[21] N. Machiavelli, *Lettere*, ed. F. Gaeta, p. 270.
[22] C. Strozz., Ser. I, 136, fo. 218r (between fos. 220 and 221), Rome, 13 May 1513.

it was he who went to the entrance of the conclave to try to
glean information,[23] and it was later to him that the Ten sent
a letter which for reasons of secrecy was not addressed to the
three ambassadors jointly.[24] The delay in Jacopo's departure
caused him to write to Machiavelli that he was 'without any
business whatsoever' and, as at Trent, just waiting for it.[25]
Vettori through lack of money was living like an ordinary
citizen, neither always wearing the long robes customary for
ambassadors in Rome, nor entertaining, nor keeping more than
the minimum number of horses, and he considered greater
expenditure unjustified, since it was to Salviati that people
turned.[26] Only when Jacopo left did Vettori decide to uphold
the standard set by him and the other ambassadors and to buy
himself a black damask jacket and another mule as the one he
had was too old to move.[27] To Paolo, Francesco complained
that Jacopo resented his presence when public business was
being conducted.[28] Perhaps Jacopo thought that Vettori took
his brother too much into his confidence. Certainly Jacopo had
received a letter which Vettori believed to have been written by
Matteo Strozzi after his return to Florence to the effect that
Paolo was talking as if he were cognizant of all the secret affairs
of state.[29] According to Vettori however Jacopo himself often
talked carelessly and once when he lost favour with the pope
through some indiscretion he had tried to blame Paolo for it.[30]
He would, Vettori maintained, have committed further indis-
cretions had it not been for him.[31] Filippo Buondelmonti's son,
Benedetto, writing from Rome shortly after Vettori's departure
considered that Vettori had been more submissive in his
attitude to the Medici than his position and the honour of the
city warranted, and he compared this servile sense of duty
unfavourably with Jacopo Salviati's behaviour, concluding that

[23] Dieci, Responsive, 109, fo. 27r, 4 March 1513.
[24] Dieci, Missive, Legaz. e Comm., 40, fo. 6v, 6 April 1513.
[25] N. Machiavelli, Lettere, ed. F. Gaeta, p. 264.
[26] See p. 87, n. 22; C. Strozz., Ser. I, 136, fo. 229 (bis)r, 16–18 June 1513.
[27] C. Strozz., Ser. I, 136, fo. 219v, Francesco to Paolo, Rome, 5 Aug. 1513.
[28] Ibid., fo. 217(b)r (between fos. 216 and 219), 'a dì 26'.
[29] Ibid., fo. 218v, Francesco to Paolo, Rome, 13 May 1513; ibid., fo. 229v, 16
June 1513.
[30] Ibid., fo. 229v, Francesco to Paolo, Rome, 16 June 1513.
[31] Ibid., fo. 225r, Francesco to Paolo, Rome, 14 Aug. 1513.

one should know how to gain esteem rather than humble one-
self. Nevertheless even then he remarked to Filippo Strozzi that
Vettori merited a pension and later the two men were to be
responsible for his further employment in Medici affairs.[32]

To form some idea of the wide range of business with which
Vettori had to deal after August 1513 one needs to read the
official dispatches from the Eight, the Ten[33] and the *Signoria*.
The ambassador is requested to answer questions on papal
policy, to give information on various foreign powers and to
appeal for papal support in disputes with neighbouring states.
Some dispatches contain petitions through the *Signoria* from
monks and ecclesiastics and from merchants for redress of losses
suffered. Leo, who personally intervened in Florentine internal
affairs, sought the ambassador's opinion on governmental
matters. He was also the channel through which ecclesiastical
concerns, for example, in connection with the pope's right to levy
a *decima*, or tithe, on the Florentine clergy, were conveyed to the
city. There was thus no apparent lack of work. Yet within
fifteen months Vettori had re-applied to the Ten for permission
to leave Rome,[34] which indicates that he was still dissatisfied
with his chances of achieving anything worthwhile for his city or
for private individuals. His reaction to circumstances on the
surface so favourable to Florence lead one to question whether
the city's expectations both public and private were in fact
satisfied by the Medici pope.

On Leo's accession the Florentines were in a state of elation.
As the instructions to the ceremonial embassy put it, they were
delighted to have on the papal throne not a stranger, but a
compatriot, a Florentine of the city's most noble and noted

[32] M.A.P., 108, No. 147, to Filippo Strozzi, Rome, 17 May 1515: 'l'ambasci-
adore merita bene et pensione perchè io intendo che egli andava ogni dì et ogni
mattina a chasa il Magnifico con pocho honore del grado aveva e della città. Io
so ben Jacopo quando ci era non faceva chosì et si vuole saper farsi stimar et non
tanto abandonatamente sottomettersi.' On 16 June 1513 Vettori himself wrote of
his attitude to the Medici, 'e non li domando mai di choxa non mi dichino. Vero è
che uso sempre quella modestia si richiede'; C. Strozz., Ser. I, 136, fo. 228v,
Francesco to Paolo; below, p. 146, n. 19.

[33] Under the Medici the *Otto di Pratica* became once more the committee which
dealt with foreign affairs. The *Dieci di Balìa*, the Ten, was not, however, replaced
by the *Otto*, the Eight, until 1514.

[34] M.A.P., 108, No. 124, Filippo Strozzi to Lorenzo, Rome, 13 Aug. 1514.

family. From the time of Peter, the first Vicar of Christ, down
to the present day no one from Florence had been worthy to be
raised to this most elevated rank but Leo.[35] Vettori regarded
the accession of Leo as an event that should bring honour and
profit to the public as well as the private interests of his city.[36]

Leo's attitude to the Florentine ambassadors seemed to
justify the city's hopes, as Vettori's description of his ease of
access to the pope and to information shows: 'In the time of
previous popes all the cardinals [at the court] had to be
contacted in order to obtain information but now it is not like
this because after the pope the treasurer[37] knows the news and
both of them see me willingly so that I shall hear the latest
reports and shall not fail to be solicitous at court. . .'[38] During
his audiences at the Vatican Vettori communicated the instructions received from the Ten directly to the pope.[39] On one
occasion when he did not follow this practice he explained to
them that it was because Leo had two cardinals with him.[40]

Exchange of opinion between the Florentine ambassador and
the pope seems at first sight to have been unrestricted. In the
spring of 1513 when it became known that a truce had been
signed between France and Spain, Leo discussed with Vettori
his views on the situation with a warning to the Florentine
Signoria to treat his opinions not as a 'secret' but as a 'top
secret' because 'the discovery that he had used words like this
could do great harm'.[41] However such confidence is no more
than another example of that duplicity noted by the Venetian
ambassador, Antonio Soriano. Later, in April 1515, Leo
warned Francis I to keep their negotiations secret 'sub poena
excommunicationis'.[42] Certainly by 1514 Vettori had realized
that Leo's frankness was more apparent than real, though
significantly he tries to excuse the pope: 'It is indeed true that

[35] Signori, Missive, Legaz. e Comm., 23, fo. 104r.

[36] O. Tommasini, ii, p. 969.

[37] Bernardo Dovizi, Cardinal Bibbiena.

[38] C. Strozz., Ser. I, 136, fo 225v, Francesco to Paolo, Rome, 14 Aug. 1513;
cp. N. Machiavelli, *Lettere*, ed. F. Gaeta, p. 270.

[39] 'secondo il nostro consueto', Dieci, Responsive, 116, fo. 103r.

[40] *Ibid.*, fo. 154r, Rome, 25 June 1513.

[41] *Ibid.*, 114, fo. 334v, Rome, 23 March 1514: 'non che secreto secretissimo . . .
perchè lo intendersi fussino decte simil parole da lui potrieno nuocer' assai.'

[42] F. Nitti, *Leone X e la sua politica* (Florence, 1892), p. 9, n. 1.

he refrains on occasion from discussing some of his thoughts, for ideas in the case of great princes are judged by results and should their plans not succeed, for princes are fallible like the rest of us, they can change them.'[43] Indeed from Vettori's private correspondence it emerges that he himself interpreted Leo's diplomatic conduct as imposing on him extreme tact, amounting to secrecy, vis-à-vis his own masters. In a letter to Paolo he wrote that he did not inform the *Signoria* of 'secret negotiations for treaties or similar matters . . . because I fear the pope may take it ill, and it is necessary for one who is here to be very careful in what he writes.'[44] The position appears more clearly from passages in two letters to Machiavelli. On 23 November he wrote: 'I write once every four days to the Ten and I relate some tired tales little worthy of note, because I have nothing else to write for the reasons which you know.'[45] About two months later Vettori gives a glimpse of the difficulty of trying to compose an acceptable 'fantasy' for the Ten which would neither reveal Leo's secret plans nor yet be so devoid of news as to insult the Ten's intelligence or to cause them to question his own lack of ability or diligence.[46]

The papal aim, as all the Florentine ambassadors together in Rome reported it, was to promote peace by settling existing disputes and concluding new alliances; from these objectives Leo would not on any account deviate.[47] To Machiavelli Vettori interpreted the papal policy as avoiding wars, 'acting as mediator, and composing and settling those which had arisen between princes'.[48] That Vettori reflects faithfully the genuine aims of the early years of Leo's pontificate would seem to be proved by Giulio de' Medici's revelation to Giuliano of the main lines of papal policy. They are given as the restoration of peace to war-distracted Christendom, the ending of the schism, and the prevention of further warfare in Italy.[49] By 1514 Vettori

[43] Otto, Responsive, 11, fo. 73r, Rome, 29 July 1514: 'è bene vero che si ritiene qualche volta di conferire qualche suo pensiero perchè le cogitationi dei principi grandi el più delle volte sono stimate da chi le intende effecti, et non riescono poi così perchè sono huomini come li altri . . . possonsi anchor mutare'.

[44] C. Strozz., Ser. I, 136, fo. 225r, Rome, 14 Aug. 1513; cp. p. 89, n. 32.

[45] N. Machiavelli, *Lettere*, ed. F. Gaeta, p. 299.   [46] *Ibid.*, p. 318.

[47] Dieci, Responsive, 115, fo. 406r, Rome, 28 May 1513.

[48] N. Machiavelli, *Lettere*, ed. F. Gaeta, p. 282, Rome, 20 Aug. 1513.

[49] F. Nitti, p. 11, Rome, 29 March 1513.

interpreted this policy as inspired by Leo's desire to establish peace between Christians so that a 'whole-hearted attack' could be launched on the Infidel.[50] In fact this aim was overlaid by more immediate concerns.

Opinions differ as to the further aims of Leo's policy. Some see him as one who wanted to promote peace mainly to preserve the temporal and spiritual independence of the Holy See;[51] others accuse him of promoting the interests of his family, in fact of nepotism and favouritism towards Florence. The Venetian ambassador in Rome, Marino Giorgi, considered that the pope wanted 'neither war nor trouble' but that his kinsmen involved him in it.[52] Vettori's official dispatches and his comments in the more intimate *Sommario* reveal a conflict of interest between international policy on the one hand and Florentine and family territorial ambitions on the other. Significantly Vettori adopts the papal point of view with regard to Leo's early policy.

Florence's dispute with Lucca which came before the pope during the early part of Vettori's mission in Rome and which the ambassador had in fact been instructed in his *commissione*[53] to discuss with Leo demonstrates this clash of interests. The Florentines had not been on the best of terms with Lucca since 1495 when the French had allowed the Lucchese after their campaign in Naples to buy Pietrasanta and Motrone which had been taken as security from the Florentines and should have been returned to them. In a long-standing boundary dispute between the Lucchese and the community of Barga in Val di Serchio, the Florentines had intervened on behalf of the Barghigiani and seized several castles on Lucchese territory.[54] When the Florentine grievances with the Lucchese, who went to great lengths to arouse sympathy for their case in Rome, were brought to the attention of the pope, he did not immediately intervene. In a letter signed by the three ambassadors then still present in Rome the Ten were informed that they had twice

[50] Otto, Responsive, 11, fo. 73r, Rome, 29 July 1514: 'una generosa impresa'.
[51] F. Nitti, pp. 62–4.
[52] E. Albèri, *Relazioni degli ambasciatori veneti al Senato*, Ser. II (Florence, 1846), iii, p. 51.
[53] Signori, Missive, Legaz. e Comm., 23, fo. 102r.
[54] G. Cambi, xxii, pp. 31–3.

brought the 'outrages' ('insolentie') of the Lucchese to Leo's
attention and had shown him the Ten's communications on the
subject but that he was loath to believe what he had been told,
'it seeming to him impossible that being so greatly inferior in
strength they should be so bold'.[55] As sole ambassador Vettori
wrote to the Ten of Leo's unwillingness to sacrifice his reputation with the European rulers in order to benefit the Florentine
government.[56] In another dispatch he quoted the pope as
saying that 'minor matters should not be allowed to give rise to
greater disturbances'.[57] A year later when Leo had in fact
adjudicated in favour of his compatriots ruling that the Lucchese
should concede Pietrasanta and Motrone to them, retaining,
however, the area in dispute with the Barghigiani, he exhorted
Vettori to inform his government that having been awarded
Pietrasanta they should not omit 'to make all possible demonstra-
tions of love towards the Lucchese both in public and in private'
so that they would rest content and he would be seen to have
honourably exercised the holy office whose function he saw as
establishing peace between all men and especially between
neighbours.[58]

In his *Sommario* Vettori approves the position taken up by the
pope at the beginning of his pontificate and he criticizes those
Florentines who were dissatisfied with the pope's adjudication.
Some citizens, he wrote, considered that the good of the city
consisted in greatly extending the boundaries of its territory, but
they did not realize 'what infamy they caused the pope to incur
with all men and how much suspicion they aroused in the
princes in forcing him in the early months of his pontificate to
permit the Florentines without any cause whatsoever to attack
their neighbours and allies the Lucchese'.[59] The pope, he went
on, 'unwillingly' allowed the Florentines to harm the Lucchese;
he was persuaded by those who, understanding little of foreign

[55] Dieci, Responsive, 116, fo. 199v, Rome, 2 July 1513.

[56] *Ibid.*, 117, fo. 194r, Rome, 12 Sept. 1513: '. . . non desidera altro che fare bene
alla cictà, ma non vorrebbe che un picholo benefitio come è questo privarlo d'un
maggiore che sarebbe quando e' principi dubitassino che lui non tenessi conto
della ragione nè della equità per beneficare Vostre Signorie'.

[57] *Ibid.*, fo. 276r: 'le cose piccole non habbino a dare disturbo alle grandi'.

[58] *Ibid.*, 118, fo. 53r, Rome, 8 Oct. 1514.

[59] *Sommario*, p. 301.

policy, saw in this cause a chance for Leo to gain favour with the Florentines.

Just as Vettori had blamed the *amici* for the unlawful tyranny of the Medici in internal politics[60] so now the responsibility for what he considered to be an injustice to the city's neighbours is also laid at their door. From neither situation was Francesco personally detached for in both his brother Paolo was involved. We have seen how he was one of those who took part in the calling of the *parlamento*; now he was among those involved in raids on the Lucchese. Paolo had factories on Lucchese territory which had been rendered inoperative by the destruction of certain woods which he had bought from some citizens of Castelluccio. In a reprisal raid his own men had made off with a number of Lucchese cattle.[61] Perhaps it was on account of his business interests in the area that he was elected commissioner on 7 October 1513 with Vieri de' Medici to receive Pietrasanta and Motrone from the Lucchese in accordance with the papal arbitration.[62]

Francesco's private views on the Lucca episode expressed to his brother are interesting and confirm the opinion expressed later in the *Sommario*. He deplores Paolo's attack on his neighbours and condemns his compatriots' demands as shortsighted and detrimental to the pope's reputation: 'I am sorry that our neighbours had to be badly treated . . . I cannot understand those of our citizens who believe that the pope should be prepared to be blamed [for their sake] by all Christian princes.'[63]

As it became apparent that the pope was not necessarily inclined to fulfil Florence's wishes, the Ten sometimes sought a more powerful intermediary than the ambassador and this they found in one of the Medici themselves. The rôle of Giuliano de' Medici in Florentine diplomacy during the short period when he

[60] Above, p. 73.

[61] B.N.F. Ginori Conti, 29, 68(23), fo. 56r, Paolo Vettori to Niccolò Michelozzi, Buti, 7 July 1513.

[62] Otto, Missive, Legaz. e Comm., 10, fo. 6v, 7 Oct. 1513, commissione to Vieri de' Medici and Paolo Vettori; G. Cambi, xxii, p. 33; B.N.F. Ginori Conti, 29, 44, fo. 3.

[63] C. Strozz., I, 136, fo. 216r, Francesco to Paolo, Rome, 24 July 1513: 'mi doleva bene havessi offessi e vicini tanto aspramente quanto s'intendeva . . . non so già questi nostri cittadini in su che si fondino a credere che il papa voglia esser biasimato da tutti e principi Christiani'. Cp. *Sommario*, pp. 301–2.

was ruler of the city has not yet been fully investigated, and some indication of it here may help to throw further light on Vettori's status as ambassador. Until Giuliano's departure for Rome in May 1513 he had been one of the Ten[64] and was referred to by them even after he had left as 'our colleague'. Instructions such as 'you will give immediate notice of it to His Holiness the Pope and to Giuliano our colleague'[65] and 'as usual, you will confer with His Holiness the Pope and with his Magnificence Giuliano'[66] frequently occur. The Ten sometimes sent letters directly to him, thus on 29 July: 'to his Magnificence Giuliano we have written about it separately',[67] and on 2 July, 'our Giuliano has been written to in private'.[68] The Ten even went further, leaving the ambassadors out altogether. In the letter of 29 July we also find: 'We speak with you about everything freely and without reserve, as we do among ourselves, and, as you will find, to our ambassadors we have kept silent on many points'.[69] It is clear that on controversial points such as the Lucchese dispute, the Ten could rely on Giuliano's active cooperation. On 9 July we learn that Giuliano took the part of the Florentines when Leo did not believe the reported insolence of the Lucchese: 'his Magnificence Giuliano forcefully reiterated the injuries which they had done us during the time he was one of the Ten', and as a result of a 'very long discourse' in which Giuliano justified the city 'very promptly', the Lucchese representative suggested coming to terms and submitting the differences with the Florentines to papal arbitration.[70]

The intervention of the Medici in Florentine foreign policy and a consequent reduction in the importance of the city's ambassadors is corroborated by evidence in the Medici correspondence. At the end of May 1513 Giuliano wrote to the Florentine second chancellor, Niccolò Michelozzi that he should send all important and secret matters direct to him for communication to the ambassadors or not as he saw fit. With regard to other letters Michelozzi should use his discretion,

---

[64] Dieci, Missive, Legaz. e Comm., 40, fo. 1v.
[65] *Ibid.*, fo. 59v, 8 June 1513.   [66] *Ibid.*, fo. 76v, 26 July 1513.
[67] *Ibid.*, fo. 107r.   [68] *Ibid.*, fo. 81v.
[69] *Ibid.*, fo. 108v, 29 July 1513: 'Parliamo con voi liberamente ogni cosa e sanza riserva, parendoci farlo con noi stessi e come vedrete molte cose habbiamo taciute con li ambasciadori.'   [70] Dieci, Responsive, 116, fo. 240r.

seeming to take due account of the ambassadors, who were all prudent men and friends of the Medici, but without endangering secrecy.[71] On the occasion of the visit to Rome of Maximilian's councillor Mathias Lang, this policy is applied to Vettori, the sole remaining ambassador. This time not only Giuliano but the pope and Cardinal Giulio are to carry on negotiations, but Vettori, characteristically, is assigned the rôle of an observer who is allowed to intervene for his city so as not to be slighted in his capacity as official ambassador.[72]

Francesco himself seems to have found it easier to approach the pope than Giuliano,[73] at least in connection with his dismissal to which we are about to turn. Vettori's brief remarks to Machiavelli about his official contact with each one may reveal the degree of his success with the different members of the Medici family. When visiting the Vatican Palace, he wrote, he addressed twenty words to the pope, ten to Cardinal Giulio and six to Giuliano. His friendship with Cardinal Giulio, later Pope Clement VII, which developed from 1519 on, may have started during this period as Vettori mentions that he sometimes dined with him.[74]

Even in the appointment and dismissal of ambassadors Florentine wishes were not overriding. Here the pope's is the controlling hand. An instance of this arises soon after Leo's accession when Jacopo Salviati was not granted permission to leave the papal court, even though the Ten had agreed to his and Strozzi's return on 19 April.[75] It was not until 5 August that

[71] B.N.F. Ginori Conti, 29, 41, fo. 15r. Rome, 28 May 1513: 'Quanto al modo dello scriver vostro qua mi occore ricordarvi questo che le cose importanti et che meritono secreto le mandiate a me et io le comunichero secondo me pare. L'altre che vi par si possino scriver ali oratori che hora l'hanno ad intender tutti dirizatele a loro et in questo bisogna giuochi la discretione la quale regna in voi in farli participi in modo che paia si tenghi conto di loro, et non vi sia pericolo del secreto, che per altro son tutti huomini veramente prudenti et amici nostri.'

[72] Lorenzo de' Medici to Card. Giulio de' Medici, 27 Oct. 1513. O. Tommasini, ii, p. 978.

[73] C. Strozz., Ser. I, 136, fo. 228r. Rome, 16 May 1513, Francesco to Paolo: 'A Giuliano si parla con più difficoltà che al papa.'

[74] N. Machiavelli, Lettere, pp. 298–9; see, also, above p. 79, his remarks to Paolo about Cardinal Giulio.

[75] The mission of Jacopo Salviati and Matteo Strozzi was expected to end with Vettori's arrival and on 12 Feb. the Ten were awaiting their return. Dieci, Missive, Legaz. e Comm., 39, fos. 145r–157v; F. Guicciardini, Carteggi, i, p. 136, Iacopo

Salviati was allowed to depart and then to accompany Lorenzo and the archbishop of Florence.[76] His earlier petitions had been ignored.[77]

The return of Francesco Vettori was not dissimilar. By 4 May 1513 the Ten had given him permission to leave, not in one letter but in four. Leo, however, delayed the ambassador's departure from week to week in spite of having expressed his willingness when first approached to let him go.[78] On 24 July Vettori remarked with characteristic resignation and self-deprecation, 'great men cannot consider the likes of me'; his wishes had been ignored so often that he expected even his servants to mock him.[79] He was not given leave at all that year. In August 1514 he was apparently again asking for permission to go back to his city.[80] but it was not until 15 May 1515 that he eventually arrived in Florence.[81]

Two possible explanations for Leo's reluctance to grant his release can be found in Vettori's political views and his suitability for the post. The delay in Salviati's departure may have resulted from Leo's desire to wait for the Medicean regime to become more stable before his return because his 'republican' views were known.[82] Similarly the pope may have been prompted to delay Vettori's departure, remembering his friendship with Soderini and Machiavelli and the moderate views which he held.[83] A more cogent reason could however be that Vettori

to Francesco Guicciardini, Florence, 8 Jan. 1513; cp. Dieci, Missive, Legaz. e Comm., 40, fo. 17r and Dieci, Responsive, 115, fo. 130v.

[76] C. Strozz., Ser. I, 136, fo. 219v. Francesco to Paolo, Rome, 5 Aug. 1513. He arrived in Florence on 10 Aug. 1513, Signori, Missive, Legaz. e Comm., 27, fo. 11r.

[77] C. Strozz., Ser. I, 136, fo. 229 (bis)v. Francesco to Paolo, Rome, 16 June 1513. Salviati is granted leave because of his wife's grave condition, but on 14 July Salviati is still in Rome and promised departure 'in pochi pochi dì', Dieci, Responsive, 116, fo. 263r.

[78] C. Strozz., Ser. I, 136, fo. 228r. Francesco to Paolo, Rome, 16 May 1513.

[79] Ibid., fo. 216v. Francesco to Paolo, 24 July 1513: 'li huomini grandi non possono havere chonsiderazioni a un par' mio.'

[80] M.A.P., 108, No. 124. Filippo Strozzi to Lorenzo, Rome, 13 Aug. 1514.

[81] Signori, Missive, Legaz. e Comm., 27, fo. 15r. Margin: 'Recessus est die 15 mai 1515.'   [82] H. Reinhard, p. 26.

[83] Vettori refers to his unpopularity with the supporters of the present regime in a letter to Machiavelli (Lettere, ed. F. Gaeta, pp. 241, 246) and to tax discrimination against his family, C. Strozz., Ser. I, 136, fo. 219v, Francesco to Paolo, Rome 5 Aug. (1513); Piero Soderini visited Jacopo Salviati when he arrived in Rome in May 1513 and Vettori was present, ibid., fo. 218v, Rome, 13 May 1513.

had become the type of ambassador required by the Medici. A diplomat with initiative was not needed since 'business comes to hand predigested' as Vettori informed Strozzi. What was wanted was a trustworthy and efficient person who would not divulge the secrets of papal policy.[84] He should not irritate the pope with too many petitions—a lesson which Vettori had learned in the course of his mission.[85] He could be pliable like Vettori, or elderly like Bernardo Rucellai who wanted to be appointed ambassador in Rome just because at his age he was unable to cope with much work.[86]

For the reasons previously shown Vettori's importance as an ambassador had been adversely affected in most spheres by the time he again applied for his mission to terminate. The original direct relationship with the pope had been undermined with Giuliano as negotiator; Leo's request for secrecy must have produced an uncomfortable position of dual loyalty. Though Vettori shared the pope's wider view of a policy for peace, he had to represent Florentine interests.

Apart from conducting official business, a Florentine ambassador had to act on behalf of private citizens. Merchants, ecclesiastics and petitioners for official posts requested his intervention. The requests of the merchants were conveyed either through the Ten or the *Signoria*. The *Signoria* for example, reported Leonardo Manelli's complaint that a quantity of grain on its way from Spain had been mistaken for French merchandise and stolen by the Genoese fleet, and he asked for a papal brief to the Community and Doge of Genoa.[87] The *Signoria* also asked on behalf of certain Florentine merchants that a letter from the pope should be addressed to the king of England to recover a ship carrying woad and other merchandise impounded by the English at Dover.[88] Another request, this time conveyed

---

[84] M.A.P., 108, No. 124. Filippo Strozzi to Lorenzo, Rome, 13 Aug. 1514: 'qui non bisognare homo fatto, atteso le faccende venirli in mano digestite, ma confidente e da farsi'. Cp. above, p. 91 for Vettori's remarks on secrecy.

[85] Below, p. 101.

[86] M.A.P., 108, No. 127. Filippo Strozzi to Lorenzo, Rome, no date: 'Bernardo Rucellai haveva fantasia venire qui oratore, non perchè le faccende meritassino tale homo . . . in oltre el non vi essere faccende lo persuadeva al venire, perchè ormai non tolerava più la faticha.'

[87] Signori, Missive, Ia Cancelleria, 57, fo. 176v, 10 Nov. 1514.

[88] Signori, Missive, Ia (seen. 87) Cancelleria, 57, fo. 142r, 12 Nov. 1513.

by the Ten with the apology that 'we are too frequently forced, though to our great displeasure, to commend to you our merchants who have suffered loss in various ways and places', concerned a merchant ship *en route* for Constantinople which had been seized by a pirate from Rhodes.[89] In the case of the woad which was sequestered at Dover, a papal brief was obtained by Vettori but this did not produce the desired effect, being followed by a request for another letter to Henry VIII for the recuperation of the merchandise which was valued at 600 ducats.[90] This time it was suggested that Giuliano de' Medici should appeal. The goods which came into the hands of the corsair of Rhodes also caused more than one papal brief to be sent out. The captured vessel containing the Florentine merchandise sailed into Messina where it awaited the arrival of the grand master of Rhodes in the hope that he would agree to the goods being sold in that island. Papal briefs were addressed to the viceroy of Sicily, to the bishop of Messina and to the governors of the territory. On this question more could not be done in Rome and an agent had to be sent to Messina.[91] The Ten expressed their gratitude for the good ambassadorial services rendered.[92]

Requests connected with ecclesiastical matters ranged from that of the zealous friars of the church of S. Croce who wanted a certain Franciscan from Montepulciano as their preacher for the coming Lent,[93] to that of the convent of S. Gallo who begged the pope for permission to grant plenary indulgence to all who came to their church and made offerings, as they needed funds to pay for the many friars expected to arrive for the meeting of the chapter after Easter.[94] There was also the appeal of certain Cistercian monks concerning disputed rights to an abbey,[95] and a query on the concession granted to a Genoese merchant to charge the Jewish merchants two per cent at

[89] Dieci, Missive, Legaz. e Comm., 40, fo. 67r, 13 June 1513.

[90] Signori, Missive, Ia Cancelleria, 57, fo. 154v, 15 March 1514.

[91] Dieci, Responsive, 116, fo. 202r, 2 July 1513.

[92] *Ibid.*, fo. 309v, 23 July 1513; Dieci, Missive, Legaz. e Comm., 40, fo. 72r, 18 June 1513.

[93] B.M. Addit Ms. 10,277, fo. 16r, 12 Feb. 1514.

[94] Signori, Missive, Ia Cancelleria, 57, fo. 185r, 23 Jan. 1515.

[95] *Ibid.*, fo. 135r, 17 Sept. 1513.

certain fairs on feast days.[96] Cases such as these do not appear to
be mentioned again and one can assume that Vettori was able
to deal satisfactorily with them. The *Operarii* of S. Maria del
Fiore thanked Vettori for the indulgence that he had procured for
the Cathedral with his 'usual prudence', though they returned
the papal brief as it contained an error in the wording.[97]

By contrast Vettori was frequently unsuccessful in his support
for those seeking official posts. Various reasons may be advanced
for this. Sheer numbers alone made it impossible to satisfy everyone. According to the historian Jacopo Pitti, the elevation of
Giovanni de' Medici to the papacy 'impregnated' almost all the
inhabitants of Florence with hopes of enrichment and aggrand-
izement.[98] Private letters such as Lionardo Bartolini's give
glimpses of 'brigades' of eager office seekers. Such a crowd had
arrived in Rome that to satisfy ten per cent would lead to
bankruptcy.[99] Vettori asked his brother to consider the number
of the pope's relations, servants and *amici* for then he would
realize how impossible it was to obtain anything.[100]

The large number of applicants for official posts is the reason
given by Vettori for his failure to meet Machiavelli's request to
him to recommend his brother Toto for a position in the papal
household, as the appointment would have little chance of
being sanctioned by the *camera*.[101] The same reason probably
accounts for Vettori's inability to help Pietro del Bene, and
Giannozzo Capponi, though he blamed himself for failing his
friends: 'I am no good at profiting myself or anyone else.'[102]
Vettori has been criticized for not doing more for his friends,
but the virtual impossibility of obtaining posts is borne out by
the fact that a man like Lionardo Bartolini,[103] left for Florence
where there would, he thought, be less competition.[104]

---

[96] *Ibid.*, fo. 164r, 26 June 1514.   [97] B.M. Add. Ms. 10,277, fo. 17r, 21 Feb. 1514.
[98] *Apologia de' Cappucci*, cit. O. Tommasini, ii, p. 72, n. 2.
[99] B.N.F. Ginori Conti, 29, 92, 6, fo. 31r, Lionardo Bartolini to Michelozzi,
Rome, 24 March 1513.
[100] C. Strozz., Ser. I, 136, fo. 218v, Rome, 13 May 1513.
[101] O. Tommasini, ii, p. 969.
[102] *Ibid.*, 'non so essere impronto da fare utile a me e alli altri' cp. C. Strozz.,
Ser. I, 136, fo. 217(bis)r, Francesco to Paolo, Rome, 'a dì 26' (July 1513).
[103] Brother of Gherardo Bartolini, treasurer to Lorenzo de' Medici.
[104] B.N.F. Ginori Conti, 29, 92, 6, fo. 43v, Lionardo Bartolini to Michelozzi,
Rome, 1 May 1513.

The fact that Leo, though willing to grant public requests, disliked being asked for private favours, undoubtedly inhibited the ambassador who wanted to remain in his good graces. According to Jacopo Nardi, the pope exclaimed that among the multitude of Florentines at the papal court there were only two who had recommended the city to him rather than their own interests; one of them, Piero Soderini, was very wise and the other, Carafulla (a noted buffoon) was quite mad.[105] Filippo Strozzi thought that Leo would not mind who succeeded Vettori provided that he did not overwhelm the pope with petitions,[106] and Vettori himself believed that Jacopo Salviati enjoyed papal favour because he had made only few personal requests.[107] He wished that he, too, had followed this policy from the beginning, and, as we have seen, he advised his brother not to petition Cardinal Giulio on behalf of his friends.[108] A letter to Paolo written in June 1513 shows the need which he felt for a reorientation in his conduct. He tried to be on good terms with everyone and especially with the pope's relatives whose danger as potential enemies he did not underrate, a caution which he shared with Lorenzo de' Medici's preceptor, Varino Favorino: 'in every pontificate . . . the papal relatives wish members of the household and papal servants ill'.[109] After about a year of cautious policy Vettori believed that he had won favour with the Medici: 'Pontifici Maximo et reliquis nostris Medicibus sum, meo iudicio, satis gratus; tamen nihil ab illis peto.'[110] One condition for carrying out this resolution was to be under an obligation to no one, and when he returned the silver which he had borrowed for his house in Rome, Vettori wrote to Machiavelli that he had done this partly because 'they used to expect me to put in a word with His Holiness on their

[105] J. Nardi, ii, p. 27.

[106] M.A.P., 108, No. 128, Filippo Strozzi to Lorenzo, Rome, 20 Aug. (1514): 'Nostro Signore aproverrà tutti quelli aproverrete voi, d'un modo non sieno persone per chiedere a ogni hora, perchè Sua Santità aborrisce molto tale parte.'

[107] C. Strozz., Ser. I, 136, fo. 218v, Francesco to Paolo, Rome, 13 May 1513.

[108] Above, p. 79.

[109] E. Mestica, Varino Favorino Camerte (Ancona, 1888), p. 82, cit. O. Tommasini, ii, p. 80; C. Strozz., Ser. I, 136, fo. 229(bis)r, 16 June 1513: 'è chostume chosì a ogni pontificato che e parenti dal papa vogliano male a' familiari e servitori. Io mi sforzerò star bene con tutti'.

[110] N. Machiavelli, Lettere, ed. F. Gaeta, p. 362.

behalf'. Initially he had complied with the lenders' demands but without success.[111]

In spite of what Vettori gives as the reason for his lack of success in securing advantages for his friends, it is likely that ultimately his failure in this direction stems from his deliberate policy of not constantly petitioning the pope and other members of the Medici family. On occasion the reason for failure may be attributed to lack of money. In the question of who would be given the lease of the alum mine which the Holy See let out to private citizens,[112] the Vettori are mentioned among those who could not afford the money.[113] Eventually the wealthy banker Agostino Chigi became the lessee on the strength of a loan.[114] As Francesco pointed out to Paolo on another occasion, some citizens were in a position to lend money to help others to obtain offices but the Vettori were not able either to give or to obtain credit.[115]

The various petitions of Machiavelli represent a special case worth investigating also for their political implications. Both Paolo and Francesco Vettori tried to deal with his predicament: Francesco, whom one would presume to have the better chance, with seeming indifference, Paolo energetically and effectively. A possible explanation may be found in their respective relationships with members of the Medici family. It seems likely that the pope to whom Francesco would have to turn was little disposed to comply with the wishes of his republican compatriot. As Cardinal Giovanni he was probably responsible for Machiavelli's loss of office[116] for it was not until 7 November

---

[111] *Ibid.*, p. 298.

[112] On venality of papal offices, P. Partner, 'The "Budget" of the Roman Church in the Renaissance Period', *Italian Renaissance Studies*, ed. E. Jacob (London, 1960), p. 258.

[113] B.N.F. Ginori Conti, 29, 92, 6, fo. 31r. Bartolini to Michelozzi, Rome, 24 March 1513: 'Hassi a dare la minera . . . i Vectori non credo che possino comparare con e danari che da altri se ne truovono'; on speculation about future of alum and salt mines, see F. Vettori to Paolo, Rome, 16 May, 1513, C. Strozz., Ser. I, 136, fo. 228r and *ibid.*, 13 May, 1513 fo. 218r: 'questa chosa vuole sollecitudine e danari.'

[114] *Ibid.*, fo. 228v. Rome, 16 June 1513: 'L'alumi . . . hebbe il Chigi . . . ma danari mette il Chigi perchè messer Lorenzo l'aiuti.'

[115] *Ibid.*, fo. 229r. Rome, 16 June 1513.

[116] C. Clough, 'Yet again Machiavelli's Prince', *Annali dell'Istituto Universitario Orientale*, Sezione Romanza, Napoli 1963, p. 211.

1512 after the *parlamento* had been called, the *Balìa* of Medici
citizens had been given full powers and Cardinal Giovanni
himself had entered Florence that Niccolò was dismissed from his
post in the chancery[117] and that he was confined to Florentine
territory by the *Signoria* three days later on a bail of 1000 florins
put up by three citizens.[118]

Machiavelli himself pinned his hopes of recovering favour and
employment with the Medici on Giuliano: it was to him that he
addressed the sonnet telling of his imprisonment as a result of
the conspiracy against the Medici on the part of Agostino
Capponi and Pietropaolo Boscoli in which he was alleged to
have been involved;[119] to him, too, that he sent a gift of thrushes
together with a further sonnet;[120] nor did he abandon his hopes
in April 1513 when he heard that His Magnificence was going
to Rome.[121] Later it was to Giuliano that he first dedicated *The
Prince*.[122]

Of the two Vettori brothers, it was Paolo who was on good
terms with Giuliano. As we have seen,[123] he had been in communication with him before the revolution and (since it was
Paolo who seems to have acted as spokesman for Giuliano on
the question of a testimonial for Francesco Guicciardini's ex-
secretary)[124] he was perhaps already majordomo of Giuliano's
household in 1513, a position he certainly held at the time of
Giuliano's marriage in 1515.[125] He was Giuliano de' Medici's
ambassador to the king of France in October 1515.[126] He expected to be made governor of the new state comprising Parma,

[117] N. Machiavelli, *Le Opere*, ed. P. Fanfani and L. Passerini, i (Florence, 1873),
p. lxxxiii.

[118] *Ibid.*, p. lxxxiv; for names of the three, below, p. 104.

[119] R. Ridolfi, *Machiavelli*, p. 137.

[120] *Ibid.*, p. 140.

[121] N. Machiavelli, *Lettere*, ed. F. Gaeta, p. 244.

[122] *Ibid.*, p. 304.

[123] Above, pp. 60–1.

[124] R. Ridolfi, *Guicciardini*, pp. 285–6, n. 10.

[125] C. Strozz., Ser. I, 10, fos. 134r–53 headed: 'Spese fatte per M. Pagholo
Vettori maiordomo dello Ill.mo S.or nell'andate di Bolongnia et in Bolongnia e
altrove'; *ibid.*, fo. 178r: 'Lista della casa del Ill.mo S.or Giuliano de' Medici.'
Paolo heads the list as 'Messer Paolo Vitori Maiordomo'.

[126] B.M. Add. Ms. 10,280, fo. 17v, cover of letter from Antonio Maria Dainero,
Florence, 14 Oct. 1515: 'Al molto M.co messer Paulo Vittori orator del Ill. S.or
Iuliano de' Medici appresso la X.ma M.tà etc'. Cp. Add. Ms. 23,721, fo. 22v,
cover of letter.

Piacenza and Modena to be headed by Giuliano.[127] It therefore
does not come as a surprise that Paolo was instrumental in
procuring Machiavelli's release from prison.[128] Rumour also
had it that Paolo was working for Machiavelli's acceptance into
Medici service, evidently against Leo's wishes.[129]

Yet Francesco Vettori is wrongly accused of being indifferent
to his friend's fate. It was he who, together with Filippo and
Giovanni Machiavelli, paid the 1000 gold florins which Niccolò
was obliged to find as surety for his undertaking not to leave the
Florentine dominion.[130] We have proof that Vettori petitioned
the pope to release Machiavelli from prison after the Boscoli
conspiracy.[131] One may argue that Vettori had taken a risk
when supporting his friend on these occasions and the suspicions
which they aroused in the pope made further intervention well-
nigh impossible. Probably, as suggested earlier, Vettori was
already associated in Leo's mind with the republican element in
Florence which he had no wish to favour.[132] Certainly Vettori
himself seems to have thought that his action in saving the life
of Piero Soderini may have been responsible for the lack of
warmth which he had hoped for from the pope.[133] Paolo's
boldness and success and Francesco's caution and comparative
failure in Machiavelli's case may therefore reflect the attitudes
to Machiavelli of Giuliano de' Medici and Leo X and the
brothers' respective relationships with them.

If Vettori was often unsuccessful in petitioning the pope for
others, he was scarcely less so on his own and his family's behalf.
Of the three types of petitioner distinguished by Lionardo
Bartolini as having claims on Leo—the relations, the *amici* and
those who had helped the Medici back to power in Florence[134]

---

[127] N. Machiavelli, *Lettere*, ed. F. Gaeta, p. 374.   [128] *Ibid.*, p. 234.

[129] Mss. Torrigiani in *A.S.I.*, Ser. iii, xix (1874), p. 231. Piero Ardinghelli to
Giuliano, Aug. 1515.

[130] Notarile antecosimiano, D. 8 (1508–15), fos. 124r, 124v. R. Ridolfi,
Machiavelli, p. 133 says 'three friends, whose names have not come down to us', but
cp. also Signori, Deliberazioni, ord. autorità, 114, fo. 119r, to which Mr Humphrey
Butters kindly drew my attention. Filippo Machiavelli was a neighbour of the
Vettori in the commune of Cepparello in the Val d'Elsa, Decima Republicana, 4,
4, 1498, S. Spirito (Nicchio) I-Z, fo. 267r.

[131] N. Machiavelli, *Lettere*, ed. F. Gaeta, p. 233.

[132] Above, p. 97.   [133] N. Machiavelli, *Lettere*, ed. F. Gaeta, p. 241.

[134] B.N.F. Ginori Conti, 29, 92, 6, fo. 43v. Lionardo Bartolini to Niccolò
Michelozzi, Rome, 1 May 1513.

—Francesco considered that his brother Paolo merited recognition in the last category.[135] It was, however, just towards those citizens to whom Leo knew that he was beholden that his policy of seeming to have little regard for Florence was particularly harsh.[136] Francesco's ambition was 'to extract from the Pope something profitable' for himself and his brother so that they could become 'first rich and then honoured',[137] but the only advantage gained was Paolo's nomination as treasurer of the *decima*, the tax levied from the Florentine clergy.[138] Not even his hopes of finding suitable husbands for his daughters materialized during this period,[139] and Francesco Guicciardini criticized him for offering them to the first suitors who appeared.[140] Vettori discouraged his brother, too, from trying to become related to the pope by marriage plans involving a daughter of Leo's sister Contessina.[141]

Moreover, any financial gain would have been more than offset by the heavy commitments which went with Vettori's office. Three months after his arrival he complained to his brother about the additional cost he would incur if his mission were to continue: he would have to attend to his clothes; provide himself with more horses and buy wine, hay and other things 'which I do not dare to do because I cannot be extravagant'.[142] He estimated that he would need at least seven horses at the cost

---

[135] C. Strozz., Ser. I, 136, fo. 216r. Francesco to Paolo, Rome, 24 July 1513: 'se non eri voi tre, credo o Firenze andava a sacho o sarebbono [the Medici] anchora fuori. Se lui non rimunerà voi tre . . . che siate causa metterlo in casa donde n'è seguito il pontificato . . .'

[136] *Ibid.*, fo. 218v. Francesco to Paolo, Rome, 13 May 1513: 'E perchè lui conosce havere obligo chon chi l'ha aiutato tornare chostì, vuole monstrare non fare molto stima di Firenze.'

[137] C. Strozz., Ser. I, 136, fo. 230r. Francesco to Paolo, Rome, 'a dì 18' (June 1513): 'trarre dal papa choxa d'utile e diventare prima richi e poi honorevoli'.

[138] Letters of thanks from both Paolo and Francesco indicate that Paolo received the post. M.A.P., 116, No. 352, Francesco to Lorenzo, 9 Oct. 1514; *ibid.*, No. 421, Paolo to Lorenzo 22 Oct. 1514; cp. M.A.P., 108, No. 124, Filippo Strozzi to Lorenzo Strozzi, 13 Aug. 1514.

[139] C. Strozz., Ser. I, 136, fo. 219v. Francesco to Paolo, Rome, 5 Aug. 1513.

[140] F. Guicciardini, *Scritti Politici e Ricordi*, ed. R. Palmarocchi (Bari, 1933), pp. 276, 307.

[141] C. Strozz., Ser. I, 136, fos. 229r–230r. Francesco to Paolo, Rome, 'a dì 18' (June 1513).

[142] *Ibid.*, fo. 228r, 16 May 1513: 'il che io non ardisco fare perchè non posso gittare via'.

of twenty-five ducats a pair, forty or even fifty ducats for cloth-
ing and another fifty or more for furnishing the house.[143] For a
while in Rome, as he told Machiavelli, he had lived sumptuously and finely, entertaining, offering two or three dishes,
eating off silver and such like, but when he realized he was
spending too much and was none the better off, he decided not
to invite anyone and to live more like an ordinary citizen.[144]
His household comprised Giuliano Brancacci, a chaplain, a
secretary, nine servants, and he kept seven horses and it ab-
sorbed all his salary. Vettori who had not been accustomed to
stint himself in his youth now had an income on which he could
barely live and dowries for his unmarried daughters had to be
provided.[145] However, he was sufficiently resigned to be able to
write to Machiavelli, 'as you know, I adapt myself to everything; I shall confine myself to the possible'.[146]

Accommodation for ambassadors was often difficult to find,
but in Rome Vettori seems to have been lucky. His first house
was near Monte Giordano.[147] Then he took over free of charge
the house of Goro Gheri, bishop of Pistoia, who had been sent to
the Romagna; this adjoined S. Michele in the Borgo towards
Monte Gianicolo, close to the Vatican and St Peter's.[148] It was
a small but pleasant house with what had once been a beautiful
garden. At the time when Vettori lived in the Borgo it was rather
solitary and he could climb up the Monte Gianicolo and walk
along little paths amongst the vines unobserved by anyone.[149]

The members of the ceremonial embassy were lodged in the
Monto Giordano neighbourhood near Vettori's first house;[150]
the arrangements made for them show that the practice of
arriving at a palace furnished solely for their visit was not
peculiar to the Valois and Tudor monarchs. Lionardo Bartolini,
who was responsible for the ambassadors' accommodation,[151]

---

[143] *Ibid.*, fo. 229(bis)r. Francesco to Paolo, Rome, 16 June 1513.
[144] N. Machiavelli, *Lettere*, ed. F. Gaeta, p. 298.
[145] *Ibid.*, p. 245.
[146] O. Tommasini, ii, p. 969.
[147] C. Strozz., Ser. I, 136, fo. 218v. Francesco to Paolo, Rome, 13 May 1513.
[148] *Ibid.*, fo. 225v, 14 Aug. 1513.
[149] N. Machiavelli, *Lettere*, ed. F. Gaeta, p. 298.
[150] C. Strozz., Ser. I, 136, fo. 218v. Francesco to Paolo, Rome, 13 May 1513.
[151] B.N.F. Ginori Conti, 29, 92, 6, fo. 36v. Lionardo Bartolini to Michelozzi,
Rome, 10 April 1513.

reported to Niccolò Michelozzi that Jacopo Rucellai had
negotiated at Leo's request with the Orsini for the ambassadors
to be lodged on the Monte Giordano.[152] The Orsini had agreed
willingly but though there was space enough for all the visitors
nothing but bare walls would await them unless arrangements
for furnishing the palace could be made quickly.

The court of Rome after the 1460s has been described by a
modern authority as 'the listening post of Italy' to which 'the
Italian states sent their most accomplished diplomats, their most
promising juniors and their handsomest and best supplied
legations'.[153] Certainly in Vettori's day it must have been one of
great splendour and full of brilliant people. The humanists,
Pietro Bembo and Jacopo Sadoleto, were papal secretaries;
Giovanni Rucellai, who was working on his play *Rosamunda*
while Vettori was in Rome, was also a member of Leo's household;[154] Cardinal Bibbiena, the Bernardo Dovizi of Raphael's
well-known portrait, was treasurer general; Ludovico Canossa
was master of the household before he became papal nuncio;
and Filippo Strozzi, like his father a great builder whose name
is perpetuated in the famous Florentine palace, held the post of
depositary of the papal chamber (*depositario*).[155] Raphael was
painting there and Michelangelo had just completed the ceiling
frescoes of the Sistine Chapel. Giovanni Corsi, Francesco da
Diacceto and Giovanni Rucellai cannot have been the only
humanists who came to Vettori's house.[156] Yet he derived little
satisfaction from this assembly of outstanding scholars, artists
and men of affairs. It makes strange reading when he says that
although the concourse in Rome was large, 'few are out of the
ordinary'. Bibbiena alone is singled out for his 'gentile
ingegno'.[157] The salacious jokes in *La Calandria* were no doubt
relished as much by the author of the *Viaggio in Alemagna* as
Vettori's jocund conversation was appreciated by Bibbiena

---

[152] *Ibid.*, fo. 46v. Lionardo Bartolini to Michelozzi, Rome, 9 May 1513.

[153] G. Mattingly, *Renaissance Diplomacy* (London, 1955), p. 106.

[154] Written in 1515. *Le Opere di Giovanni Rucellai*, ed. G. Mazzoni (Bologna,
1887), p. xvii.

[155] P. Paschini, *Roma nel Rinascimento* (Bologna, 1940), p. 411.

[156] P. Kristeller, 'Giovanni Corsi', *La Bibliofilia*, xxxviii (1936), p. 249; for
Giovanni Rucellai, N. Machiavelli, *Lettere*, ed. F. Gaeta, p. 299.

[157] N. Machiavelli, *Lettere*, ed. F. Gaeta, p. 300.

when the two men were together in France.[158] Vettori's dissatisfaction with the rest of the concourse perhaps stemmed from his dislike of court life:[159] he found the letters of his contemporaries little else but 'ceremonies, lies and fables' and he wondered how their authors had attained any rank whatsoever.[160]

Vettori's term of office as Florentine ambassador in Rome lasted for two years during which his appointment was frequently renewed.[161] Florence had expected too much of a Medici pope, for, although Leo was not ungenerous to his relations and compatriots, he was not prepared to make constant concessions to family or Florentine interests. Nor was he willing to take the Florentines entirely into his confidence. While making the familiar Medici gesture of consulting the citizens, he would generally carry out his own policy. A Florentine ambassador had direct access to this most illustrious member of his city but had little important business to do with him. Negotiations were not primarily carried out by Vettori: vital policy was frequently dealt with by members of the Medici family; the ambassador was but the channel through which communications and requests both public and private were conveyed. He had some influence but little power. Patronage was undoubtedly an important aspect of his office, but here Vettori's deference to Leo's dislike of private petitions limited his effectiveness. Neither a resplendent figure himself nor the head of an impressive legation, Vettori would not fit Garrett Mattingly's description of the diplomats sent to the 'listening post of Italy', but the renewals of his term of office may indicate that he had become the type of ambassador required by the Medici now that Florentine affairs were linked with papal policy. His tenure of office in France will show the position of a Florentine ambassador outside Italy in this early period of Medici domination in Rome and Florence.

[158] B.M. Add. Ms. 10,280, fo. 24r. Bibbiena to Vettori, Angers, 27 July 1518: 'non vorrei che voi vi foste partito di qua tanto m'era grata la iucondissima vostra conversatione'.

[159] Above, p. 9.

[160] N. Machiavelli, *Lettere*, ed. F. Gaeta, p. 300.

[161] Signori, Missive, Legaz. e Comm., 27, fos. 17r, 17v, 18r.

CHAPTER VI

Florence, France and Lorenzo (1515–19)

THE PAPAL CONTROL over Florentine external and internal
affairs and the rivalry between different members of the Medici
house which determined Vettori's activities in Rome formed the
background to his connection from 1515–19 with France and
with the young Lorenzo de' Medici.

Francesco Vettori arrived in Florence from Rome with
Lorenzo on 15 May 1515[1] and was almost immediately recognized by Francesco Guicciardini as the citizen most in favour
with the young ruler after Filippo Strozzi.[2] This close relationship must have been established in Rome, probably in connection with the manoeuvres for Lorenzo's appointment to the
captaincy of the Florentine forces which should be seen in the
context of papal and Florentine relations with France.

Francis I, who had succeeded Louis XII on New Year's Day
1515, resolved to fulfil his predecessor's ambition to recapture
Milan. In December 1514, when Louis XII was still alive, the
pope, through Vettori, had asked for Machiavelli's advice on
the best policy to pursue in the event of a French invasion and
attack on the city. Machiavelli had counselled that neutrality
would be dangerous and, since a French victory was almost
certain, an alliance with Louis was advisable, provided that
Venice took the same course.[3] Louis' death, however, saw the
pope still uncommitted either to France or to her enemies.
Although in February Leo brought Florence into the anti-
French league comprising the emperor, the king of Spain and
the Swiss, for which the duke of Milan ceded to him his rights
over Parma and Piacenza, the pope himself remained outside

[1] Signori, Missive, Legaz. e Comm., 27, fo. 15r. Margin: 'Recessus est die 15 mai
1515.'
[2] F. Guicciardini, *Carteggi*, i, p. 247. Francesco to Luigi Guicciardini, Florence,
6 June 1515; *ibid.*, p. 251, 4 July 1515.
[3] N. Machiavelli, *Lettere*, ed. F. Gaeta, p. 361.

the League and continued negotiations with the French until he finally joined the coalition against France in mid-July 1515.[4]

While still uncommitted to either side, Leo made preparations for war: on 10 January he chose his brother Giuliano as the commander-in-chief of the papal troops[5] and in mid-April informed the Eight through Vettori that he wished the Florentines to raise 700 men-at-arms.[6] Although this proposal was ill-received, the Florentines nevertheless complied with his wishes. Once the decision to raise troops had been taken, the question of commanders was bound to arise. When the Eight consulted the pope on this question, they received from Vettori the answer that His Holiness had not yet made up his mind.[7] But if the pope was undecided, his nephew was not. He wished to command the Florentine forces himself.

Vettori's account in his *Sommario* of the way in which Lorenzo had himself appointed captain general provides a clue to the writer's attitude towards the pope's nephew and towards the French. He states that Giuliano de' Medici had promised the captaincy and a large salary to his brother-in-law, the count of Geneva. Whereupon Lorenzo saw in this proposition a slight to his honour and, thinking that the Florentines would resent the great expense in which they would be involved, sought the title of captain for himself, though without the troops or the salary. In this way he could frustrate Leo's and Giuliano's scheme. The pope, according to Vettori, disliked this idea but consented, provided that Lorenzo obtained the approval of the Seventy which he reckoned he would not get. However, Lorenzo who had discussed the matter with them beforehand, obtained their consent, much to the pope's displeasure. But once faced with this *fait accompli*, Leo insisted that instead of having the empty title Lorenzo should be given charge of the troops.[8]

In an article on Lorenzo's appointment to the captaincy of the Florentine forces, Giorgetti has shown that, contrary to Vettori's statement, Lorenzo wanted not only the title but also

---

[4] L. Pastor, vii, p. 111 notes that 'Nitti (60) says that Leo X joined the anti-French league definitely on 14 July 1515; Brosch (i, 43) names the 15th and Balan, Boschetti (I, 90) 17 July.'

[5] H. Reinhard, p. 44.

[6] A. Giorgetti, 'Lorenzo de' Medici', *A.S.I.*, Ser. iv, xi (1883), p. 201.

[7] *Ibid.*, p. 202.   [8] *Sommario*, pp. 306–7.

the troops and a salary.[9] Letters to Lorenzo of 20 and 21 April from Galeotto de' Medici, in charge of the government of Florence during the young Medici's absence in Rome, reveal that Lorenzo had already asked for 500 troops in line with papal wishes and was trying to ensure that the authority for hiring them was in the hands of the Eight. Galeotto succeeded in getting this concession from the *Balìa* but the Council responsible for a commitment of this kind was in fact the Seventy. On 28 April they passed a provision giving full authority to the Eight to engage up to 500 men-at-arms. Without a special law abrogating in his favour an existing provision of the Republic which denied the post of captain or *condottiere* to any private citizen, Lorenzo could with the votes of the Eight only and with every semblance of legality assume the rank at which he aimed. According to Giorgetti, both Leo and Lorenzo wanted to raise troops, but the pope objected to Lorenzo's name being associated with the *condotta*, or hiring of troops, and to his assuming the title of captain.[10] Vettori's argument that Lorenzo wanted to save the Florentines money and assume the title to thwart the pope's plans thus seems fallacious.

The ground having been well prepared in Florence, Lorenzo returned to the city in May, accompanied, as we know, by Vettori, to superintend the final steps in the fulfilment of his ambition. On 23 May at a meeting of the Council of Seventy the gonfalonier, Roberto di Giovanni de' Ricci,[11] recommended Lorenzo as captain general of the Florentine forces and commissioned the Eight in virtue of the recently passed provision to proceed as quickly as possible with the hiring of troops. Before leaving Rome, Lorenzo had already arranged for the payment of certain commanders he wanted whose names he had listed.[12]

Vettori's account reflects the rivalry between Giuliano and Lorenzo already noted in previous chapters, and this rivalry is also alluded to by Parenti in his history and by Lorenzo himself in his correspondence with his secretary.[13] Two letters from Benedetto Buondelmonti to Filippo Strozzi, however, indicate

[9] 'Lorenzo de' Medici', pp. 194–215.
[10] *Ibid.*, pp. 205–6.
[11] B. Masi, *Ricordanze*, ed. G. Corazzini (Florence, 1906), p. 154.
[12] A. Giorgetti, 'Lorenzo de' Medici', pp. 207–8; pp. 211–12.
[13] *Ibid.*, p. 204, n. 1.

opposition to Lorenzo's intention from another quarter of which Vettori makes no mention. Buondelmonti states that Jacopo Salviati and his wife Lucrezia, Leo's sister Contessina and her husband Piero Ridolfi, Luigi Ridolfi and Cardinal Bibbiena opposed Lorenzo's plan because they regarded it as potentially despotic. The writer, though, considered the move expedient for the security of the regime on which depended his own safety and that of the other pro-Medici citizens. It should, he advised Strozzi, be carried out as quickly as possible.[14]

Vettori favoured Lorenzo's plans. On the strength of a conversation which Bernardo Rucellai had had with a certain woman informant (who may well have been Lucrezia Salviati), Buondelmonti reported that Francesco had encouraged Lorenzo to take the step he had. He also reported Paolo as saying that his brother favoured Lorenzo's intention.[15] The minutes of the meeting of the Seventy on 23 May show that Vettori approved of Lorenzo's proposal to become captain saying that it should be carried out as soon as possible.[16] On 2 June Vettori was elected one of the Eight[17] charged with hiring the mercenaries and was very probably a party to the decision of 3 July to increase the captain's salary.[18]

If, as indicated, Vettori's account in his *Sommario* of Lorenzo's designs does not accord with the true facts it is very probable that he wished to give it a more republican interpretation than the truth warranted, his intention being to exculpate Lorenzo from the charge of despotism and himself from the consequences of being implicated in it. His explanation of Lorenzo's desire to lead the troops personally in the field once they had been raised for him, is also given on favourable grounds: Lorenzo acted in the interests of the pro-French Florentines, again in opposition to the pope.

The young Medici, Vettori would have us believe, did not wish the Florentine forces to oppose France which he knew they would be forced to do if they were dispatched to Lombardy. He

---

[14] M.A.P., 108, No. 148, 17 May 1515; *ibid.*, No. 146, 19 May 1515.

[15] *Ibid.*, No. 147. Two important women in Roman political life at this time were Lucrezia Salviati and Contessina Ridolfi. Lucrezia was the more vocal of the two; see also No. 147 and A. Giorgetti, 'Lorenzo de' Medici', p. 203.

[16] Otto, Delib., Partiti, Condotte, 11, fo. 9v.

[17] Tratte 84, fo. 81r.   [18] A. Giorgetti, 'Lorenzo de' Medici', p. 209.

therefore told the pope that the Florentines would not send their troops without their captain; this he regarded as tantamount to preventing their departure for he was certain that the pope would not wish him either to leave Florence or to be in the same camp as Giuliano. Leo was spared a decision when Giuliano's illness forced him to send his nephew in his brother's place. Lorenzo, Vettori writes, accepted 'unwillingly' since he feared that in acting against France he would antagonize the Florentines, the city's merchants would suffer, and Francis I, if victorious, might take his state from him. Only 'constrained by the papal command' did Lorenzo assemble his own and the papal troops and set out from Florence for Lombardy on 16 August in company with Cardinal Giulio de' Medici who was going to Bologna to take up his appointment as papal legate.[19] With Lorenzo, though the writer does not say so, went Francesco Vettori, appointed by the Eight as *commissario* of the Florentine forces.[20]

Examination of letters between certain members of the Medici family confirms the papal opposition to Lorenzo's intentions. On 29 June 1515 Leo conferred on Giuliano the supreme command over the ecclesiastical forces.[21] The Florentine companies were expected to join the papal army in order to carry out the joint defence of Parma and Piacenza. Lorenzo, however, refused to put his contingents under Giuliano's command and urged the pope early in July to give him permission to accompany Giuliano in the field at the head of the Florentine forces.[22] Leo, however, wanted Lorenzo to remain in Florence and would have preferred to send Cardinal Giulio rather than Lorenzo to replace Giuliano during his illness.[23] It was not until the beginning of August that he conceded Lorenzo's wishes, now appointing him commander over the entire papal army.[24]

Beneath Lorenzo's opposition to the pope lay an important difference of approach to France. Leo wished to direct Florentine foreign policy in union with that of the papacy,[25] but

---

[19] *Sommario*, pp. 306–8; *Ricordo*, p. 281; H. Reinhard, p. 56.
[20] Otto, Delib., 6, fo. 25v Patente 15 Aug. 1515.
[21] H. Reinhard, p. 52.   [22] A. Giorgetti, 'Lorenzo de' Medici', p. 213.
[23] A. Zobi, *Delle Nozze del Magnifico Giuliano de' Medici con la Principessa Filiberta di Savoia* (Firenze, 1868), pp. 74, 79, 86.
[24] *Ibid.*, p. 93.   [25] H. Reinhard, p. 52.

Lorenzo presented to his uncle the dangers for Medici rule in Florence of the anti-French policy which Leo was likely to adopt. In his anxiety to win the pope's consent to his command of the Florentine forces Lorenzo had pointed out that if the fortunes of war went against the pope and Francis I were victorious, a revolution in Florence and his own expulsion might result. Leo replied on 16 July that if what Lorenzo had reported was true, then this was all the more reason for him to remain in Florence. In any case he had not yet decided against France.[26]

The potential danger to the Medici party in Florence emerges from the correspondence between Alfonsina and her son and between the Eight and the pope after Lorenzo's departure for Lombardy.[27] Already then a critical situation had developed: the French had crossed the Alps six days before,[28] and having bypassed the Swiss forces defending the gateway to Italy at Susa, had captured their leader Prospero Colonna on the day Lorenzo left and were fanning out over northern Italy.[29] Lorenzo's mother Alfonsina, 'blushing with shame' at the thought of her son's delayed departure and the inadequacy of the papal forces, besought him to consider carefully that Francis I had arrived in Italy with a following of 80,000 and that Florence was devoted to the crown of France. She exhorted him not to repeat the errors of his father Piero whose obstinate opposition to France had earned the Medici nineteen years' exile. 'That owl Bibbiena', she went on with reference to Cardinal Bibbiena's anti-French influence at the Curia, 'must not be allowed to ruin them a second time.'[30] On the 18th the Eight themselves warned the pope that Francis I could cause a revolution in the city;[31] in fact only four days later Leo himself learned from a report sent by Ludovico Canossa, his legate in France, that Francis was in contact with the anti-Medici elements in Florence.[32] Yet on 27 August the pope countered his

---

[26] A. Giorgetti, 'Lorenzo de' Medici', Doc. IV, p. 317.
[27] Lorenzo and Vettori left Florence on 16 Aug., B. Masi, p. 154.
[28] A. Giorgetti, 'Lorenzo de' Medici', p. 215.
[29] *Sommario*, p. 308; A. Verdi, *Gli ultimi anni di Lorenzo de' Medici, Duca d'Urbino* (Este, 1905), p. 12.
[30] *A.S.I.*, Ser. v, viii (1891), p. 189; M.A.P., 137, No. 652, 11 Aug. 1515.
[31] H. Reinhard, Doc. II, p. 90.
[32] *Ibid.*, Doc. III, p. 91, P. Ardinghelli to Alfonsina, Rome, 22 Aug.

nephew's letter in which he had complained of the ruin to which his uncle's policy was leading him with the admonition not to harbour the French in his heart nor to be so ready to throw himself at Francis' feet; Lorenzo should rather consider the 'liberty of Italy'; the papal and Florentine forces together could defeat the French.[33]

Inside information of this kind affords an explanation for Vettori's interpretation of Lorenzo's action; it also contributes to our understanding of his own behaviour as *commissario* as he relates it in his history.[34] Once the Florentine contingent had joined forces with the papal army assembled at Piacenza, strategy dictated a joint advance of the confederates over the river Po to reinforce the Swiss based on Milan, and a limited advance was in fact advocated by Cardinal Giulio, but such a policy ran counter to the wishes of the Florentines who were determined at all costs to avoid offending the French. Lorenzo under pressure from the Spanish viceroy Cardona, who would otherwise have held him responsible for the loss of Milan, proposed to cross the river with all the troops under his command. This decision, which Lorenzo reported to his mother in a letter written in Vettori's hand, was vigorously opposed by Alfonsina,[35] who because she knew how unpopular it would be, did not communicate it to the Eight.[36] According to his account in the *Sommario*, Vettori too, acting in his capacity as *commissario*, protested that under no circumstances were the Florentine government willing for their troops to attack the French. The government was quite content for Florentine troops to defend the papal territories of Parma and Piacenza but they were to advance no further. If Lorenzo wished to cross the Po, he must do so as commander of the papal forces only; the Florentine contingent would not be permitted to go with him, nor would Lorenzo be given pay either for himself or for the men. Such boldness especially from his friend Vettori apparently took Lorenzo by surprise and he dropped his plan of involving Florentine troops in attacking the French but still intended to

---

[33] A. Verdi, p. 13.
[34] *Sommario*, pp. 309–10.
[35] M.A.P., 137, No. 672, Alfonsina to Lorenzo, Florence, 10 Sept. 1515.
[36] *Ibid.*, No. 674, Alfonsina to Lorenzo, Florence, 12 Sept. 1515.

cross the river with the papal forces.[37] But this design did not materialize owing to the viceroy's withdrawal.

Vettori's account of this episode gives an accurate account of the wishes of the Florentines and it is sufficient to cite the Eight's letter to him of 2 September to show the type of calumny which he wanted to refute. It was being said in the French army, the Eight wrote, that the Florentines had sided against the French and that they had sent Lorenzo and the Florentine troops into Milanese territory to defend it against the king of France. Vettori, the Eight went on, had not only seen the untruth of these allegations but had demonstrated it to all the world.[38]

Francis' victory at Marignano on 13 September which resulted from the failure of the armies of the pope and of the viceroy to join forces with the Swiss seemed to make an attack on the ecclesiastical territories of Parma and Piacenza imminent. That Francis agreed to peace terms with the pope instead was due to the skilled diplomacy of the papal legate Ludovico Canossa and to French fears of an English invasion.[39]

During these negotiations Lorenzo seems to have been much more eager than the pope to come to an understanding with Francis.[40] The peace terms signed by Canossa and the duke of Savoy on 20 September[41] were approved by Francis I at Pavia on 9 October and by Leo at Viterbo on the 13th,[42] yet only five days later rumour reached Milan that the pope was no longer willing to confer in person with the French king. Francis, angered by this rebuff, determined to use the influence of Lorenzo, Cardinal Giulio and Giuliano with Leo to reverse this decision. The man the king chose as his emissary to the three Medici was Paolo Vettori.[43] Paolo was then in Milan as Giuliano's ambassador to the French court[44] but on 19 October he met Cardinal Giulio in Bologna who urged him to convey Francis' request to Leo and assured him of Lorenzo's support.[45]

[37] *Sommario*, p. 310.   [38] Otto, Missive, Legaz. e Comm., 11, fo. 128r.

[39] L. Pastor, vii, pp. 122–4; *Sommario*, p. 313.

[40] A. Verdi, p. 16; L. Pastor, vii, p. 123; L. Madelin, *France et Rome. La Pragmatique Sanction* (Paris, 1913), p. 120; cp. M.A.P., 137, No. 658.

[41] Otto, Responsive, 12, fo. 301r.

[42] A. Buisson, *Le Chancelier Antoine Duprat* (Paris, 1935), p. 109.

[43] M.A.P., 110, No. 98, F. Pandolfini to Lorenzo de' Medici, Milan, 18 Oct. 1515; A. Verdi, p. 17.   [44] M.A.P., 110, No. 98 and above, p. 103, n. 126.

[45] *Ibid.*, 113, No. 183. Cardinal Giulio to Lorenzo, Bologna, 19 Oct. 1515.

By 22 October the cardinal could inform Lorenzo of the pope's consent to a meeting with the French king.[46]

Francesco Vettori's views on the Franco-imperial power contest expressed in the *Sommario* show a significantly pro-French bias. It is true that he had experience by then of the imperial victories and particularly the sack of Rome, but his preference for the French has been evident before and is a typically Florentine attitude. He regrets that Francis did not follow up his victory which would have made him master of Italy, and he bitterly deplores the 'bad luck' which prevented Italy from coming into the hand of such a 'good and excellent Prince' under whose protection she could have enjoyed many years of peace. It was an 'evil fate' for Italy which led Francis to enter into peace negotiations with the papal legate. Vettori's account suggests that it was principally Leo who wanted peace; it obscures the fact that Lorenzo was more eager for it than the pope and omits Paolo's commission.[47]

The peace settlement and the prospect of a meeting in the near future between Leo and Francis made the dispatch of Florentine ceremonial ambassadors to the French king a matter of urgency. These had been appointed in June which was even then considered late, Francis having been on the throne since January. The Eight had explained to Francesco Pandolfini, the Florentine ambassador in France, that they had delayed making the appointments until Lorenzo's return from Rome which was later than anticipated. Now that they had been created they were expected to depart within the month.[48] From June onwards however their dispatch became the subject of anxious correspondence between the Eight, the pope and members of the Medici family.

The three ambassadors were Francesco Vettori, Vieri de' Medici[49] and Filippo Strozzi. In his *Sommario* Vettori gives the fighting in Lombardy as the reason why they did not immediately leave Florence.[50] This is what the Eight told Pandolfini,[51]

[46] *Ibid.*, No. 184.

[47] *Sommario*, p. 313; see also above, p. 66, and below, p. 136.

[48] Signori, Missive, Legaz. e Comm., 27, fo. 19r, 12 June 1515; Otto, Missive, Legaz. e Comm., 11, fo. 110v, 15 June 1515.

[49] Vieri de' Medici did not go as he was at Pietrasanta. M.A.P., 137, No. 659.

[50] *Sommario*, p. 314.   [51] Otto. Missive, Legaz. e Comm., 11, fo. 125r.

but as a general statement it is misleading since it obscures the fundamental cause of delay which was the opposition of the pope. As late as 18 August the Eight asked Leo for permission to send the ambassadors appointed in June;[52] this was refused by him on 20 August,[53] but yielded on 22nd in a moment of panic caused by Canossa's news that Francis I was in contact with the anti-Medici element in Florence.[54] Four days later the Eight informed the pope[55] and Vettori[56] of the imminent departure of the ambassadors. Vettori was instructed to obtain Lorenzo's approval of the arrangements. He nevertheless refers to the Florentine decision finally to dispatch the ambassadors as 'by order of the pope'.[57] By the end of August Leo had evidently again changed his mind for the departure of the ambassadors was once more postponed.[58] The matter remained in abeyance until the proposed meeting between the French king and the pope after Francis' victory at Marignano. By 15 October Filippo Strozzi had joined Vettori in Reggio and Francesco wrote to the Eight saying that they were ready to leave whenever the Eight thought fit.[59] He reminded them however that according to the original arrangement a third ambassador was needed. This letter crossed with one informing Vettori that Lorenzo de' Medici had been put forward.[60] He had not however been the choice of the pope, who had wanted to send one of the 'leading citizens', his brother-in-law Jacopo Salviati for instance. Alfonsina, who together with Giuliano de' Medici and Jacopo Salviati was governing Florence in Lorenzo's absence,[61] had objected that the two ambassadors would be joined by Francesco Pandolfini, the resident ambassador to the king, and three would be

---

[52] *Ibid.*, fo. 120v.

[53] Otto, Responsive, 12, fo. 194r; F. Nitti, Doc. II, p. 210, Cardinal Giulio, Rome, to Giuliano de' Medici and Jacopo Salviati in Florence.

[54] H. Reinhard, Doc. III, p. 91; Doc. IV, p. 91.

[55] Otto, Missive, Legaz. e Comm., 11, fo. 124r.

[56] *Ibid.*, 124v.

[57] Otto, Responsive, 12, fo. 220r, 25 Aug. 1515: 'Per una di V.S. de' 24 intendo che per ordine di N.S. quelle sono resolute a mandare li oratori al X.mo.'

[58] M.A.P., 137, No. 663, Alfonsina to Lorenzo, 30 Aug. 1515; Otto, Missive, Legaz. e Comm., 11, fo. 126v.

[59] Otto, Responsive, 12, fo. 368r.

[60] Otto, Missive, Legaz. e Comm., 11, fo. 141r. Messer Luigi de' Rossi had been suggested instead of Vieri de' Medici but is now replaced by Lorenzo.

[61] H. Reinhard, pp. 56–7.

sufficient. She too disapproved the Eight's decision to send Lorenzo,[62] as the pope had done. They however cited the example of Lorenzo the Magnificent who had represented his city at Naples and elsewhere, precedents which they felt the pope would appreciate.[63] Lorenzo, to whom Vettori communicated the Eight's preference, expressed his desire 'to satisfy the city in everything'; he had sent to Florence for a letter of credence to the French king, which he would use or not as he thought fit.[64] Leo, on being consulted by Francesco Pandolfini on the Eight's behalf, considered that his nephew should go as a private person but act as an ambassador on his arrival.[65] This attitude recalls his similar dislike of Lorenzo's acceptance of the title of captain. Ultimately on 17 October Lorenzo was elected ambassador[66] and on the 21st, four months after he had been appointed, Francesco Vettori left Reggio with him and Filippo Strozzi to carry out the ceremonial part of what was later to be extended into a resident embassy in France.[67]

During the ceremonial part of his mission to the French king Vettori, as initially in Rome, was only one of a number of ambassadors whose principal function was to do honour to the new ruler. With the Eight's permission, the three ambassadors usually sent a joint letter back to Florence.[68] Vettori's name stands under Pandolfini's but above Strozzi's. Lorenzo de' Medici did not sign. Occasionally Vettori wrote in his own hand on behalf of Strozzi and himself,[69] or even on his own.[70] At other times Francesco Pandolfini was the scribe for the letter common to all three ambassadors and Francesco Vettori made additions.[71] Once Pandolfini would seem to be the author of the letter as well as its scribe.[72] Since it is not easy to establish who was the author of each letter and because our primary interest is in Vettori, the information (mostly concerning the progress of French negotiations with the Swiss, and the Venetian attack on

[62] M.A.P., 137, No. 700.
[63] Otto, Missive, Legaz. e Comm., 11, fo. 141r.
[64] Otto, Responsive, 12, fo. 375r. [65] M.A.P., 110, No. 97.
[66] Signori, Missive, Legaz. e Comm., 27, fo. 19v.
[67] Otto, Responsive, 12, fo. 381r.
[68] Otto, Missive, Legaz. e Comm., 11, fo. 144r.
[69] Otto, Responsive, 12, fo. 393r–v. [70] *Ibid.*, fo. 453r–v.
[71] *Ibid.*, fo. 444r–v. [72] *Ibid.*, fo. 395r: 'ad me Francesco Pandolfini'.

Brescia) which the three ambassadors sent back to Florence will not be discussed. Brief reference will however be made to that part of the correspondence which deals with the choice of city where Francis and Leo were to meet, as this throws further light on the relations between the various members of the Medici family and between Florence and France. Vettori's future is intimately bound up with these two points.

The conversations between the French king and the pope took place in Bologna. Had Leo, Alfonsina and the Eight had their way, the agreement signed there might have been known as the concordat of Florence, for no sooner had the Eight received news of Leo's intended parley with Francis than they wrote to Roberto Acciaiuoli, their ambassador in Rome, instructing him to recommend Florence as a place of meeting.[73] On 17 October Roberto replied that the pope himself did not object to this suggestion but some of the cardinals apparently considered Florence a summer rather than a winter meeting place, on account of the shortage of wood, wine and meat which made it in their opinion impossible in December.[74] Francesco Vettori and his colleagues were ordered to persuade Francis I of the desirability of Florence as a meeting place.[75] Lorenzo opposed this choice, his ostensible reasons being that Francis' presence in Florence would cause the city great expense and that the king might want the city for himself if he saw its great beauty.[76] We may assume the real reason to be his fear of the Florentine pro-French party, which according to Parenti had written a letter to Francis inviting him to the city 'which on several occasions had received from his ancestors liberty from the tyranny of many'.[77] Alfonsina, who had learned from Paolo Vettori of Lorenzo and Cardinal Giulio's disapproval on the strength of the first two reasons, wrote to Lorenzo that she herself could not think of anything in the world which would bring Lorenzo greater reputation and honour than to have a king of France in his house, and who would kiss the feet of and pay

[73] A. Verdi, p. 17.

[74] M.A.P., 110, No. 97. A. Verdi, p. 18. Bologna on the other hand was known as 'fat Bologna', M. Bishop, *Petrarch and his World* (London, 1964), p. 29.

[75] Otto, Missive, Legaz. e Comm., 11, fo. 143v; *ibid.*, Responsive, 12, fo. 395r.

[76] M.A.P., 137, No. 707.

[77] Parenti, Istorie, cit. A. Verdi, p. 18.

homage to his uncle. As to the cost, she cited the precedent of Charles VIII's visit to the city which had not involved it in greater expense than intended. His fear of Francis' desire to possess Florence on account of its beauty drew from her, a Neapolitan by birth, the remark that there were many other cities in Italy as beautiful as Florence and if the king wanted everything lovely he would want the whole of Italy.[78] Alfonsina must have convinced her son for Lorenzo joined the Florentine ambassadors in attempting to persuade Francis to come to Florence.[79] Francis, however, declined on the ground that he was in the middle of negotiations with the Swiss in which a delay of two or three days might be harmful: Florence would, therefore, be too far away. Moreover he wanted the discussions to take place as soon as possible and the choice of Florence as a place of meeting would mean their postponement because he did not want to enter the city with any less ceremony than Charles VIII and that would require some weeks' preparation.[80]

Already before the meeting in Bologna had taken place, the Eight had written to ask Lorenzo which of the ambassadors at present with the French king he thought should accompany him to France.[81] His answer to the question is not extant, but we must assume that he suggested Vettori. After the meeting, Lorenzo, Vettori and Filippo Strozzi accompanied Francis to Milan, then early in January Strozzi, in response to the Eight's orders, accompanied Lorenzo to Florence while Vettori set out for France following after the young king who returned to his native land post-haste.[82]

The existence of two sets of official correspondence from Vettori in France—one to the Eight and another to the Medici —raises questions about his status and the nature of his activities there. His letters to the Eight and their replies are to be found in the official register of the time. On the other hand, his letters to Lorenzo de' Medici or to his secretary Goro Gheri are an incomplete collection among the Medici and the Strozzi papers in Florence and the Vettori papers in the British Museum,

[78] See pp. 120, n. 76.
[79] Otto, Responsive, 12, fo. 391r.   [80] *Ibid.*
[81] Otto, Missive, Legaz. e Comm., 11, fo. 155v.
[82] Otto, Responsive, 12 ,fo. 494r; Otto, Missive, Legaz. e Comm., 12, fo. 4v.

London. Even a summary glance at the two sets of correspondence shows a certain difference between them. The letters to the Eight are largely confined to reports of news; those to Lorenzo or to Goro Gheri contain more personal views and though fewer in number form a more interesting series. Both are relevant to an understanding of the relationship between the Medici and Florence with regard to foreign affairs.

That Vettori used two standards can be seen from a letter to Goro Gheri: 'I consider it an advantage that I can tell you everything I have in mind without reserve, whereas writing to others I should proceed with greater caution.'[83] On one occasion he expressed concern to Gheri about the dryness of his reports to the Eight.[84] At least once Vettori wanted to confide some point to Gheri only; Gheri however thought this inadvisable and forwarded Vettori's letter to messer Baldassare da Pescia, another of Lorenzo's secretaries, to show it to Lorenzo, 'because from patrons nothing must be kept secret'.[85] In a letter dated 1 November 1517 to Gheri he includes a proviso that a suggestion made should not be discussed 'with any citizen in Florence' as he was certain it would meet with disapproval.[86] Although one could quote other examples which show that Vettori wrote more fully to Lorenzo than he did in his letters to the Eight,[87] the basic difference between the two sets arises from the fact that he was employed by the Eight chiefly as an information agent, the negotiations being conducted by the papal emissaries, whereas he was used by Lorenzo in connection with his marriage negotiations.

Vettori's function as information agent emerges from the first letter, dated 19 January 1516, addressed to him alone in Milan instructing him to depart for the court and to let them know 'daily' everything that occurred. Anyone going to France via

---

[83] C. Strozz., Ser. I, 9, fo. 9r, Paris, 2 March 1517: 'mi pare conveniente potere dire a voi tutto quello intendo senza rispecto che havendo a scrivere ad altri andrei con più riguardo'.

[84] Lettere di Goro Gheri, I, fo. 177r, 9 Dec. 1516.

[85] Ibid., I, fo. 198r, 21 Dec. 1516: 'perchè a patroni non si ha ad occultar niente'.

[86] M.A.P., 142, No. 161, 1 Nov. 1517, below p. 131, n. 149.

[87] Cp. Gheri's comment, 1 Jan. 1517: 'io piglio tanto piacere di questi sua un poco extesi advisi quanto di cosa nessuna perchè sono di qualità che aprono la mente a molte cose che importano assai'. Lettere di Goro Gheri, I, fo. 291r.

Florence would be used to send him information which could serve as an excuse to go to court and so to find out what was going on.[88] Vettori saw the wisdom of this for normally he had no business to conduct for the Eight which necessitated speaking to the king.[89] To Lorenzo Vettori wrote on 5 February 1516 that the papal nuncio could inform him better than he of the likely changes of policy after the king of Aragon's death because Canossa had talked at length with Francis while he, 'not having anything to negotiate', had only paid his respects to the king.[90]

The death on 23 January 1516 of Ferdinand of Aragon was one of the events of European importance which occurred while Vettori was in France. The Florentine ambassador's reports on it enable us to assess his ability as an information agent and to compare the content of the dispatches which he sent to the Eight with those which he wrote to Lorenzo.

News of Ferdinand's death, which was learned from a captured courier coming from the papal nuncio in Spain, reached the French court probably on 3 February.[91] In the reporting of this event there is little difference between the accuracy and speed of Vettori and that of the Venetian ambassador, Giovanni Badoer. Both wrote to their respective governments on the same day—5 February—but while Vettori correctly assumed, with the king of France, that the news was true, Badoer was doubtful.[92] In his letter to the Eight Vettori reported the satisfaction of the French king and commented in his usual cautious way that it was difficult to conjecture what would happen since everyone spoke according to his own convictions, some believing that the king would attack Navarre, others Naples. Badoer also did not make any personal comment or conjecture; he does however give more information about the projected attack on Naples, mentioning the various promises of infantry if it were undertaken.

Ferdinand's death was an event of considerable importance to the papacy and therefore to Florence, as the concordat of

[88] Otto, Missive, Legaz. e Comm., 12, fo. 5v.
[89] Otto, Responsive, 12, fo. 504r, 27 Jan. 1516.
[90] A. Desjardins, ii, p. 765.
[91] Otto, Responsive, 12, fo. 509r, Avignon, 5 Feb. 1516.
[92] M. Sanuto, Diarii, xxi (Venice, 1887), 522, Badoer to Venice, Avignon, 5 Feb. 1516.

Bologna had put Leo under obligation to support the king should he attack Naples.[93] Vettori's letter to Lorenzo dealing on the subject is more explicit than the dispatch to the Eight written on the same day. The king of France, Vettori reported, had written to the pope; he would like to seize the kingdom of Naples immediately and had 600,000 crowns ready for the expedition— a fact which the Florentine ambassador found difficult to believe. Francis relied on the difficulties which Ferdinand's successor, the Archduke Charles would face in Spain and the preoccupation of the English king with Scottish affairs. What should the pope do? Vettori pointed out that if the king of France were in possession of Naples and Milan, Italy would be at his mercy; on the other hand the archduke, the prospective emperor, already in possession of Flanders and inheriting terri- tories from the king of Spain, would be more powerful than France if he added to these the kingdom of Naples, and thus greatly to be feared. Neither ruler was desirable in Naples but Vettori could see no alternative.[94]

Lorenzo undoubtedly favoured papal support for the French enterprise. On 9 February Vettori received a letter from Lorenzo which caused him to hurry to the court and carry out its instructions even before the king's *levée* was complete.[95] Vettori had interpreted his commission as offering Lorenzo's services for the French attack on Naples and wanted to prevent Francis from taking Prospero Colonna into his service so that the command could be given to Lorenzo. Vettori soon realized that the captaincy of the French forces was reserved for one of their own leaders and asked Lorenzo if it was his intention to lead the papal contingent and, if so, should Francis request this position for him from the pope? Lorenzo's reply enables us to see his ambitions, his regard for Vettori and the influence which he thought he could wield over his uncle.[96] He highly com- mended Vettori for the prudence with which he had carried out his commission, though he had misunderstood it on two points. Lorenzo's intention was to serve the French king by command-

[93] A. Desjardins, ii, p. 764.
[94] *Ibid.*, pp. 765–7.
[95] *Ibid.*, p. 767.
[96] M.A.P., 109, No. 42, cit. A. Verdi, p. 23 (though the ambassador is Vettori not Pandolfini as Verdi thought).

ing whatever number of papal and Florentine troops Francis
saw fit to put under him, provided such a number was in keeping with his honour; it was not his wish that Francis should beg
the command from Leo for he considered this not in keeping
with his honour and his relationship with the pope which was,
he thanked God, rather that of being able to beg favours for
others. The attack on Naples did not materialize. The pope, at
first willing to support the French enterprise, retracted following
the news of the emperor's arrival in northern Italy and Francis
had to focus his attention on the defence of Milan.[97]

We turn now to the negotiations for Lorenzo de' Medici's
marriage. These provide further illustration of the close connection between Florentine and papal affairs and of Vettori's
relations with the papal legate and with Lorenzo.

The subject of marriage had been raised by Lorenzo himself
as early as February 1514 and may be considered at that stage
as an aspect of the rivalry with his uncle Giuliano.[98] In connection with the negotiations then in progress with Spain and
Savoy for Giuliano's marriage, Lorenzo wrote to his mother that
she should help forward Giuliano's interests in order that his
own could then be considered; she should remind the pope that
when all had been done to Giuliano's satisfaction, Leo should
not forget him. Alfonsina, highly critical of her brother-in-law's
social aspirations, which she thought exceeded Cesare Borgia's
in his early days, maintained that Lorenzo could not be made
to wait until all Giuliano's demands had been satisfied.[99]

Like Giuliano's, Lorenzo's marriage plans were conditioned
by his ambition for a state. Contemporaries expected the pope
to make territorial provision for his relatives. When he was
considering for Giuliano a daughter of the house of Cardona,
Leo had told the Spanish ambassador that he would require a
territory in the kingdom of Naples worth 12,000 ducats.[100]
Papal ambitions for Lorenzo, which only became known nine
months after Giuliano's death, were not dissimilar.

The death of his brother in March 1516 caused the pope to
recommend his nephew to Francis I,[101] but it was not simply a

---

[97] A. Verdi, p. 23.   [98] O. Tommasini, ii, pp. 993–4.
[99] Ibid., p. 999.   [100] Ibid., p. 982.
[101] A.S.I., Ser. iii, xx (1874), p. 30, 22 March 1516.

case of Lorenzo taking Giuliano's place in the connection established with France as negotiations for a French bride for him
had begun before Giuliano's death severed the link forged with
the house of Savoy. Almost as soon as Vettori arrived in France
in January 1516 he reported to Lorenzo on the prospects of a
marriage with the house of Navarre.[102] In the same month
Francis' mother Louise had requested the king of Navarre to
send his daughters to Lyons for inspection.[103] Further information is given on the kingdom of Navarre in the letter which
Vettori wrote to Lorenzo about the possible effects of the king of
Aragon's death.[104] At the end of this year Cardinal Giulio's
letters to the papal legate, Ludovico Canossa, reveal what the
pope's territorial ambitions were. On 30 December the cardinal
wrote that Leo would like Francis to give his nephew a fief or
secure him an annual income of 12,000 ducats.[105] These
requests were repeated during the following month,[106] but
during the spring and summer of 1517 no more than passing
allusions to the marriage negotiations are found, probably
owing to preoccupation with the conquest of the duchy of
Urbino and with Lorenzo's serious injury during this campaign.
In May 1517 Canossa left France and was replaced in September by the new legate Giovanni Staffileo, bishop of Serbenico.
At about this time the subject was raised again in letters which
are now addressed jointly to Staffileo and Vettori. Owing to the
diplomatic device of sending two different letters—one to be
shown openly to the French king and one which Staffileo and
Vettori were to keep to themselves—we can ascertain the pope's
real intentions.[107] The official letter to the king made no mention of the actual amount of the dowry but confined itself to the
hope that Francis would not fail to provide for the lady honourably by giving her a fief or the money to buy one. A fief in
France was to be preferred.[108] The secret letter dated 18
October warns the two negotiators that the pope did 'not want
the woman without the dowry' and categorically stated that the
dowry must be as large as possible. If the negotiators were skilful

[102] A. Desjardins, ii, p. 761.
[103] D. Moulton Mayer, *The Great Regent* (London, 1966), p. 94.
[104] A. Desjardins, ii, p. 773.
[105] *A.S.I.*, Ser. iii, xx (1874), p. 250.   [106] *Ibid.*, p. 253.
[107] *Ibid.*, p. 403.   [108] *Ibid.*, p. 402.

a state with an income of 20,000 ducats might be obtained, though an income of 10,000 ducats would be acceptable as a basis for a settlement.[109]

As regards the state, whether given directly by the French king or bought with money provided by him, the pope wished it to be in France rather than anywhere else as this would be more secure.[110] It was largely on account of uncertainty about the future of Navarre[111] that the negotiations for a daughter of that house were transferred to a daughter of the count of Boulogne whose lands were in Auvergne. From the spring of 1518 onwards after terms had been drawn up for Lorenzo's marriage to this girl attention centred on the choice of a fief. Francis offered the duchy of Valentinois in the Dauphinate but, significantly for the contemporary reputation in Italy of Cesare Borgia, Leo and Cardinal Giulio considered that the title of Duke Valentino 'stank'.[112] The pope had an additional reason for rejecting this duchy: it was crown property and Francis might be able to claim it back, as Louis XII had done in the case of Cesare Borgia.[113] Leo insisted that every effort be made to have all privileges and documents correctly drawn up so that no quarrels could arise in the future concerning the territory which had been alienated; research was undertaken to find out the regional custom and law with regard to the territory in question. Ultimately the county of Lavaur which Francis was prepared to make into a duchy, was accepted.[114] The income of 10,000 ducats eventually agreed upon was the lowest figure at which the pope had been prepared to negotiate.[115] In addition to the *donativum* expected from a bridegroom, in connection with which a palace outside Florence was requested, Lorenzo was to give his bride an annual income of 4000 ducats.[116]

[109] *Ibid.*, p. 403.   [110] *Ibid.*, p. 403; A. Desjardins, ii, pp. 761, 773.

[111] B.N.F. Ms. G. Capponi, Cassetta 4, 1, insert 10, Vettori to Lorenzo, 3 March 1517.

[112] Acq. e Doni, 1, insert 10, Baldassare da Pescia to Lorenzo, 7 Feb. 1518: 'Io vi dirò el vero quello di Valentinoys lo hanno in abominatione et dà loro nel naso per quello che vostra Ex.a sa.'   [113] M.A.P., 142, No. 159, 10–11 March 1518.

[114] L. Passy, i, p. 220, n. 1. It was made into a duchy with an income of 10,000 ducats annually but not until Feb. 1519, only 3 months before Lorenzo's death.

[115] M.A.P., 142, No. 117, 4–5 Jan. 1518 and 'li articoli di maritaggio' (a copy of terms enclosed); above, n. 109.

[116] *Ibid.*, No. 229 and 'li articoli di maritaggio', *Ibid.*, No. 282.

Brides were merely pawns in the territorial and financial game. Lorenzo did not seem to mind what match was made so long as it did not make trouble for him;[117] a minor consideration in the eventual choice between the second daughter of the king of Navarre and the daughter of the count of Boulogne had been speed: provided that neither had a defect of mind or body which would prevent marriage, then choice should be made of whichever one would bring the negotiations most rapidly to a close.[118] Only the ages, but not the names of the daughters of the house of Navarre are ever given,[119] and when Cardinal Giulio dispatched the mandate empowering the negotiators in France to come to terms, a blank was left in it for the name of the girl.[120] Even when, eighteen months after the beginning of the negotiations, Madeleine de la Tour, daughter of the deceased count of Boulogne was at last chosen, Lorenzo complained that he had not been given the name and surname of the lady.[121] Although careful inquiries had evidently been made about the physical merits of the girls and the elder daughter of the house of Navarre had been eliminated as humpbacked,[122] the girls had never appeared in court, even though ordered to do so.[123] Neither Vettori nor Staffileo had in consequence seen them or the girl with whom they eventually contracted the marriage on Lorenzo's behalf.

So much for the expectations of the marriage. We may now examine Vettori's rôle in the negotiations for it and in particular try to establish his position with regard to the papal nuncios, Ludovico Canossa and Giovanni Staffileo.

Apart from what is most probably an allusion to Lorenzo's matrimonial intentions in Leo's recommendation of his nephew to the French king after Giuliano's death,[124] the letters written on the pope's behalf in the spring of 1516 contain no reference to any marriage negotiations. Vettori's letters to Lorenzo, on the other hand, contain from the very moment of his arrival in

---

[117] O. Tommasini, ii, p. 994, Lorenzo to Alfonsina, 14 Feb. 1514: 'et sia qual parentado si vuole, che a me non dà briga'.

[118] A.S.I., Ser. iii, xx (1874), p. 404.

[119] A. Desjardins, ii, p. 761.

[120] A.S.I., Ser. iii, xx (1874), p. 403.

[121] A.S.I., Ser. iii, xxi (1875), pp. 208–9.   [122] A.S.I., Ser. iii, xx (1874), p. 408.

[123] M.A.P., 142, No. 174, 5 Dec. 1517.   [124] See p. 125, n. 101.

Lyons information about the house of Navarre.[125] It would seem that Vettori was responsible for the preliminary investigations and the papal nuncio for the subsequent negotiations. It is to Canossa and to the papal chamberlain Latinus Benassaius, sent specially to inform the nuncio of the pope's demands,[126] that Leo's views on the state and the dowry are communicated on 30 December 1516.[127] The instructions about the marriage aims contained in the letter of 9 January 1517 were likewise addressed to Canossa and Latinus with no reference to Vettori.[128] However, when Canossa left France in May 1517,[129] Vettori conducted the negotiations with the house of Navarre,[130] and after the arrival of the new nuncio in September 1517, communications from Rome were generally addressed to both.[131]

Relations between Vettori and Canossa had been good, and their friendship continued long after both had completed their mission to France.[132] Vettori had formed a high opinion of Canossa's skill as a negotiator after the battle of Marignano.[133] When he had departed from Milan for Bologna ahead of the French king he assured Lorenzo that Canossa, who had remained with Francis, would deal ably with any questions that might arise since his good qualities were such as to enable Leo and Lorenzo to put more trust in him than anyone.[134] No mention is made of any friction between Canossa and Vettori who apparently accepted his subordinate position without resentment. *Vis-à-vis* Staffileo Vettori's position should have been different; he had negotiated alone and instructions were directed to both, but his letters to Lorenzo's secretary Goro Gheri show that the new nuncio treated him as his inferior: negotiations were carried on either by Staffileo alone or with Vettori in a subsidiary rôle. On 5 November Vettori wrote that he was waiting for the nuncio 'to execute the commission';[135]

[125] A. Desjardins, ii, p. 761.   [126] *A.S.I.*, Ser. iii, xx, p. 244.

[127] *Ibid.*, p. 250.   [128] *Ibid.*, p. 253.

[129] *Ibid.*, p. 395, last letter before Canossa's departure.

[130] *Ibid.*, p. 404.

[131] With the exception of an important interlude in November when Staffileo alone is the recipient, below, p. 130.

[132] G. Ruscelli, *Lettere di Principi*, ii (Venice, 1575), fos. 26v–28r, 30v–31v.

[133] *Sommario*, p. 313.   [134] M.A.P., 123, No. 323.

[135] M.A.P., 142, No. 166, 16 Nov. 1517: 'aspectavo el nuntio per exeguire la commissione'.

on the 16th he could not say anything about the dowry except what he had heard from the nuncio and this information he was sure Staffileo had already communicated to Rome.[136] At the beginning of December Vettori had not heard from Gheri since 25 November but the nuncio had had joint letters from Cardinal Giulio and Lorenzo de' Medici instructing him to delay negotiations until Thomas de Foix, seigneur de Lescun, the brother of the French governor of Milan, had arrived.[137] Staffileo, who had daily conferences with Francis, as we know from a conversation Vettori had with the grand master, did not give Vettori particulars of these interviews as he wanted to send them to Rome himself.[138] Four days later we learn that because the queen mother had been ill Vettori had not talked with her, but the nuncio had spoken to her in her bed chamber.[139] The nuncio spoke to the king 'aside' on 13 December.[140] After the arrival of Thomas de Foix, it was the nuncio who replied when asked at the meeting at which de Foix was present whether he and Vettori had a *mandato* giving them the power to negotiate. Staffileo discussed the proposed terms of the marriage agreement one by one knowing all the technicalities whereas Vettori did not.[141]

If, as seems to be the case, the nuncio took the lion's share in negotiations, one would like to know how this came about. Vettori's letters to Goro Gheri in November 1517 direct us to the root of the trouble. The ambassador says that when Staffileo arrived he did his best to see that he was honoured both by Francis and by the queen mother Louise.[142] But then while the nuncio travelled with Francis to Moulins, Vettori staying behind with Louise, he received the secret letter of 18 October addressed to both of them.[143] Staffileo replied without explaining Vettori's absence with the result that the next letter was addressed to him alone. At this Staffileo became so proud that he began to ignore Vettori, persuading himself, according to Francesco, that Lorenzo had lost confidence in his ability and even loyalty. The fact that two further letters were addressed to

---

[136] *Ibid.*
[137] *Ibid.*, No. 173, 1 Dec. 1517.
[138] *Ibid.*
[139] *Ibid.*, No. 174, 5 Dec. 1517.
[140] *Ibid.*, No. 177, 13 Dec. 1517.
[141] *Ibid.*, No. 148, 22 Jan. 1518.
[142] *Ibid.*, No. 233, no date.
[143] *Ibid.*, No. 169, 25 Nov. 1517; for letter of 18 Oct., above, pp. 126–7, n. 109.

both of them was interpreted by Staffileo as mere formality as
they were short and in his view procured at Vettori's request.[144]
Francesco felt the need for Gheri's intervention in his favour
with Lorenzo and Alfonsina,[145] and he explained to him why he
had not accompanied the king to Moulins. He was ill and could
not ride strenuously; Francis had been away only eighteen
days, and the nuncio was quite capable of attending to any
business that might occur.[146] He described the nuncio as a *uomo
da bene* and in common with the rest of this class, out for honour
and gain. His ambition was a cardinal's hat. In conclusion
Vettori stated that he did not mind if the nuncio wrote to Rome
thus taking all the credit for himself, for he was certain that
Lorenzo realized he was doing all he could.[147]

One of Vettori's attempts to define his sphere of duties proves
that he considered himself the personal agent of Lorenzo de'
Medici. He would not, he wrote to Gheri, be so presumptuous
as to want to share the transaction of papal business with
Staffileo or to detract from his honour; all he wanted was 'to
intervene in the marriage negotiations for which the Duke sent
me here'.[148] Slowly Vettori must have come to the conclusion
that at least for the present there was no need for a resident
Florentine ambassador at the court but that Lorenzo's personal
affairs would best be served by a personal representative. This is
written in a letter previously mentioned in which Gheri is asked
not to discuss his suggestion 'with any citizen in Florence' on
account of the disapproval it would arouse.[149] Gheri felt compelled to clarify the relative positions of Vettori and Staffileo as
far as the marriage negotiations were concerned. In the impending discussions with Lescun, he wrote, Vettori must be present
'although the nuncio will be there', because concerned as he
was 'with the interests of the Duke and his house, his Excellency
and Madonna Alfonsina will know that nothing to the benefit of

---

[144] *Ibid.*, No. 233, no date.
[145] *Ibid.*, No. 167, 17 Nov. 1517; No. 177, 13 Dec. 1517.
[146] *Ibid.*, No. 165, 13 Nov. 1517.
[147] *Ibid.*, No. 167, 17 Nov. 1517.
[148] *Ibid.*, No. 182, 29 Dec. 1517.
[149] *Ibid.*, No. 161, 1 Nov. 1517; '... et vi dirò una cosa ma non vorrei che
conferissi con nessuno cittadino costì perchè sono certo dispiacerebbe che io
crederrei che fussi bene non tenere qua huomo fermo ma quando il Duca accadessi
ci mandassi uno in nome suo'. See above, p. 122, n. 86.

the Duke will be allowed to be overlooked'.[150] Four months later Vettori complained to Lorenzo that the nuncio wished to demonstrate that he was undertaking 'the business not only of His Holiness but also of your lordship and that I am here to no purpose'. He revealed little to Vettori 'even though your lordship regards me as his servant as he has always done'.[151]

Vettori provided Lorenzo with essential information about the brides. His favourable reports on Madeleine's income,[152] relations,[153] and lands[154] must have satisfied Lorenzo and been instrumental in the eventual choice of this young lady as his bride. We know that Vettori had formed the view that his marriage to one of the daughters of the king of Navarre would have been both unprofitable and impolitic. A daughter of that house would have had only what her father could give her; she could not have had anything from her relations; her two brothers could contribute nothing and her uncle was 'the poorest man in the world'.[155] When he had acted as negotiator between the departure of one papal legate and the arrival of the next at a time when negotiations were still being carried on with the house of Navarre, the choice between the two elder daughters had been left to him.[156] Further proof of Vettori's involvement with Lorenzo's affairs may also be gauged from the fact that he suggested Poggio a Caiano as a gift to his bride[157] and that the duke sent him to Auvergne to hand over the ring to Madeleine, which was tantamount to a marriage ceremony by proxy. This episode represents the climax in Vettori's status as Lorenzo's personal agent. The letter in which the duke gives him his instructions is confiding and personal in tone and betrays the trust of the young man in the older.[158] The diamond

---

[150] Lettere di Goro Gheri, I, fo. 412r, G. Gheri to Vettori, 19 Nov. 1517: 'perchè benchè qui sia el nuncio, per havere Lei quello interesse che ha col Signor Duca et con questa casa, la Sua Excellentia et la Signora di Madonna pensano che se voi ve ne troverrete, che non resterà cosa alcuna indietro per benefitio di Sua Excellentia che non sia da voi ricordata e proposta'.

[151] B.N.F. G. Capponi, Cassetta 4, 1, insert 16; 'per volere mostrare fare le faccende non solo di N.S. ma quelle di V.S. et io son qua per niente, pure ad me rileva poco pure che V.S. mi tenga per servidore come ha facto fino a qui'.

[152] M.A.P., 142, No. 177, 13 Dec. 1517.   [153] Ibid., No. 117, 4–5 Jan. 1518.

[154] Ibid.   [155] B.N.F. G. Capponi, Cassetta 4, 1, insert 10.

[156] A.S.I., Ser. iii, xx (1874), p. 404.

[157] M.A.P., 142, No. 229, no date.   [158] B.M. Add. Ms. 23,721, fos. 11r, 14r.

ring which he sent was one of the Medici antiques chosen by the
pope and would be followed by more jewellery and brocade.[159]
The letter to his bride of which he sent copies to Vettori, the
ambassador should deliver or not as he thought fit or as custom
dictated. He relied on Vettori as a married man to find the
appropriate words for such an occasion as he himself was 'new
to such ceremonies'.[160] Vettori's co-operation was also enlisted
to win the desired French support for Lorenzo's political ambitions (tantalizingly referred to only as 'some plans of ours'); in
exchange Lorenzo was prepared to aid French demands at the
papal court.[161]

The pope was not satisfied with the marriage settlement and
little pleased with the two ambassadors who had negotiated it.
Vettori's self-justification, contained in a letter to Gheri, is
mainly based on the curtailment of his power by Staffileo and on
illustrations of the way in which the nuncio sought to prove to
the French his higher position. A re-reading of his letters,
Vettori said, would show that he had never held out hopes
which had not been fulfilled. He had besides been a 'minister
with little authority'; even in his presence Staffileo had boasted,
'I have the mandate, I have the letters [from Rome]', so that
Vettori could imagine what he said in his absence. In fact
Frenchmen had told him that in order to win greater credit the
nuncio had said Vettori was there to intervene in the negotiations only at his, Staffileo's, pleasure. Vettori concluded by maintaining that what had been achieved was more due to him than
the nuncio and that there was nothing in the world he would not
endure to safeguard Lorenzo's interests. He must have felt that
blame could not be meted out equally to both ambassadors for
he asked Gheri to make an exception of him when the pope
complained about the negotiators.[162]

A characteristically Florentine concern to save money and

---

[159] *Ibid.*, fo. 10v, cp. B.N.F. G. Capponi, Cassetta 4, 1, insert 12, Gherardo
Bartolini to Lorenzo de' Medici, 6 March 1518 on jewels for Madeleine.

[160] B.M. Add. Ms. 23,721, fo. 11r.

[161] *Ibid.*, fo. 14r: 'come noi speriamo socto l'ombra di sua Maestà havere a
riposare et colorire qualche disegno nostro così potete pensare che da noi non
habbia a mancare di servirli et compiacerli di ciò che sapranno domandare. . .'
For the French demands, see below, p. 140.

[162] M.A.P.., 142, No. 156, 25 Feb. 1518.

admirable administrative ability mark Vettori's handling both
of the marriage ceremony by proxy in Auvergne and the actual
ceremony at Amboise. In travelling to Auvergne he prevented
his French escort from entertaining their friends at Florentine
expense but also deprived posterity of a portrait of Madeleine
by a pupil of Leonardo through choosing instead a less costly
artist. On his return to Amboise Vettori, like the most efficient
Best Man, advised the prospective groom on matters of practical importance: since the wedding would be taking place in
Lent, it would be expedient to bring a dispensation;[163] life was
extremely expensive in France, so a comparatively small escort
of about a hundred horses would save money, better spent on
presents, and avoid the imputation of arrogance;[164] cloth of
gold was out of fashion for the present but serviceable great-
coats (*giubboni*) and tunics (*saioni*) were the thing. As to presents,
for Francis he recommended a pair of fine horses and some scent
of which the king was very fond; for Louise a beautiful picture,
and for the queen and for Francis' sister Marguerite a fine mule
each. A generous donation to the grand master was advisable
because his friendship should be cultivated as he was a man of
great importance and would be even more powerful if Louise's
ill health caused her to withdraw from affairs of state.[165]
Antoine du Prat and Robertet must also be remembered. And,
finally, since jousts are being arranged and Lorenzo will perhaps
be asked to participate, Vettori would remind his patron 'to
arrange for your own arms to be brought for to joust with other
people's I do not think is very safe'.[166]

His wedding was not the only object of Lorenzo's journey.
Francis I had invited him to stand proxy for Leo X at the
baptism of his child, should it be a boy.[167] The birth was
anxiously awaited during February while Vettori was at
Amboise, and on 2 March the Florentine ambassador reported
the arrival of a son.[168] Nine days later he wrote to Lorenzo that

[163] *Ibid.*, No. 154, 8 Feb. 1518; *ibid.*, No. 157, no date.

[164] *Ibid.*, No. 157, no date; *ibid.*, No. 156, 25 Feb. 1518; B.N.F. G. Capponi,
Cassetta 4, 1, insert 10.

[165] M.A.P., 142, No. 156, 25 Feb. 1518.

[166] B.N.F. G. Capponi, Cassetta 4, 1, insert 10: 'ricordo a quella il fare portare
l'arme sua che a giostrare con quelle d'altri non credo sia molto sicuro'.

[167] M.A.P., 142, No. 157, no date.   [168] *Ibid.*, No. 158, 2 March 1518.

he should come quickly for it was not fitting that the baptism of
one who was to be king of France should be long delayed.[169] In
mid-April Lorenzo arrived for the ceremony which took place
on the 26th.[170] For four months the court was *en fête*. The baptism was followed by banquets and dancing in which the king
himself took part. Jousts began on 1 May and were held daily
until August. Festivities were the only topic of conversation,[171]
and at their outset, on 2 May, Lorenzo was married.[172] No
letter of Vettori's describing the event appears to be extant, but
this loss is redeemed by the detailed account from the Venetian
ambassador of the nuptial banquet which Vettori attended,
seated on the right of the king, as was Lorenzo. The feast,
accompanied by music and held in a great hall specially erected
and sumptuously decorated for the occasion, lasted about three
hours and was followed by two hours' dancing.[173]

Shortly before the festivities began Vettori, who according to
his later admission had been longing to leave France, received
the king's permission to depart, but by now was sorry to leave.[174]
He was replaced by his friend Jacopo Gianfigliazzi, who
arrived on 27 April,[175] and who, after accompanying Francis
from Amboise to Angers, travelled with Lorenzo to Auvergne
to settle the details of the division of his bride's possessions.[176]
Vettori went with the court to Angers where a short illness
detained but did not prevent him from paying one more visit to
Auvergne before journeying to Lyons whence he accompanied
Lorenzo to Florence.[177] He reached the city on 27 August,[178]

[169] *Ibid.*, No. 159, 10–11 March 1518.

[170] Otto, Responsive, 17, fo. 315r, 15 April 1518; *ibid.*, fo. 309r.

[171] *Ibid.*, fo. 316r.

[172] M. Sanuto, *Diarii*, xxv (Venice, 1889), 412.

[173] *Ibid.*, 407 and 412–13.

[174] B.N.F. Magliab. VIII, 1402, fo. 42r. Vettori to Francesco del Nero, 21
Aug. 1520: 'et fai chome io quando ero in Francia che ogni dì scrivevo volerme
partire et non hebbi mai la peggior nuova che quando intexi era facto lo scambio';
Otto, Responsive, 17, fo. 315r.

[175] Otto, Responsive, 17, fo. 318r; for Vettori's friendship with J. Gianfigliazzi,
see N. Machiavelli, *Lettere*, ed. F. Gaeta, pp. 310–11; to Gheri Vettori confessed
displeasure at Jacopo's appointment 'non perchè non lo iudichi sufficientissimo a
exequire quello li sarà commesso' but because he would be needed in Florence.
M.A.P., 144, No. 96, 3 April 1518.

[176] *A.S.I.*, xxiii (1876), p. 406.   [177] Otto, Responsive, 17, fos. 336r and 356r.

[178] Signori, Missive, Legaz. e Comm., 28, fo. 19r.

ten days in advance of, and probably to prepare for, the state entry of the young duke and his bride.[179]

Lorenzo's policy for Florence after his return from France provides another example of those differences of opinion with the pope of which we have already had evidence in the episode of the captaincy and prior to the battle of Marignano.[180] Vettori's account is biased in Lorenzo's favour because of his personal involvement.

Vettori states that after having been in Florence for a month following the nuptial festivities, the duke set off to meet Leo, who was then at Montefiascone, to discuss with him three points: he wanted to leave his duchy of Urbino to the Church, to relinquish his captaincy of the Florentine forces, and to rule Florence as a citizen, as he had always meant to do. But Alfonsina, strongly objecting to her son giving up his title, frustrated the successful conclusion of these discussions by sending word to him that she was dangerously ill and if he wanted to see her alive he should come immediately. The 'good son', believing his mother, set off post-haste. As a result of his strenuous journey he fell ill a few days after his return and died after six months' intolerable suffering on 4 May 1519.[181]

Vettori's facts are corroborated from other sources. From the correspondence between the young duke and his secretary we learn that Lorenzo's departure had to be postponed for ten days on account of Alfonsina's illness[182] but that, his mother's condition having improved, he arrived at Montefiascone on 5 October.[183] On 27 October in a letter from the port of Palo, Lorenzo informed Gheri that the papal party (which included Cardinal Giulio de' Medici and himself) would be travelling to Magliana, the pope's hunting lodge, and would leave there for Rome on Saturday.[184] Evidently something—and there seems no reason to believe that it was not a communication from the already sick Alfonsina—caused Lorenzo to leave Rome on the

---

[179] B. Masi, *Ricordanze*, p. 235, 7 Sept.

[180] Above, pp. 110ff. and 116.   [181] *Sommario*, p. 328.

[182] Lettere di Goro Gheri, IV, fo. 284v; *ibid.*, fo. 288v, 6 Oct.

[183] *Ibid.*, fo. 290r; M.A.P., 144, No. 208, Lorenzo to Gheri, Montefiascone, 5 Oct. 1518.

[184] M.A.P., 144, No. 227, 27 Oct., from Palo: 'Arrivamo hiersera qui a Palo et ꭒomani ciene andiamo a la Maglana et sabbato in Roma.'

day he arrived, for on 30 October (which was a Saturday) Benedetto Buondelmonti wrote from there that he had 'visited many cardinals and excused Your Excellency's hasty departure'.[185]

The question which remains to be investigated is whether Vettori's reporting on the discussions between the pope and his nephew is equally correct. Lorenzo's alleged plan to return to a less despotic type of rule needs to be checked against other sources. A number of leading Florentines considered that the purpose of Lorenzo's journey was to obtain papal approval for the establishment in Florence of a principality in name as well as in reality. Already before the duke's return from France the more 'republican' element which had been anxious after the return of the Medici in 1512 again voiced fears of Lorenzo's despotic intentions and registered disapproval by denying support.[186] Jacopo Salviati, for example, did not consider it necessary for the city to send ambassadors to welcome him and gave further proof of his discontent by retiring from the circle of Lorenzo's intimate advisers to papal protection in Rome.[187] It is likely that he resorted to this step after a meeting called by the duke a day or two after his return.[188] Another of Lorenzo's adherents, Lanfredo Lanfredini, also showed his opposition by feigning illness and retiring to his house.[189] With this antagonism to the duke Francesco Vettori was significantly not associated. Indeed he and Filippo Strozzi now replaced Jacopo and Lanfredo among Lorenzo's intimate advisers[190] and the duke took them with him to Rome in what was considered to be his 'final attempt to win the Pope's consent to make Florence a principality'.[191]

---

[185] B.N.F. G. Capponi, Cassetta 4, I, insert 45, Rome, 30 Oct.: 'Io ho visitato molti Reverendissimi e fatto la scusa della partita repente di V.ra Ex.a.'

[186] G. Cambi, xxii, p. 151; F. Nerli, p. 131; S. Ammirato, vi, lib. 29, p. 48.

[187] G. Cambi, xxii, p. 151; F. Nerli, p. 131.

[188] Lettere di Goro Gheri, IV, fo. 283, 30 Aug., Florence: 'S. Ex.a. verrà qui hoggi o domane per starci 2 giorni per visitare e vedere questi cittadini et amici poi se ne tornera al Poggio.' Cp. Parenti, Istorie, B.N.F. II, IV, 171, fo. 140v.

[189] F. Nerli, p. 131.

[190] G. Cambi, xxii, p. 151; F. Nerli, p. 131; S. Ammirato, vi, lib. 29, p. 48.

[191] F. Nerli, p. 131; B. Cerretani, Sommario, B.N.F. II, IV, 19, fo. 52r: 'et Francesco Vettori et Filippo Strozzi in questa tornata facevano quello che volevano'.

Ten days after Lorenzo's death Vettori wrote to his brother
Paolo that he and Filippo Strozzi were alleged to have counselled the duke in France to make himself lord of Florence and
to have won the king's approval but not that of the pope and
Cardinal Giulio who so far from being won over were antago-
nized. Vettori recounts the reactions of Jacopo Salviati and
Lanfredo Lanfredini with which we are familiar but denies all
accusations against Lorenzo because he believed 'the duke not
only did not intend to put such a thing into operation' but also
'had not even thought of it, for without actually being lord of
the city [he] disposed of it as he wished'.[192]

Unfortunately for the truth of Vettori's statement a letter
written by Benedetto Buondelmonti to Lorenzo from Rome
appears to implicate Francesco in some plan of the duke's of
which the pope disapproved. Writing on 30 October, Benedetto
confirms that Vettori was there on that day which makes it
almost certain that he had travelled to Rome with Lorenzo as
Nerli says.[193] Vettori has suppressed this fact in his writings.
Benedetto states that Vettori, having stayed behind after the
duke's precipitate departure, sought an interview with Cardinal
Giulio. The topic discussed at the interview is not mentioned
but the cardinal was requested by Vettori to bring some
important point to the pope's attention.[194] Reconstructing the
situation it seems likely that Vettori asked Giulio on Lorenzo's
behalf to communicate to Leo the results of certain deliberations between Giulio and Lorenzo which Lorenzo could not now
present to the pope himself. Benedetto's letter indicates that
Cardinal Giulio was willing to try to win over the pope to what
Lorenzo desired should take effect.[195] Vettori, Benedetto continued, would be given the opportunity to see the cardinal in a
couple of days' time and would inform the duke of the results of

---

[192] O. Tommasini, ii, p. 1067.

[193] F. Nerli, p. 131.

[194] B.N.F. G. Capponi, Cassetta 4, 1, insert 46: 'Mons. R.mo mi ha questa sera
detto che essendo rimasto Francesco Vettori avanti di suo partire vuole parllare
con secho et vuole che parlli con N.S.'

[195] *Ibid.*, 'molto si dimostra volere operare quanto potrà con N.S. quello che V.
Ex.a desidera habbi effetto et che questo rimosso da ogni altra chosa farà che in
tutto quello chonoscerà essere da V. Ex.a desiderato operà quanto saprà et potrà
perchè oltre al piacer et far utile ad V. Ex.a confessa ingenuamente chosì essere il
il suo bixogno.'

Giulio's conversation with Leo. In fact by 2 November at latest he must have instructed Lorenzo's chancellor ser Bernardo Fiamminghi (whose arrival in Florence Gheri mentions on 5 November) to report to his patron on the outcome of it.[196] Vettori could have given further details himself as he was expected to leave Rome on 4 or 5 November.[197] One more mention of him in a letter from Benedetto to Lorenzo written on 5 November shows that he departed out of favour with the pope. When Benedetto dined with Leo that evening he did his best to restore his compatriot to Leo's good graces.[198]

Nerli[199] and Cerretani[200] state that the pope was opposed to Lorenzo extending his authority, and the rumour to which Vettori referred in the letter to his brother that he had not won over the pope to Lorenzo's plans is another pointer in this direction. It is unfortunate that we have no evidence on the outcome of the interview between Cardinal Giulio and the pope which took place at Vettori's instigation, but if everything is considered, Leo must have opposed Lorenzo's design, knowing how the Florentines would react and always wanting to be himself the undeclared overlord of Florence. In the end Lorenzo's death removed the thorny problem for the time being.

Lorenzo was undoubtedly ambitious. Take the question of his relinquishing the duchy of Urbino, mentioned by Vettori as one of the topics under discussion between him and

---

[196] Lettere di Goro Gheri, III, fo. 168v: 'Ser Bernardo è arrivato questa sera dal quale ho inteso quanto mi advisate che lui veniva instructo da Francesco di quanto haveva parlato con Monsignore Reverendissimo; et voleva parlassi con Nostro Signore. . .'

[197] M.A.P., 143, No. 165, Benedetto Buondelmonti to Goro Gheri, Rome, 3 Nov. 1518.

[198] B.N.F. G. Capponi, Cassetta 4, I, insert 53, Benedetto to Lorenzo, Rome, 8 Nov: 'Essendo questa sera ad tavola N.S. d'una cosa in un'altra si parllò di lui nonobstante che lui sia in quello concetto che io ho advisato V. Ex.a. Io feci offitio buono laudandolo quanto sapevo ad chausa tanto più entrassi in animo ad S. B.ne et in amore.'

[199] F. Nerli, p. 131.

[200] B. Cerretani, Sommario. B.N.F. II, IV, 19, fo. 51v: 'Lorenzo andò a Roma al Papa dal quale fu veduto et ricevuto salvaticamente . . . perchè S. Santità haveva ruminato che la prima cacciata et mali loro del 1494 si causò da modi di suo padre . . . l'havere a farsi capo nella città cosa odiosissima, il volere dare lo stato d'Urbino appresso dall'altri sua et rovina di tutto lo stato loro. . . Queste cose movevano Sua Santita a tanto odio . . . che non lo poteva vedere et lo licentiò che si tornassi alla città dove tornato stava di tanto mala voglia quanto poteva.'

his uncle. What Lorenzo really wanted was to exchange the duchy for the Romagna.[201] Again Vettori has only given half the truth.

As to Lorenzo's intention to give up the captaincy, one could remark that it might not have suited him to be in the paid employment of a city that he wanted to dominate as an absolute prince. Although *condottieri* not infrequently ended up as princes in other Italian states, the position of Florence with its republican institutions might have appeared different to Lorenzo. Also the pope was perhaps to be expected to comply with his plans if he had no troops under his direct control. And the fact that he had no military power behind him would make his position more acceptable to the Florentines. This seems almost the only explanation for Vettori's highly controversial statement.

During his meeting with the pope Lorenzo petitioned him in favour of Francis I. Leo was to concede to the French king the right to impose the tenth on the French clergy;[202] he also persuaded the pope to extend the term of office of the French legate, Cardinal Adrien Gouffier for a year, which went against Leo's wishes.[203] Moreover he dissuaded the pope from a plan which he considered detrimental to his good relations with France. Leo had intended to ask the king of Spain for a fief for Lorenzo in the realm of Naples but the latter considered this impolitic and the pope agreed to transfer his plan to his other nephew Ippolito.[204] It was rumoured, according to Vettori, that the French king had given his consent to Lorenzo's designs for Florence[205] and, seeing what an eager representative of his interests he had in the duke, Francis can only have favoured a strong rule in the city by his new supporter.

Vettori in attempting to depict as unambitious a ruler who, but for the reluctance of the pope and his early death, would probably have established an even more despotic government than he had done, also wants to defend his own rôle as Lorenzo's intimate counsellor. During Lorenzo's illness he was constantly

[201] A. Verdi, p. 105; G. Ruscelli, i, fo. 34v.

[202] A. Verdi, p. 104, n. 3; L. Pastor, vii, p. 241.

[203] *A.S.I.*, Ser. iii, xxv (1877), pp. 387ff.; A. Verdi, p. 110, n. 1; B.N.F. G. Capponi, Cassetta 9, vii, insert 26; B.M. Add. Ms. 23,721, fo. 13v.

[204] A. Verdi, p. 103.

[205] O. Tommasini, ii, p. 1066.

at Poggio a Caiano, as a letter of Giovanni Corsi to Paolo Vettori reveals,[206] and he was the 'gran maestro' to whom anyone who sought Lorenzo's favour would have to turn.[207] Both for his position of trust and for his share in Lorenzo's affections, Vettori would be likely to incur the hatred of the duke's possessive mother. That this was reciprocated, the markedly hostile attitude to her in his writings indicates.[208]

After his return from France Francesco had a vested interest, as it were, in Lorenzo's power. Luigi and Jacopo Guicciardini state that a number of the friends of the regime borrowed substantial sums from the commune, and the Eight who were in office for the six months from December 1518 to June 1519 paid out a great deal of money under the heading of expenses on legations to wipe out at least part of their debts to the commune. Among the recipients of such money, as Jacopo Guicciardini wrote, and official records prove, were Francesco and Paolo Vettori.[209] Francesco Vettori's son in law, Francesco Scarfi, was evidently aware of his father-in-law's political and financial dependence on Lorenzo, for during the duke's illness he became insistent upon the payment of his wife's dowry. Vettori's fears of his patron's death and his comment that if it occurred he would have 'to live in reduced circumstances with such little money [as I have] in some place far from here', prove Scarfi's anxiety justified.[210]

Francesco Vettori was one of the few who wrote favourably of Lorenzo after his death; even Filippo Strozzi related that there were not many who mourned him in their hearts.[211] Jacopo Guicciardini reported that even in the countryside people impugned Lorenzo's desire to make himself lord of Florence and Francesco Vettori was hounded by the gossip of the disgusted populace.[212] Cerretani, stating that the city criticized those who

---

[206] C. Strozz., Ser. III, 145, fo. 108r; B.M. Add. Ms. 10,280, fo. 8v.

[207] B.M. Add. Ms. 10,277, fo. 156r.

[208] *Sommario*, p. 328; *Vita d'Lorenzo* in O. Tommasini, ii, p. 1061; letter to Paolo, 14 May 1519, *ibid.*, p. 1067.

[209] F. Guicciardini, *Carteggi*, iii, pp. 47, 50; Otto, Condotte e Stanziamenti, 12, fo. 32r; Otto, Deliberaz., Partiti, Condotte, 12, fo. 18r.

[210] C. Strozz., Ser. III, 145, fo. 108r.

[211] G.-B. Niccolini, p. xxxvi.

[212] F. Guicciardini, *Carteggi*, iii, p. 51, Florence, 20 June 1519.

CHAPTER VII

In Cardinal Giulio's Administration
(1519-1523)

WHATEVER the truth regarding Lorenzo's intentions for the government of Florence, his death marked the beginning of a new chapter in the city's history. The internal and external problems of Florence usually associated with Leo X's demise in December 1521 or Clement VII's accession in November 1523 were already emerging in 1519. For the pope to find a new ruler for the city was difficult since he was now the only surviving legitimate male descendant of Lorenzo the Magnificent. In foreign policy the concordat concluded with France at Bologna and the *rapprochement* following Lorenzo's marriage were abandoned by Leo in favour of an alliance with the emperor. Florence which had maintained commercial links with France and always inclined towards that country suffered from the disastrous consequences of Leo's reorientation. For Francesco Vettori, too, these four years contain the seeds of change: they show the painful dissolution of his political ties with France, his growing friendship and political partnership with Filippo Strozzi and his increasingly more intimate association with the cardinal, who as pope was to become his patron.

To replace his deceased nephew as ruler of Florence, Leo chose his cousin Cardinal Giulio de' Medici, an illegitimate child of Lorenzo the Magnificent's brother Giuliano. As in 1512, the pro-Medici citizens acted to strengthen the existing regime. This time Francesco Vettori was foremost among them. In a letter to Paolo he said that he had been expecting Lorenzo's death for some weeks and, realizing that the pro-Medici citizens were few and could not afford to be caught unprepared, he had on several occasions drawn the attention of Goro Gheri and others to the need for protective measures. Gheri refused to believe that Lorenzo's illness was fatal, or if it were, that there was cause for alarm, but Luigi [della Stufa],[1] Piero Ridolfi, Pandolfo Corbinelli and Filippo Strozzi shared Vettori's fears and persuaded Gheri to provide 200 infantry to forestall any attempt at revolution. As a result of these precautions, when Lorenzo died the city remained quiet. But, according to Vettori, the responsibility for safeguarding the continuance of the Medici regime in this way was attributed solely to him and Strozzi. They were accused of acting for their own protection, thereby increasing the unpopularity they had already incurred as the alleged accomplices of Lorenzo's despotism. Cardinal Giulio had been given the same account of Vettori's activities on his journey from Rome to Florence, which had roused his suspicion, Vettori thought, even though he did not entirely believe it.[2]

To establish precisely Vettori's responsibility for the security of the regime at this period is perhaps impossible. He had been called to *pratiche* on Lorenzo's return to Florence in 1515,[3] and Nerli says that the 'citizens of the *pratica*' ordered the Palazzo della Signoria to be fortified and the guard to be doubled.[4] He was then also a member of the Eight,[5] and their records of payment for extra bread, wine and cheese[6] and munitions[7] for additional troops in the palace from 4 to 8 May prove Nerli's statement correct. But these records show that it was not Vettori alone who took the decision. Other members of the Eight were Pandolfo Corbinelli and Luigi della Stufa, both mentioned by Vettori as having tried to convince Gheri of the need for armed protection.[8]

The continuance of Medici government having been assured thanks to the prompt action of its leading supporters in protecting it by force, Cardinal de' Medici, as was to be his practice also after his accession to the papacy, dissociated himself from the unpopularity of the measures taken. No sooner was Lorenzo's funeral over than he assembled the principal citizens to discuss

---

[1] 'Messer Luigi' must be Luigi della Stufa.
[2] O. Tommasini, ii, pp. 1066-7, 14 May 1519.
[3] F. Guicciardini, 'Ricordanze', in *Scritti Autobiografici e Rari*, pp. 76-7.
[4] F. Nerli, p. 132.   [5] Tratte, 84, fo. 81v, 7 Dec. 1518 for 6 months.
[6] Otto, Delib., Partiti, Condotte, 12, fo. 27r.   [7] *Ibid.*, fo. 33r.
[8] Tratte, 84, fo. 81v; O. Tommasini, ii, p. 1066.

the reform of the government and reallocated many of the public offices among a wider range of citizens.[9] He gained popularity by his readiness to grant audiences[10] so that even a convinced republican like the historian Jacopo Nardi writes of his 'extreme patience' and of the favourable Florentine opinion now formed of him obliterating the reputation gained him by his administration of the pope's affairs in Rome.[11] However, when it became known a month after Cardinal Giulio's arrival that he would soon have to return to Rome, fears of another crisis were roused and rumours in the city were rife as to his deputy.[12] The choice between Goro Gheri and Silvio Passerini, cardinal of Cortona, was resolved by Cardinal Giulio in favour of the latter on the grounds that the Florentines would more readily submit to a cardinal than to Lorenzo's former secretary. Nevertheless a rivalry between the two men, with its potential threat to stable government, ensued, only to be removed after Giulio's intervention from Rome in favour of the cardinal.[13]

As could be expected, Vettori's political defamation resulted in a temporary eclipse of his career; he did not hold any political office during the first nine months after Lorenzo's death, the only public post to which he was appointed—to be one of the *Sei della Mercanzia*[14]—being of a largely commercial nature. Indeed shortly after the duke's death he considered retiring to his villa.[15] Yet, despite Francesco's popular disrepute and despite Cardinal Giulio's tendency to reckon with public opinion, he never quite dropped Vettori. A month after Lorenzo's death Guicciardini names Francesco Vettori, Filippo Strozzi and Jacopo Salviati as already being closely associated with the cardinal.[16] In the latter part of October, the month in which Cardinal Giulio departed for Rome, Vettori considered following him in November and was encouraged in this plan by Benedetto Buondelmonti whose letter to Vettori from Rome

[9] J. Pitti, 'Istoria Fiorentina', *A.S.I.*, i (1842), p. 119; F. Nerli, p. 133.
[10] F. Guicciardini, *Carteggi*, iii, p. 48, Luigi to Francesco Guicciardini, 19 June 1519.
[11] J. Nardi, ii, p. 61.
[12] See n. 10.
[13] F. Nerli, pp. 134–5; B. Cerretani, Sommario, B.N.F. II, IV, 19, fo. 56r.
[14] Tratte, 84, fo. 152r, Aug.–Dec. 1519.
[15] C. Strozz., Ser. I, 136, fo. 72r, B. Buondelmonti to F. Vettori, 8 July 1519.
[16] See n. 10.

suggests that his chances of gainful and honourable employment would thereby be increased.[17] A letter of Filippo Strozzi's written in January 1520 reveals that he was in Rome then[18] and another from Vettori to Strozzi later that year indicates that he and Buondelmonti were largely responsible for his engagement in Medici affairs.[19] Cerretani holds him, Strozzi and Salviati responsible for the letter which Cardinal Giulio wrote to Goro Gheri ordering him to submit to Cortona.[20] On 24 January Strozzi reported that Vettori would return to Florence in the following week with Lorenzo's former treasurer, Gherardo Bartolini, and Cardinal de' Medici, should he depart then, or else without him, but Vettori and Gherardo may well have joined the number of notables who accompanied the cardinal on 6 February when he set out on his slow journey by litter.[21]

Three months later Francesco is once more in the Palazzo della Signoria. He was elected one of the priors[22] and Cardinal Giulio's reliance on him was such that a month earlier he had asked him if he wished to be gonfalonier.[23] For some reason connected with his uncle Bernardo,[24] Vettori declined. The offer was repeated at the time when Vettori's name was proposed for prior by the *accoppiatori*. Vettori suspected in their proposal of him a design on the part of Jacopo Salviati and Pandolfo Corbinelli, both *accoppiatori*,[25] to foist Pandolfo's brother, Niccolò Corbinelli on Cardinal Giulio for the post of gonfalonier, which in fact he obtained at the next election.[26] Vettori asked Filippo Strozzi to find out from Goro Gheri the

[17] C. Strozz., Ser. I, 136, fo. 78v, 28 Oct. 1519.

[18] C. Strozz., Ser. III, 108, fo. 14v, 24 Jan. 1520 'In Roma'.

[19] *Ibid.*, fo. 148r: 'E vi parrà bene che io sia spelagato in buon porto che poi che voi et Benedecto mi havete voluto mettere a fare le faccende de' Medici et mandarmi oratore in Francia et in Hispagnia, sia stato facto de' signori priori. . .' No date but the reference to F. Vettori's appointment as prior assigns it to 1520. Cp. C. Strozz., Ser. I, 136, fo. 78v, B. Benedetto to F. Vettori, Rome, 28 Oct. 1519, speaks of 'l'andar in Francia' and 'qualche altro disegnio'.

[20] B. Cerretani, Sommario, B.N.F. II, IV, 19, fo. 56r.

[21] C. Strozz., Ser. III, 108, fos. 13r and 14(bis)r, Filippo to Lorenzo Strozzi, Rome, 24 Jan. and 6 Feb. 1520.

[22] Tratte, 94, fo. 11r, 1 May 1520.

[23] C. Strozz., Ser. III, 108, fo. 148r, F. Vettori to F. Strozzi, no date but on internal evidence 1520.

[24] Bernardo was not drawn for any of the three major offices at this time. Tratte, 342, fo. 84v (priors), fo. 85v (16 *gonfalonieri*), fo. 87v (12 *buonuomini*).

[25] Tratte, 84, fo. 44r.   [26] Tratte, 132, fo. 264r.

motives behind his election as prior,[27] but unfortunately Gheri's reply is not known to us.

The year 1520 not only witnessed Vettori's renewed ascendancy in Florentine political affairs but also the initial phase of Machiavelli's entry into the service of the Medici and the change in foreign policy referred to previously.[28] That Machiavelli's connection with the Medici was due to Strozzi intervention is common knowledge; it may be possible to show that Vettori also had a part to play. This and the political association of the Strozzi and the Vettori at various times between 1520 and 1537, as indeed on several occasions previously, may justify a brief survey of the Strozzi-Vettori relationship at this juncture.

Filippo Strozzi's connections with Francesco Vettori date back to the early years of Leo's pontificate when both were in Rome in an official capacity, as they were some years later in Lombardy. They had both attended the duke's marriage at Amboise[29] and had both returned with Lorenzo to Florence. Both were in Rome at the time of Lorenzo's hasty return to Florence, that is during the time of the crucial interview between Cardinal Giulio and Leo. During the weeks before Lorenzo's death both are mentioned as the duke's counsellors. The onus of Lorenzo's autocratic aims fell on both after his death. It was Filippo who had encouraged and aided Vettori's further employment by the Medici in 1519–20. After the death of Alfonsina, Filippo's mother-in-law, in February 1520 relations between Cardinal Giulio and Filippo became strained as Filippo's wife Clarice was defrauded by the cardinal of a large part of her mother's inheritance.[30] In this delicate matter he turned to Vettori for help. In a letter from Rome to his brother Lorenzo he suggested a consultation between the two and virtually put this affair into their hands: 'seeing that there is no time to write to and fro, I have decided to put myself in the hands of those whose love and intelligence make them for me superior to all others'.[31] Filippo offered Vettori hospitality in

[27] See p. 146, n. 23.

[28] Above, p. 143.

[29] G. Cambi, xxii, p. 134; G.-B. Niccolini, p. xxxvii.

[30] G.-B. Niccolini, p. xxxvii.

[31] C. Strozz., Ser. III, 108, fo. 32r, 26 Feb. 1520; cp. F. Vettori to P. Vettori, 14 May 1519, O. Tommasini, ii, p. 1067.

Rome,[32] and looked after his financial interests.[33] The life of Lorenzo, which Francesco wrote soon after the duke's death,[34] is dedicated to Clarice Strozzi. Through the brothers of the two men the Strozzi and the Vettori families were linked, Paolo Vettori having married Lorenzo Strozzi's daughter Francesca.[35] Even the litigation which ensued after Paolo's death between Francesca's brother Matteo and Paolo's brothers Francesco and Giovanni did not disrupt the friendship between Filippo and Francesco.[36]

The proposed co-operation between Lorenzo Strozzi and Francesco Vettori on behalf of Filippo points to a good understanding and to a mutual trust, which may lend weight to the following interpretation. In previous letters when Filippo had written to his brother alone he generally employed the familiar *tu*, but when he had meant to include Francesco Vettori he used *voi*. The appearance of the plural form in Filippo's letter of 17 March approving his brother's action in recommending Machiavelli to Cardinal Giulio could consequently be taken to refer to Lorenzo and Francesco rather than in a general way to Lorenzo's friends in the Rucellai gardens, as Ridolfi suggests.[37] Given the known personal friendship between Machiavelli and Vettori one is tempted to go even further and to wonder if Vettori's high esteem for his friend encouraged and activated Lorenzo.

In her foreign policy after 1519 Florence was treated as an adjunct of the papacy even more than under Lorenzo who had maintained a certain independence. She was an unwilling partner to Leo's eventual opposition to France, a policy bitterly resented and responsible for at least one serious threat to

[32] C. Strozz., Ser. III, 108, fo. 49r, F. Strozzi to F. Vettori, 31 Oct. 1520.

[33] *Ibid.*, 'la provisione vostra per questo anno è passata in forma vene harete che non è mala faccenda perchè in fatto io non so come senza un simile aiuto voi possiate passare la vita vostra honestamente'. See also, below, p. 165.

[34] Written between 1519 and 1523, see *Vita di Lorenzo* in O. Tommasini, ii, p. 1063.

[35] Above, p. 2.

[36] Below, p. 185 and C. Strozz., Ser. III, 108, fo. 66r, F. Strozzi to F. Vettori, Rome, 10 March 1526.

[37] Letters were shared between them: C. Strozz., Ser. III, 108, fos. 35r, 36v. For Lorenzo's recommendation of Machiavelli: fo. 40v; R. Ridolfi, *Machiavelli*, p. 177 and p. 306, n. 2.

Cardinal Giulio's rule. After Lorenzo's death the pope's chief concern (since he no longer had a nephew to provide for) was to extend the papal territory.[38] He added Pesaro and the duchy of Urbino and hoped to recover Parma and Piacenza and to annex Ferrara. As a counterweight to the increasing imperial power, he would have liked an alliance with France but although a secret treaty was signed between France and the papacy in October 1519,[39] Francis I's refusal to abandon his protégé the duke of Ferrara and his generally overbearing attitude[40] determined the pope to regain the independence of the Holy See by driving the French from Italy. This line of policy inevitably led to a closer co-operation with Charles V from whom he also hoped for help in suppressing the anti-papal Lutheran revolt.[41]

Between October 1520 and January 1521 negotiations with France dragged on while Leo began to seek an agreement with the emperor. On 29 May 1521 the pope signed a secret contract with Charles which needed only the occasion of a French attack on the territory of the Church a month later to be made public though it was given out that the alliance had only then been signed.[42] War in northern Italy soon followed. In August Parma was invested by the allies, but not taken.[43] At the end of September Cardinal de' Medici was appointed legate to the army.[44] On 19 November an allied force of papal, Spanish and Swiss troops captured Milan from the French.[45] This news, which seemed to herald the success of Leo's policies, reached the pope on 28 November. Three days later he died.[46]

Leo's death caused great rejoicing and renewed activity among his enemies.[47] Francesco Maria della Rovere recovered the whole of the duchy of Urbino save the fortress of San Leo which remained in Florentine possession; Orazio and Malatesta Baglioni, two sons of Giampaolo Baglioni, who had been exiled from the papal territory of Perugia, on 6 January captured the

[38] *Sommario*, p. 331; L. Pastor, vii, p. 282.
[39] L. Pastor, viii, p. 3.   [40] *Ibid.*, p. 10.
[41] *Ibid.*, p. 14.   [42] *Ibid.*, pp. 35, 43.
[43] F. Guicciardini, *St. d'It.*, iv, pp. 100–8; L. Pastor, viii, p. 50.
[44] L. Pastor, viii, p. 52.   [45] *Ibid.*, p. 54.
[46] *Sommario*, p. 338; L. Pastor, viii, pp. 58, 67.
[47] L. Pastor, ix, p. 2.

city with the help of the duke of Urbino and moved against Siena. From Rome Francesco Soderini, cardinal of Volterra, the brother of the erstwhile gonfalonier, anxious to redeem his family's fortunes in Florence, plotted to bring Tuscany back into alliance with France. Aided by less French money than he would have liked but spurred on by ambition, the cardinal launched an attack against Siena under the leadership of the *condottiere* Renzo da Ceri. By this means he hoped to bring down the Sienese government headed by Cardinal Petrucci and to see it replaced by one with whose help he could eventually overthrow the Medici in Florence.[48]

Meanwhile the question of Leo's succession was dividing the cardinals in Rome. Cardinal Giulio de' Medici, resplendent in the glory of his recent conquest of Milan, wealthy, and important through his connections with Florence, appeared to have a good chance of becoming pope, even though fear that the papacy should begin to be vested in one family caused reluctance in some quarters. Time would have been on the side of those who favoured the election of Cardinal Giulio since his opponents were united only in their intention to frustrate it; but time was not to be had. The revolution in Perugia, threatening as it did the downfall of the government in Siena, led the chief of Cardinal Giulio's supporters, Cardinal Petrucci, to call for a quick outcome to the conclave so that he could return to Siena. Appreciating Cardinal Petrucci's situation and also the fact that the fall of the Sienese government would endanger his own regime in Florence, Cardinal Giulio was unable effectively to promote his own candidature. The conclave's ultimate choice of Adrian seems to have been impulsive—or as some said inspired —rather than deliberate, the result in fact of the inscription of his name on a voting slip with the intention of delaying rather than seeking a conclusion. But a discussion of Adrian's merits, followed by a gradual accumulation of votes, led, to the surprise of all concerned, to his election.[49]

During the period under discussion, 1519–23, Medici diplomatic policy gave Vettori an opportunity to exercise his administrative and executive ability. After Lorenzo's death

---

[48] J. Pitti, 'Istoria Fiorentina', in *A.S.I.*, i (1842), pp. 125–6.
[49] F. Guicciardini, *St. d'It.*, iv, pp. 144–5.

when Leo united the duchy of Urbino with the states of the Church, he granted San Leo, the duchy's chief fortress, and the territory of Montefeltro to the Florentines as an indemnity for the 350,000 ducats which they had paid to the Church in the course of Lorenzo de' Medici's acquisition of the duchy in 1516.[50] What could be more indicative of the high esteem in which the Medici held Vettori than that it was he who was appointed 'Commissioner and Mayor (*Sindaco*) of the Commune and to take possession of the territory of Montefeltro, which His Holiness the Pope conceded to this Republic'.[51] The fact that he had been associated with Lorenzo at the time when he proposed the return of the duchy of Urbino to the Church and that he had had previous military and administrative experience of subject towns must have further recommended him. His election was approved by the Hundred and took effect on 22 July.[52] He left Florence the following day, and his original appointment having been prolonged by two further months,[53] he returned to Florence on 20 November.[54]

After his return from Montefeltro Vettori three times held a major political office in Florence which associated him with the foreign or domestic policy of his city. During these terms of office Cardinal Giulio's absences resulted in periods of great responsibility for Vettori in which he showed himself determined to ensure the safety of the regime.

In the very month after his arrival in Florence Vettori became a member of the Eight for part of the time that Cardinal Giulio was papal adviser in Rome,[55] but Giulio departed for Lombardy in September 1521, leaving the cardinal of Cortona in charge of the government,[56] and two months later Vettori as gonfalonier had to safeguard the regime in conjunction with Cortona during the critical period of the unpopular attack on

[50] G. Cambi, xxii, p. 167; J. Pitti, 'Istoria Fiorentina', p. 119; G.-B. Niccolini, p. xxxvi.

[51] *Ricordo*, p. 282.

[52] Signori, Missive, Legaz. e Comm., 27, fo. 23v; G. Cambi, xxii, p. 167.

[53] Signori, Missive, Legaz. e Comm., 27, fo. 24r.

[54] *Ibid.*, fo. 23v.

[55] Tratte, 84, fo. 82r; followed by 6 months' office as *Conservatore di Legge* in which he was initially especially concerned with private petitions: Tratte, 84, fo. 15r; Signori e Collegi, Delib. sp. autorità, 41, fos. 177r and 179v.

[56] F. Nerli, p. 134.

the French in Milan and during the crisis following Leo X's death.[57] The members of the *Signoria* took every precaution against revolution and imprisoned all suspect citizens.[58] On learning of the pope's demise the Medici partisans insisted on Cardinal Giulio's immediate return. Again as in 1519, seeing that the crisis was over, Giulio dissociated himself from an unpopular measure by releasing the imprisoned citizens.[59] Nerli praises Vettori and Cortona for the provision they had made for the security of the regime,[60] but Pitti maintains that the authors of the order to imprison the opponents of the Medici were publicly reprimanded for acting for party motives rather than for the good of the city.[61]

Major responsibility for the imprisonments must rest with Vettori. During most of his first month of office as gonfalonier he was ill and he participated in few of the *Signoria*'s deliberations in the Palazzo della Signoria.[62] Even when he was chosen chairman (*prepositus*) of the meetings on 12 November, he obtained permission for a colleague to act in his place.[63] It is therefore significant that Vettori should have been present on 3 December, the day on which the decision to imprison the suspect citizens was taken.[64] Given that the preservation of the Medici regime was the aim, Vettori's and Cortona's measure seems fully justified considering that the Medici government was not protected by guards, extra forces or fortresses and threatened by enemies on the Sienese border.[65] This could have been the moment for disaffected supporters to join the opponents to overthrow the regime, as did in fact happen in 1527. The course of action taken proves the supporters' satisfaction with Cardinal Giulio's administration. The leading rôle which Vettori played proves him committed to the Medici at this time.

Nevertheless Leo X's foreign policy was hard for a Florentine

[57] Tratte, 94, fo. 11r, 1 Nov. 1521; Tratte, 132, fo. 266r.
[58] J. Pitti, 'Istoria Fiorentina', p. 121.
[59] *Ibid.*; *Sommario*, p. 340.   [60] F. Nerli, p. 135.
[61] J. Pitti, 'Istoria Fiorentina', p. 121.
[62] Signori e Collegi, Delib. ord. autorità, 123, fos. 155r, 155v, 156r; C. Strozz., Ser. I, 137, fo. 154r, Ludovico Alamanni to Luigi Guicciardini, Florence, 15 Nov. 1521.
[63] Signori e Collegi, Delib. ord. autorità, 123, fos. 156r–v.
[64] *Ibid.*, fo. 162r.   [65] F. Nerli, p. 135.

to accept. Vettori's ill health seems to have been to a large extent engendered by the depression from which he had suffered ever since the pope forced upon his compatriots an anti-French orientation.[66] As a member of the Eight from December 1521 to June 1522 Francesco was one of those responsible for the measures to protect his city from the results of the revolution in Perugia with its threat to Siena, immediately after Leo's death. In response to the wishes of Cardinal Giulio, who feared for his own authority in Florence and hoped to increase his chance of becoming pope by defending the territory of the Church, the Florentines raised forces for the defence of Perugia.[67] But having found by 5 January that 'the whole city' under the leadership of Gentile Baglioni had decided to come to terms with the aggressors,[68] the Eight turned their attention to the protection of Siena. In discussions held between Cardinal de' Medici and the leading citizens, it was decided to attempt to contain the war in Siena by sending troops in support of Cardinal Petrucci's government.[69] As Cardinal de' Medici and the cardinal of Cortona then departed for the conclave, the responsibility for the execution of this decision fell upon the Eight.[70] They sent Guido Vaina to Siena with 100 light cavalry and money to engage more forces on the spot;[71] on 19 January they agreed the terms for the hire of Swiss troops.[72] By such measures the Eight saved the government of Cardinal Petrucci and therefore that of Cardinal de' Medici. They also quashed Cardinal Francesco Soderini's attempt to engender a revolution in Siena with the help of armed forces, declaring themselves ready to chase his *condottiere* Renzo da Ceri 'right home'.[73]

On the occasion of a request from the imperialists for financial assistance, the Eight instructed their ambassador in Rome that the war in Lombardy and the punitive measures against Perugia and Siena had caused the Florentines enormous expense

[66] G. Ruscelli, ii, pp. 26–7, F. Vettori to Canossa, 12 Feb. 1522.

[67] F. Guicciardini, *St. d'It.*, iv, p. 141.

[68] Otto, Missive, Esterne, Legaz. e Comm., 15, fos. 7r–v (6 Jan.), 10r (7 Jan.) to Galeotto de' Medici.

[69] F. Nerli, p. 135.   [70] *Ibid.*, p. 136.

[71] F. Guicciardini, *St. d'It.*, iv, p. 147.

[72] Otto, Delib., Partiti, Condotte, Stanziamenti, 12, fo. 162v.

[73] Otto, Missive, Esterne, Legaz. e Comm., 15, fos. 113v (2 May), 122v (10 May), 123r.

since they had had to double their forces and all this through no fault of their own. They were being treated as they were entirely out of a desire to force them over to the French.[74] Yet, as the Eight had complained earlier,[75] they had received no help whatsoever from the imperialists nor from the Sacred College, who had even protested when the Florentine forces, after saving Siena, had entered Perugian territory to try to reinstate Gentile Baglioni and to expel those who had rebelled against the Church.[76]

Vettori's loyalty to the cardinal was beyond question but his sympathy with France caused him much anguish. To remedy the damaging effects of the rupture with France he and his colleagues, disturbed like him by the anti-French policy enforced on Florence, decided to send Francesco Altoviti to the French court to explain the position. The *Signoria* requested Vettori to give Altoviti a letter of recommendation to his old friend Ludovico Canossa. This letter expresses the dilemma of all pro-French Florentines and of the writer in particular.[77]

Vettori stated that he had done all he could to prevent a breach with France but his authority and his influence had been insufficient for success. Leo, the originator of the policy, was now dead, but the city continued to be in a situation more painful than the writer could describe. The object of Altoviti's mission was to seek Canossa's aid in restoring the Florentines to Francis' favour, for once the king, the most just and prudent prince not only of his own day but for many years past, had heard the explanations of the 'poor Florentines', he would accept them once more for the true friends and servants which they had always been. Their helplessness in a situation governed by Leo's Swiss and Charles' Spanish troops and by the Sienese threat on their borders had forced them to do what Leo wished; but the Florentines themselves were innocent and their magistrates had made no alliance with the emperor nor had they signed any declaration against France. The economic motive behind the Florentines' desire to be on good terms with France is evident

[74] *Ibid.*, fos. 122r–v.
[75] *Ibid.*, fo. 27r.
[76] *Ibid.*, fos. 40r, 41r; F. Guicciardini, *St. d'It.*, iv, p. 148.
[77] G. Ruscelli, ii, fos. 26v–28r.

from Vettori's request to Canossa to do the best he can for the city's merchants.

Canossa's reply contains a reference to Vettori's inherent pessimism; he trusted that Vettori's ill health was not as serious as he made out, for he remembered his habit of minimizing the good and exaggerating the bad. As regards the foreign situation, so long as Leo was alive, Canossa had always believed the Florentine justifications and he liked to think that the French did too. After the pope's death it had been generally hoped that the Republic would give proof of her long-standing friendship with the kings of France. If this had happened, there would be no need now for any explanations on Canossa's part, but the city's failure to respond made many think that the desired negotiations had no other object than to win time to see the outcome of affairs in Lombardy. Canossa, however, was certain that the *Signoria* in their wisdom and experience appreciated the need for French support.[78]

There is no reference to Francesco Altoviti's mission in any of the letters written either by the Eight or by the *Signoria* during February 1522; nor does he appear to have been given a *commissione*. In May, however, the Eight admit to Galeotto de' Medici, the Florentine ambassador in Rome, following an allegation from Don Juan Manuel, the imperial ambassador in Rome, that a man had been sent to France for discussions with Francis I.[79] This man, however, is likely to have been Benedetto Buondelmonti whom Cardinal de' Medici had dispatched secretly to Francis I in response to a request by the merchant Piero Spini on behalf of the French king. He was to offer to place at Francis' disposal 40,000 ducats on the recapture of that part of the duchy of Milan which he had lost in November.[80]

It is difficult to account for the sending of envoys to France by the Eight and the cardinal at such short intervals but the conclusion which suggests itself is that Vettori's letter to Canossa was delivered to him by Francesco Altoviti who had no power to negotiate. Canossa then brought the content of Vettori's letter to the knowledge of Francis I who, sensing that

[78] *Ibid.*, fos. 30v–31v.
[79] Otto, Missive, Esterne, Legaz. e Comm., 15, fo. 115v.
[80] J. Pitti, 'Istoria Fiorentina', p. 121.

the cardinal might agree to negotiations in view of the growing Florentine discontent, sent word to the cardinal directly, using as his agent a Florentine resident merchant, Piero Spini, where-upon the cardinal, having agreed with the Florentines on the sum of money and conditions to be offered in negotiations, dis-patched Buondelmonti to the French court. This view is sup-ported by Jacopo Pitti who interprets the cardinal's approach as dictated by the desire to maintain his reputation in Florence and also to eliminate the danger of a revolution in support of France.[81] If this interpretation is correct, Vettori played a decisive part in the attempt to re-establish diplomatic relations with France. From Cardinal Giulio's point of view the negotia-tions were probably not intended to lead to an alliance: he was an imperialist at heart[82] and French power in northern Italy was weak.

It is most likely that Cardinal Giulio's encouragement of the Florentines' desire for political reform was also merely pre-cautionary. A number of citizens, pro-French and encouraged by the French-supported threat from Siena, had begun to demand the introduction of a more republican form of govern-ment. Then, emboldened by the Florentine military success, discussion about reform became more widespread and even descended to particulars,[83] although no direct intervention in their favour by the French could be expected after the collapse of Francesco Soderini's enterprise. The knowledge that by April a large part of the city (three quarters according to Cerretani's estimate)[84] was against him led the cardinal to placate the opposition by inviting open discussion of reform and by receiv-ing memoranda on the subject by individual citizens. The main topics discussed were the same as in 1502 and 1512, that is the length of the gonfalonier's term of office, the introduction of an aristocratic senate composed of life members, and the re-opening of the Great Council. Some citizens even went so far as to suggest names of candidates for the office of gonfalonier which they wished then as in 1512 to be an annual appointment. Among those mentioned were Roberto Acciaiuoli and Francesco Vettori, both of whom, significantly, had been ambassadors in

---

[81] *Ibid.*   [82] M. Tucker, 'Gian Matteo Giberti', *E.H.R.*, xviii (1903), p. 30.
[83] F. Nerli, pp. 136–7.   [84] O. Tommasini, ii, p. 449, n. 1.

France.[85] Vettori himself, together with such convinced Medici partisans as Pandolfo Corbinelli, Piero Ridolfi, Gherardo Corsini, Matteo Niccolini, Lorenzo Morelli and Filippo Strozzi, was opposed to reform on the grounds that it would endanger the regime and cause the ruin of its supporters.[86] This appears to have been the common attitude among those who had been responsible for the Medici's return to power,[87] and the desire on the part of Francesco Vettori, Pandolfo Corbinelli, Piero Ridolfi and Filippo Strozzi to safeguard the regime is similar to that at the time of Lorenzo's death. There is no mention of Vettori's name among those who submitted memoranda to the cardinal although reform schemes from his hand exist for later periods.

In May a plot to kill Cardinal de' Medici was discovered. Battista della Palla, Zanobi Buondelmonti and Luigi Alamanni, the brother of Ludovico with whom Vettori had been friends since 1520 when they had served as priors together,[88] were among those implicated. Nerli acknowledges the influence of Machiavelli's writings on them and refers also to their connection with Cardinal Soderini.[89] The failure of this plot gave Cardinal Giulio the opportunity to strengthen his position in Florence and to put an end to the discussions on reform. Although Francesco Vettori was in no way associated with the planned assassination, he had been singled out as a likely sympathizer by those intrepid spirits intent on restoring the Republic with French support. According to the evidence given by a conspirator called Niccolò Martelli during the trial, Cardinal Soderini was in touch with Alfonso Strozzi, Niccolò Capponi, Niccolò Valori, Giovan Vittorio Soderini and Tommaso Soderini. Jacopo Salviati, too, was said to have been approached but to have considered the time not yet ripe. To Roberto Acciaiuoli and Francesco Vettori however (whose names we have seen mentioned during the recent discussions on reform for the office of gonfalonier) Francis I himself was alleged to have written as to personal friends.[90]

[85] F. Nerli, p. 137.   [86] O. Tommasini, ii, p. 449, n. 1.
[87] J. Pitti, 'Istoria Fiorentina', p. 123.
[88] R. von Albertini, pp. 438–9; Tratte, 132, fo. 263v.
[89] F. Nerli, p. 138.
[90] Giornale Storico degli Archivi Toscani, iii (1859), pp. 240, 258, 266.

Owing to his allegiance both to Francis and to Cardinal
Giulio, Vettori's position must have been very difficult and it is
perhaps at this time that he refused the pension which the
French king had granted him as a reward for his embassy in
1515–18. According to the author of the *Azioni*, Vettori argued
that as a supporter of the Medici his allegiance was with the
imperialists and that he did not consider it honourable to accept
money from an opposing power.[91] Vettori's account of the plot
in the *Sommario* is not sympathetic to the rebels whom he
describes as 'certain young men with greater desire for liberty
than prudence'; they would not, he thought, have succeeded in
establishing a republican form of government but only a licentious and tyrannical one. He exonerates Cardinal de' Medici
from all blame for punitive action against the offenders; this was
carried out solely to satisfy the imperialists who had declared
that anyone trying to change the regime in Florence should be
punished mercilessly as an enemy of the emperor.[92] Had
Vettori's loyalty to the Medici been doubted, he would not have
been appointed *podestà* of Pistoia three months after the plot[93]
nor would he have been elected once more a member of the
Eight soon after his return to Florence.[94]

This term of office, from December 1522 to June 1523, once
again coincided with a crucial period in the foreign affairs of
Italy and in Medici expectations. Owing to Adrian's delicate
health a fresh papal election was likely to occur soon and the
Habsburg–Valois struggle was intensified by the prospect. In
Rome, already during the spring and summer of 1523 the
imperialists were taking steps to strengthen their position:
Cardinal Soderini was imprisoned in April;[95] Venice was
reconciled with the emperor in July,[96] and Adrian was persuaded to join the League against France in August. Charles V,
Henry VIII, Francesco Sforza and Cardinal Giulio undertook
to raise forces to stem the latest French invasion of Lombardy.[97]
During July Charles V informed the duke of Sessa, his ambassador in Rome, that were a conclave to occur every effort should

[91] *Raccolto delle Azioni*, p. 275.
[92] *Sommario*, pp. 342–3.
[93] Tratte, 71, fo. 6r.
[94] Tratte, 84, fo. 82r.
[95] L. Pastor, ix, p. 187.
[96] *Ibid.*, pp. 193–4.
[97] *Ibid.*, p. 206.

be made to secure the election of Cardinal Giulio de' Medici as his support of the imperialists in the past could be expected to continue in the future.[98] However when Adrian died on 14 September, Cardinal Giulio was far from certain of success, despite the imperial favour towards him. All the French cardinals were against him.[99] Events in the states of the Church, too, gave cause for alarm as Alfonso, duke of Ferrara, taking advantage of the vacancy in the Holy See, captured Reggio and Rubiera and threatened Modena.[100]

On 31 August the Eight sent Paolo Vettori to Francesco Sforza in Milan with the Florentines' first contribution to the League against the French,[101] and at the beginning of October, Francesco Vettori, whose term of office as a member of the Eight had expired, was asked by Cardinal Giulio through his adviser Nicholas Schönberg to forecast the outcome of the conclave.[102] Significantly Vettori's past connection with the French court still made him suspected of being pro-French, but he assured the Cardinal that 'while this spirit rules this body' he would write and say all that he considered of use to him. Although the French cardinals had arrived, Vettori did not think their numbers sufficient to elect their own candidate but they were, he thought, sufficient to delay the election of a pope. This in itself would achieve Francis' purpose which Vettori saw as cutting the imperialists off, during the vacancy, from the financial aid which a pro-imperial pope would provide. The troops in Modena would then mutiny and the duke of Ferrara, doubting the adequacy of his own forces, would call in the French troops near Cremona to capture Modena and possibly even other territories.

Vettori's assessment of the situation in the States of the Church was pretty astute. During the interregnum no pay was forthcoming for the Spanish troops in Modena and the city would have fallen to the duke of Ferrara had it not been for the exertions of Francesco Guicciardini, the city's governor.[103] The

[98] Ibid., p. 231.
[99] Ibid., p. 232.
[100] F. Guicciardini, St. d'It., iv, p. 197; L. Pastor, ix, p. 245.
[101] Otto, Missive, Esterne, Lett. e Istruzioni (1480–1532), 16, fos. 85r and 86r.
[102] C. Strozz., Ser. I, 136, fos. 207r–208v, F. Vettori to Schönberg, Florence, 9 Oct. 1523.   [103] F. Guicciardini, St. d'It., iv, pp. 197ff.

longer the vacancy, however, the greater the likelihood that the
city would be seized. Vettori suggested that at present the only
way to control the situation was to allow the duke to take
Modena but on condition that he provided a sum of money
which would be used to force the French troops stationed near
Cremona to withdraw after a surprise attack carried out in
conjunction with the imperial troops under the marquis of
Mantua and the Venetian forces in northern Italy. The
imperial troops would then unite in Milan and issue forth to
conquer the French. Objections from the College of Cardinals
to the loss of a territory of the Church were to be expected but
the imperialists among them would approve if they knew that it
was in the emperor's interests.

Vettori's prediction for the future was gloomy: Cardinal
Giulio de' Medici's pro-imperial reputation had helped considerably until now but doubts were being cast on it. The joint
campaign of Charles V and Henry VIII against France had
begun too late for much progress to be made this winter. But for
the propensity of the Italian towns to revolution, defeat for
France seemed credible, yet if France had money and if a pope
were not elected quickly to support the war, there was no knowing what might happen.

The end of the conclave and the election on 19 November of
Cardinal Giulio to the papacy proved Vettori's fears unfounded.
The respect which the cardinal had won as the adviser of Leo X
and as the ruler of Florence caused general satisfaction with his
election and high hopes for the future. The duke of Ferrara gave
up his designs on Modena; the Florentines anticipated advantages from another Medicean pontificate.[104] The Vettori's
fortunes had already for some time been in the ascendant.
Francesco's many honourable appointments have been discussed. A month before he ceased to be a member of the Eight,
he had been appointed to the *Otto di Guardia*,[105] a term of office
which was followed immediately by his election in October as
one of the twelve *procuratori*[106] responsible for internal and

[104] L. Pastor, ix, pp. 242–7.

[105] Tratte, 84, fo. 88r.

[106] Tratte, 84, fo. 49v; for the office of *Dodici Procuratori*, N. Rubinstein, *The Government of Florence under the Medici*, pp. 199–200.

especially financial affairs. Paolo had been prior in the previous summer.[107] Many Florentines must therefore have agreed with Filippo Strozzi who considered the Vettori family most influential. A letter which he wrote to Francesco seeking his patronage for a relation, begins 'I know how much the Vettori can do in Florence'.[108] Who could have foreseen the tragic events of the next few years and the collapse of all the hopes which the election of Pope Clement VII had raised?

[107] Tratte, 132, fo. 268v May–June 1523.
[108] C. Strozz., Ser. III, 180, fo. 112r, 2 May 1523.

CHAPTER VIII

For Pope or Florence (1523–7)

THROUGHOUT Vettori's association with the Medici there are signs of a conflict between his loyalty towards his patron and his loyalty towards his city. Though less marked before his closer connection with Giulio de' Medici, these signs are evident as early as his first mission to Rome.[1] Vettori's situation is not unique, since many other upper class citizens who served the Medici faced similar problems of divided loyalty. After 1513 Florence virtually ceased to be ruled from within the city. From the accession of Leo X onwards Florence, as an adjunct of the papacy, became merely a small part of the pope's European-wide diplomacy. Employment by the Medici might offer a citizen greater opportunities as a papal servant, a lieutenant of the papal forces or a commander of the papal galleys after 1512, but whereas between 1434 and 1494 such employment had usually corresponded with the interests of Florence, in the later period it frequently conflicted with them. In the case of a clash between papal and Florentine aspirations the *uomo da bene* might find himself in the dilemma of choosing between the loyalty and self-interest which bound him to a patron and the loyalty and ambition which governed his attitude towards his city. This was the dilemma which faced Francesco Vettori and several of his compatriots in the years 1523–7.

The immediate problem of the early months of Clement's pontificate was to decide how Florence should be governed now that its ruler had been made pope. Since the only two male descendants of Lorenzo the Magnificent were not only illegitimate but minors, the Florentines hoped to be allowed at last to govern themselves. The way in which a decision on this issue was reached illustrates the relations between the pope and the leading citizens; it is indicative, too, of Vettori's dual rôle as a papal servant and a Florentine.

[1] Above, pp. 90–1.

Soon after the new pope's election a formal embassy of congratulation was sent by the Florentines to Rome. It consisted as at the time of Leo X's accession of ten principal citizens who joined the resident ambassador.[2] This time Francesco Vettori was among those who came from Florence. Like Leo[3] Clement used the opportunity of the presence in Rome of these additional ambassadors for consultations on the question of the city's future government. The newcomers made their official entry on 6 February 1524;[4] the ceremonies of the public audience on the 15th were followed the next day by a secret audience in which the ambassadors communicated their instructions to Clement;[5] then on 21 February after a splendid papal banquet all the ambassadors from Florence, together with Jacopo Salviati who had joined them in Rome and Piero Ridolfi who was not an ambassador,[6] met Clement for secret discussions in which each was asked freely to express his views.[7] Nerli and Varchi reveal the pope's policy: those present should request 'on their own initiative' either Alessandro or Ippolito, the bastard sons respectively of Lorenzo, duke of Urbino, and Giuliano, duke of Nemours, as their new ruler. If the young men were not to be made 'absolute lords' of Florence, they should at least be given 'special authority', but the Florentines and not the pope were to appear as the authors of this plan.[8] The semblance of free choice offered to this meeting is typical of Medici methods and will be observed again during the years 1530–2.

Despite the papal attempt to soften resistance by the banquet, the meeting following it produced not one opinion but three. Some were in favour of having one of the young Medici as ruler; others hedged, and a few dissented.

Francesco Vettori was one of the dissenters. He wanted the

---

[2] Elected 14 Dec. 1523. The resident ambassador was Galeotto de' Medici. Jacopo Salviati was likewise in Rome, Signori, Missive, Legaz. e Comm., 27, fos. 29v–30r. Credentials in Vatican Archives, Armadio I, 18, 2574; names in B. Varchi, i, pp. 63–4.

[3] Above, p. 75.

[4] Signori, Missive, Legaz. e Comm., 27, fos. 29v–30r; F. Vettori and Lorenzo Strozzi arrived in Rome on 3 Feb., Otto, Responsive, 33, fo. 38r.

[5] Otto, Responsive, 33, fo. 111v.

[6] *Ibid.*, fo. 103r; F. Zeffi, 'Vita di Lorenzo Strozzi' in L. Strozzi, *Le Vite degli Uomini Illustri della Casa Strozzi* (Firenze, 1892), p. xix.

[7] *Sommario*, p. 349; F. Zeffi, p. xix.   [8] F. Nerli, pp. 141–2; B. Varchi, i, p. 64.

city to be led by a gonfalonier. According to his account in the *Sommario*, he, Roberto Acciaiuoli and Lorenzo Strozzi maintained that it was 'neither honourable nor profitable' for the city to be governed by Silvio Passerini, the cardinal of Cortona in whose charge Ippolito and Alessandro were to be sent to Florence. The Florentines had respected Cardinal Giulio not as cardinal but as a member of the Medici family. The cardinal of Cortona, however, came from one of Florence's subject towns and would not have the city's interests at heart. If Ippolito was Clement's choice, let the youth be allowed to study or to amuse himself until he was of age and in the meantime permit the citizens to govern themselves with an annually appointed gonfalonier; in this way they would see their political status respected.[9] Varchi mentions that Vettori supported Jacopo Salviati's view that the ancient laws and present government of the city should not be changed. Among those who knew of the pope's secret intention and supported it were Alessandro Pucci and Palla Rucellai.[10]

If, as Francesco Zeffi says, Francesco Vettori and Lorenzo Strozzi lost favour with the pope as a result of their opposition to his plan,[11] Vettori's fall from grace can only have come at the end of the embassy (perhaps accounting for his early departure) and it must have been only temporary, for signs of esteem mark the early part of his stay in Rome, and his close association with Clement continued for most of the pontificate. His accommodation is indicative: he was among those lodged on the first floor of the Cancelleria which was reserved for the most senior members of the embassy[12] and was given one of its seven principal gold-decorated rooms.[13] Vettori received from Francesco del Nero the details of the annual reform of the *Monte*[14] and discussed them personally with Clement,[15] even though the

---

[9] *Sommario*, pp. 349–50; F. Zeffi, p. xx confirms Vettori's attitude but says he and Lorenzo Strozzi would have liked either a life-gonfalonier or a three-year appointment.   [10] B. Varchi, i, p. 65.   [11] F. Zeffi, p. xx.

[12] C. Strozz., Ser. III, 108, fo. 76r. F. Strozzi to Lorenzo, Rome, 8 Jan. 1524.

[13] B.N.F. II, IV, 344, fo. 31r. Document describing allocated rooms.

[14] Otto, Missive, Legaz. e Comm., 16, fo. 227r, 10 Feb.: 'già più giorni siamo intrati nella nuova riforma da farsi della ciptà la quale per antiqua consuetudine suole essere expedita per tucto el presente mese', cp. B. Varchi, iii, p. 37.

[15] C. Strozz., Ser. I, 136, fo. 235r. F. Vettori to Francesco del Nero, Rome, 16 Feb. 1524.

subject had been raised with the pope by all the ambassadors together.[16] Since Vettori left Rome before his colleagues, it was from him, as they wrote, that the Eight would be informed of 'everything that has been negotiated and executed here by us'.[17]

The financial support Vettori received from Clement must be taken as another token of the pope's esteem. A year after the ceremonial embassy Filippo Strozzi was once again working to supplement his friend's income,[18] this time by trying to obtain for him the salary of one of the recently instituted sinecures of the papal court known as the *Cavalieri di San Pietro*. He informed Francesco that the pope had not raised any objection to giving him the next vacancy, of which he, Strozzi, had the disposal. One became vacant two months later and Filippo duly nominated his friend.[19] During the siege of Florence in 1529–30, while Vettori was at the papal court, he drew a large income from the archbishopric of Florence and fifteen crowns a month from the treasurer Francesco del Nero from the Roman office known as the *Ripetta*.[20] From 1530 onwards he received an annual pension in recognition of his services to the pope.[21]

Despite the tacit or expressed disapproval of several of the members of the ceremonial embassy, the cardinal of Cortona was appointed governor in May 1524; the two young Medici arrived in Florence in August, and Ippolito, having been made eligible for all public offices at Clement's express orders,[22] ruled the city under the cardinal's guidance, while Alessandro stayed at the Medici villa of Careggi in the care of Rosso Ridolfi.[23] The Venetian ambassador Marco Foscari describes prevailing conditions in Florence. The 'signori Medici', as he termed them, ruled 'extremely despotically', according to the wishes of the

---

[16] Otto, Responsive, 33, fo. 103r, 21 Feb. 1524.

[17] *Ibid.*, fo. 26r, 27 Feb. 1524: 'Domattina . . . si invierà Francesco Vettori del quale le S.V. saranno raguagliate di tutto quello si è negociato et exeguito qua per noi.'

[18] Above, p. 148.

[19] A. Bardi, 'Filippo Strozzi', pp. 48–9, n. 4.

[20] G. Busini, *Lettere*, Lettera Nona, p. 69; *Raccolto delle Azioni*, p. 278.

[21] F. Vettori to Bartolomeo Lanfredini, Florence (April–May 1533) refers to the pension he has had from the pope for the last three years. R. von Albertini, p. 454. Renewal of this pension in 1533 by Clement, Vatican Archives, Armadio 29, vol. 82, fo. 163r, 30 June.

[22] J. Pitti, 'Istoria Fiorentina', p. 133.   [23] B. Segni, iii, p. 294.

pope but in the name of the cardinal of Cortona and Ippolito de'
Medici. The *pratiche* and other consultations took place in the
Medici residence, to which all business was referred except some
matters of little importance which passed through normal
channels. The ordinary councils of the city did not meet; the
Medici imposed the taxes; ambassadors, after a preliminary
audience with the *Signoria*, negotiated with the cardinal and
Ippolito only; almost all the letters were addressed to the
cardinal and all were delivered to the Medici palace. Only
Medici supporters approved by the pope were elected to the
important offices. By sending young Ippolito and the cardinal
to rule Florence, Foscari went on, Clement made himself unpopular even with the ordinary citizens who wanted as their
temporal ruler neither the pope, nor a child nor a citizen from a
subject town. The despotism of Ippolito and the cardinal, the
taxes, and the way in which offices were distributed made the
regime so unbearable, Foscari reported, that even Medici
sympathizers who had staked much in support of it were
alienated.[24]

Francesco Vettori's position in the cardinal of Cortona's
administration differed from that of the other citizens of his
class and experience for two reasons: unlike Filippo Strozzi,
Jacopo Salviati, Francesco Guicciardini and Paolo Vettori, he
spent most of his time in Florence, and unlike Matteo Strozzi,
Luigi Guicciardini and Niccolò Capponi, he did not withdraw
from the cardinal's government.[25] Indeed he was constantly
employed in the chief offices of the city: he was a member of the
Eight annually[26] and was twice chosen by this body to present
their views to the pope;[27] he was an *accoppiatore*;[28] and in
November–December 1524 he was a prior.[29] Of those most
closely connected with the Medici government in Florence only
Matteo Strozzi (with whom Vettori was to be associated
politically in 1527 and after 1530) was a member of the Eight
as frequently as Vettori,[30] Niccolò Capponi having been a

[24] E. Albèri (1839), Ser. II, i, pp. 43–4 and 73–4.   [25] B. Segni, iii, p. 295.
[26] Tratte, 84, fo. 82v: June–Dec. 1524; Dec. 1525–June 1526; his appointment in
June 1524 was his fourth tenure of that office since Dec. 1518, v. fos. 81v, 82r.
[27] Below, pp. 171, 179.   [28] Tratte, 84, fo. 44v.   [29] Tratte, 94, fo. 11v.
[30] Except for 1524 Matteo was elected annually from 1523–6 inclusive, Tratte,
84, fos. 82v, 187r.

member only once,[31] and, as already stated, Jacopo Salviati, Francesco Guicciardini and Filippo Strozzi not being available.[32]

Undoubtedly Cortona's trust in Vettori was based on the pope's high opinion of him, and Cortona expected Vettori to promote Clement's interests. When, for example, Vettori suggested that the Florentines should safeguard the security of the city themselves in view of the parlous situation of the pope, the cardinal is reported to have exclaimed, 'is this what one expects, Francesco, from someone who has been so favoured and rewarded by the Pope?'[33] Basilio in Vettori's dialogue *Il Sacco di Roma* stating 'when the Pope asked me in which citizen Cortona most confided, I told him I believed he confided in me more than in anybody else', truthfully describes the author's position in those years.[34]

Despite the special position which Vettori held in the cardinal's administration, he was critical of it, as he had been of Medici government in 1512. He probably had the cardinal's shortcomings in mind when he made Basilio say in the *Sacco* that the ruler of Florence should be a man of great intelligence, born and bred in the city and with the knowledge of individual citizens which enables him to discuss with each one his particular interests.[35] In December 1524 he wrote to Paolo that the cardinal was most diligent 'but he was not born here and he does not understand our ways'.[36] Although a narrowly-based republican form of government was his ideal, Vettori's political thinking was realistic and at times cynical. It was all right, he also wrote in this letter, to use gentle methods when the sea was calm but when the future was uncertain he would adopt the rigorous methods necessary for a strong government. Referring to Clement's anxiety concerning the large number of citizens proposed for the Council of Seventy, Vettori criticized the cardinal's lack of firmness in allowing too many names to be submitted. He should seek advice from a small inner council of

[31] Tratte, 84, fo. 82v.

[32] J. Salviati's name appears annually from 1514–22 but not thereafter, Tratte, 84, fos. 81r, 81v, 82r.   [33] B. Segni, iii, p. 303.

[34] *Sacco*, p. 416. For identification of Vettori with Basilio, v. R. Hughes, Francesco Vettori, thesis submitted for Ph.D., University of London, 1958, p. 303.

[35] *Sacco*, pp. 416–17.   [36] C. Strozz., Ser. I, 136, fo. 209v.

five or six citizens. Vettori follows up this idea after 1530 in advocating a small group of councillors as advisers to Duke Alessandro.[37] As early as 1512 the use of force had had a place in Vettori's political thought,[38] and he became more convinced of the need for it as popular resistance to the Medici regime increased; by 1527 he was of the opinion that there were no such things as free republics; all governments were tyrannies.[39] In Florence no citizen was concerned with liberty but only with his own profit. Brutus and Cassius had not been moved by patriotism and liberty but by ambition and the desire for gain.[40]

Varchi divides the pro-Medici citizens dissatisfied with the cardinal's administration into two parties: those who did not object to the Medici despotism, but found fault with Cortona's administration, and those who found the Medici acceptable as 'capi e superiori' but not as 'principi e padroni'. The latter group, to which Nerli assigns Vettori, pointing to his friendship with Strozzi and his relationship by marriage with Niccolò Capponi, really wanted government by the *ottimati*.[41]

The Florentines were certainly restive but the city's revolt against Clement was the direct result of his diplomatic policy with its incipient military dangers and its crippling financial burdens. From the beginning of his pontificate both Francesco and Paolo Vettori were closely associated with this diplomacy.

Already at the time of the Florentine ceremonial embassy to Rome the financial aspects of the alliance between the pope and the emperor, inherited by Clement from Adrian VI and costing him 15,000 ducats monthly in contributions to the imperial forces,[42] were brought up for discussion by the ambassadors. From August 1523 Florence had paid her contribution. On the 31st the Eight had informed their resident ambassadors in Rome that they had sent Paolo Vettori to Milan with Florence's first payment,[43] and in the following month Clement wrote to Francesco thanking him for his support in raising money.[44] By

---

[37] Below, pp. 243, 250.   [38] Above, p. 78.   [39] *Sommario*, p. 293.

[40] *Sacco*, p. 426.   [41] B. Varchi, i, pp. 70–2; F. Nerli, pp. 142–3.

[42] *Sommario*, p. 347.   [43] Otto, Missive, Esterne, Legaz. e. Comm., 16, fo. 86r.

[44] Acq. e Doni, 59, insert 3 (6), Card. Giulio de' Medici to F.V., Rome, 15 Sept. 1523: 'Francesco del Nero ci ha fatto intendere quanto in le cose che occurreno vi siate mostrato propitio et favorevole et maxime in la provisione del danaro il che ci è stato molto grato, pregandovi a favorire questa decima de' preti . . . perchè

February 1524 Paolo was the apostolic nuncio in Milan[45] to whom the Eight had written about the initial payment of a new Florentine contribution.[46] Francesco with the resident and two other ceremonial ambassadors discussed personally with Clement such financial exactions which were already beginning to make the pope unpopular in Florence.[47]

Clement's foreign policy was hesitant and vacillating. In order to bring peace to Italy and to restore freedom to the papacy he seems to have had a genuine desire to preserve a neutral position in the struggle between France and the Empire,[48] but his oscillation between these two powers caused Guicciardini to believe in the successive influence over him of the radically opposed views of his two principal advisers, the pro-French Gian Matteo Giberti and the imperialist Nicholas von Schönberg.[49] Before 1525, when Vettori was again sent to Rome, Clement allied with France. He gave as a reason for not renewing the league with the emperor in April 1524 the desirability of neutrality on the part of the Father of Christendom so that he might command respect for a summons to war against the Infidel.[50] But after the repulse of the imperial invasion of France in the summer of 1524 and the subsequent French counter-offensive resulting in the recapture of Milan in October, the Valois ruler seemed to be more formidable than the Habsburg and by 30 October Clement had sent his pro-French adviser, Gian Matteo Giberti, to seek an agreement with Francis I.[51] However, on subsequent information of a French setback he redirected him first to find out from Lannoy, the imperial viceroy and commander-in-chief, and from the marquis of Pescara, another of the imperial commanders, on what terms they would be prepared to sign an armistice. But Giberti found both sides unwilling. Undeterred Clement made one more effort

cavando el predecto Francesco da preti predecti 10,000 ducati provederà lui al resto di questa seconda paga.'

[45] Otto, Missive, Esterne, Legaz. e Comm., 16, fo. 222v.

[46] Ibid., fo. 223r, 3 Feb. 1524, to Galeotto de' Medici.

[47] Otto, Responsive, 33, fo. 66r. Ambassadors to Otto, Rome, 7 Feb. 1524: 'Questa sera il R.mo Turitano et Mag.ci Lorenzo Morelli, Francesco Vettori et Galeotto de' Medici ne hanno parlato con N.S.' ('ne' refers to the 'pagamento').

[48] L. Pastor, ix, p. 253.

[49] F. Guicciardini, St. d'It., iv, pp. 330–1; L. Pastor, ix, p. 254.

[50] C. Roth, The Last Florentine Republic, p. 8.   [51] L. Pastor, ix, p. 266.

to bring about an armistice. For this mission he employed Paolo Vettori who set off from Rome on 22 November to contact Lannoy but whose task was doomed to failure from the start, according to Francesco, because of the personal ambition of the Constable Bourbon to become duke of Milan.[52] The alliance which Clement concluded with France the next month placed the papacy (and perforce Florence) on the losing side when on 24 February 1525 Francis I was defeated and captured by the imperialists at Pavia. The pope was now in an extremely precarious position, his independence being virtually lost with Milan and Naples under imperial control. In these circumstances he was faced with the problem of whether to join with England, Venice and the duke of Milan to form a league against the emperor or to come to the best possible terms with him. As in the previous year, Clement consulted Florentine opinion; again Francesco Vettori was sent to Rome, this time alone.

Vettori would be acceptable to the pope. At the end of December while he was serving his city as prior, his brother Paolo, perhaps acting on Clement's instigation, as Francesco's answer seems to imply, invited him to come to Rome.[53] In November Alessandro Pazzi had put forward such a suggestion. If this, too, was inspired by the pope, the invitation is couched in flattering but heavily veiled terms.[54] But whoever suggested Vettori, clearly he did not go as a private citizen: 'the Pope understands', wrote Gian Matteo Giberti to the Eight on 3 March 1525, 'Francesco Vettori sent by your lordships should be here tomorrow; as soon as His Holiness has heard from him the proposals made in your name, he will see that you are informed of what occurs'.[55]

[52] G. Ruscelli, ii, fo. 61v. Sanga to Ludovico Canossa, 29 Nov. 1524; *Sommario* p. 354.

[53] C. Strozz., Ser. I, 136, fo. 209r. Francesco to Paolo, 'in palazzo a dì 29 dicembre 1524': 'e quanto al venire chostì io la farei tanto volentieri quanto è ragionevole non per altra causa che per vedere N.S.'

[54] B.M. Add. Ms. 10,277, fo. 197r. Alessandro Pazzi to F. Vettori, Ex Urbe, 1 Nov. 1524 (wrongly ascribed to Piccolomini): 'sichè havete ad havere non solo caro di venire qua per mantenervi in la gratia Sua [of the Pope] ma ancora molto più per vedere un principe tanto grande et tanto sapiente verso di voi si bene volto et animato, reputando dare a S.tà. piacere assai nel vedervi (mihi crede)'.

[55] Otto, Responsive, 33, fo. 215v: 'Secondo N.S.re intende Francesco Vettori mandato dalle S.V. doverà essere qui domani, dal quale inteso che Sua S.tà. harà le proposte facte in nome d'esse li farà rispondere quello occurrerà.'

Three extant documents show the arguments which led
Vettori and the Eight to advise Clement not to join the proposed league against Charles V; because one of them is undated, however, it is difficult to establish the degree of Vettori's
responsibility for his city's adoption of a resigned and negative attitude to the defence of Italian independence which
contrasts with the bold approach of Guicciardini and
Machiavelli.[56]

Vettori arrived in Rome on 6 March.[57] From a copy of a
letter which he wrote the next day to Roberto Acciaiuoli, a
member of the Eight, we learn that he had an audience with
Clement immediately.[58] After reporting to the Eight what the
pope had told him about his current relations with the imperialists, Vettori's letter presents the arguments for and against
adherence to the league asking on the pope's behalf for the
Eight's advice. Firstly, a financial agreement with the emperor
would be difficult for the pope owing both to his and the
Florentines' lack of money, and, secondly, if payment were
made, it was likely that, having attacked France with success,
the emperor would then turn to the conquest of Italy, which
deprived of money would be defenceless. Hence to come to
terms with the emperor would be to make the imperialists
masters of both France and Italy. To prevent this a league of
the pope, the Venetians, the Florentines and the duke of Ferrara
had been suggested for offensive action against the emperor,
and 'many of the cardinals and other great prelates and
officials favoured this policy'.[59] This course seems 'dangerous',
Vettori went on, because experience frequently showed that
'leagues of many parties (*pezzi*) bear little fruit', for 'everyone

[56] On Guicciardini, R. von Albertini, p. 245; for Machiavelli's views, see
below, p. 178.
[57] Otto, Responsive, 33, fo. 336v, Galeotto de' Medici to the Eight, Rome,
6 March 1525, Vettori 'arrived this morning'.
[58] Arch. Ricasoli, Florence, Carte Acciaiuoli, F. Vettori to R. Acciaiuoli, Rome,
7 March 1525 (copy). I am grateful to Dr Gino Corti for telling me of the existence
of this letter and of the reply to it, see p. 172, n. 65. For members of the Eight,
including Acciaiuoli, Tratte, 84, fo. 82v; F. Vettori was not a member at this
time.
[59] 'et però era chi ricordava che si facessi una lega papa, venitiani, fiorentini,
Duca di Ferrara et altri d'Italia gagliarda . . . et molti di questi cardinali et altri
grandi prelati et uficiali sarebbono in questa oppinione'.

intends to spend the minimum and gain the maximum'.[60] The Venetians would seek advantage for themselves out of the fighting in Lombardy and, once having gained what they wanted, would not care if the emperor were to retire from there towards Tuscany where the Florentines with their 'weak city' would be the first to fear him.[61] The pope, Vettori continued, therefore wished to be advised whether to come to an agreement with the emperor, giving him money on the best possible terms, or to enter the league thus adopting 'this bold course which could be honourable and for the health of all Italy'.[62] Although one senses that Vettori considers it inadvisable to join the league, in this letter to Acciaiuoli he does not actually commit himself to either course: 'To tell you the truth, Roberto, I am much confused in this matter, for in giving the money I see great difficulty and, moreover, that we shall help to bring about our own ruin; in the other course I can see so many uncertainties and dangers that I fear it will anticipate that ruin.'[63] Vettori says he will await the Eight's reply, but he does nevertheless advise them that if they decide to adopt the way of financial agreement with the emperor, they should stress the city's weakness.[64]

The extant copy of Acciaiuoli's reply to Vettori dated 12 March sets out the Florentine reasons for advising an agreement with the emperor as the less 'deadly' of the two evils.[65] It also, incidentally, corroborates Foscari's report on the conduct and personnel of Medici government in Florence. Vettori's letter was discussed at a meeting held in the cardinal of Cortona's

---

[60] 'Questo partito pare pericoloso perchè spesso si vede che queste leghe di molti pezzi fanno pocho fructo et che ogni huomo pensa spendere il meno che può et trarre il più che può.'

[61] '... et havendo noi fiorentini la città debole saremmo e primi che haremmo a temere'.

[62] '... questo partito audace et che potrebbe essere honorevole et a salute di tutta Italia'.

[63] 'Io a dirvi il vero Ruberto mio in questa materia sono molto confuso perchè nel dare e danari veggo dificultà grande et in oltre aiutiamo la ruina nostra: in questo altro partito mi occorrono tanti dubii e pericoli che temo decta ruina non s'anticipi.'

[64] 'monstrate la deboleza della città'.

[65] Arch. Ricasoli, Florence, Carte Acciaiuoli, R. Acciaiuoli to F. Vettori, Florence, 12 March 1525 (copy). The letter speaks of the choice between two deaths.

room by a small number of acceptable citizens, only three of
whom were members of the Eight. Acciaiuoli names them as
messer Matteo (Niccolini), Lorenzo (Morelli),[66] Gherardo
(Corsini),[67] Jacopo (Gianfigliazzi?),[68] Piero (Ridolfi),[69] Matteo
(Strozzi),[70] Palla (Rucellai) and himself. The weaknesses of
the Florentine external and internal situation, and the selfish
attitude which made the Italian city states of the renaissance
such an easy prey to foreign invasion are all reflected in the
cautious and negative policy which the Florentines advise.
They would have liked to assent to the more 'glorious', 'reasonable' and 'magnanimous' course, concentrating Italy's forces
and liberating the country once and for all from foreign armies[71]
but 'turning from universal concerns to particular conveniences
and inconveniences, as everyone must do',[72] and to an estimate
of their own strength, it seemed to Clement's Florentine
advisers that 'necessity' induced them to abandon the honourable course, leading to immediate death, and to adopt the other,
which although leading ultimately to the grave, at least extended the period of life.[73] They knew perfectly well that their
internal political weaknesses were the obstacle to the 'more
magnificent plan' for the Italian cause but nature taught self-
preservation before death for the common safety.[74] Florence

[66] A member of the ceremonial embassy to Rome and participant in private
discussions with Clement (see above, p. 169), therefore likely to be at this meeting.

[67] A member of the Eight, and therefore likely, though Gherardo Bartolini is
also possible. For G. Corsini, see also above, p. 157.

[68] A member of the Eight in 1526 with whom Vettori corresponded; a staunch
Medicean and therefore likely to be the Jacopo referred to here, as Jacopo Salviati,
another possibility, was in Rome.

[69] A Medicean and a member of the Eight.

[70] One of the inner circle of Cortona's government.

[71] 'la intentione et desiderio nostra saria di accostarsi a quel partito che tiene in
se più del glorioso, più del ragionevole, et più del magnanimo che ci si porge avanti
et questo è restrignere tucte le forze italiane, et liberarsi una volta da questi
exerciti ultramontani'.

[72] 'Nondimeno ritirando poi la mente dalle cose universale alli commodi et
incommodi particulari, come in facto debba far ciaschuno . . . la necessità c'induce
ad lasciar da parte questo partito.'

[73] 'el quale se bene ci può conducere alla fossa, non dimeno ci da più vita et più
agio a respirare'.

[74] 'Et conosciamo benissimo che la debolezza dello stato nostro è causa
d'impedire quel disegno più magnifico per le cose d'Italia, ma la natura c'insegna
pensar prima alla sicurtà della vita nostra che apporci alla morte per la sicurtà
universale.'

was without her own forces, and by the time she had negotiated the conditions for hiring them and found the captains to lead them, the Venetians being so 'boastful and vexatious' and the duke of Ferrara so 'mean and punctilious',[75] the imperial forces would be upon them. Then finding the Florentines disarmed, her government financially and morally weak, her citizens discontent and her cities disaffected and ill-fortified, ruin would shortly follow.[76] Resistance would mean filling the Florentine dominion with soldiers, and suffering as much damage from friend as from foe. Nor could Florence bear the expense of war. For all these reasons therefore the advisers at the meeting concluded that the slower death was the safer, for in the preceding interval much could happen to change the situation. The letter ends with the warning that in coming to terms with the emperor, Clement should commit the Florentines to the smallest possible money payment.

In its conclusions, in its stress on Florentine financial and internal weakness and in its distrust of the Venetians, Acciaiuoli's letter resembles Vettori's and was undoubtedly influenced by it.[77] But the views expressed in our third document, an undated 'discourse' in Vettori's hand[78] preserved among the papers once belonging to the Strozzi, whose title 'Discorso di Francesco Vettori se fusse meglio fare una Lega o vero accordare con l'Imperatore' is not contemporary, also resemble those in Roberto Acciaiuoli's letter. The document (whose small initial letter gives it the appearance of a draft or a copy) opens with the remark that 'we understand from your ['*tua*'] letter of the 3rd that the Pope would like to know whether to form a league comprising the Pope, the Venetians, the Duke of Ferrara, and the Florentines . . . or rather to come to terms with the Emperor

---

[75] 'i Vinitiani vantaggiosi et fastidiosi come sapete, et el Duca di Ferrara avaro et puntuoso in e tituli del capitano'.

[76] 'Et trovandoci disarmati, le terre infecte et non forte, lo stato qui debole et senza nervo et senza danari li animi de ciptadini et chi mal contento, siamo certi che in brevissimi giorni desoleremo questa ciptà.'

[77] Speaking of Vettori's letter of 7 March, Acciaiuoli wrote: 'Et havendo bene ponderato el contentato d'epsa ci pare che la S.tà. di N.S. ci ponga davanti el partito, tanto ben digestito et con tanta considerazione examinato, che ci monstra la resolutione men difficile che non haremo hauto senza quel discorso et apparentia di lume.'

[78] C. Strozz., Ser. II, 86, fos. 229r–30v.

or his agents on the least wretched terms possible'. As the battle of Pavia took place on 24 February and the terms of agreement between Charles and Clement were signed on 1 April,[79] the 3rd referred to can only be 3 March. As Vettori arrived in Rome on 6 March, he cannot have written the document in Florence. The use of the pronouns *tua* and *noi*, as employed by the Eight to Galeotto de' Medici,[80] suggests a communication from this magistracy to Galeotto in Rome, copied subsequently by Francesco Vettori, but, as it is not entered in their register, it probably came from Roberto Acciaiuoli, who was a member of that office.

Like Acciaiuoli's letter of 12 March, the document in Vettori's hand acknowledges that for the pope to oppose Charles' ambition to dominate Italy by giving his support to a league against the emperor would be a 'glorious enterprise'; it also shares the letter's resigned and negative attitude in pointing out that 'what seems glorious is not however practical'. Italy was so sick that the 'strong medicine' of war which could win her liberation could also mean her sudden death. The choice between two forms of death is also here, though the choice of the slower death is placed neatly, and without examples, in the context of the familiar Florentine diplomatic practice of playing for time: 'to take advantage of time is sometimes appropriate'.[81] More precise illustrations are given by this writer of the financial, military and political factors which in his view make a war against the emperor an impractical undertaking. Money is recognized as 'fundamental for war', but both the principal adherents to the league, the pope and Venice, are shown to be financially embarrassed. Here, however, the reasons for the pope's lack of money are explained: he entered on his pontificate with an empty treasury, and he is taken to be unwilling to resort to extraordinary means of making money. The Florentines are reported since 1521 to have spent more than 600,000 ducats, lost over 200,000 at sea, and to be owed at least 700,000 in France. Venice, too, in the last fifteen years had had nothing

---

[79] Otto, Responsive, 37, fos. 37r–v.

[80] Otto, Missive, Legaz. e Comm., 16, fo. 222r, 2 Feb. 'Per la tua . . . de xxx . . .'; fo. 221v: '. . . se havanti ti occuressi alcuna cosa . . . con la solita tua prudentia' etc.

[81] cit. R. von Albertini, p. 245, n. 4.

but expenditure and losses, though her strong island position and excellent constitution placed her politically in no danger either from external attack or internal revolution; this could not be said of the pope, riddled as both the papal states and Rome were with faction. No mention is made of Florence's political weaknesses. Venice's ambitions in Lombardy are not referred to, nor her lack of regard for Florence. The writer merely points out how useless the Venetian forces would be if they were cut off, as was likely, by the imperial forces sent up from Naples into Lombardy.

Taken altogether the advice given in this letter, with its more statesmanlike omission of the vindictive references to the Venetians and to the political weakness of Florence, and with its stress on the difficulties in the papal states—of more immediate concern to Clement—would seem to indicate that it was meant for the eye of the pope.[82]

From Galeotto's dispatch to the Eight of 6 March we know that Clement was already inclined towards agreement with Charles,[83] and the appraisal of the situation from the Eight put to him by his trusted adviser Vettori must have confirmed him in his opinion. By 10 March the pope had clearly made up his mind to come to terms with the emperor: on that day he sent Paolo Vettori to the duke of Albany, some of whose troops having withdrawn from an intended campaign in Naples were in the neighbourhood of Rome, to advise him to leave Italy with his forces and not to await the fury of the enemy.[84] Albany complied and left from Civitavecchia for France. On 1 April a defensive and offensive treaty was concluded between the pope and the imperial viceroy.[85] Before this date, sometime before the end of March, Vettori returned to Florence.[86]

The excessive power which the defeat of Francis I and the capitulation of Clement had given to the emperor brought a

---

[82] 'S. Stà che intra le terre sue ha la factione et in Roma medesima.'

[83] Otto, Responsive, 33, fo. 336v.

[84] Otto, Responsive, 33, fo. 346r. Galeotto de' Medici, Rome, 14 March 1525. Nicholas Schönberg to Paolo Vettori, Rome, 16 March 1525, Phillips Ms. 921 now in the Archivio di Stato, Florence.

[85] Otto, Responsive, 37, fos. 37r–v.

[86] C. Strozz., Ser. I, 136, fo. 234r. F. Vettori to Francesco del Nero, Rome 11 March 1525: 'et penso venirmene di questa altra settimana, et facci poi lo imperadore quello che vuole'. O. Tommasini, ii, p. 1149.

predictable anti-imperial reaction. Charles did not honour the
terms of his agreement with the pope,[87] and Clement, in
common with many Italians, feared that the emperor would
conclude one with his royal prisoner. This seemed the more
likely when, in June, Francis was taken to Spain.[88] Only a
month later therefore, the earliest of the anti-Habsburg negotiations, which were to lead to the formation of the League of
Cognac in the following spring, were opened. In August Louise
of Savoy, in her son's absence, negotiated a treaty of alliance
between France and England.[89] Her ambition, however, was to
win the pope and Venice to the French side. But Clement was
as usual undecided, and the Venetians refused to commit themselves before the pope. Clement's main preoccupation was the
freedom of Milan, which on the seizure in October of Duke
Francesco Sforza's chancellor, Girolamo Morone, allegedly for
plotting against the emperor, and on the retreat of the duke into
the citadel, had fallen under imperial control.[90] No agreement
had been reached about its surrender before the emperor had
made the political error which finally brought the League into
being. In March 1526 when Francis I arrived on French soil, no
one expected him to abide by the exigent terms of the peace of
Madrid which had purchased his freedom.[91] In little over a
month Clement sent Paolo Vettori to the French court, ostensibly to congratulate the king on his liberation but in fact also
to discover Francis' intentions. If he meant to keep faith with
Charles, Paolo was to say nothing further. If, however, he was
undecided, Paolo was to make known the pope's desire for an
alliance and to urge him to action. Paolo was only forty-nine
but being already in poor health, according to his brother, he
fell ill on the journey and died in Florence.[92]

The negotiations with Francis were continued by Capino da
Capo; by 8 April he was able to report that France had been
won for the League;[93] and on 22 May the Holy League of
Cognac consisting of Clement VII, Francis I, Venice and Duke
Francesco Sforza was formed. The outcome could only be war

---

[87] *Sommario*, p. 356; L. Pastor, ix, p. 282.

[88] L. Pastor, ix, p. 284.

[89] *Ibid.*, p. 285.

[90] *Ibid.*, p. 291.

[91] *Ibid.*, p. 299.

[92] *Sommario*, p. 361.

[93] L. Pastor, ix, pp. 300–1.

and in June Clement made preparations. Francesco Guicciardini was appointed lieutenant of the papal forces and among those taken into the papal and Florentine service was Giovanni de' Medici, father of Cosimo the future duke of Florence.[94] Despite the highest expectations, in no sector of the war which the pope had planned were the forces of the League successful.[95] Milan was not liberated, and the diversionary attacks planned against the imperialists in Siena and Genoa likewise failed. Even worse, the Colonna attack on Rome, sparsely garrisoned after the peace agreement with them on 20 August, brought their hostile troops into the city and caused Clement's ignominious retreat into Castel S. Angelo to be followed on 21 September by a humiliating truce with the imperialists which demanded that Filippo Strozzi and a son of Jacopo Salviati be given as hostages to the imperial envoy Don Ugo da Moncada.[96]

Vettori committed to paper his own thoughts on the situation in Lombardy and was also a link in the chain of communication by which Machiavelli's views were conveyed to the pope. On 5 August he wrote to Niccolò that he had sent his letter to Rome to Filippo Strozzi to use as he thought fit,[97] and three weeks later Strozzi told Vettori that he had shown it to Clement.[98] In this letter Machiavelli had suggested a diversionary attack on Naples as part of the war against the emperor. Vettori considered a further offensive inadvisable in view of the previous failures at Milan and Siena. His cautious, logical assessment contrasts significantly with the daring planning of his friend. The pope, too, was against Machiavelli's diversion, which was in fact not undertaken, and it would be interesting to know whether Vettori had been voicing Clement's view or vice versa; the latter presupposes that either Filippo Strozzi or the cardinal of Cortona had conveyed his comment to Clement. Vettori believed, as he had done a year earlier, and still did when he wrote the *Sommario*, that shortage of money was the fatal weakness of the war against the emperor.[99] As an example he dis-

---

[94] *Sommario*, p. 363.

[95] War plan: L. Pastor, ix, p. 308; its failure, *ibid.*, pp. 317–24. F. Guicciardini, *St. d'It.*, v, Lib. XVII, chaps, iii–vii; *Sommario*, pp. 363–7.

[96] *Sommario*, pp. 367–9; L. Pastor, ix, p. 334.

[97] O. Tommasini, ii, p. 1242.   [98] *Ibid.*, p. 1245.   [99] *Sommario*, p. 363.

cusses the Colonna's incursion and shows that the pope exposed Rome in order to save money.[100] He considered, writing to Machiavelli in August, that the pope had conducted the war 'con ragione' and that no one could say that he was moved by passion.[101]

In Florence the effect of these events diminished Clement's prestige and stimulated a desire to clarify the city's position vis-à-vis the pope. Particularly disturbing even to the most committed Medici supporters was the failure to recapture the citadel of Milan, the retreat of the Florentine forces from before Siena,[102] and the papal retreat into Castel S. Angelo. Consequently in October the Eight selected a special envoy to go to Rome to make their views known to Clement. As in the previous year, the man chosen was Francesco Vettori.[103] The main purpose of the mission was to inform the pope of the Eight's desire to be consulted before he took decisions; this was coupled with a warning not to burden the city with further expense as his reputation among the citizens was declining and they could not be pressed any further. Vettori was also to broach a new point: the Florentines' wish to be governed in Florence and not from Rome.[104] In his Sommario Vettori calls the mission a condemnation of Clement's 'lack of prudence and courage' by 'those who judge events', in fact 'by most men'.[105]

Vettori arrived in Rome in the evening of 17 October.[106] That same night he was received by Clement and on the following day he had two further audiences with him. According to Vettori's account in the Sommario Clement was not at all pleased with the Eight's communication but 'since Francesco was his confidant', he thought he had told him this out of affection, and, because he considered him to be 'too cautious', he underestimated the gravity of the situation in Florence which Vettori had brought to his attention.[107] This is not entirely borne out

[100] Ibid., p. 367.

[101] O. Tommasini, ii, p. 1243; cp. Sommario, p. 363; below, pp. 222–3.

[102] Sommario, pp. 366ff. Otto, Missive, Legaz. e Comm., 18, fo. 59v.

[103] Otto, Missive, Legaz. e Comm., 18, fo. 84r, 10 Oct. 1526 to Galeotto de' Medici; Sommario, p. 370.

[104] Ibid., fos. 86r–87r, 23 Oct. 1526, fo. 86v: 'Firenze si governi in Firenze'.

[105] Sommario, p. 370.

[106] Otto, Responsive, 46, fo. 40r, 17 Oct., Galeotto to Eight; ibid., fo. 1r, Rome, 19 Oct. 1526, Vettori to Eight.   [107] Sommario, p. 370.

by the official dispatch to the Eight of 19 October.[108] The pope,
Francesco reported, quite appreciated the Eight's desire to be
informed and consulted before he took any decision: he had, in
fact, asked for the *Signoria*'s advice on several occasions since the
cardinal of Cortona's arrival. After assurances of his affection
for Florence, he justified the war as having been forced on him
by the emperor's aspiration to dominate Italy,[109] subdue the
Holy See and degrade Florence. He then defended the decision
to capture Milan as reasonable, but admitted failure. This had
shown him that the war was to be a long one and had determined the diversionary attack on Siena and the eventual agreement with the Colonna which had meant a saving of 15,000
ducats a month. He did not promise to consult the Eight on all
occasions but evaded this request by saying that he had always
ordered his agents in Lombardy, France and at the imperial
court (Francesco Guicciardini, Roberto Acciaiuoli and Baldassare da Castiglione respectively) to keep Florence informed.

Clement's answer to the request for greater self-determination
is conciliatory. The pope first told Vettori that he was sometimes worried when he intervened in the appointment of
Florence's magistrates but he had borne with the work entailed
to eliminate dissension between citizens. Nevertheless he
appreciated the request for 'Florence to be governed in
Florence', and would always approve any decision taken there,
provided that it was for the preservation of the regime and the
benefit of the city. The Eight could discuss this with Cortona,
Ippolito, the *accoppiatori*, or other citizens. Vettori had the
impression that Clement was very willing to approve anything
on which the Florentines were in agreement. He does not refer
to this part of his mission in the *Sommario*, presumably because
the pope's answer contradicts his assessment of the effect which
the demands of the Eight had on Clement. The only possible
explanation for Clement's concessions to a demand from
Florence amounting to a basic change of policy is that he did
realize the implications and the danger of the situation.

---

[108] Otto, Responsive, 46, fos. 1r–2v.

[109] Cp. R. Acciaiuoli in A. Desjardins, ii, p. 681: 'Let the Emperor rule Italy and
he will rule the world', and Wolsey's remark that Charles wanted to be master of
the world with the pope as his chaplain, E. Armstrong, *The Emperor Charles V*, i
(London, 1902), p. 164.

For their part the Eight were pleased to learn of the pope's consent. As the allocation of offices would lead to dispute, they decided to have the majority of cases settled by the cardinal of Cortona and Ippolito who was now old enough to begin to take control of the government as the regime required. The pope should be left the decision of the most important matters and they thought it advisable to keep Clement fully informed.[110]

Francesco Vettori's behaviour in Rome illustrates the dual rôle in which Florentines were liable to find themselves as servants of the pope and citizens of Florence. The Eight wanted Vettori to encourage the pope not to observe the truce with the imperialists which followed the Colonna raid. He was to urge Clement whenever possible to help the League in Lombardy, for a victory there would strengthen his hand in the negotiations for peace.[111] Vettori as a representative of the Eight faithfully conveyed these views to Clement, but at the same time in his capacity as servant of the pope he felt obliged to contradict them. Accordingly he encouraged Clement to summon forces to Rome so that he would not again be surprised by the Colonna, but warned him against attacking them or sending the naval captain Andrea Doria to blockade Genoa from the sea, which the pope considered he could do without breaking the truce.[112]

In replying to the Eight through Vettori, Clement said that he was concerned only with finding some way of bringing about peace with a view to future action against the Turks, and he understood that Charles' intention was the same. Meanwhile he proposed to keep the status quo as long as the imperialists did the same. In contradiction of his reply to the Eight and against Vettori's warning he attacked and occupied the Colonna castles and sent Andrea Doria to Genoa.[113]

During the truce Clement began negotiations for peace with the imperialists. In these Vettori was involved as the pope's confidential servant. In a letter of 26 October 1526 Vettori informed the Eight that Clement was sending Nicholas Schönberg,

---

[110] Otto, Missive, Legaz. e Comm., 18, fo. 87r, 23 Oct. 1526.
[111] Otto, Missive, Legaz e Comm., 18, fos. 86r-v.
[112] B.R.F. Ms. Moreni, 98, fo. 69v, F. Vettori to Jacopo Gianfigliazzi, 25 Dec. 1526; cp. *Sommario*, p. 371.   [113] *Sommario*, p. 371.

archbishop of Capua, to Naples to negotiate for peace and while he was writing Schönberg actually left.[114] Three letters written by Vettori to the archbishop for the pope and several letters from Filippo Strozzi to Vettori show the futility of these negotiations and the frustration of a Florentine like Strozzi who fearing for his life and liberty saw revolt as the only solution to the situation.

None of these three letters to Schönberg has a date, but internal evidence, for instance the arrival of Giovanni Bandini, which is mentioned in the first one and in a dispatch of the Florentine ambassador to the Eight dated 19 December, assigns it to this month and possibly also to this day.[115] On similar evidence the last one was written at the end of December.[116] The fact that Vettori was chosen to conduct the correspondence in preference to Gian Matteo Giberti, whose pro-French sympathies made him unacceptable to the imperialists, proves that Vettori was no longer suspected of such leanings.[117]

The first letter to Schönberg, in which Clement reiterates his previous loyalty to the emperor and his present hope of a treaty having convinced himself of Charles' good intentions towards all Christians, the Church, Italy and himself, points out the advantages which the emperor would derive from extending the truce for another six months: Charles could prepare for a renewed attack on France in the spring and in any case no decisive action could be fought during the present season. His forces could be maintained with relatively small expenditure and even if some were disbanded, additional troops could quickly be drafted from Germany. The pope makes it clear in this letter that he is prepared to abandon his allies.[118] It will be noticed that Clement has merely asked for the prolongation of the truce; he has made no offers of either financial or territorial advantage to the emperor as guarantees.

[114] Otto, Responsive, 46, fo. 6ov.

[115] G. Ruscelli, ii, p. 98; Otto, Responsive, 46, fo. 155r; cp. Strozzi's receipt of a letter from Vettori dated 19 Dec. under cover of one to Schönberg, C. Strozz., Ser. III, 108, fo. 97r.

[116] G. Ruscelli, p. 100, acknowledgment of letters dated 24 [December].

[117] *Ibid.*, ii, p. 98.

[118] *Ibid.*, p. 98v; the arguments now presented in favour of a truce are based on those previously used by France and Venice against it, Otto, Responsive, 46, fos. 60–1, 26 Oct. 1526.

By the time the third letter was written the emperor had made known his conditions for an extended truce; these included the surrender of Pisa and Livorno and a large sum of money. The pope answered that he considered the terms offered tantamount to war. If the emperor was determined to rob him of everything, he would have to get it by force.[119]

Vettori's personal view can be pieced together from a number of extant letters during the mission. In November he was one of a minority in Rome in favour of peace, even if the conditions were hard.[120] In December his view, still unchanged, was shared by the pope, who 'confessed' to Vettori that there was no remedy but peace.[121] By January, or possibly at the end of December, having learned the emperor's conditions, he had changed his opinion, and the operative factor was his concern for Florence. In a private letter dated 25 December to his friend Jacopo Gianfigliazzi, a member of the Eight, he professed that 'the city should suffer as little as possible'.[122] In the papal letter to Schönberg the point of view of the Eight was taken (unlike a few weeks before when Vettori gave personal alongside official advice to Clement) and it was argued that Pisa and Livorno could not be pledged for the maintenance of the truce 'primarily because the Florentine Signory do not wish it'.[123] Nor could money be given, as the pope was poor and Florence 'wretched and in desperate straits'.[124] His friend Ludovico Canossa put the reasons for Vettori's change succinctly when he wrote in a letter to him on 12 January 1527 that it seemed strange that as soon as the viceroy had demanded Pisa and Livorno the Florentines—and from the beginning of the letter it is clear that he included Vettori in this accusation—opposed such an agreement and suddenly considered that the means for conducting the war were available, almost as if they expected the pope to ruin the Church for the sake of Florence.[125]

[119] G. Ruscelli, ii, fo. 100r–v.

[120] B.R.F. Ms. Moreni, 98, fo. 66v, F. Vettori to Jacopo Gianfigliazzi, 7 Nov. 1526. Vettori says that 90 per cent of Roman opinion favours war; cp. *Sommario*, pp. 370–1.

[121] B.R.F. Ms. Moreni, 98, fo. 69v, F. Vettori to Jacopo Gianfigliazzi, 25 Dec. 1526.   [122] *Ibid.*, fo. 70v.

[123] G. Ruscelli, ii, fo. 100r; cp. above, p. 181, n. 112.   [124] *Ibid.*, fo. 99r.

[125] C. Strozz., Ser. I, 137, fos. 167v–168r, L. Canossa to F. Vettori, Venice, 12 Jan. 1527: 'se vui siete tale quale io vi tengo che nella patria vostra nè forse

The fate of Francesco Vettori's friend Filippo Strozzi, who was to play an important part in the future events of the city, was intimately linked with papal diplomacy. After the agreement of 21 September which followed the Colonna threat to Rome, he was kept prisoner in the Castel Nuovo in Naples as Don Ugo da Moncada's hostage.[126] While Vettori was in Rome, Strozzi, who was allowed to receive visitors and letters, kept him informed about the negotiations between the imperialists and the papal envoy. As their chance of success receded and with it the likelihood of his own release, Strozzi became desperate. As early as October the pope had attempted to get him freed, offering Alessandro de' Medici in his stead.[127] Another attempt was made in November, likewise without success.[128]

Finding that Schönberg's mission had failed, Strozzi wrote to Battista della Palla and Zanobi Buondelmonti concerning Vettori's imminent departure that it was better if he helped Florence in her need.[129] Very probably Strozzi's devoted wife Clarice had sought Vettori's help for her husband's release both in Florence, before she left for Rome to goad the pope into action,[130] and later in Rome. His departure caused her such distress that she fell ill. Her remark to Francesco del Nero that they had first taken away her husband and now Francesco Vettori indicates his close ties with this family,[131] as does also Filippo's to Vettori thanking God for friends like him and

altrove non si truovano molti simili a vui, ben vi confesso che mi (168r) è parso assai strano quando da diversi luoghi ho inteso che subito che'l Vice Re domandò Pisa et Lyvorno cominciasti vui Signori Fiorentini che havevate prima tanto persuaso l'accordo a dire che non era bene d'accordarsi et che non mancherebbe il modo di far la guerra et come non si parla più de le terre vostre tornate in sull'accordo, quasi come se al Papa convenghi ruinare la Chiesa purchè salvi le cose di Firenze'.

[126] C. Strozz., Ser. III, 127, fo. 220r: 'Promessa del Cardinale Pompeo Colonna a Filippo Strozzi di farlo liberare dal Castelnuovo dove è tenuto ostaggio, qualora la città di Firenze si sottragga al dominio mediceo', 21 Feb. 1527. Below, p. 187.

[127] *Calendar of Letters, Despatches and State Papers relating to the Negotiations between England and Spain* (ed. G. Bergenroth), iii, part 1 (1525–6), (London, 1877), p. 981.

[128] *Ibid.*, p. 994, 5 Nov.; p. 1008, 16 Nov.; p. 1018, 22 Nov.

[129] C. Strozz., Ser. I, 99, fo. 18r. F. Strozzi to Battista della Palla and Zanobi Buondelmonti, 'in Castello', 17 Jan. 1527.

[130] G.-B. Niccolini, pp. xl–xli.

[131] C. Strozz., Ser. III, 145, fo. 114r. Francesco del Nero to F. Vettori, Rome, 17 Jan. 1527.

Francesco del Nero who were more devoted to his interests than he deserved.[132]

How highly Filippo Strozzi and Francesco Vettori rated each other's friendship and political partnership can be gauged from the fact that a law suit between the Strozzi and Vettori families did not sever their ties. Since Paolo's death on his mission to the king of France, proceedings had been going on to secure for Giovanni Vettori part of Paolo's inheritance that Matteo Strozzi, brother of the widowed Francesca, claimed for her. The case caused Vettori, who hated litigation,[133] much anxiety. At one time he feared arrest; the pope had been consulted and showed disapproval and the family whom the Vettori were fighting was one of the most important and influential in Florence.[134] When Vettori's departure from Rome in January 1527 was determined, Filippo Strozzi recommended him to co-operate with Matteo so that both together could concern themselves with his affairs.[135] The good relations which Vettori established with Matteo after his return to Florence proved their worth in the events of 1527 and after 1530. It seems that Vettori suffered financial losses, which he could ill afford, in connection with this law suit,[136] but he rated political affairs higher than personal animosity.[137]

By the turn of the year 1526–7 several other leading Florentines besides Filippo Strozzi had come to realize that the pope's position was desperate and that little help for their city could be expected from Rome. The most frequently mentioned names in connection with the dramatic events of 1527 are those of Niccolò Capponi and members of the Salviati, Guicciardini and

[132] A. Bardi, 'Filippo Strozzi', p. 52.
[133] B.R.F. Ms. Moreni, 98, fo. 70v.
[134] O. Tommasini, ii, p. 1244, F. Vettori to N. Machiavelli, 5 Aug., 1526; *ibid.*, p. 1246, F. Strozzi to F. Vettori, 26 Aug. 1526.
[135] A. Bardi, 'Filippo Strozzi', p. 56.
[136] C. Strozz., Ser. V, 1209, fo. 151r. F. Vettori to F. Strozzi, 1 Aug. 1528: 'sendo in villa dove mi sono ridotto a stare . . . perchè Matteo per haver governato questa heredità di Pagolo a modo suo è suto causa che mio fratello si tiene male satisfacto di me et havendo la casa comune ho preso il partito che io vi dicho di sopra'. Cp. *Sacco*, p. 442 where Basilio (Vettori) speaks of his poverty on account of 'certi privati potenti' who have taken the greater part of what he had; above, p. 167, n. 34, for identity of Basilio.
[137] R. von Albertini, p. 438, F. Vettori to Bartolomeo Lanfredini.

Vettori families.[138] Filippo Strozzi's personal danger and
Jacopo Salviati's fears for his son's fate (though the latter was
not handed over)[139] gave these two citizens special incentives
for taking the initiative. On 30 December Filippo wrote to
Vettori, 'this bark of St Peter is sinking; it is time to jettison a
part to save the rest with their lives. If you believe that it cannot perish, I will soon enlighten you to the contrary.'[140] This
allusion to revolt was followed in January by a precise reference
to revolution.[141]

Strozzi became the centre of intrigue for the exiles and his
collaborator in Florence was Vettori. Varchi reports that
Zanobi Buondelmonti, together with Battista della Palla,
travelled from Siena, where they were in exile for their part in
the 1522 conspiracy against Cardinal Giulio de' Medici, to
Naples to discuss with Filippo Strozzi measures so that the city
should not 'in the wake of Clement's obstinacy and indifference
become a prey to the barbarians'.[142] On 17 January Strozzi
wrote to Battista della Palla and Zanobi Buondelmonti giving
them news of the bad state of affairs in Florence and information
about certain of the '*amici*', including Vettori.[143] Other letters
show the extent of his correspondence with potential rebels. One
already referred to mentions the expectation he had of Vettori's
co-operation after his return to Florence and the rôle which he
himself hoped eventually to play there.[144] With Palla and
Buondelmonti Strozzi discussed the means for his release and
informed them that Vettori had left Rome and would undertake
for the city 'everything expected of a good citizen'. He was
aware of what was going on and he, Strozzi, would keep him
informed of future plans. This letter contains interesting details.
The writer was to return to Florence from Rome by sea and
river. Use would be made of the 4000 infantry in the city which
however would need additional fortification. It still lacked a
leader and he would use the first opportunity to show the
citizens that he had 'that mind and will which should be the
mark of every *uomo da bene*'. In his castle prison he was con-

[138] *Calendar of Letters, Despatches and State Papers*, iii, part 2 (1527–9), pp. 27–8;
C. Roth, pp. 21, 34, n. 53; M. Sanuto, *Diarii*, xliv, 583.

[139] G.-B. Niccolini, p. xl.   [140] A. Bardi, 'Filippo Strozzi', p. 51.

[141] *Ibid.*, p. 55.   [142] B. Varchi, i, p. 111.

[143] C. Strozz., Ser. I, 99, fo. 18r.   [144] *Ibid.*

stantly reading Livy and Aristotle, the former for practical
advice, the latter for the conception of the civic virtues apper-
taining to an upper-class citizen.[145] Already in January, as a
letter to Lorenzo shows, Filippo considered that since there was
no hope of an agreement between the viceroy and the pope, it
would not be long before a revolution occurred in Florence.
Those thinking of reprisals against him as a Medici sympathizer and relative of the pope misunderstood him. If he were
in Florence his actions might already have demonstrated what
he could at present only express in words.[146] Cardinal Colonna's
undertaking dated 21 February to release Filippo Strozzi as
soon as Florence was withdrawn from Medici domination
establishes that Strozzi came to an agreement with the imperialists to effect a change of government in Florence.[147]

Zanobi Buondelmonti and Battista della Palla conducted a
propaganda campaign from Siena, tempting the hungry Florentine *Signori* with the offer of grain if they would free themselves
from Medici domination.[148] An entry for April 1527 in Sanuto's
Diarii records Zanobi Buondelmonti in Bourbon's camp and the
presence of exiled Florentines at the viceroy's camp. It also
mentions rumours among the Florentines that the city had come
to an understanding with the imperialists.[149] Already in January
Strozzi himself had expressed hope of active assistance from the
exiles in Siena.[150] He urged his brother Lorenzo to convey to
them his trust in their patriotism.[151]

Initially when Strozzi's plans for a secession of Florence from
Rome began to take shape, probably at about the time when all
hope for Schönberg's negotiations for a truce had to be abandoned, sometime towards the end of December, Vettori's
attitude was one of doubt and caution. He feared the consequences of a revolution supported by the rabble and exiles, and
he feared for his personal safety, presumably partly because he

[145] *Ibid.*, fos. 19r–21r.
[146] C. Strozz., Ser. III, 108, fo. 101r. 5 Jan. 1527, 'in castello'.
[147] Above, p. 184, n. 126.
[148] B.N.F. II, III, 433, fo. 8; C. Roth, p. 22 and p. 34, n. 61.
[149] M. Sanuto, *Diarii*, xlv, 26; C. Roth, p. 21.
[150] C. Strozz., Ser. I, 99, fo. 20, 30 Jan. 1526 'in castello'.
[151] C. Strozz., Ser. III, 108, fo. 101v. F. Strozzi to Lorenzo, 5 Jan. 1527 'in
castello'.

had been in the government when Cardinal Giulio banned these citizens. However when Strozzi had assured him of their goodwill towards him, writing that they would not wish to return without him in the city, and that they had great faith in his 'ability, sound judgment and intelligence',[152] Vettori must have been won over. Lorenzo Strozzi wrote in his biography of his brother Filippo that it was Francesco—according to common opinion one of the foremost and wisest of Florence's citizens—who suggested to Filippo that he should undertake secret negotiations on behalf of the city for an agreement with imperial agents in Naples. According to this agreement Filippo was to be set free against a surety of 50,000 crowns, presumably to take an active part in bringing about the revolution, but he would return to Naples if it had not occurred within three months. If the revolution broke out, he would be considered completely free.[153] That the Eight came to an agreement with the viceroy and the duke of Bourbon for the release of Filippo on payment of a certain sum of money is evident from his comment on this fact in a letter to his brother.[154] In the event, however, Filippo Strozzi was set free as a result of the humiliating agreement with the viceroy made by the pope himself on 15 March 1527.[155]

One more leading Florentine citizen needs to be introduced whose collaboration with Strozzi and Vettori was of vital importance in connection with the revolts of 1527. Niccolò Capponi's position was different from that of Filippo Strozzi, Francesco Vettori, Jacopo Salviati and Francesco Guicciardini in that he was not a papal servant. It is interesting to notice that Niccolò Capponi was a brother-in-law of Filippo Strozzi and Francesco Vettori, as family ties played an important part in the risings of 1527, many of the leaders being related by blood or marriage.[156] He was foremost among those who repeatedly requested self-determination for Florence from the pope. Probably in December during an interview with the cardinal of

---

[152] A. Bardi, 'Filippo Strozzi', p. 55.

[153] G.-B. Niccolini, p. xlii.

[154] C. Strozz., Ser. III, 108, fo. 107r. 16 April 1527; Cardinal Colonna's promise, above, p. 184, n. 126.

[155] G.-B. Niccolini, p. xliii; L. Pastor, ix, p. 371

[156] B. Segni, iii, p. 286; F. Nerli, p. 143.

Cortona he said that since the pope seemed determined upon war and the ruin of Italy, the time had come for the citizens to think of the peace of their afflicted city.[157] In January he asked for papal permission for Florence to govern herself,[158] to conduct her foreign policy separately from the pope's and to make an agreement with the imperialists. By April he was negotiating with the viceroy, probably to secure imperial forces to support, if need be, the city's move against the Medici.[159] In May Capponi and Vettori collaborated in the final stage of Strozzi's return to the city.[160]

The revolution in May 1527 which finally brought about the downfall of Medici government was preceded by a number of minor clashes. The first one occurred in November 1526 while Vettori was in Rome. The serious reverse of the papal forces and the death of the Medici captain, Giovanni delle Bande Nere at Borgoforte, near Mantua, had caused consternation in Florence and brought into the open a group of young aristocrats under the leadership of Piero Salviati who demanded arms, ostensibly to defend the city but also with a rising against the Medici in mind. They were supported by all who desired a more broadly-based government, but in particular in the *pratiche* and magistracies by Piero's cousin, Niccolò Capponi, his brother-in-law, Matteo Strozzi, and Luigi Guicciardini, the brother of the historian.[161] A dangerous situation arose when they came to blows with the civic guard.[162] Their request was refused and this concluded the first incident. At the end of March 1527 when Bourbon's forces moved in the direction of Tuscany, the request for arms was renewed, this time it was hoped with active support from the gonfalonier, Luigi Guicciardini.[163] But Guicciardini, unwilling openly to defy Cortona, resorted to clandestine consultations in his house in which he promised the issue of arms to those heading the sixteen companies into which the youths had divided themselves following the precedent of the ancient civic

---

[157] B. Segni, iii, p. 297.

[158] G. Ruscelli, ii, fo. 206v. Bishop of Pola to Niccolò Capponi, Rome, 15 Jan. 1527.

[159] *Ibid.*, p. 209v; C. Roth, p. 34, n. 50.   [160] Below, pp. 194–5.

[161] B. Varchi, i, pp. 103–4; B. Segni, i, pp. 7–8; F. Nerli, p. 145.

[162] F. Nerli, pp. 146–7; B. Varchi, i, pp. 104–5.

[163] F. Nerli, p. 148; B. Varchi, i, pp. 105, 116; B. Segni, p. 8.

militia.[164] On the other hand, Cortona consulted with some citizens in the Medici palace and was told by Niccolò Capponi that the gravity of the situation called for an official meeting in the Palazzo della Signoria, the traditional seat of government, and not in the Medici palace where Cortona resided.[165] This incident was equally inconclusive, and Bourbon's forces continued to advance. By 16 April the starving and ill-paid soldiers over whom their leaders had lost control had reached Florentine territory.[166] In the face of this danger Florence took the initiative and renewed her alliance with the League. The duke of Urbino, who was promised San Leo if he hurried to the defence of the city, was within four miles of the walls on 26 April.[167]

On that day another incident occurred. On the news that the distribution of arms had been conceded,[168] the companies and a large number of citizens had assembled in the churches of their respective quarters when the rumour spread that the cardinal of Cortona had left the city and 'taken God with him'. In fact, oblivious of the highly explosive situation, he had gone with Ippolito and Cardinals Ridolfi and Cibo, whom the pope had sent during the winter to Florence to strengthen the regime,[169] to a meeting with the leaders of the League and with Francesco Guicciardini, the lieutenant of the papal forces.[170] The weird combination of a row between a soldier and a man selling him a cap and a mule bolting triggered off the explosion.[171] The populace and the companies surged into the square outside the Palazzo della Signoria. To the accompaniment of the time-honoured cry of 'popolo e libertà', the young men seized the palace whose guard fled to a nearby church.

This spontaneous rising ran into grave difficulties. Ironically a carefully worked out plan for a serious rising on the next day existed but could have no bearing on this situation.[172] Only Francesco Vettori and Luigi Guicciardini took action. Having failed in his address from the rostrum to quell the tumult, the gonfalonier returned into the palace and the *Signoria* who had

[164] B. Varchi, i, pp. 117, 120; J. Nardi, ii, p. 114.
[165] F. Nerli, p. 148; B. Varchi, i, p. 118.
[166] *Sommario*, p. 375; F. Guicciardini, *St. d'It.*, v, p. 128; L. Pastor, ix, pp. 374–7.
[167] *Sommario*, p. 377.   [168] J. Nardi, ii, p. 114.
[169] B. Varchi, i, pp. 105–6.   [170] *Ibid.*, pp. 119–20; J. Nardi, ii, p. 114.
[171] J. Nardi, ii, pp. 114ff.; B. Varchi, i, pp. 120–1.   [172] C. Roth, p. 31.

been hastily summoned were asked to pass a resolution to banish the Medici.[173] Apparently this sudden proposition left them speechless. It was, according to Varchi, Vettori who broke the silence with the remark, echoing Tacitus, that this was a time for deeds not words, with the result that the voting box was passed round and the black beans indicated a unanimous vote in favour of expelling the Medici. A notary was found—the same who had drawn up the terms of 1512—and a formal resolution was composed: the Medici were to be banished, prisoners released and the constitution of 1512 restored.[174]

After these deliberations, the members of the *Signoria* retired to the rooms in the palace which they inhabited during their two months' term of office. Vettori with other leading citizens withdrew into the gonfalonier's room.[175] Once more his positive and circumspect action contrasts with the confusion and indecision of the others present: he drew up letters of credence for Bartolomeo Cavalcanti, who was to go as messenger to the duke of Urbino, to emphasize that the city did not intend to depart from its devotion to the pope and the Church, nor from its adherence to the League but only to free itself from the present form of Medici government.[176] Such a sentiment illustrates Florence's close association with the pope and the predicament of those citizens who were his servants. Perhaps because of his unique relationship with Clement and Cortona Vettori felt compelled to explain the city's position.

In the heat of events, defence measures such as guarding the city gates and garrisoning the palace had been ignored:[177] the Medici returned through one of the unguarded gates and the Piazza della Signoria was soon held by the advancing infantry. The palace was besieged and many within might have lost their lives had it not been for the intervention of Francesco Guicciardini who headed the infantry and had entered Florence with the returning Medici.[178] The terms of surrender of the Florentine citizens to the League were agreed between him and Vettori but opinions differ on their exact rôles. There is, too,

[173] J. Nardi, ii, pp. 115–17.   [174] B. Varchi, i, pp. 123–4.
[175] J. Nardi, ii, p. 118; B. Varchi, i, p. 126.
[176] J. Nardi, ii, p. 118; B. Varchi, i, p. 140.
[177] F. Nerli, p. 149.   [178] *Raccolto delle Azioni*, pp. 277–8.

some confusion with regard to the activities of the other mediator, Federigo da Bozzolo.

The first assault on the palace by the infantry who returned with the Medici had been driven off, largely owing to Jacopo Nardi's initiative in hurling missiles on the attackers from the palace battlements,[179] but a second onslaught was planned before nightfall to prevent the defenders from being reinforced under cover of darkness. While artillery was being brought up for the preliminary bombardment, Federigo da Bozzolo, a captain in the pay of the French, left the palace as a self-appointed peace-maker.[180] It would seem (following Cecil Roth's reconstruction of the events)[181] that Bozzolo had entered the palace at the height of the fray with the intention of pacifying the rioters, had met with no success, but did not manage to get out again and was thus at the mercy of both defenders and attackers. By offering to sue for peace he was allowed to leave the palace. Once outside, however, he intended to double-cross the defenders by advising the cardinals to attack but was dissuaded by Francesco Guicciardini, who acted as a patriot and at the same time as a protector of his brother and his friends. On Guicciardini's initiative the cardinal of Cortona agreed to send Bozzolo back to negotiate an agreement. His offer met with a mixed reception: the ardour of the young men for the fight conflicted with what Varchi is pleased to call the cowardice of the old.[182] Both his age and his reactions in similar situations in the past make it certain that Francesco Vettori would be in favour of a settlement and do his best to persuade all present of the wisdom of such a course. At any rate it was he who negotiated with Francesco Guicciardini, and the author of the *Azioni* attributes the decision to accept the terms of the capitulation to Vettori's efforts.[183] The part which each man played in these negotiations has been disputed. Varchi claims that Guicciardini drew up the agreement.[184] Vettori claims to have written it.[185] The verbs used by Varchi for Guicciardini and by Vettori of his action are 'dettare' and 'scrivere' respectively. The

---

[179] J. Nardi, ii, pp. 119–20; B. Varchi, i, pp. 130–1.

[180] B. Varchi, i, pp. 131–2, 134–6.   [181] C. Roth, p. 29.

[182] B. Varchi, i, p. 136.   [183] *Raccolto delle Azioni*, p. 278.

[184] B. Varchi, i, p. 137.   [185] *Sommario*, p. 378.

distinction to be made between the man responsible for a
dispatch and its scribe has often been referred to in investigating
authorship of diplomatic correspondence. When speaking of the
letters of credence given to Bartolomeo Cavalcanti, Nardi
says specifically that they were 'written and composed' ('scritte
e dettate') by Vettori.[186] If we reject his double claim, it would
follow that the terms of agreement were drawn up by Guicciardini and written down by Vettori. Alternatively, since
Vettori was one of the rebel citizens within the palace and
Guicciardini was with the forces of the League outside, as Roth
suggests, both could have been engaged from their respective
sides.[187]

The first of the revolts of 1527 had come to an end. By the
terms of the armistice the resolutions which the insurgents had
passed were annulled; all those who had taken part in the rising
were pardoned.[188] Francesco Vettori, together with Matteo
Strozzi and Niccolò Capponi, the other older leaders, went to
the Medici palace to excuse himself for the disorders which had
ensued.[189] As one who had been trusted by both Clement and
the cardinal, his position must, to say the least, have been
extremely uncomfortable and frightening.

The events of 26 April 1527 might perhaps have been
Florence's last bid for liberty if the military situation and the
arrival of Filippo Strozzi, freed from his imprisonment, had not
provided her with both the opportunity and the leader for
another revolt. The sack of Rome by the imperial troops under
Bourbon and the imprisonment of Clement VII in Castel S.
Angelo deprived Cortona of the likelihood of help from Rome,
and the treatment which Filippo Strozzi received at the hands
of the pope alienated him from the Medici cause. With the
ratification of the treaty between the pope and the imperialists
on 29 March, Strozzi was free to leave Naples.[190] On his arrival
in Rome he excused himself with Clement for the contact which
he had had with the rebels. The pope seemed to accept his
excuse, but neither thanked him for the inconvenience which he
had suffered on his behalf nor apologized for breaking the truce

[186] J. Nardi, ii, p. 118.   [187] C. Roth, p. 342.
[188] B. Varchi, i, p. 137.   [189] J. Nardi, ii, p. 121.
[190] L. Pastor, ix, pp. 371–2.

with Don Ugo da Moncada and thus putting his life in danger.
Clement further angered Strozzi by withholding a cardinal's hat
from his son. Filippo's earlier passion to show his compatriots
the mind and will of a true upper-class citizen was now inflamed
by the papal injury to his pride. Although no one was allowed
to leave Rome on Clement's express orders, Clarice obtained
permission to convalesce in Florence and to be accompanied by
her husband and their sons.[191] Strozzi departed on 4 May, two
days before the arrival of Bourbon's forces and the subsequent
sack, news of which reached Florence on the 12th.[192]

The reaction of the city, whose major interest in Rome was
financial, is described by Vettori. All the enemies of the Medici
were angry, especially as the sack had involved Florence in a
loss of many hundreds of thousands of ducats for which everyone
blamed the pope. Politically the scene was one of dismay and
fear. The Medici party could only remain in power through
force and for this a garrison of at least 3000 was needed, which
in the exhausted state of the city's finances Vettori reckoned she
could not afford. Therefore (having in effect concluded that the
regime was untenable) the Medici supporters, according to
Vettori, decided to put the honour and benefit of the city before
their personal welfare and persuaded the cardinal to relinquish
power.[193] Although Vettori's report is clearly coloured by his
desire to give the best possible interpretation of the course taken
by the *amici*, it leaves the reader in little doubt that papal
servants and Medici supporters had no further use for Medici
domination.

Strozzi led Florence's second attempt to end the Medici
regime, but without the support of Francesco Vettori, Niccolò
Capponi and members of the Strozzi family he might not have
succeeded. Having reached Livorno on his return journey,
Filippo wrote to his brother Lorenzo to sound Alfonso Strozzi,
Capponi and Vettori as to whether his appearance in Florence
was advisable.[194] At the same time as he received Capponi's
answering letter asking him to come to help free Florence from

---

[191] G.-B. Niccolini, p. xliii; B. Carnesecchi, 'L'Assedio di Firenze', pub. M. Lupo
Gentile in *Studi Storici*, xiv (Pisa, 1905), pp. 449, 450–1.
[192] *Sommario*, p. 381.   [193] *Ibid.*
[194] Ed. A. Bardi, 'Filippo Strozzi', p. 58, 11 May.

the Medici, Filippo received one from the cardinal of Cortona likewise soliciting his support. He decided to send his wife to Florence to find out the position.[195]

In the city the will of Vettori and the other leading citizens prevailed. When Clarice Strozzi reached Florence she was immediately visited by relatives and friends and, having heard their wishes, encouraged them, promising all possible help in so honourable an undertaking. The next morning she was taken by litter to the Medici palace where she had a meeting with the cardinal at which Vettori and Capponi were present. Greeting Cortona with the words, 'O Monsignor, Monsignor, where have you led us? Do you think that your methods are those of the great members of our house?' Clarice spoke so forcefully that Vettori and Capponi had to intervene. Later that morning she induced Ippolito de' Medici to leave the city voluntarily rather than wait until he was expelled. The conversation was cut short by an arquebus being fired outside the door, the result of a tumult in the palace and, one gathers, also in the city. Hence, protesting at being expelled, she left by the back door for her own house, and wrote to her husband to return forthwith.[196]

Vettori and Capponi who were present when the arquebus was fired, took fright and left the city for the comparative safety of Empoli. On their way they met Filippo Strozzi who must have awaited his wife's report not far from the city. On hearing the news of the firing incident, he and Vettori stayed at the Capponi villa at Legnaia while Capponi and Lorenzo Strozzi sought further information.[197]

Strozzi left for Florence on the following morning and was welcomed by the young men who wanted to overthrow the regime. Earlier on Clarice had been recalled to the Medici palace. In her presence the cardinal of Cortona had sent a deputation to the Palazzo della Signoria (where a pro-Medici government was still in office) to inform the magistrates that Florence was free to choose her own form of government, for he had resolved to surrender his power.[198] At the meeting which followed the news of the step taken by the cardinal, it was

[195] G.-B. Niccolini, p. xliv.
[196] B. Varchi, i, pp. 151–3.   [197] G.-B. Niccolini, pp. xlv, xlvi.
[198] G.-B. Niccolini, p. xlvii; B. Varchi, i, p. 154.

decided to banish the Medici from Florence. Vettori, who took an active part in the discussions, acted as mediator between the *Signoria* and the League and explained to the Venetian ambassador Foscari 'in suitable words' what had taken place.[199] Once again he was the official mouthpiece of the citizens as he had been after the abortive April rising.

Although Cortona and Ippolito had ceded to the *Signoria* the right to form a government of their choice, Ippolito evidently thought that the support of Filippo Strozzi (whom he received while the *Signoria* was discussing the message conveyed to them by the deputation) and his associates Capponi, Matteo Strozzi and Vettori could still reverse the situation. The *Signoria* was Medicean and 3000 paid soldiers were available to guard the Medici palace, the Palazzo della Signoria and the city gates.[200]

There is little doubt that if these four men had changed their minds and had not acted as Florentine patriots, the Medici regime need not have capitulated so quickly. Piero Nofri, captain of the 3000 infantry, considered that he could keep control of the city if money could be raised to pay the men, and according to Segni and Varchi, the cardinal of Cortona could have produced a substantial sum from his own resources.[201] As mentioned before, Vettori maintained in the *Sommario* that the city could not raise the money for the troops necessary to safeguard the regime owing to her great losses.[202] His rather summary dismissal of this important point fails to record the fact that Strozzi (or, as Segni claims, Capponi) had seized the money which could have been used to finance continuing military support for the Medici regime.[203] Nor does he mention that it was Strozzi, too, who dismissed the guard from the Palazzo della Signoria.[204]

Although Filippo Strozzi complied with Ippolito's request and agreed to go to the Palazzo della Signoria to do what he could for the Medici, by the time he arrived the decision to restore the city to republican government had already been taken. Strozzi returned to the Medici palace and told Ippolito that he had no intention of attempting anything which would detract

---

[199] M. Sanuto, *Diarii*, xlv, 139–41. [200] B. Varchi, i, p. 155.
[201] B. Segni, iii, p. 302; *ibid.*, i, p. 13; B. Varchi, i, pp. 154, 159.
[202] *Sommario*, p. 381. [203] B. Varchi, i, p. 153; B. Segni, iii, pp. 302–3.
[204] B. Varchi, i, pp. 157, 159.

from the favour which the young Medici had won with the people by giving them their liberty and he suggested that he should stand by his original concession. Ippolito and the cardinal demanded a copy of the proceedings in the palace and Filippo reported their request to the *Signoria* who sent them the conditions drawn up by the *pratica*.[205] It was at this point that Filippo dismissed the guard from the Medici palace and together with Niccolò Capponi advised Ippolito and the cardinal of Cortona to leave Florence for Poggio a Caiano. The *Signoria* appointed two commissioners to accompany the Medici out of the city. They were joined by Filippo Strozzi and, according to one account, by Francesco Vettori.[206]

[205] *Ibid.*, pp. 56–8.
[206] B. Varchi, i, pp. 159–60; B. Segni, i, p. 18 gives Vettori's name.

CHAPTER IX

Between Pope and Popolo (1527–30)

THE PROVISION passed by the pro-Medici *Signoria* on 16 May, the day before Ippolito and Cardinal Cortona left the city, shows the type of government which the leading citizens would have liked.[1] It would have differed little in composition from that before the revolution. The *Signoria* was to remain in office until the end of its term. The restoration of the republican Great Council was not to take place until a month later and in the meantime the government was to be in the hands of a council of 120. The 120 were to be elected by the existing magistracies and were to take over the duties of the Council of the Hundred. Perhaps this body was inspired by the 140 which Leo X had wanted in 1513.[2] In any case, together with the *Signoria*, the Seventy and the *Balìa*, it was to elect a committee of twenty to be responsible for the reorganization of the Great Council. In this way the power of the Medici party would have continued through the influence of the new council of 120 on the executive and of that of the twenty on the Great Council. Critics considered that Filippo Strozzi and other citizens concerned intended to establish a form of government which they called 'putting the state in store' until they could see what happened to the pope.[3] Whatever designs the principal citizens had in mind were, however, frustrated. At daybreak on 18 May malcontents assembled in the *Piazza* protesting against the government.[4] The *Signoria* met but, despite concessions, including the dismissal of the Eight of Ward (*Otto di Guardia*) responsible for state security, the clamour increased and Niccolò Capponi had eventually to promise to advance the date of the opening of the

---

[1] Details of the constitution of 16 May and of the reforms between 18 and 31 May are taken from C. Roth, pp. 45–54 and Appendix, Documents 2 and 3, pp. 349ff.

[2] Above, p. 81.

[3] B.N.F. II, III, 433, fo. 147r, Piero Giugni, 'Caso del Venerdì 1527'.

[4] B. Varchi, i, pp. 165–6.

Great Council,[5] and after some discussion the *Signoria* issued a proclamation calling for a meeting of it in three days' time. Accordingly amid much rejoicing the Great Council met on 21 May, a month earlier than originally planned.[6] During the next ten days the real constitutional revolution took place. As in 1494 and 1512, so in 1527, slight immediate change in the constitution eventually gave way to a more radical settlement. The Eight of Ward were appointed from members of the new regime; the Medicean Eight (*Otto di Pratica*) were replaced by the Ten (*Dieci di Libertà e Pace*), the republican equivalent. The members of the Eighty (*Ottanta*) retired and a fresh election took place. The committee of twenty chosen (as a concession on the part of the 120) in the Great Council instead of by the existing Medicean councils, decided, as their functions entitled them, upon the conditions of office of the gonfalonier. He was to be elected for one year, with the possibility of re-election for a second term. With the election of Niccolò Capponi to this office on 31 May, the constitutional work of the revolution was accomplished.[7] The oligarchical constitution of 16 May had favoured the optimates but after the revisions the leaders of that class would have been politically deprived had it not been for the attitude towards them of the new gonfalonier.

As we have seen, Niccolò Capponi was one of those who like Francesco Vettori had been a prominent member of the cardinal of Cortona's government but had revolted against the Medici when all else failed. By birth and kinship Capponi belonged to the new ruling group of the optimates but his past connection with the Medici led their friends (the *Palleschi*) to hope for toleration in the new regime. Capponi himself seems also to have hoped for the continued support of the Savonarola-inspired republican element (the *Piagnoni*) whose votes combined with the more moderate of the other two parties had secured his election.[8] What Varchi refers to as 'the party, or rather faction, of Niccolò, or of Capponi' was thus a coalition and a centre party.[9] It contained young men such as Piero

[5] B. Segni, *Vita di Niccolò Capponi*, p. 307; B. Varchi, i, p. 167.

[6] J. Nardi, ii, pp. 127–8; B. Varchi, i, p. 170. Provision of 20 May in C. Roth, Appendix 3, pp. 351–3; deliberations of 22 May, C. Roth, p. 50.

[7] B. Varchi, i, pp. 175, 189–91; C. Roth, p. 53.

[8] B. Varchi, i, pp. 207–15; C. Roth, pp. 61–2.   [9] B. Varchi, i, p. 208.

Salviati,[10] whose father Jacopo's republican inclinations have frequently been pointed out before; Capponi's own son, Piero,[11] and the young aristocrat Alamanno Pazzi,[12] son of Antonio who, like Francesco Vettori, had been a member of the Florentine ceremonial embassy to Clement VII in 1524, but, unlike him, had not opposed the pope's intention to send to Florence the two young Medici, Alessandro and Ippolito.[13] But older men too were associated with it: Matteo Strozzi and Roberto Acciaiuoli from among the inner circle of the former Medici government;[14] the *Pallesco*, Francesco Serristori,[15] and perhaps, too, Jacopo Guicciardini, who was later to support Capponi's extreme republican successor, the gonfalonier Francesco Carducci.[16] In opposition to the centre party were the more extreme republicans, the *Arrabbiati*, drawn largely from the lower classes but including also some of the less moderate or more ambitious *Piagnoni* and a few of the more unruly members of the upper classes. Before long their leader, Baldassare Carducci, was to epitomize anti-Medici sentiment.

The domination of the Savonarolan republicans gave Capponi's government a distinct 'theocratic tinge':[17] sumptuary laws were passed regulating luxury in dress; gambling was prohibited and censorship of books introduced. In addition, many anti-Medicean measures were taken as a concession to the *Arrabbiati*. One was the Great Council's appointment of the *Sindachi del Comune*,[18] five citizens detailed to examine the public accounts, later to be known as the *Tribolanti* (tormentors) owing to their severity.[19] Their examination was to be taken back to the beginning of the Medici regime in 1512. Anyone found, through fraud or favour, to be in debt to the state was in their power.[20] Another commission of five citizens was the assessor of the *balzello* (extraordinary tax) of 70,000 to 80,000 ducats which particularly hit wealthy pro-Medici citizens.[21] The *Quarantia*

[10] *Ibid.*, p. 502; B.N.F., Ms. Ginori Conti, 29, 32, insert 3, fo. 13r for members of 'questa setta capponescha', see below, p. 237, n. 76.

[11] B. Varchi, i, pp. 256–7.

[12] *Ibid.*, p. 502; below, p. 237, n. 76. [13] *Ibid.*, p. 64, above, p. 163, n. 2.

[14] Above, p. 173. [15] Below, p. 237.

[16] F. Nerli, p. 189; below, pp. 219, 221. [17] C. Roth, p. 62.

[18] Provvisioni, 206, fo. 3r, 4 June 1527; B. Varchi, i, p. 219.

[19] B. Varchi, i, p. 253; C. Roth, p. 65. [20] C. Roth, p. 65; below, p. 204.

[21] *Ibid.*, p. 65; Provvisioni, 206, fo. 7r 11 June 1527.

(an extraordinary judicial tribunal) which had been in force at the time of Piero Soderini, could also be a powerful weapon in the hands of extremists. On account of the greater number of members it was considered less susceptible to pressure than the smaller *Otto di Guardia*, and although right of appeal did exist from it to the Great Council, a sentence passed by the *Quarantia* could be quashed only by a two-thirds majority.[22]

Had it not been for Niccolò Capponi's particular policy towards the pope, to which reference will be made later,[23] the position of Francesco Vettori in the Republic would have been politically most frustrating. We saw that he had been one of those who drew up the new constitution on the day before the Medici left the city,[24] and Busini confirms the importance of Vettori at this juncture, mentioning that he was one of the very few citizens responsible for the reform of the constitution.[25] But he was given no official position after May 1527, although he was well disposed towards the gonfalonier, who called him in to give advice in the *pratiche*. He was not one of the Ten, although his brother Giovanni was elected both in December 1527 and in December 1529.[26] He was not a member of the Eight of Ward, though he had served twice before 1527.[27] He had on four occasions before May 1527 been one of the twelve *procuratori* but the office had now been abolished.[28] However, he does seem to have had some share in the legislation in the Great Council for the re-introduction of the *Quarantia*.[29]

As after Lorenzo de' Medici's death, again Vettori's connections with the previous regime made him suspect. For one who had worked with the cardinal of Cortona and who had been more or less continually resident in Florence the situation must have been more delicate than, say, for Filippo Strozzi who had been away and who had been treated as a saviour on his return. Busini maintains that suspicion limited the action of those few citizens, of whom Vettori was one, who undertook the immediate

---

[22] C. Roth, pp. 65–6.
[23] Below, pp. 206 ff.
[24] Above, p. 196; M. Sanuto, *Diarii*, xlv, 139–41.
[25] G. Busini, *Lettere*, p. 8.   [26] Tratte, 84, fos. 48v, 46r.
[27] Elected Sept. 1518 and May 1523. Tratte, 84, fos. 86v, 88r.
[28] Elected Oct. 1518, Oct. 1523, Oct. 1525, April, 1527. Tratte, 84, fos. 52v, 49v, 50r; above, p. 160.   [29] G. Busini, *Lettere*, p. 49.

reform of the constitution.[30] When he wrote to Lanfredini in July he refrained from telling his friend even such news as he had, in order to avoid having to render account before any magistrate either for works, words or letters.[31] He was then living for safety's sake outside Florence, as were Francesco and Luigi Guicciardini.[32]

An example of the kind of situation for which the previous servants of the Medici might be blamed is provided by the quarrel over the transfer to the new republican government of the fortresses of Pisa and Livorno in accordance with the terms of the agreement drawn up the day before the Medici left the city. As we have seen, Filippo Strozzi with two commissioners had accompanied the Medici out of Florence. He was also to superintend the reversion of the two fortresses.[33] According to Varchi, Ippolito de' Medici and Cardinal Passerini wrote to the castellans informing them that they had surrendered the government of the city to the *Signoria*, and ordering the handover to whoever was appointed by the *Signoria* to take charge. The castellans however refused to act without first receiving authorizations in accordance with their instructions (*contrassegni*).[34] Since only the pope knew their formula, the transfer of the fortresses to the new regime was in effect withheld. The resulting dispute was to cause the Florentines much trouble and Vettori and Strozzi were held responsible, Vettori less so since he merely accompanied the Medici and their escorts as far as San Donato in Polverosa.[35] Busini, who hated Vettori, considered that if any one man was responsible for the castellans' resistance to the Republic's regaining the fortresses, it must be Vettori who, he maintained, was always considered 'astute and dissimulating'.[36] Certainly Vettori was not ignorant of what was

---

[30] *Ibid., Lettere*, p. 8.

[31] R. von Albertini, p. 422; cp. similar attitude of Roberto Acciaiuoli, C. Strozz., Ser. I, 137, fos. 269r, 270r, letter to Jacopo Salviati, Florence, 12 Feb. 1528: 'non vi ho scripto . . . dubitando non nocere a noi et a me'.

[32] F. Guicciardini, 'Ricordanze' in *Scritti Autobiografici e Rari*, ed. Palmarocchi, p. 95. Guicciardini sent his wife to Venice.

[33] B. Varchi, i, p. 160; B. Segni, i, p. 19.

[34] B. Varchi, i, p. 160; cp. corroboration of Varchi's statement in C. Strozz., Ser. I, 353, fo. 50v, cp. B.N.F. II, III, 433, fos. 17r, 18r.

[35] B. Varchi, i, pp. 160, 171; B. Segni, i, p. 18.

[36] G. Busini, *Lettere*, p. 7.

going on. Giovanni Corsi, a convinced Medicean,[37] who together with a commissioner and the captain had entered the
fortress of Pisa to try to persuade the castellan, Paccione, to
surrender it, wrote to Vettori on 18 May appealing for his
help.[38] Corsi believed Paccione's refusal to hand over without
the *contrassegni* to be due to a desire to await the outcome of
events in Rome. Similar difficulties were expected in Livorno.
The fact that Corsi appealed to Vettori to see that the *contrassegni* were sent shows that he thought Vettori was in a position
to get them dispatched, but we do not know whether he did
what Corsi asked for. Strozzi we know was hoodwinked when he
enlisted the help of Ippolito in the matter but was subsequently
blamed for allowing him to escape from Pisa to Lucca.[39] His
reputation was tarnished by this episode; on his return from
Pisa he was virtually ignored by the government. After the
death of his wife in May of the following year, he left Florence
for France.[40]

For Vettori, as for several of his class, the period of republican
government brought financial ruin. Antonio Soriani, the Venetian ambassador in Rome, reported that taxation weighed
particularly upon the partisans of the Medici.[41] In June and
October 1527, and in May of the following year, Francesco
Guicciardini had to contribute to the forced loan, and in 1529
he had to run into debt in order to pay.[42] By 1529, if not before,
Vettori himself had to contribute heavily to the *balzello*, as
emerges from a letter he wrote from Bologna. It makes pathetic
reading. 'In Florence', he informs Bartolomeo Lanfredini, 'they
have again imposed a *balzello*, that is the *Signoria* has imposed it
on whom it chooses to. I am taxed at fifty ducats for whose payment I shall sell some strong boxes and chests which were in
Siena and which you have often seen. I have nothing else in the
house and little remains to me except my wife, [Madda]lena,
and because she knows that I have no money, she has pawned
all her clothes and mine.' His wife had had money transferred to

[37] R. von Albertini, p. 110, n. 1.
[38] C. Strozz., Ser. I, 98, fo. 252r.
[39] B. Varchi, i, pp. 172–4; G.-B. Niccolini, pp. li–liv.
[40] G.-B. Niccolini, p. liv.
[41] C. Roth, p. 65.
[42] *Ibid.*; R. Ridolfi, *The Life of Francesco Guicciardini*, pp. 181–2.

the Capponi in Siena where Bindo [Altoviti] was instructed to pay Vettori 150 ducats, of which he had already used fifty.[43]

As far as judicial discrimination is concerned, Vettori seems to have been more fortunate than others. Benedetto Buondelmonti was accused as early as 1527 by the *Tribolanti* of being 1000 crowns in the debt of the state. When his men tried to resist the sequestration of his goods, Buondelmonti was arrested. The matter was judged an affair of state and referred by the Eight of Ward to the *Quarantia*, by whom Buondelmonti was sentenced to four years' imprisonment.[44] Francesco del Nero, treasurer before the Medici expulsion, was prosecuted by the *Sindachi del Comune*,[45] the appointed auditors of public accounts of the period 1512–27, although Filippo Strozzi had persuaded Niccolò Capponi to burn one book of accounts for which Francesco was answerable, in order to avoid this calamity.[46] That during Niccolò Capponi's two terms of office no proceedings were taken against Vettori may have been due to the great care he took to avoid being summoned by the magistrates.[47] He may also have been saved by being related to Rinaldo di Filippo di Bertoldo Corsini, who perhaps helped to get Francesco del Nero's incriminating account book destroyed. In the summer of 1528, as del Nero informed Strozzi, Corsini was appointed one of the five *Sindachi del Comune*.[48] He was the grandson of Vettori's aunt Bartolomea Vettori and Bertoldo Corsini,[49] and del Nero hoped that through him Vettori might be useful in the matter of a book of accounts kept at the time of Roberto de' Ricci's treasurership under Lorenzo, duke of Urbino.[50] Since Roberto's name was a cover for Filippo Strozzi's *de facto* tenure of the

[43] R. von Albertini, p. 424.   [44] B. Varchi, i, pp. 254–5.

[45] B. Carnesecchi, 'L'Assedio di Firenze', pub. M. Lupo Gentile in *Studi Storici*, xiv (Pisa, 1905), pp. 456–7.

[46] B. Segni, iii, p. 312.

[47] Above, p. 202.

[48] C. Strozz., Ser. V, 1209, fo. 118r, Florence, 28 June 1528, Francesco del Nero to Filippo Strozzi.

[49] B.N.F. Ms. Passerini, 3. 8., fo. 69r. Bartolomea was Piero Vettori's sister.

[50] Above, n. 48 and p. 200: 'E nuovi sindachi furono Bernardo da Verrassano, Raffaello Mazzinghi, Carlo Bellacci, Rinaldo Corsini et Erasmo Marucelli a quali Batista ha dato notitia di ciò ch'è scripto in sul quel mio libro a tempo di Ruberto de' Ricci et datine loro la ciptà . . . io credo si domandi Carlo in mia racomandatione, . . . et Francesco Vettori sarebbe buono con Rinaldo Corsini che è suo nipote per conto del libro a tempo di Ruberto de' Ricci.'

office of treasurer,[51] Vettori would undoubtedly be concerned about the fate of any accounts kept at that time. It was therefore presumably in connection with this matter that he had spoken to Rinaldo in August 1528 and that he had high hopes of Rinaldo's help, as he wrote to Strozzi.[52] When Vettori was in the end summoned before the Eight of Ward, it was not on account of his activities in the earlier years of the Medici restoration but on a charge of associating with Clement VII.[53]

As often before, events outside Florence influenced her domestic policy. At the time of the revolt against the Medici Florence was a member of the League of Cognac, but the leaders of the revolt had already conspired with the imperialists;[54] and in June when the vital issue of the city's future diplomatic policy was discussed, the new gonfalonier considered an alliance with the victorious emperor to be safer for the city than a reaffirmation of the one with France. So strong, however, was the republican tradition of the association of the two lilies (tinged as it was by memories of Savonarola) that Capponi had to yield. On 22 June 1527 Florence took the fatal decision to remain a member of the League of Cognac, with the obligation to supply a contingent of 4000 foot soldiers and 400 horse.[55]

The error of this decision was not, however, immediately apparent. Partly as a result of the French sending an army in the pope's support, Charles V agreed on 26 November to release Clement from his captivity.[56] The pope could therefore be expected to view with favour the military successes of the French forces under Lautrec; but within an ace of victory Lautrec's army, to which the Florentines had loyally made their contribution, was decimated by plague in the summer of 1528. The city of Naples, which had seemed about to fall to the besiegers, was

---

[51] M. Parenti, Istorie, B.N.F. Ms. II, IV, 171, fo. 115v, May 1515: Filippo Strozzi replaces Galeotto de' Medici in Lorenzo's favour. Lorenzo takes from Galeotto the 'conto del depositario' and gives it to his brother-in-law Filippo Strozzi, although 'in facto' 'col nome fussi di Ruberto de' Ricci'; also, above, p. 141.

[52] C. Strozz., Ser. V, 1209, fo. 151r, Florence, 1 Aug. 1528, F.V. to Filippo Strozzi: 'Ho parlato a Rinaldo Corsini et mi promette molto bene et io l'ho per buono et per huomo che non promettessi quello non volessi fare, nondimeno non ardisco promettermi delli huomini et maxime in questi tempi.'

[53] Below, p. 220.   [54] C. Roth, p. 69.

[55] B. Segni, iii, p. 316; B. Varchi, i, pp. 176–88; C. Roth, pp. 70–1.

[56] L. Pastor, ix, ch. 12 and p. 463.

saved for Spain, and in August Lautrec's retreating remnant capitulated.[57] Italy's future now lay in the hands of Charles V.

Florence had made her choice, but the pope had not committed himself to France, and little political acumen was now required to forecast that he would eventually come to terms with the emperor, as he in fact did at Barcelona in June 1529. He was also likely to insist on the restoration of his family to Florence as the price of an alliance with Charles. In fact, the settlement of 29 June 1529 was sealed by Charles V's promise to give the hand of his illegitimate daughter Margaret to Alessandro de' Medici, who was to be ruler of the city.

Ever since Clement's release from Castel S. Angelo in December 1527 an agreement between pope and emperor, which would spell disaster for the Republic, was a possibility Niccolò Capponi had foreseen and tried to forestall by a *rapprochement* between his city and the pope. Owing to the fierce opposition of the *Arrabbiati* to such a policy, negotiations had had to be secret. The success of the policy had also depended on collaboration with many of the former Medici supporters. The effect of foreign affairs upon Niccolò Capponi's policy gave the optimates the influence in his government which offset to some extent their lack of power. If the discovery of Capponi's negotiations with Clement had not brought about the gonfalonier's downfall, possibly before long a government of optimates would have been established with papal connivance. It would undoubtedly have been more broadly based than that which was to come into being after the fall of the Republic when the pope was in a victorious position.

Capponi's contact at the papal court was Jacopo Salviati, now one of the pope's most confidential servants.[58] Owing to the need for secrecy, Capponi had maintained only an indirect association with Salviati. One of those through whom news was passed between Florence and Orvieto, whither the pope had fled on his release from captivity, must have been Ugo Gambara, the governor of Bologna.[59] In a letter of 24–5 December 1527

---

[57] F. Guicciardini, *St. d'It.*, v, pp. 209–10, 228–30; L. Pastor, x, pp. 24–5.

[58] B. Segni, iii, pp. 319–20; B. Varchi, i, p. 487.

[59] B. Varchi, i, p. 507; B.N.F., II, III, 433, fo. 197r, decoded fo. 207r; signature 211r; J. Nardi, ii, pp. 147–51; C. Roth, Appendix 5, pp. 355–6. Roth does not give

written to Salviati, Gambara mentions an interview with Niccolò Capponi in which the gonfalonier had said in so many words that if the pope did not insist on ruling Florence himself but let affairs rest in the hands of the leading citizens, there would be many upper-class citizens who with papal support would bring matters to 'a good end'. What this 'good end' might have been is indicated by the Venetian ambassador Foscari's allusion to an understanding with the pope after a revolution in favour of the optimates.[60] Donato Giannotti's *Discorso sopra il fermare il governo di Firenze* written for the gonfalonier indicates the type of government they were visualizing.[61] Giannotti recognized that every government depended for existence on the satisfaction of its supporters and since 'men live contentedly and quietly when they obtain or see the way to obtaining their desires', the government which gave its supporters the opportunity to satisfy their wishes would be considered the best. Accordingly, realizing that some citizens desired liberty, others honour and the most ambitious the position of prince, he believed that the best type of constitution for Florence would be one combining elements of popular liberty with the upper-class desire for honour. He suggested a pyramid structure with a Great Council at the base, a gonfalonier for life as its apex and in between twelve *procuratori* and an aristocratic senate of a hundred. In the letter to Zanobi Bartolini which accompanied the definitive version of this *Discorso* in 1530, Giannotti wrote that the pope could elect the senate, the *procuratori* and the gonfalonier on the first occasion, provided that members of these bodies were elected in accordance with the proposals made in his discourse on subsequent occasions. 'In this way', he went on, 'the Pope will be able to place the government in the hands of his friends to the satisfaction and contentment of the city.'[62]

Violent opposition to Capponi's policy on the part of the

the name of the writer; the version in cipher (fo. 197r) is, however, signed by Gambara and its cover addressed to Salviati in Orvieto (fo. 211v).

[60] M. Foscari, *Relazione* in E. Albèri, Ser. II, i, p. 76.

[61] D. Giannotti, *Opere politiche e letterarie*, ed. F.-L. Polidori, i (Florence, 1850), pp. 3–15; R. Starn, *Donato Giannotti and his Epistolae* (Travaux d'humanisme et Renaissance, 97, 1968); for an analysis of this *Discorso*, R. von Albertini, pp. 113–15; cp. F. Gilbert, 'The Venetian Constitution' etc. in *Florentine Studies*, ed. N. Rubinstein, p. 498, n. 1 for dating.   [62] D. Giannotti, *Opere*, i, p. 2; pp. 3–6.

Arrabbiati had caused the gonfalonier to rely increasingly on the optimates. In the *pratiche* he had drawn upon their experience to such an extent that in August 1528 a law had been introduced which abolished his freedom to summon to them anyone he wished.[63] Henceforth a *pratica* had to consist of twenty citizens (the *Arroti*) elected twice annually in the Great Council, together with past and present members of the Ten.[64]

Given Vettori's relationship with Capponi and their and Strozzi's participation in the revolution, it is not surprising to find that Vettori was one of those whose advice the gonfalonier had sought in the *pratiche* held before the reform of August 1528. Segni's information on this point is of interest for he shows that Niccolò Capponi was bound by ties of friendship or relationship to all the optimates who had been foremost in the government of the Medici and to those who had been friends of the pope, and that it was with their help that he had restored Florence to liberty. In consequence it had appeared to him unjust to ill-treat by word or deed those whose honour and long experience in affairs of state warranted their participation in the councils of the Republic. For this reason Francesco Vettori, Matteo Strozzi, Francesco Guicciardini and others like them were summoned to the *pratiche*.[65]

Lack of evidence makes it difficult to establish with any precision Vettori's views on Capponi's policy and even whether he had been involved during the summer of 1528 in the secret negotiations with the pope reported by the Ferrarese ambassador.[66] According to Segni, such citizens as Francesco Vettori, Francesco Guicciardini, Roberto Acciaiuoli and Filippo Strozzi who were reckoned to be great friends of the pope were very well disposed towards Niccolò Capponi for whose integrity and goodness they had great respect. Whatever their feelings for the Medici, they would not have lifted a finger for them while Capponi was gonfalonier.[67] It is tempting to assume (but there

[63] J. Nardi, ii, p. 147.

[64] C. Roth, p. 116; 1st election 28 Aug.; J. Pitti, 'Storia Fiorentina', i, p. 157; B. Varchi, i, pp. 486–7; J. Nerli, pp. 186–7; F. Gilbert, 'The Venetian Constitution' p. 498, n. 1.

[65] B. Segni, i, pp. 40–1; J. Pitti, i, p. 145.

[66] A. Rossi, *Francesco Guicciardini e il governo fiorentino dal 1527 al 1540*, i (Bologna, 1896), p. 118, n. 2, dispatch 14 Aug. 1528.   [67] B. Segni, i, p. 159.

is no evidence) that Vettori knew about Capponi's later negotiations with the pope and that he had been consulted on the proposed new constitution—he must have been considered an expert administrator by now. His relationship with Rinaldo Corsini, who is mentioned by Varchi as one of Capponi's party,[68] may have been an added recommendation. Rinaldo was one of the priors in November–December 1528,[69] and was to sponsor the decision to decapitate Jacopo Alamanni,[70] the headstrong ringleader of Capponi's opponents whose threats had sent Filippo Strozzi into exile.[71]

Whatever the extent of Vettori's involvement in Niccolò's attempted *rapprochement* with Clement, the fall of the gonfalonier in April 1529, on the discovery of his secret negotiations with the pope, and the subsequent election of the more extreme republican, Francesco Carducci, removed his main link with the regime and, since the extreme republicans were so bitterly opposed to those of his class, made the chance of further association with the government unlikely.[72] Indeed only two months after Capponi's downfall Vettori gave vent to his political and social frustration in a letter to his friend Filippo Strozzi.[73] Through no fault of his own, Vettori wrote, he seemed to become more suspect every day. For this reason he refused to tell Strozzi even private news as this would, he says, inevitably involve some discussion of public matters which would harm Strozzi and himself. Socially, the new laws against gambling made life very tedious for one who was indulgent towards it[74] and whose great delight was a game with Machiavelli. As he relates, he was himself willing to run the risk of an offence against the law by playing, but others were not. The religious character of the regime was also a potential danger to Vettori; his boredom with ancient history and the works of Livy made him curious to read Erasmus and other works printed in Germany or the Low Countries, but his fear of being considered a Lutheran with its

[68] B. Varchi, i, p. 454; above, p. 204.
[69] Tratte, 94, fo. 12r.   [70] B. Varchi, i, p. 454.
[71] *Ibid.*, i, p. 392; B. Segni, i, pp. 75–6; later, Alamanni seized Giachinotto Serragli, the go-between employed by Capponi in his correspondence with Jacopo Salviati, see J. Nardi, ii, p. 148; F. Nerli, p. 173.
[72] For the fall of Capponi, see C. Roth, pp. 115–29.
[73] C. Strozz., Ser. V, 1209, fo. 73, 1 June 1529.   [74] Above, p. 9.

attendant penalties prevented him from doing so. It was at this
time, as Vettori mentions, that Antonio Brucioli, who had been
involved in the plot against Cardinal Giulio de' Medici, was
arrested on a charge of heresy and also for his political opinions.
He had read the works of Luther to some young men and disputed about the Faith with the friars of St Mark's; in addition,
he was thought to have written to the king of France declaring
that the government of Florence had come into the hands of the
people and that the aristocrats were held in such suspicion and
were so badly treated that if something were not done, the
Republic would not long survive.[75]

Exasperation with life in Florence and a longing to see Strozzi
are probably sufficient explanation for the desire Vettori expressed to join his friend in Venice where the latter intended to
go and summon his son.[76] It would be interesting to know
whether any political motive underlay their projected visits.
Perhaps not, since at a time when Alessandro de' Pazzi's request
for a permit to go to Rome aroused controversy in the *pratiche*,[77] Vettori seemed to think he would have no difficulty in
obtaining the necessary permission to travel to Venice. On the
other hand, a plot on behalf of the Medici by Florentine
citizens living there had been suspected only the previous
month[78] and Vettori and Strozzi may have wanted to establish
contact with these compatriots.

Vettori may not have been granted permission to go to Venice
and, as we shall see, the next months proved important ones
both for him and the city, culminating in his dispatch to the
pope at Bologna in September 1529.

This embassy was necessitated by the alliance between pope
and emperor against Florence which Niccolò Capponi had tried
to prevent. The treaty of Barcelona was followed just over a
month later by the peace of Cambrai (5 August)[79] in which
Francis for the return of his two hostage sons had promised to
abstain from interference in Italian affairs and renounced all his

---

[75] C. Strozz. *Inventario*, i, p. 369, Ciaio Ottaviani, notary, Florence, 29 May
1529; B. Varchi, i, pp. 530–4; C. Roth, p. 135; for life of Brucioli, v. G. Spini, *Tra
Rinascimento e Riforma. Antonio Brucioli* (Firenze, 1940).

[76] Above, p. 209, n. 73; in 1528 F. Guicciardini had already sent his wife there,
above, p. 202, n. 32.

[77] C. Roth, p. 135.   [78] *Ibid.*   [79] L. Pastor, x, pp. 59–60.

rights in the peninsula, thus leaving his loyal Florentine allies to the mercy of the emperor. Shortly after, Charles came to Italy to establish his control and on 13 August news reached Florence that he had arrived at Genoa on the previous day.[80]

Owing to the division of opinion between those who favoured reconciliation with the pope and the emperor and those who opposed it, determined to defend Florentine liberty at any price, considerable confusion had prevailed in the city for some months, the more so as the true facts of the diplomatic situation were difficult to establish. From France Baldassare Carducci, kinsman of the gonfalonier and a supporter of the League with that country even after the peace of Cambrai, wrote such sanguine accounts of France's goodwill towards Florence that when rumour of the signing of the peace reached the city Bartolomeo Cavalcanti had to be sent to France to try to ascertain the truth. The result was that the Florentines then received conflicting reports and did not know which to believe.[81]

Discussions on what position to adopt *vis-à-vis* the emperor were no less confused and controversial. Nerli maintains that talks with Charles V on the city's behalf which Luigi Alamanni was willing to undertake, never had a chance to begin as optimates like Matteo Strozzi, who would have favoured such a course, were not called to the *pratiche* which considered the matter.[82] Even when the emperor had actually arrived in Italy, the ambassadors sent to him were chosen from the two opposing camps: Niccolò Capponi and Matteo Strozzi being mentioned as having favoured and Alfonso Strozzi and Tommaso Soderini as having opposed the mission.[83] The four could not even write a joint report to Florence on the imperial reactions to their embassy.[84] This is not perhaps surprising, as the emperor did not wish to offend his new ally the pope on account of the threat from the Turkish advance in Austria, and was not prepared to enter into discussions with the Florentines before they had come to an agreement with Clement.[85]

With Francesco Carducci strongly against reconciliation with the pope, evidence of bitter political controversy may be

[80] *Ibid.*, p. 68.   [81] F. Nerli, pp. 185, 186.
[82] *Ibid.*, p. 187.   [83] *Ibid.*, pp. 187-9.
[84] *Ibid.*, p. 191.   [85] L. Pastor, x, p. 69.

expected in the appointments, instructions and dispatch of the ambassadors who in the autumn of 1529 were eventually sent to Clement.

Two widely separated military movements, one in Austria and the other in Tuscany, explain why an implacable pope agreed to receive the ambassadors and an increased number of Florentines inclined to the view that they should be sent. Clement was urged by Charles V to come to terms with his compatriots because the emperor wanted to terminate a war in Tuscany which was engaging part of his forces and costing him money, both needed to stem the Turkish advance on Vienna;[86] dismay at the successes of the imperial troops under their leader the prince of Orange within Florentine territory impelled Carducci to seek the advice of those optimates whose recent treatment and whose past career made them desire reconciliation with the pope.[87]

The question of sending ambassadors to Clement was raised in a *pratica* held on 11 September[88] and discussed in further ones on the 15th and 16th, with the usual embargo on the optimates still applying.[89] But the capitulation in the middle of September to Orange's forces first of the city of Cortona and then of Arezzo so unnerved the gonfalonier that he called to the next *pratica* held on 19 September certain pro-Medici citizens whose views he had hitherto not sought.[90] On this occasion the majority, with the exception of Francesco Carducci and a few extreme supporters, decided in favour of the immediate dispatch of Pierfrancesco Portinari and Andreuolo Niccolini, two of the four ambassadors who had already been appointed.[91] Among the optimates invited was Francesco Vettori. As one would expect he spoke out in favour of dispatching Portinari 'quickly' and giving him a colleague.[92] He advised that the wishes of the pope be discovered, and that he should be induced to arrange for a halt in the advance of the troops. Carducci and his sup-

---

[86] F. Guicciardini, *St. d'It.*, v, p. 282.

[87] F. Nerli, pp. 192–3.

[88] Cons. e Prat., 71, fo. 8or–v.

[89] *Ibid.*, fos. 81r–82r (15 Sept.); fos. 82v–83v (16 Sept.).

[90] F. Nerli, pp. 192–3; Cons. e Prat., 71, fos. 84r–87r.

[91] Cons. e Prat., 71, fo. 86v.

[92] Cons. e Prat., 71, fo. 86v.

porters were overruled and Pierfrancesco Portinari was hastily dispatched to Clement.[93]

By the time the next *pratica* was held on 22 September the appointment of Vettori as an ambassador was evidently under discussion. He was not present, as he was then outside the city. Various speakers expressed the opinion that Jacopo Guicciardini and Andreuolo Niccolini, the other two ambassadors already appointed, should be sent immediately. It was Luigi Soderini, representing the Sixteen *Gonfalonieri*, who first mentioned the name of Vettori as a desirable ambassador, saying that if he could not be sent (on account of his absence from Florence) then the other two should go. Lorenzo Lapi, on behalf of the *Dodici Buonuomini* also gave it as his opinion that Francesco Vettori being 'delayed', Jacopo Guicciardini and Andreuolo Niccolini should depart. Lorenzo Segni, speaking for the members of the *pratica*, expressed the same view, adding that Jacopo Guicciardini should be given a *mandato libero* to allow him to come to an agreement with the pope.[94] So strong, however, was the feeling on the part of the extreme republican elements against any kind of agreement with Clement that Lorenzo Segni was threatened on leaving the *pratica* and Lionardo Bartolini, one of the *Gonfalonieri* (a 'complete plebeian', who later bought Francesco Vettori's house for a paltry sum)[95] warned him that he would be torn to pieces if he ever made such remarks again.[96]

Perhaps Vettori had had a similar experience as a result of his speech in the *pratica* of 19 September. The explanation for his absence from Florence during such critical days is that he had fled. One is reminded of 1512 when he wanted to flee and of 1527 when he and Niccolò Capponi went to Empoli. A letter written by his brother-in-law, Giuliano Capponi, on 20 September makes it clear that by that date Vettori had already left. 'I understand', Capponi begins, 'that because of the fear that overcame you on account of the words used by some presumptuous fellow, you decided to depart to avoid unpleasantness.' The writer then expresses his displeasure because he does

[93] Dieci, Missive, Legaz. e Comm., 48, fo. 44r, Portinari's instructions.
[94] Cons. e Prat., 71, fo. 88r.   [95] Below, p. 220.
[96] F. Nerli, p. 195; B. Segni, iii, p. 361.

not think it wise for Vettori to run the risk of being exiled; he had nothing to fear since there was talk of sending him to Rome and Lorenzo Segni had assured him that this question had just been discussed; he could benefit both himself and his city by undertaking the mission.[97] This letter, though bearing no address on the outside, supports Varchi's remark that Vettori had 'fled to Pistoia'.[98] The appointment of Vettori, who departed on 23 September, the day after the *pratica*, was a conciliatory gesture of Florence towards the pope.[99]

Carducci's attitude is revealed by the type and content of the instructions given to the ambassadors. Nerli reports that the gonfalonier, who was unable to oppose the appointment of the ambassadors, would not allow their instructions to be discussed by the Council of Eighty or the members of the *pratica* in case they should be too favourable to the pope.[100] The anti-papal sentiment and makeshift character of these instructions—Portinari's dated 20 September,[101] Guicciardini's 22nd,[102] and Vettori and Niccolini's together 23rd[103]—lend support to Nerli's statement since otherwise more conciliatory documents might have resulted. Portinari's brief, signed in the name of the Ten and their secretary Donato Giannotti is anything but submissive in character. It emphasizes the willingness of the city to recognize the pope as the Good Shepherd of all Christians and the particular protector of Florence but Clement is also informed that although the city has not behaved in the way expected of her, it is not for him to reprove and persecute her but like a good father to correct the errors of his children by friendly persuasion rather than by severe punishment; for, whereas the one engenders charity and benevolence, the other produces hate and enmity. Since Florence has not failed in any ecclesiastical duty towards the Holy See, the pope should order the arms taken up against the city and his *patria* to be laid down and see to it that the emperor advances no further into the Florentine dominion. To stop the imperial armies is obviously

---

[97] B.N.F. Magliab. XXV, 552, fo. 1r.
[98] B. Varchi, ii, p. 146; F. Nerli, p. 196.
[99] *Francesco Ferruccio e la guerra di Firenze*, p. 428; C. Roth, p. 172.
[100] F. Nerli, pp. 193-4.
[101] Dieci, Missive, Legaz. e Comm., 48, fo. 44r.
[102] *Ibid.*, fo. 47v.   [103] *Ibid.*, fo. 48v.

the chief aim of the mission as conceived by Carducci and the
Ten: 'first we desire you to do all you can to induce His Holiness
to halt . . . the army of the Prince of Orange'.[104] But this is not
to be achieved at the cost of a change of government. In the
event of discussions which might lead to an alteration in 'our
liberty and the present free and pacific government' Pierfrancesco Pandolfini is to emphasize that he has received no
instructions on this point and that he will hear nothing of it.

As their heading indicates,[105] Jacopo Guicciardini's instructions are an appendage to those given to Portinari. They, too,
reiterate the determination to preserve the liberty of Florence
at all costs: the ambassador is to discuss and agree with anything the pope wants provided he lets the city enjoy 'our liberty
with the present government and dominion';[106] for this the
Florentines have determined to give their lives.

That the instructions for Francesco Vettori and Andreuolo
Niccolini are likewise an adjunct to the main set given to
Portinari[107] can similarly be seen from their heading 'Given next
. . . to Francesco Vettori and Andreuolo Niccolini to be communicated to Pierfrancesco Portinari and Jacopo Guicciardini',
and also by their command that the latter two ambassadors let
the newcomers see their previous orders. This last set of instructions adds nothing new to the previous ones except for a reference to an answer from the prince of Orange received by a
Florentine mission which had been sent to him on 12 September
in an attempt to stop his further advance.[108] The prince had
informed Florence that he had had injunctions not to undertake
any negotiations with the city unless the Medici were received
back with the authority they had had before their expulsion in
1527. This, the instructions say, does not correspond with the
pope's proclaimed good intention towards the city and its
liberty and is against both human and divine law particularly in
one who, as pope, should seek the universal good of all men and
especially of his native city. Since the Florentines desire to come
to terms with him under honourable conditions, now is the time
for the pope to show to the world his clemency and benignity.

[104] *Ibid.*, fo. 45r.   [105] *Ibid.*, fo. 47v.
[106] *Ibid.*, fo. 48r: '. . . la nostra libertà col presente governo et dominio'.
[107] Above, p. 214, n. 101.   [108] C. Roth, p. 170.

Jacopo Guicciardini left Florence on 22 September. Vettori
and Niccolini followed on the 23rd.[109] Their party eventually
comprised about twenty people including Vettori's nephew
Bernardo, his son-in-law, Francesco Scarfi, Luigi Capponi, the
son of his brother-in-law, Giuliano, his friend Bartolomeo
Lanfredini, Jacopo Guicciardini's son Angelo and his brother
Girolamo, Andreuolo Niccolini's son and Antonio Portinari and
some of Pierfrancesco Portinari's servants.[110] By 24 September
the travellers had safely reached Siena despite the Spaniards
who were blocking the road and who had captured some
merchants only the day before. Here a friend informed them
that the Spaniards would certainly take them prisoners if they
advanced and they sought the advice of messer Bardo (probably
Altoviti)[111] who told them that they needed a safe-conduct from
the duke of Amalfi, Alfonso Piccolomini. A bugler and twelve
cross-bowmen, who would have to be paid and given all
expenses, would accompany them across Sienese territory. The
ambassadors apologize to the Ten for this and also for the fact
that they could not travel with the desired speed. Should they
be captured, however, they would suffer harm and the *Signoria*
dishonour.[112] Vettori later reckoned that the episode had cost
him sixty crowns.[113] In all they paid 200 crowns.[114] News of the
Florentine ambassadors' plight reached Rome and the pope
sent a *commissario* to escort them[115] and also a safe conduct on
5 October, probably solicited by the two Florentine ambassadors already there.[116] By 8 October the Ten feared some mis-

[109] Dieci, Missive, Legaz. e Comm., 48, fo. 49r.

[110] Vatican, Armadio 40, vol. 25, fos. 24r–25r, papal safe-conduct for the party
at Siena, dated 5 Oct. 1529.

[111] Florentine ambassador in Siena, B. Varchi, i, p. 535.

[112] Dieci, Responsive, 151, fo. 64r. This letter in Vettori's hand is dated 24 Nov.,
but this is obviously an error since it is signed by him and Andreuolo Niccolini who
was with him at the time and there is also a letter of 1 Oct. from the Ten which
refers to this incident, Dieci, Missive, Legaz. e Comm., 48, fo. 57v; cp., also, Dieci,
Responsive, 151, fos. 16r, 18v.

[113] B.N.F. Magliab. XXV, 552, fo. 32r, Bologna, 26 Nov. 1529, Francesco to
Giovanni Vettori.

[114] Dieci, Responsive, 151, fo. 16r, Rome, 7 Oct.

[115] *Ibid.*, fo. 18v. Jacopo Guicciardini, Pierfrancesco Portinari, Rome, 5 Oct.
1529.

[116] Above, n. 110 and p. 215; also, Dieci, Responsive, 151, fo. 18v: 'per più
cautele si è obtenuto un altro spaccio da S. S.tà medianti il quale pensiamo ne
verranno sicuri'.

hap had befallen Vettori and Niccolini as they had had no news of their arrival.[117] But by 7 October they had actually reached Rome only to find that Clement was leaving that day for Bologna to meet Charles V.[118] Owing to the military situation in the Florentine dominion, the pope travelled through the Romagna instead of by the shorter route through Tuscany.[119] The two ambassadors already in Rome, Jacopo Guicciardini and Pierfrancesco Portinari, had decided to travel with the pope, and Vettori also determined to follow him if his health would allow. Andreuolo Niccolini, however, said that he was too old and ill and would remain in Rome, returning to Florence as soon as safety permitted.[120] Nevertheless, all four ambassadors apparently followed Clement for on 22 October they all signed the dispatch from Imola.[121] Andreuolo Niccolini's signature has a very debilitated look and Vettori's, too, is thin and rather faint.

Immediately after the arrival in Rome of Vettori and Niccolini, all four ambassadors went to Clement who gave them the same answer as he had previously given Portinari and Guicciardini—he could not alter the agreement which he had made with the emperor. On 16 October, in their first audience after their departure from Rome, the four ambassadors tried again to persuade the pope to stop the damage which the city was daily suffering from the imperial forces under the prince of Orange, but they found Clement's mind unchanged: though he regretted the sufferings of his native city, he could not abandon his agreement with Charles.[122] Four days later the pope was at Cesena[123] and here, as a result of the letters which he had received from the emperor and the prince of Orange urging him to come to terms with his compatriots,[124] and in response to the appeals of the exiles headed by Francesco Guicciardini,[125] he conceded the Florentine ambassadors another interview. This

[117] Dieci, Missive, Legaz. e Comm., 48, fo. 61r.
[118] Dieci., Responsive, 151, fo. 16r.
[119] Ibid., fo. 18v; cp. L. Pastor, x, pp. 76, 77.
[120] Ibid., fo. 16r.   [121] Ibid., fo. 12r.
[122] Ibid., fo. 16r, 7 Oct.; fo. 14r, 16 Oct.   [123] L. Pastor, x, p. 78.
[124] A. Bardi, 'Carlo V e l'assedio di Firenze', in A.S.I., Ser. V, xi (1893), pp. 64–6; G. de Leva, ii, pp. 575–6; A. Rossi, Francesco Guicciardini, i, p. 146.
[125] A. Rossi, Francesco Guicciardini, i, pp. 145–56; 150–1.

time he was prepared to indicate the terms on which he would be willing to come to an agreement with the city, and Francesco Nasi was sent with them to Florence, but the gonfalonier did not communicate them to the councils or the *pratiche*.[126] They were, however, communicated to the Ten who viewed them with suspicion and instructed the ambassadors to return to Florence if they were being kept by mere words, leaving Pierfrancesco Portinari behind to negotiate with the emperor.[127] The Ten's feelings are summed up in the curt comment, 'seeing such obstinacy in His Holiness towards his native city, no more time is to be lost with him but on the contrary turn all your attention to the emperor and make every effort to placate him and to come to some honest settlement'. On 13 November Andreuolo, Francesco and Jacopo were instructed to return to Florence;[128] Pierfrancesco Portinari remained to continue negotiations with the emperor.

There is no doubt that by now feeling on both sides was too strong for much hope of agreement. Other dispatches of the time show the willingness of the Florentines to defend their liberty 'with their possessions and their blood', to sacrifice their villas on the outskirts of the city and to give their money.[129] In the Great Council each citizen wrote down the amount which he could afford to give for the city's defence, and the young men cut down all the trees for a mile around Florence. Quantities of orange and cedar trees were used in the defences.[130] The city was prepared for a siege.

Following the failure of Portinari's negotiations with the emperor, he, too, was recalled and was back in Florence by 11 December.[131] Guicciardini and Niccolini had already arrived in the city by 22 November,[132] but Vettori, who had not aligned himself with his colleagues in the discussions with Clement, did not dare to return and stayed in Bologna.[133] He

---

[126] F. Nerli, pp. 203–4; B. Segni, i, pp. 210–11; no mention of Nasi in relevant vol. of Cons. e Prat., 71, fos. 118v–120r.

[127] Dieci, Missive, Legaz. e Comm., 48, fos. 68r, 69r–v.

[128] *Ibid.*, fo. 75v.

[129] Dieci, Missive, Legaz. e Comm., 48, fo. 54v, 28 Sept. 1529 to Baldassare Carducci; cp. F. Nerli, p. 189; Dieci, Missive, Legaz. e Comm., 48, fo. 55, 29 Sept. 1529 to Bartolomeo Gualterotti.   [130] B. Carnesecchi, p. 467.

[131] Dieci, Missive, Legaz. e Comm., 48, fo. 87r.

[132] *Ibid.*, fo. 77r.   [133] F. Nerli, p. 204.

had acted in his usual rôle of mediator between the pope and his compatriots. He had tried to win acceptance for the proposed papal terms and attempted when they had been refused to placate the anger of the pope which had been roused by his fellow ambassador, Jacopo Guicciardini, the follower of Francesco Carducci. Guicciardini had informed the pope, doubtless in an offensive manner, that since the Republic had been unable to come to any agreement with him to free herself from the great destruction being caused by the armies, the decision had been taken to recall the ambassadors with a warning that the Republic was determined to defend herself to the point of death. This speech had produced in the pope a fit of anger plainly visible in his face. Jacopo would have said more had he not been interrupted by Clement and others present who had restrained him. One of those present had been Vettori who had tried to soften Jacopo's words and to calm Clement's wrath. The pope, shouting, had declared that he had no intention of taking away the Florentines' liberty even though he knew it to be tyranny.[134]

In remaining with Clement Vettori fully realized, as a remark to Bartolomeo Lanfredini shows, that this would mean exile.[135] It appears, however, both from his letter to Lanfredini, dated 19 November, and from one to his brother Giovanni, dated 26 November, that he had fallen ill. To Giovanni, Francesco wrote that although he feared his enemies he was not greatly concerned with the danger from them as they could not take from him many years of life, but he could not return as he was unable to ride and in fact in Bologna where everyone rode he had to walk.[136] Francesco Guicciardini told his brother Luigi that a certificate signed by two doctors had been sent to Florence to corroborate Vettori's statement, but that he was doubtful if this would be accepted.[137] He was right. From Vettori's letter to Giovanni we must assume that the *Signoria* had already condemned him. By December, according to a letter of Francesco del Nero to Filippo Strozzi, the Florentines were

[134] B. Segni, i, pp. 210–11, 217–19.
[135] R. von Albertini, p. 424.
[136] B.N.F. Magliab. XXV, 552, fo. 32r, Bologna, 26 Nov. 1529.
[137] G. Canestrini, *Op. ined.*, ix (Firenze, 1866), pp. 139–40.

beginning to detain certain citizens of whom Giovanni Vettori was one,[138] but it was not until June 1530 that Francesco was actually tried before the *Quarantia* and condemned as a rebel.[139] Bernardo Segni recounts that Vettori's goods and his house were bought by Lionardo Bartolini—the 'plebeian' who had threatened Lorenzo Segni—for only 560 ducats although they were actually worth 4000.[140] Francesco's house, the Casa de' Cerri, outside the walls of Florence was occupied for the defence of the city and the oak trees in which he snared birds were cut down.[141]

The reactions of Francesco Guicciardini and Filippo Strozzi to Vettori's decision throw some light on the reasons for it and on their respective characters. Guicciardini's attitude was fatalistic. He did not know if Vettori's medical certificate would be accepted but 'this is a game which injures all the Florentines and for one reason or another everyone will be ruined; so the Fates of our city have decreed'.[142] Via Filippo Strozzi, Giuliano Capponi tried to warn Vettori of the disastrous results of his decision but Strozzi himself upheld Francesco's choice knowing that it had not been fortuitous but reasoned.[143] Vettori's own attitude is gloomy and more specific than Guicciardini's. Instead of Guicciardini's Fates, Vettori refers to human vices: 'cursed be the ignorance and ambition that have led us to remain outside and me especially whom exile finds old, sick and poor'.[144] With characteristic resignation he writes to his brother, 'it has seemed fit to my *Signori* to condemn and exile me without first citing me. *Patientia!*' He had, he said, always done what he could for the *patria* and he would continue to do so while his spirit dominated his frail body. Giovanni should not attempt to help because it would be useless.[145]

Had Vettori returned to Florence, his chances of escaping either death or imprisonment would most likely have been slim.

---

[138] C. Strozz., Ser. V, 1209, fo. 27r, Rome, 8 Dec. 1529: 'A Firenze si attende a sostenere ciptadini et pigliarli criminalmente come harete inteso et in particolar di Giovanni Vettori.'

[139] C. Roth, p. 252, n. 39. [140] B. Segni, i, p. 219.

[141] R. von Albertini, p. 424. F. Vettori to B. Lanfredini, Bologna, 19 Nov. 1529.

[142] G. Canestrini, *Op. ined.*, ix, p. 140, Bologna, 3–4 Dec. 1529.

[143] A. Bardi, 'Filippo Strozzi', p. 59. [144] R. von Albertini, p. 424.

[145] B.N.F. Magliab. XXV, 552, fo. 32r, Bologna, 26 Nov. 1529.

Several of his compatriots are reported to have been beheaded for favouring agreement with the pope.[146] Giovanni Vettori was condemned to prison in February 1530 in the Palazzo del Podestà and remained there for the duration of the siege.[147] Andreuolo Niccolini was elected one of the Ten, and Jacopo Guicciardini's nephew, Niccolò, was one of their number for Francesco Vettori's own quarter of S. Spirito. The choice of such men summed up for him the whole spirit of the regime. With offices filled by Carducci's supporters and with such an extreme republican government Florence was no place for him.[148] He was not alone in his choice of exile: Matteo Strozzi had not returned from his summer mission to the imperialists at Genoa but had gone to Venice instead;[149] Niccolò Capponi had died in exile;[150] Filippo Strozzi was in Lucca in the winter of 1529;[151] Francesco Guicciardini was in Bologna and Roberto Acciaiuoli also was outside Florence.[152]

Vettori and those of the Florentines who were in Bologna were at the hub of European diplomacy. For four months pope and emperor resided under the same roof—that of the Palazzo Pubblico—in apartments connected by communicating doors.[153] They discussed not only the fate of Florence, but the investiture of the duchy of Milan, the settlement of the dispute between Venice and the pope, and between the pope and Ferrara, and it was in Bologna and not in Rome that the emperor's coronation took place.[154]

Busini stated that Vettori was one of the pope's councillors, and from two extant letters of this period it is evident that he was in close contact with Clement.[155] He was also well informed on details of negotiations as is shown by the precise information

---

[146] Cp. F. Nerli, p. 221; B. Segni, i, p. 213.   [147] F. Nerli, p. 219.

[148] R. von Albertini, p. 424.

[149] A. Bardi, 'Filippo Strozzi', p. 60.   [150] B. Segni, i, p. 203.

[151] A. Bardi, 'Filippo Strozzi', p. 61; C. Strozz., Ser. V, 1209, fo. 27.

[152] F. Guicciardini was in Bologna by the time Vettori arrived; he and Roberto Acciaiuoli were in Rome with Vettori during the latter part of the siege, see B. Segni, i, p. 301. A. Rossi, *Francesco Guicciardini*, i, p. 170, n. 1.

[153] R. von Albertini, p. 423; G. Romano, *Cronaca del soggiorno di Carlo V in Italia* (Milano, 1892), p. 124; F. Guicciardini, *St. d'It.*, v, p. 282; J. Brewer, *Letters and Papers, foreign and domestic, of the reign of Henry VIII*, iv, part III, 1529–30 (London, 1876), p. 2706, No. 6065.   [154] L. Pastor, x, pp. 84–99.

[155] G. Busini, *Lettere*, p. 69; R. von Albertini, p. 422, F. Vettori to Bartolomeo Lanfredini, Bologna, 19 Nov. 1529; *ibid.*, p. 424 to same, Rome, 26 June 1530.

he gives on discussions between the emperor and the prince of Orange (who arrived in Bologna on 13 November),[156] though in this case Pierfrancesco Portinari probably kept him informed. Also Vettori could report that the emperor was advising Clement 'almost against his will' to allow the war against Florence to be restarted and the emperor had consulted his doctors and masters of theology about the justice of such action. In his account Vettori emphasizes the papal point of view, or what Clement wished the Florentines to take as his point of view. There is, for instance, no mention in contemporary chronicles of the emperor's learned consultations, and the imperial correspondence nowhere reflects papal reluctance to wage war against Florence but rather Charles' acquiescence in Clement's desire for the submission of Florence in order that his friendship with the pope might not be jeopardized.[157] Only in a letter from Francesco Gonzaga, the marquis of Mantua's ambassador, does the view expressed by Vettori emerge. On 13 November he reported that the pope had bitterly lamented the unfortunate events in Florence and had said that participation in 'this ball' was forced upon him against his will.[158] According to Vettori, imperial justification for the war was threefold: firstly, the Florentines, holding Florence and the dominion as a vicariate from the emperor, in acting against him had forfeited their legal rights; secondly, in refusing to grant the benefits requested by the pope and in taxing the clergy without papal permission, the Florentines were excommunicate and any Christian prince therefore had the right to persecute them, and thirdly, there was no greater nor more cruel tyranny than a tryannical *popolo*. The third reason sounds remarkably like Clement's comment to the Florentine ambassadors on the occasion of Jacopo Guicciardini's outburst.[159] Commenting on the situation, Vettori changes the papal metaphor of a ball into one with which he was more familiar, and remarks that the game cannot go well, whichever turn it may take. As in his correspondence with Machiavelli in 1526, he adopts the

[156] G. Romano, *Cronaca*, p. 132.

[157] A. Bardi, 'Carlo V', pp. 44, 57; cp. Charles V to Margaret of Austria, 16 Nov. 1529, *ibid.*, p. 31; *ibid.*, p. 44, report of Louis de Praet to Granvelle; *ibid.*, pp. 34, 44: F. Guicciardini, *St. d'It.*, v, p. 282.

[158] G. Romano, *Cronaca*, p. 131, n. 2.   [159] Above, p. 219.

criterion of *ragione*: he has seen so many illogical and unforeseen things happen that he does not want to judge the outcome of the present conflict. His pro-papal bias is reflected in his irritation with the situation as it has developed: had it not been for this cursed Florentine affair, he writes, Clement VII, despite all other adversity, would have been the most glorious pope for many years.[160]

The impression of someone close to the source of decisions is also conveyed by Vettori's report in the same letter to Bartolomeo, on the settlement between the pope and Venice. On 10 November the Venetian government gave full powers to their ambassador, Gasparo Contarini, to restore Ravenna and Cervia to Clement VII.[161] Vettori is therefore quite accurate in his report from Bologna on the 19th that the Venetians were secretly negotiating to come to terms with the pope, returning to him Ravenna and Cervia. His report of the arrival of the duke of Milan and the belief that Milan will be restored to him is equally correct. Even English affairs, important of course at this period on account of Henry VIII's desire for a divorce from the emperor's aunt, Catherine of Aragon, receive Vettori's attention. He refers to the fall of Wolsey from power.[162] In view of Vettori's closeness to the centre of activity, it is tantalizing that we have so little evidence of his personal opinions on events and no indication of the advice, if any, that he gave to the pope.

In addition to their diplomatic negotiations in settlement of the affairs of Italy, pope and emperor were concerned with the question of Charles V's coronation in Bologna. Since imperial coronations normally took place in Rome, doubt had been expressed about its validity.[163] According to a letter which Charles wrote to Margaret of Austria on 13 February, he had evidently taken counsel on this point in both Bologna and Germany.[164] Only three days before Roberto Roffia, Vettori's secretary,[165] had sent him from Rome a book on the coronation

---

[160] R. von Albertini, p. 423; cp. Vettori's view in the *Sommario* that Clement had had bad luck; on this, v. F. Gilbert, *Machiavelli and Guicciardini*, pp. 251–2.

[161] L. Pastor, x, pp. 86–7.   [162] R. von Albertini, p. 423.

[163] L. Pastor, x, pp. 89–90, n. 4.   [164] A. Bardi, 'Carlo V', p. 35.

[165] Roffia went with Vettori to France and became tutor and then secretary to Lorenzo de' Medici's bride, B.R.F. Ms. Riccardiana, 2240, fo. 74r, Giuliano Brancacci to F. Vettori, Florence, 3 March 1518, and C. Strozz., Ser. I, 10, 'Nota

of the king of the Romans printed in Italian, which shows how closely Vettori associated himself with every problem discussed and how he liked to form his views from a knowledge of the sources.[166]

Within four weeks of his coronation the emperor left Bologna for Germany and nine days later, on 31 March, the pope likewise departed. By 12 April he was back in Rome.[167] In Bologna he had daily expected to hear of the capitulation of his native city but Florence continued to hold out against the siege which had begun in October until after the failure of Francesco Ferruccio's gallant attempt in early August to raise it.[168] Not until 12 August was the city forced into surrender.

The war against Florence cost the pope vast sums of money so that he had to resort to every expedient: he borrowed money wherever he could; Filippo Strozzi, for example, lent him considerable sums; he pawned the papal jewels and he apparently considered abandoning the campaign altogether.[169] Added to the threat of bankruptcy were the reproaches of other Christians for such an undertaking against his compatriots, the fear that Florence might be sacked and, in the summer, the knowledge that France and England might help the Florentines.[170] In April Clement was in despair and when the French envoy, Gabriel de Gramont, bishop of Tarbes, urged him to come to terms with his compatriots, he expressed the wish that 'Florence had never existed'.[171]

More than one source indicates that the Florentine exiles were among those who advised the pope to continue the war until total victory had been achieved, from fear that they would otherwise be made to suffer for having sided with him.[172] Segni

della famiglia di Madama' (written on cover in F.V.'s hand, fo. 170v) where F.V. has added at bottom of list (fo. 161v) 'Roberto fiorentino segretario'. Roberto may have been Vettori's 'scriptore' in Rome (N. Machiavelli, *Lettere*, ed. F. Gaeta, pp. 298, 326) since many of the dispatches from Rome seem to be in the same hand as those from France; also, M.A.P., 111, No. 181: 'Roberto Rophia, apud oratorem florentinum' to Augustino Vespucci, Rome, 18 Aug. 1513; see also begging letter of Roffia to Vettori, C. Strozz., I, 137, fos. 273r–273v, 14 April 1526.

[166] Acq. e Doni, 59, insert i (7), Roberto Roffia to F. Vettori, Rome, 10 Feb. 1530.   [167] L. Pastor, x, p. 99.

[168] F. Guicciardini, *St. d'It.*, v, pp. 296–7; C. Roth, pp. 310–15.

[169] B. Segni, i, p. 265; L. Pastor, x, p. 100.   [170] L. Pastor, x, p. 100.

[171] The bishop of Tarbes to Francis I, *A.S.I.*, Appendice, i (1842), p. 476, cit. C. Roth, p. 259.   [172] B. Segni, i, p. 265; L. Pastor, pp. 99–100.

specifically accuses Vettori of having urged the pope soon after his return to Rome not to abandon the siege and of having assured him that the cause was 'most just' and worthy of papal involvement: it was a cause worth dying for.[173]

Whatever the nature of Vettori's counsel—and we must bear in mind that by the summer of 1530 Vettori was receiving a papal pension—there is no doubt that he was one of the small group of Florentine papal advisers in Rome at this time. Francesco Gonzaga wrote to the duke of Mantua that business was conducted at the papal court by the usual people. The names he gives are Cardinal Sanga, Jacopo Salviati, Francesco Guicciardini and Francesco Vettori.[174] Sanga had taken the place of Giberti among the pope's chief counsellors,[175] Salviati had been a close adviser since the papal residence in Orvieto, Guicciardini had held the post of 'Lieutenant General in the army and whole state of the Church with fullest and almost absolute power';[176] evidently Vettori is here associated with the most influential and trusted advisers. Bartolomeo Cavalcanti, the Florentine ambassador sent to Clement in August to negotiate the terms of capitulation, wrote that he had not omitted to perform his duties on behalf of the city with Francesco Guicciardini, Roberto Acciaiuoli, Roberto Pucci and Francesco Vettori.[177]

---

[173] B. Segni, i, pp. 265; cp. p. 178.
[174] A. Rossi, *Francesco Guicciardini*, i, p. 164, n. 2.
[175] L. Pastor, x, p. 11.
[176] F. Guicciardini, *St. d'It.*, v, p. 20, cit. R. Ridolfi, *Francesco Guicciardini*, p. 150.
[177] Balie, 53, fo. 15v, 18 Aug. (1530), cit. A. Rossi, *Francesco Guicciardini*, i, p. 170, n. 1.

CHAPTER X

Papal Victory (1530–2)

WHEN FLORENCE capitulated on 12 August 1530 those citizens who had supported the pope could be expected to take control. Indeed after their return from Rome Filippo Strozzi, Francesco Guicciardini, Roberto Acciaiuoli and Francesco Vettori were to be foremost in the city, but only Bartolomeo Valori, who had been the pope's commissary with the imperial forces during the siege, was on the spot to take immediate command. On 20 August a proclamation was issued calling a *parlamento*[1] and, as in 1512, the *Signoria* under the threat of foreign troops agreed to create a *Balìa*.[2] The twelve citizens chosen included Mediceans or partisans such as Ottaviano de' Medici or Luigi della Stufa but also others, creatures to a greater or lesser degree of Bartolomeo Valori.[3] At their first meeting, held on the same day, the *Balìa* placed the members of the old *Signoria* under guard and dissolved the Eight of Ward and the Ten. On 1 September the new *Signoria*, nominated as during the Medici regime, took office.[4] The government of Florence, temporarily headed by Bartolomeo Valori who established himself in the Medici palace,[5] began to apply itself to the problem of economic and political reconstruction.

The immediate task was to obtain money to get rid of the ravaging armies, both hostile and allied. By the agreement of 12 August the cost to Florence of the evacuation of the imperial army was 80,000 ducats.[6] In addition, there were the outstand-

[1] Balie, 48, fo. 114r; Provvisioni, 209, fos. 31r–32v, 20 Aug. 1530; Bannum pro Parlamentum, 20 Aug., cit. C. Roth, p. 338, n. 23.
[2] Text of decree nominating the *Balìa* in P. Falletti-Fossati, *L'Assedio di Firenze* (Palermo, 1885), i, pp. 462–8, cit. C. Roth, p. 338, n. 24.
[3] Provvisioni, 209, fo. 32r–v, names of 12 of *Balìa*; also, Balie, 51, fos. 93r–v.
[4] F. Nerli, p. 242; C. Roth, p. 334.
[5] C. Strozz., Ser. I, 59, fo. 74v. Niccolò to Luigi Guicciardini, Florence, 24 Nov. 1530.
[6] L. Cantini, *Legislazione toscana* i pp. 32–4, (Firenze, 1800).

ing claims of her own mercenaries to be met. One of the last acts of the Great Council on the day after the capitulation had been to pass a provision to raise a forced loan of 100,000 ducats from five citizens paying equal parts.[7] Within six months these loans were to be repaid by 100 other citizens who in their turn were to be reimbursed by 300 more. Already by 23 August however these contributions had to be supplemented by an additional loan of at least 25,000 ducats.[8] Eight days later thirty-five or more citizens were designated to lend 70,000 ducats to be repaid from the income on customs duties and tolls.[9] On 24 August[10] and on 8 September[11] a house tax was imposed to be raised ward by ward on all buildings except hospitals, monasteries and other institutions devoted to pious purposes, and on the 13th five citizens were appointed to collect outstanding money owing on these two imposts.[12] On 10 September when the *Balìa* sent Bartolomeo's nephew, Francesco Valori, to appeal to the pope for financial help, 46,000 ducats were still needed to rid Florentine territory of foreign troops.[13] In a further appeal to Clement of 1 October the *Balìa* referred to the 'intolerable expense' of keeping the *Lanzknechts* in wood, vinegar, oil and salt, quoted as over 17,000 ducats a month, and to the extensive damage to household goods and floors by the soldiers billeted in private houses.[14]

Demands for loans were not confined to those living in Florence. Some of the largest payments in fact came from the exiles. As early as 21 August, one day after the *Balìa* had been created, Jacopo Salviati was asked to contribute and was instructed to tax Florentine citizens resident in Rome and to appoint the firm of Bindo Altoviti as bankers for part of the sum raised from them.[15] On the same day the *Balìa* also wrote to Filippo Strozzi in Lucca asking him for a loan and charging him to collect taxes from the exiles there.[16] Luigi Guicciardini, commissario in Pisa, was instructed to collect from his

[7] Provvisioni, 209, fos. 26r ff., 13 Aug. 1530; C. Roth, p. 331.
[8] Balie, 48, fo. 118r.
[9] Balie, 51, fo. 19r.
[10] Balie, 51, fo. 8r.   [11] Balie, 48, fo. 132r.
[12] Balie, 48, fo. 140r.   [13] Balie, 51, fo. 43r.
[14] Balie, 52, fo. 3r.   [15] Balie, 51, fo. 1r.
[16] Balie, 51, fo. 1v; cp. Balie, 48, fo. 134r.

compatriots[17] and similar requests were made to Florentines in Ferrara and Venice.[18]

Although Vettori must have been one of those exiles in Rome from whom Salviati was instructed to collect money, there is no record of any contribution made by him. Letters written during the early part of September by those of his immediate family who had remained in Florence prove that they suffered great hardship. Francesco's uncle Bernardo Vettori had to contribute 35,000 ducats to the forced loan of 31 August.[19] He was so worried by his deplorable financial position and was living so miserably that he feared that he would drop down dead before long; his daily diet consisted of a little bread and a few figs. The family was obliged to supply the Spanish and German troops with bread and had none for itself. The house tax, too, caused the family much distress. Rinieri Lotti, left in charge of the family house with Francesco in Rome and Giovanni as *commissario* in Volterra,[20] was away with the imperial forces when the demand for payment came and the wretched Maddalena, Francesco's wife, did not know what to do realizing that heavy fines were imposed in the case of unpaid taxes.[21]

By 8 September the Spaniards and Germans who made up the bulk of the imperial army left Florence escorted by Rinieri Lotti,[22] who had been appointed Florentine *commissario* to them on 30 August.[23] The Italian contingent followed some days later.[24] The latter had received the sum of 46,000 ducats in cash, and brocades to the value of 12,000 ducats contributed by many Florentine families, including the Vettori, in lieu of money.[25] Even so, payments fell short of what was due. In November Vettori reported payment of the last instalment owed to the Germans. The troops of Fabrizio Maramaldo, whose presence had prevented the autumn sowing, had also been bought off and were expected to depart shortly. What 'a splen-

---

[17] Balie, 51, fos. 44r–v, 10 Sept.

[18] Balie, 51, fo. 49r (bis).

[19] C. Strozz., Ser. I, 98, fo. 94r. Bernardo to Giovanni Vettori, 2 Sept. 1530.

[20] Balie, 51, fo. 3v, 'patente' for Giovanni Vettori, 22 Aug. 1530.

[21] Balie, 51, fo. 11r, proclamation 27 Aug., and, above, n. 19.

[22] A. Rossi, *Francesco Guicciardini*, i, p. 188.

[23] Balie, 51, fo. 16r.   [24] A. Rossi, *Francesco Guicciardini*, i, p. 190.

[25] *Ibid.*, p. 190, Francesco Gonzaga to Duke of Mantua, Rome, 7 Sept.; C. Strozz., Ser. I, 98, fo. 106r Bernardo to Giovanni Vettori, Florence, 6 Sept. 1530.

did thing' it would be to have cleared the countryside of soldiers, Vettori remarked, but added that the city was left without men, money or grain.[26]

The presence of enemy troops on Florentine territory had prevented the return from Rome of the leading citizens until mid-September. The newly-elected gonfalonier, Giovanni Corsi,[27] had attempted to travel to Florence early in the month but when he reached the Certosa skirmishes between Spanish and German imperialist troops had forced him to turn back to the Chianti valley where he was on 2 September awaiting an escort to conduct him safely into the city.[28] Because they had considered it unsafe to attempt the journey, Francesco Vettori and Roberto Acciaiuoli were still in Rome on 6 September.[29] Francesco had intended to return earlier but he was particularly worried by the presence of the soldiers as he was obliged to travel in a litter and was therefore less mobile than on horse-back.[30] Nevertheless, he must have arrived in Florence towards the middle of September, for on 16 November he told Bartolomeo Lanfredini, in whose house he had been staying, that he had been there nearly two months.[31] Francesco Guicciardini returned from Rome on 24 September,[32] and Filippo Strozzi from Lucca probably about the same time, for Segni writes, 'Once things were more settled there returned to Florence those citizens who had been in Lucca as neutrals and those heads of the Medici government who had been in Rome as exiles, namely Francesco Vettori, Francesco Guicciardini, Filippo Strozzi and Roberto Acciaiuoli, in whose authority and counsel the Pope had great faith.'[33] Matteo Strozzi, who had been living in Venice, did not apparently came back to Florence until

[26] R. von Albertini, pp. 425, 427. F. Vettori to B. Lanfredini.

[27] Tratte, 94, fo. 24v, 1 Sept. 1530.

[28] C. Strozz., Ser. I, 98, fo. 92r, Palla Rucellai to Giovanni Vettori, 2 Sept. 1530; cp. Balie, 51, fo. 31v, 4 Sept.: 12 of *Balìa* give permission for Giovanni Corsi to postpone his arrival until 16 Sept.

[29] C. Strozz., Ser. I, 98, fo. 108r, Roberto Acciaiuoli to Giovanni Vettori, Rome, 7 Sept. 1530.

[30] *Ibid.*, fo. 107r. F. Vettori to Giovanni, Rome, 7 Sept. 1530.

[31] R. von Albertini, p. 427.

[32] R. Caggese, *Firenze dalla Decadenza di Roma al Risorgimento d'Italia*, iii (Firenze, 1921), p. 7.

[33] B. Segni, i, p. 301.

January 1531.[34] The fact that certain of the important Medici supporters remained outside the city instead of returning to take office in time of need caused critical comment. Vettori himself had earlier excused Bartolomeo Lanfredini and Francesco del Nero, whose presence in Rome he knew to be indispensable, but even he seemed surprised that none of the relations of the two Florentine cardinals, Ridolfi and Salviati, was in Florence when they ought to hold leading positions in the party. Luigi Ridolfi, for example, preferred to remain at Certaldo for fear of Maramaldo's troops. The absence of other exiles such as Jacopo Salviati, Lorenzo Strozzi, Roberto Pucci and Rafaello Girolami who were still in Rome, Vettori did not resent. As he wrote, he himself was prepared to die rather than to see the Medici cause defeated, and though he would have liked as many associates as possible, he was prepared to collaborate with those available. Other members of the party though felt let down.[35] One cannot but admire the determination and patriotism, or perhaps ambition, which led this timid and by now infirm man of fifty-six to exchange the comparative peace of his life in Rome for the discomforts which he must have known would await him in Florence. To the lack of food must be added the fear of the plague, of which his wife mistakenly thought she was a victim,[36] and the housing shortage. He was obliged to spend two months in Bartolomeo Lanfredini's house[37] and only managed in January 1531 to get possession of that part of his house which had been confiscated and sold after his banishment.[38]

The conditions to which the exiles returned can be appreciated from a letter which Francesco Guicciardini wrote soon afterwards. Words failed him, he reported to Bartolomeo Lanfredini, to describe the misery and ruin of the city and its surrounding countryside. Houses for many miles around Florence and in many places in the dominion were destroyed;

[34] B.N.F. Magliab. XXV, 552, fo. 145r. F. Vettori to Giovanni, Florence, 17 Jan. 1531.

[35] R. von Albertini, p. 426. F. Vettori to B. Lanfredini, Florence, n.d. (end Oct. 1530).

[36] C. Strozz., Ser. I, 98, fo. 106r.

[37] C. Strozz., Ser. I, 136, fo. 213r. Francesco to Giovanni, 29 Nov. 1530.

[38] B.N.F. Magliab. XXV, 552, fo. 145r.

the peasantry had decreased to such an extent that the lower classes scarcely existed; grain would be short in the coming year and there was little chance of sowing for the next. The disaster that Florence had suffered seemed beyond endurance.[39] Three months later Jacopo Guicciardini could still write to his brother Luigi that the city's sources of income were severely reduced, dues yielded little, salt less and contracts nothing; there was no lack of food but the cost of living was high.[40]

The first task which had to be tackled was economic reconstruction. Commerce had to be restored, the city provisioned, fortifications and bridges built and repairs undertaken. Finance continued to be the main preoccupation. In October 1530 Jacopo Guicciardini wrote to Luigi that four people had been elected to find money for public expenditure; one of them was Francesco Vettori and two of his colleagues were Roberto Acciaiuoli and Andrea Minerbetti, Jacopo could not remember the name of the fourth.[41] Francesco Guicciardini, however, could: he was Filippo Machiavelli.[42] Francesco Guicciardini informs us that these citizens were to suggest economies in the administration. As many redundant offices as possible outside Florence were to be vacated, and fortresses which were not needed should be closed, because 'without retrenchment there is no hope whatsoever that the city and the countryside can survive'. Vettori's preoccupation with Florence's financial position emerges from a letter to Bartolomeo Lanfredini in December.[43] He had always understood, he remarked, that a prince, a republic or a government which was not economically viable would come to grief. He advocated reducing the staff of the Palazzo della Signoria and military expenditure. In a memorandum, hitherto unnoticed, in the Biblioteca Nazionale, headed 'Expenses which could be cut partly this year and partly in the following one', Vettori lists further suggestions.[44] To transfer the centre of studies (*studio*) from Pisa to Florence would mean a saving of 3000 ducats; to dispense with Pisa's *bargello*, or chief constable, 1000, and with the *bargello* in the countryside

[39] A. Otetea, *Dall'Assedio di Firenze al secondo convegno di Clemente VII e Carlo V* (Aquila, 1927), p. 3.
[40] C. Strozz., Ser. I, 59, fo. 198r, 16 Dec. 1530.
[41] C. Strozz., Ser. I, 59, fo. 127v.   [42] A. Otetea, *Dall'Assedio*, p. 8.
[43] R. von Albertini, p. 430.   [44] B.N.F. II, III, 433, fo. 137r.

round Florence 2000. No money should be spent on walls because money, not walls, was the city's best defence. Interesting from a political as well as from the economic point of view is Vettori's attitude to the *Guardia*, or armed guard. In December he considered the preservation of the regime necessitated its maintenance respectively in Florence, Pisa and Livorno,[45] but by the following spring he protested that the pope was ruining Florence by putting her to the expense of its increase.[46] He estimated the cost at 3000 ducats a month, or 36,000 ducats per annum.[47] As Vettori stated in one of his memoranda addressed to the pope, 'every effort will have to be made to reduce other expenses'.[48]

Not only the finances but the revictualling of the city appear to have come within Vettori's sphere of activity. In November he wanted Filippo Strozzi to become one of the officials of the *Abbundanzia*,[49] an office concerned with the provisioning of the city, and urged him to return from Rome for this purpose. Although Strozzi did not remain in Florence, he accepted the nomination to the office[50] and played an extremely useful part in it by giving large credit facilities. By January 1531 Vettori wrote to his brother Giovanni that hunger had been averted to some extent thanks to the money lent by Filippo Strozzi but that the office was so deep in debt that its bankruptcy seemed inevitable.[51] By 14 December the officials had already spent 5000 ducats, all on Filippo's credit.[52]

Parallel with economic reconstruction ran political reform. The first of the terms of the capitulation had stipulated that Florence's form of government should be settled by the emperor within the next four months, saving always the liberty of the city. But before the decision was taken on the type of ruler and his powers certain matters of immediate practical concern came under consideration.

[45] R. von Albertini, p. 430.

[46] B.N.F. Ginori Conti, 29, 32, insert 3, fo. 13v, Benedetto Buondelmonti to Giovanfrancesco Negrini, Florence, 5 April 1531: 'et Francesco Vettori molto largamente biasima che la guardia si sia cresciuta et usa dire che N.S. rovina questa città afatto con darlli et tenerlla in tanta spesa et la advilisce et dice che la non serve ad nulla'.   [47] R. von Albertini, p. 431.

[48] *A.S.I.*, i (1842), p. 441; below, p. 240.   [49] A. Bardi, 'Filippo Strozzi', p. 64.

[50] Tratte, 85, fo. 198v., elected 20 Sept. 1530 until 1 July 1531; G.-B. Niccolini, p. lviii.   [51] C. Strozz., Ser. I, 98, fo. 127r.   [52] R. von Albertini, p. 432.

After the return of the exiles in v
faith, authorizing them to admini
with Baccio Valori',[53] the *Balìa* i
considered to be too small and
Florence, Filippo Strozzi was c
urgency of enlarging it.[54] He t
lists of citizens to be included
tactics at work in dictati
appearance that the Flor
the lists started betwee
on Strozzi's arrival or
following day on the
names suggested; th
From the combin
agreed upon by a
with names not

e criticized the lists sent from Rome
nd considered that they contained
ch family, which could cause ill
fully represented. Also, since men
r the profit derived from it and
many, it was better to satisfy a
e gained by a large *Balìa* but
were then not promoted to
a large *Balìa* in 1444 the
honour and profitable
had returned him and
The present govern-
rned by a powerful
existence. Disap-
nly add to those
popularity of a

the election of *accoppiatori* did not take place until March 1531.[62]
The number elected was twenty-four, twelve serving from
March to October and the other half from October to April of
the following year. The complications of drawing up the first
electoral registers of the new regime can be judged from the fact
that in May 1531 the task was expected to take several more
months.[63]

For reasons consistent with those given for limiting the size of
the *Balìa*, Vettori opposed a large scrutiny council denying that
new adherents could be won in this way and anticipating too
many disputes.[64] With the good of the regime in mind he wrote
to Lanfredini in December that he would not take it amiss if the
pope did not consider him for the office of *accoppiatore*, in view of
the many competitors. However, he was elected for the second
six months of the year.[65]

An office of exceptional political importance, particularly
before the election of the augmented *Balìa*, was that of the
Eight. After the capitulation the outgoing foreign committee of
Ten had urged on Clement the need to institute immediately a
new foreign committee, meaning the restoration of the office of
the Eight as in previous Medici regimes. They considered that
the twelve members of the *Balìa* could not deal with everything.[66] On 26 September Francesco Vettori, Francesco Guicciardini, Roberto Acciaiuoli, Corso delle Colombe, Palla
Rucellai, the gonfalonier, Giovanni Corsi, as well as Luigi
della Stufa and Bartolomeo Valori (who were already members
of the *Balìa*) were elected.[67] By November this office was in
overall control and especially Vettori, Guicciardini, Acciaiuoli
and Valori had great authority.[68]

There can be no doubt that Vettori's standing in Florence
had never been higher than after his return from exile. There

[62] Balie, 55, fos. 1r–v.   [63] Balie, 54, fo. 71r.
[64] 'confutationi'. R. von Albertini, p. 436. F. Vettori to B. Lanfredini, 14 March
1531.
[65] R. von Albertini, p. 432. F. Vettori to B. Lanfredini, 14 Dec. 1530; Tratte,
85, fo. 186r.
[66] Balie, 52, fo. 1v, 6 Sept. 1530.   [67] Balie, 49, fo. 27r, 26 Sept. 1530.
[68] C. Strozz., Ser. I, 59, fo. 65r(bis), Niccolò to Luigi Guicciardini, Florence,
20 Nov. 1530: 'gli Otto di Pratica governono el tutto et Messer Francesco ci ha
autorità assai, così Roberto et Francesco et questi altri, et maxime Bartolomeo
Valori'; cp. *ibid.*, fo. 74v Same to same, 24 Nov. 1530.

was a time, he wrote in March 1531, when he would have had
to go four times to the church of S. Spirito during Lent before
he could find a friar to hear his confession; now he had hardly
arrived there before a friar came to hear him. Formerly when he
required a notary he had to wait a whole day and although he
paid well they would hardly listen to him and took so little
trouble that he lost his case; now, wanting to bring a law suit
against his daughter Maria's father-in-law, Martino Scarfi, to
recover her dowry, he was waylaid by two notaries asking
when he wished to begin. In the past he had to send four times
for a doctor (whose ministrations would leave him prostrate)
and the apothecary would demand payment in advance for his
medicine; now three or more doctors answered his call and the
apothecary gave him credit.[69]

Enthusiastic as Vettori was immediately after his return to
serve his city, he was less willing to accept office a few months
later, if one is to believe certain remarks in his letters to his
brother Giovanni. According to these he had not wanted to be
a member of the *Balìa* or the Eight because he was a sick man
and could only appear at the palace with difficulty, but people
did not believe him.[70] He found being a member of the Eight
irksome because of the constant demands on the office for
money.[71] But it should perhaps be borne in mind that Vettori
was inclined to complain,[72] and that his brother Giovanni may
conceivably have been jealous of him.[73]

The first few months after the capitulation also witnessed
an increasingly close co-operation between Francesco Vettori
and Francesco Guicciardini which was to last to the end of the
former's life.[74] As this friendship had a bearing on future policy
it may be useful briefly to trace their relationship up to date.

[69] R. von Albertini, pp. 433–4 F. Vettori to B. Lanfredini, 1 March 1531.

[70] C. Strozz., Ser. I, 136, fo. 227v, Florence, 26 Nov. 1530: 'et li huomini
maledici . . . pensono et dicono che io fuggo'.

[71] *Ibid.*, 98, fo. 127r, F. Vettori to Giovanni, 5 Jan. 1531: 'io non mi pentì mai di
choxa che facessi tanto quanto d'havere consentito d'essere delli Octo di Pratica
perchè non ho choxa che mi dia più molestia all 'animo che quando mi è chiesto
danari et in questo uficio non ho da altro'.

[72] Above, pp. 9, 85ff., 155.

[73] R. von Albertini, p. 428, F. Vettori to B. Lanfredini, 16 Nov. 1530.

[74] F. Gilbert, *Machiavelli and Guicciardini*, pp. 242–3, discusses their relationship
for the period around 1527.

Before Machiavelli's death in May 1527, Vettori and Guicciardini had not been close to one another, both seeking his friendship rather than each other's. In the crisis of that spring both had chosen to support the Republic rather than the Medici but when their previous connections with the Medici made them suspect to the republicans, both had eventually retired to their villas, Vettori to write his *Sommario* and Francesco Guicciardini to collect material for the *Storia d'Italia*.[75] They had both reappeared on the political scene on the side of the pope whom they served together in Bologna and in Rome. From there they had both returned to Florence after the end of the siege and were both highly influential in the new Medici regime. In spring 1531 both came in for attack from Benedetto Buondelmonti who accused them of associating with a group of young men whose fathers had belonged to Niccolò Capponi's faction in 1527.[76] Buondelmonti was influential in Rome and though there is no proof of the pope having taken note of his rather envenomed attacks,[77] Vettori writes in a letter to Lanfredini, also meant perhaps for Clement's eyes, 'whatever people may say, no one knows better than Guicciardini how to preserve the regime'.[78] Guicciardini, too, evidently respected Vettori highly, for in the following year he considered arranging a marriage alliance between one of his two still single daughters and Vettori's nephew Bernardo, but the poor financial prospects of such a union must have caused him to abandon the idea as he later sought other suitors for the two girls.[79]

[75] R. Ridolfi, *Francesco Guicciardini*, pp. 190–2.

[76] B.N.F. Ginori Conti, 29, 32, insert 3, fo. 13v, Benedetto Buondelmonti to Giovanfrancesco Negrini, Florence, 5 April 1531. Benedetto writes that he has several times informed Clement of 'quello mi pare di questa setta capponescha . . . io so bene che oggi ha vigore quanto havessi mai . . . et so che molti giovani che sono di tal setta sono molto ristretti insieme et da Francesco Vettori et dal Guicciardino trattenuti molto'. He lists its members as the sons of Niccolò Capponi; Jacopo Guicciardini, Matteo Strozzi, Alamanno de' Pazzi and his two sons; Piero Salviati, Roberto Acciaiuoli and (Francesco) Serristori. For Francesco Serristori, v. J. Nardi, ii, p. 115; B. Varchi, i, p. 135; above, p. 200.

[77] *Ibid.*, Buondelmonti says Vettori is a 'traitor'. The two had evidently quarrelled: Vettori objected to Buondelmonti becoming an official of the *Monte* and a member of the Eight, R. von Albertini p. 435; see also, pp. 436, 438.

[78] R. von Albertini, p. 441.

[79] R. Ridolfi, *Francesco Guicciardini*, p. 223; A. Otetea, *Dall'Assedio* p. 127, F. Guicciardini to B. Lanfredini, Bologna, 2 March 1532; R. von Albertini, p. 442, F. Vettori to B. Lanfredini, 20 May 1531.

Like Francesco Guicciardini and Roberto Acciaiuoli, Vettori
was greatly impressed by the number of Medici opponents. In
November he said that it would be impossible to remove all
enemies of the Medici, too few citizens would be left.[80] In
December he estimated that at least two-thirds of the citizens
were enemies of the party, not counting those who had been
imprisoned.[81] He wished for his brother Giovanni's presence to
support the regime more adequately than he was able to.[82] To
Bartolomeo Lanfredini, as we have seen, he had expressed the
view current among Medici supporters that the regime was in
need of certain prominent Mediceans who had delayed their
return.[83]

Clearly the bitterness of those who had valiantly defended
their liberty towards those who in their eyes had betrayed the
city and deserted to the pope could not be assuaged immediately, but the punishments meted out by the returning exiles,
which were so severe that they were still recalled by chroniclers
a generation later,[84] removed any chance of appeasement.
Moreover, the Medici *amici* added to the number of their
enemies by enforcing the return of property belonging to the
Church, the guilds and the exiles which had been sold during
the Republic.[85] After a conversation with the pope Filippo
Strozzi let it be known that Clement was not opposed to violence
on the part of the Medici partisans, though he was careful to
dissociate himself from it.[86] He knew that the hatred of the
Florentine populace against the ruling citizens would make
these even more dependent on his protection and was liable to
cause discord between them.[87] Bartolomeo Valori's apparent
unawareness of the danger to the Medici government from its
many opponents caused disagreement between him and Guicciardini and Vettori, both of whom believed severity to be

[80] R. von Albertini, p. 428, F. Vettori to B. Lanfredini, 16 Nov. 1530.

[81] *Ibid.*, p. 430, Florence, 8 Dec. 1530.

[82] C. Strozz., Ser. I, 136, fo. 227r, 26 Nov. 1530.

[83] Above, p. 230.

[84] F. Gilbert, 'Alcuni discorsi di uomini politici fiorentini e la politica di Clemente
VII per la restaurazione medicea,' in *A.S.I.*, xciii, 2 (1935), p. 16.

[85] A. Rossi, *Francesco Guicciardini*, i, p. 239; R. Acciaiuoli's first *parere* in *A.S.I.*,
i (1842), p. 447.

[86] R. Caggese, iii, p. 7; F. Nerli, p. 248.

[87] F. Nerli, pp. 248–9.

indispensable for the safety of the regime.[88] In November 1530, for example, Vettori complained to Bartolomeo Lanfredini that no attempt had been made to extract from Fra Benedetto da Foiano, inspired leader of the republicans, an account of his activities through questioning or torture, even though he had been arrested and handed over to the pope two months earlier. 'You give us a bad example', Vettori declared.[89]

All the measures discussed so far have been of the immediate practical nature necessary to tide over a confused, post-war situation. But the authority of Baccio Valori, of his successor Schönberg and of those exiles who acted in the name of the pope was merely temporary and the final form of Florence's government had still to be settled in accordance with the terms of the capitulation to the emperor. On 28 October Charles V had issued an imperial bull in Augsburg pardoning the city for its rebellion and restoring its privileges and liberties, though declaring that the magistrates should be elected as under the former Medici regime. Alessandro, his future son-in-law, was recognized as head of the state, and on 7 February the *Balìa* elected him as one of their number and made him eligible for all offices.[90] The youth returned to the city on 5 July and on the following day the imperial representative, Juan Antonio Muxetola, read the imperial bull in the Palazzo della Signoria before the assembled magistrates.[91] The precise nature of Medici government in Florence and the exact extent of Alessandro's power was, however, decided by the pope, who in accordance with his accustomed practice of wanting his will to appear to be that of the leading citizens—'to throw the stone but hide his hand', as Lorenzo Strozzi put it[92]—asked for opinions orally from those in Rome and by means of written memoranda (*pareri*) from those in Florence and elsewhere. At the end of hostilities the sympathy of Vettori and the other exile leaders was with Clement to whom they had wanted the city to be surrendered rather than to the imperialists,[93] but when it

[88] G. Canestrini, *Op. ined.*, ii, p. 376; R. von Albertini, p. 413, F. Vettori to Francesco del Nero.   [89] R. von Albertini, p. 428.
[90] Text in P. Falletti-Fossati, i, pp. 465–7; cp. C. Roth, p. 336.
[91] B. Varchi, ii, pp. 568–71.   [92] G.-B. Niccolini, p. lxii.
[93] B. Cavalcanti to Florentine *Balìa*, Rome, 18 Aug. 1530, cit. R. Caggese, p. 5; B. Varchi, ii, p. 509.

came to discussion of the type of government to be established in Florence, their ways began to diverge once more. The eight extant memoranda, three by Vettori, two by Roberto Acciaiuoli, and one each by Alessandro de' Pazzi and Francesco and Luigi Guicciardini, show that the absolute rule desired by the pope was by no means the type of government desired by the majority of the principal citizens.[94]

Felix Gilbert has shown that these *pareri* fall into two distinct groups connected with discussions between Clement and certain citizens in Rome in 1531 and 1532 respectively.[95] The earlier set was on the whole concerned with problems of an immediate, practical and economic nature. Vettori's so-called 'second' *parere* was partly of this type. As we have seen,[96] he was actively engaged in the re-establishment of the Florentine economy; in this 'second' *parere*, as in the financial memorandum preserved in the Biblioteca Nazionale and in the note sent to Bartolomeo Lanfredini, reference is made to military expenditure, Malatesta Baglioni being cited in all three, in the first two the expense being given as 5000 ducats.[97] The 'second' *parere* in making the remark that 'since we are not able to do without the *Guardia* which costs 3000 a month, every effort will have to be made to reduce other expenses', seems to allude to Vettori's disagreement with the pope on this matter in April 1531 and thereby to corroborate Professor Gilbert's opinion that it was written then and was in fact the first of Vettori's memoranda.[98] But while it is likely that the emphasis placed by the leading citizens on economic matters in these early memoranda was intended to deflect Clement from absolute government in Florence,[99] it is also probably true that though Vettori did not want Alessandro as absolute ruler of his city any more than his colleagues did, he was nevertheless more in favour of a very narrowly-based government and of the use of force to preserve it.

Vettori's approach to politics is thoroughly materialistic. In

[94] Published in *A.S.I.*, i (1842), pp. 420–67.
[95] F. Gilbert, 'Alcuni discorsi', p. 14.
[96] Above, pp. 231–2.
[97] B.N.F. II, III, 433, fo. 137r; R. von Albertini, p. 431; *A.S.I.*, i (1842), p. 441.
[98] F. Gilbert, 'Alcuni discorsi', p. 14; above, p. 232.
[99] F. Gilbert, 'Alcuni discorsi', p. 19.

the 'second' *parere* his basic assumption, which is not new to his political thought, is that the Medici party depends for its existence on its members' hopes of material gain; hence for its maintenance only one choice is open—to win friends by the offer of profitable political office, or to use force.[100] The profit motive as a basis for party membership must derive from Vettori's experience in Medici government since 1512 but by the time of the last Florentine Republic he had come to the conclusion that since distribution of office was the clue to stability, no republican form of government could hope to survive in Florence unless either the city's income doubled or the number of citizens was cut by half.[101] As we have seen, concern over the paucity of profitable offices for supporters determined his attitude towards the size of the post-war *Balìa* and to the *squittino*.[102] In the 'second' *parere* after an opening analysis of the number and type of the Medici party's enemies, which he regards as the essential preliminary to a decision on the type of government to be adopted, Vettori concludes that the number of enemies is far in excess of the number of profitable offices that can be offered so that since 'the love of the populace towards the prince proceeds from the profit to be gained (*utile*)' and profits are inadequate, 'we are obliged to consider keeping the regime in power by force'.[103]

The need to hold the state by force had also not been absent from Vettori's earlier thought. In 1513 Francesco had considered it advisable to retain the *Guardia*,[104] and his fears for the safety of the Medici regime probably brought him close to Paolo's recommendation in a memorandum to Cardinal Giovanni before he left Florence: 'Your ancestors, beginning with Cosimo and continuing down to Piero depended for their ascendancy more on their industry than on force, but you must rely more on force than on hard work because you have more enemies and fewer means of satisfying them.'[105] Vettori's own solution for the safety of the Medici party in the 1530s—the use

[100] *A.S.I.*, i (1842), pp. 437, 42.
[101] B. Varchi, i, p. 367; *Sommario*, p. 293; *Sacco*, pp. 425–6.
[102] Above, pp. 233–5.
[103] *A.S.I.*, i (1842), p. 438.
[104] C. Strozz., I, 136, fo. 221r. Francesco to Paolo, Rome, 17 Feb. 1513.
[105] R. von Albertini, p. 345.

of force and a reduction of the number of offices so that those which remained could be paid and profitable—amounts to a rationalization of the absolutism which, as we shall see, the pope and his friend Filippo Strozzi wanted him to accept.

Concern with the size and the nature of the opposition to the Medici characterizes a letter which Vettori wrote to the treasurer Francesco del Nero in which he likewise suggests the solution of government by force. Von Albertini has published this letter without dating it, though he points out that it has close similarity with the *parere* of April 1531.[106] The appearance in it of a criticism of Bartolomeo Valori's over-confident attitude towards the political situation makes it clear that the letter was written before the end of 1530 when Bartolomeo was recalled as the chief papal representative in Florence and replaced by Nicholas Schönberg, who arrived there on 29 January 1531. It would therefore appear to be an early expression of the opinions put forward in the 'second' memorandum. Opening with the words, 'For many years this regime will be viable only if maintained by force' the letter goes on to seek the cause of the resistance to the Medici. The cause which Vettori suggests—the love of pleasure (*volupta*) which draws all men— is characteristic not only of his materialistic but also his often moralistic attitude to political events and reminds one that he liked to read not only history but theology. In the *Sommario*, for instance, the sack of Rome is considered to be God's punishment for the vices of the Romans,[107] and, as we saw, for his own exile in 1529 he had blamed not fate but the vices of ignorance and ambition.[108]

Everything now turns on the type of force to be adopted, and here, too, there is similarity between the letter to the treasurer and the 'second' *parere*. Vettori's suggestion in the *parere* is reminiscent of Aristotle or of Machiavelli.[109] Alessandro should be a despot without appearing to be one: 'We are obliged to adopt a method whereby Alessandro is indeed master and does whatever he wills but the city can still, fancifully, be called "free".'[110] With echoes of Paolo's memorandum, Francesco

[106] R. von Albertini, pp. 411–13.   [107] *Sommario*, p. 381.
[108] Above, p. 220.   [109] N. Machiavelli, *Il Principe*, ed. A. Burd, p. 289.
[110] *A.S.I.*, i (1842), p. 439.

maintains that the methods of Cosimo and Lorenzo the Magnificent are no longer practicable because there are insufficient *amici*, and because the main consideration must be the security of the Medici party; hence, whether he be regarded as a tyrant or merely the leading citizen, Pandolfo Petrucci, the ruler of Siena, must now be the exemplar.[111] Vettori would keep the *Guardia*, well organized and well paid and with a good captain;[112] the Colleges would be abolished, and the *Signoria* reduced to five. The Eight, the *Otto di Guardia*, ten *accoppiatori* and thirteen *procuratori* would be appointed and the government would be carried on by the *Balìa*. The *squittino* would be solely for effect since the *accoppiatori* would select whom they pleased regardless of the election results. Citizens who did not obey would be deprived of office, for 'we are obliged to maintain the government by fear.'[113]

Professor Gilbert maintains that, although the *pareri* of Francesco Vettori and Francesco Guicciardini more or less sanctioned absolutism, nevertheless they made little mention of constitutional change, economic problems, as already mentioned, taking first place. This seems to be less true of Vettori than Guicciardini. Vettori seems to have been concerned with constitutional reform from the beginning: the earliest of his *pareri* already contains the germ of propositions developed in the last. Although in April 1531 he does not, for instance, actually suggest the abolition of the *Signoria*, this is in fact implied by his proposal to reduce it to five members; and in the already-mentioned letter to the treasurer Francesco del Nero, as well as in a letter of 1 March 1531 to Bartolomeo Lanfredini he considers its complete abolition.[114] In his contemporary tenth Discourse Guicciardini, on the other hand, is less close to absolutism. Like Vettori he is aware both of the large number of Medici opponents and of the pressing need for money but unlike him he is definitely against the use of force. On this latter point Guicciardini's views are closer to those of Jacopo Salviati,

---

[111] *Ibid.*, p. 439; cp. Machiavelli's and other contemporary references to P. Petrucci, N. Machiavelli, *Il Principe*, ed. A. Burd, pp. 330–1, n. 26. Vettori himself knew and admired Petrucci's minister, Antonio da Venafro, when he was at the imperial court in 1508, *ibid.*, p. 347; above, p. 33.

[112] *A.S.I.*, i (1842), p. 439.

[113] *Ibid.*, p. 440.   [114] R. von Albertini, p. 433.

whereas, as one would suspect from their close friendship, those of Vettori are similar to Strozzi's: Guicciardini declared, 'I do not believe that there is anyone so mad who would not be of the opinion that the regime which has some friends is more secure than that founded entirely on force',[115] and Jacopo Salviati is reported to have said that the most secure principate was built on the affections of the people.[116]

As is well known, Filippo Strozzi wanted to protect the Medici regime by building a fortress to whose construction Jacopo Salviati was strongly opposed.[117] Strozzi may, however, have been influenced by a recommendation of Vettori's since, as John Hale has pointed out, 'The first hint of a citadel' occurs in a letter which Vettori wrote to Filippo in February 1532.[118] In connection with a suggested security measure of confiscating arms, Francesco remarked to Strozzi, 'I should like to see them in a secure place; a fortress would be suitable, either where the *capitani* have already started work, or somewhere else.' Where in fact the captains of the Guelf party had started work, as Professor Hale shows, and a further comment at the end of Vettori's letter corroborates,[119] was outside the Porta alla Giustizia. This fortress, Vettori now recommended should be 'finished'. But by the autumn he felt it was inadequate and suggested building another: 'having made a trifling fortress which cannot be taken without artillery', he wrote to Bartolomeo Lanfredini, 'it would be still better to build another which could be defended by artillery'.[120]

Absolutism Guicciardini would have introduced only as slowly as possible.[121] Unlike Vettori, he does not suggest a reduction of the *Signoria*, nor any other constitutional measures, but is content to point out that enemies must be suppressed and that the government must not fall for lack of money. He expressed the fears of all the leading *ottimati*, however, when he

[115] G. Canestrini, *Op. ined.*, ii, p. 382.

[116] F. Nerli, p. 260.   [117] *Ibid.*; B. Segni, i, pp. 342–3.

[118] J. Hale, 'The End of Florentine Liberty: The Fortezza Da Basso', in *Florentine Studies*, ed. N. Rubinstein (London, 1968), p. 506; L. Ferrai, *Lorenzino de' Medici e la Società Cortigiana del Cinquecento* (Milan, 1891), p. 452.

[119] J. Hale, 'The End of Florentine Liberty', etc., p. 506; L. Ferrai, p. 454.

[120] R. von Albertini, p. 450; cit. J. Hale, p. 510.

[121] G. Canestrini, *Op. ined.*, ii, p. 379.

wrote what they now knew from their experiences during the last Republic and after the capitulation to be true, that 'no one ... who is regarded as a friend of the Medici can have a chance in a million to remain alive if the government is restored to the populace'.[122]

Only later in the year 1531, after the failure of their attempt at political autonomy were the *ottimati* forced to adhere to the papal plan for Florence. During the winter of 1531-2, when Clement was more certain that the leaders of the *ottimati* were moving into line with his intentions, he again requested their written opinions.[123] To this later period belongs Vettori's so-called 'first' *parere* which was, however, written in February 1532.[124] It contains the logical development or repetition of several views already expressed in the 'second'. The central idea of the 'first' *parere* is the abolition of the *Signoria*. Experience of past revolutions has shown that it was within the *Signoria* that they had begun; its removal would, therefore, render the enemy harmless, but what about the means of gaining supporters? In 1532, as in 1531, Vettori would win them by providing opportunities for honour and gain: if the *Signoria* is abolished, the money saved on it can be distributed among the other offices like the *Dodici Buonuomini*, the *Otto di Pratica*, the *Otto di Guardia* and the *Conservatori di legge*, which until now have been unsalaried. In this way profit could be attached to offices of honour, but these offices would be very few and the government very narrowly based. In a letter of 17 October 1532 to Bartolomeo Lanfredini Vettori again refers to Petrucci's government: 'I maintain that we must govern the city as Pandolfo governed Siena and in a yet more despotic manner, and even then it will hardly do.'[125] Hatred of those citizens whose policy had in Vettori's view led to the devastation in 1530 led to the conclusion that the city must be ruled with a 'rod of iron'. Just as in 1531 he had condemned the *voluptà* of the young men, so now to Lanfredini he wrote: 'We are dealing with the most wretched, the most obstinate and the most ignorant men in the world who

---

[122] M. Rastrelli, i, p. 240.

[123] F. Nerli, pp. 259-60; F. Gilbert, 'Alcuni discorsi', pp. 13, 19-21, 23.

[124] *A.S.I.*, i (1842), pp. 433-6; for the dating, F. Gilbert, 'Alcuni discorsi', pp. 3-24.   [125] R. von Albertini, p. 449.

do not care if they lack bread, wine and all the necessities of life or if they allow to be despoiled, or themselves despoil, villas and possessions through their competition and obstinacy. If we think that they would not do the same again, we deceive ourselves.'[126] If anyone should object, Vettori went on, that he was not a good Christian, his answer would be that the Gospel precept was to love one's neighbour; he did not know of a better love, or one that did more good, than to see that the city did not fall again into the hands of these licentious, raving, evil and ignorant men. Stripped of its not uncommon condemnation of the young by the elderly, Vettori's attitude betrays the same basic concern with the practical application of the Gospel in daily life which we have already detected in the biography of his father and in the *Viaggio*.[127] It is close, also, to Machiavelli's views on the political effects of the *materia corrotta*, which in its worst stage of corruption requires to be disciplined by force, even by a despot.

In contrast, Guicciardini continued to stress the need to move slowly towards absolutism, obviously in the hope of avoiding the final step altogether. In his *parere* of January 1532,[128] which Professor Gilbert has shown to be a more theoretical and polished version of the seventh Discourse,[129] Guicciardini says, 'I do not see that total reduction to an absolute type of rule offers at present either greater power or security; it is one of those things which when they have to be done, I believe, should be taken unhurriedly and when the opportunity occurs, and in such a way that it comes almost of its own accord.'[130] This statement is subtly different from the opening words of Vettori's *parere* of February 1532: 'Since it is not Our Lord's pleasure that the duke become absolute ruler of the city, it is necessary that it be governed by magistrates who have the name while the duke in fact has the power',[131] and some way removed from Vettori's conclusion that since men will not be content with having office in name but not in fact, it is better to abolish a magistracy like the *Signoria* altogether. The solution which Francesco Guicciardini proposes differs from Vettori's by placing more emphasis on the carrot than on the stick, more that is

---

[126] *Ibid.*

[127] Above, p. 6.

[128] *A.S.I.*, i (1842), pp. 453–8.

[129] 'Alcuni discorsi', p. 10.

[130] *A.S.I.*, i (1842), p. 456.

[131] *Ibid.*, p. 433.

on the careful distribution of offices with the object of winning friends than on the abolition of organs of government. Offices, Guicciardini maintained, should be so distributed that those who received them were bound to the party because they would be so hated by the populace (*l'universale*) that they could not be safe under a 'popular' government; his maxim would be not to reward any opponent unless it was necessary for the purpose of extracting the maximum gain (*frutto*) from him. He did not consider it a matter of vital importance whether the *Signoria* was abolished or not.[132]

Roberto Acciaiuoli, too, was much less insistent on the need for force than Francesco Vettori.[133] His problem seems to have been to try to find some way of winning over the neutrals to support of the party. Like Vettori he appreciated the difficulty of this owing to the lack of money, but, unlike him, he wanted to abolish the *Guardia* which he reckoned would amount to a saving of 30,000 ducats per annum.[134] If there were a way of rewarding friends without touching the public revenues, Roberto Acciaiuoli would welcome it, but he is against the use of force and restriction of the size of the government. Like Francesco Guicciardini, he sought the solution of 'good order': 'I fear too great compulsion would crack us, and I believe that the establishment of good order would be just as secure as force'.[135] In general, however, Roberto admits to being unable to offer counsel and prefers to leave the solution to others: 'What the remedies to these dangers are, I am not able to see because my eyes cannot perceive in this darkness; and I would rather someone else did the inventing because the more I think about it, the more confused I become.'[136]

Luigi Guicciardini seems to approach most closely to Vettori in his proposals for the arrangement of offices.[137] He suggests thirty, or better, forty citizens be responsible for carrying out the *squittino*. From among their number the Eight are to be appointed; the Eight of Ward must include one of them as must also the *Conservatori di legge*. So that this large number of citizens did not have to assemble on every occasion, ten citizens were to

[132] *Ibid.*, p. 458.   [133] *Ibid.*, pp. 448–52.
[134] *Ibid.*, p. 450.   [135] *Ibid.*, p. 452.
[136] *Ibid.*, p. 449.   [137] *Ibid.*, pp. 459–67.

be chosen by the duke to act for them. Luigi advocates the removal of the *Signoria*, the *Dodici Buonuomini*, and the gonfalonier. Like Vettori he considers the *Signoria* a cause of revolutions and like him, too, he thinks the money for their maintenance could be distributed elsewhere. He also wants a council of Two Hundred. Luigi Guicciardini's suggestions, like Vettori's, approximate to the final constitutional settlement of April 1532. Like Vettori (but unlike Acciaiuoli) Luigi Guicciardini considered the *Guardia* to be of great importance, but differed from Vettori in wanting to increase it. There is in Luigi's writing, too, a pale reflection of Vettori's bitterness against the young men opposed to the Medici. Luigi did not think that any grace or favour would remove the feelings which the opponents of the Medici harboured. They would always use every opportunity to try to return to the way of life they wanted. The supporters of the Medici must rise or fall with the fortunes of that house. Fresh measures must be taken to secure the regime against the hundred or so remaining suspects among whom were the most courageous and pertinacious young men.

Vettori supported absolutism because, given the political and economic conditions of the time, he believed that for the *amici* it was the only safe solution. But he supported it also because he knew it was the will of the pope for whom, despite all that had happened, in December 1530 he still had 'the greatest regard' and whose life he considered compared so favourably with those of past popes that he could 'find few who have so many good qualities as Clement'. This was not flattery but 'the real truth'.[138] Vettori was prepared to collaborate with Clement and to execute his policy for Florence also out of friendship for Filippo Strozzi who in his turn, according both to his brother and to Benedetto Buondelmonti, was anxious to propitiate the pope for his actions in 1527 by doing everything possible in his cause.[139] Strozzi was, therefore, the obvious link between Vettori and Clement, and between Florence and Rome. During the enlargement of the *Balìa* the pope's preferences were, as we have seen, conveyed to Vettori and Florence through Filippo

---

[138] R. von Albertini, p. 429.
[139] G.-B. Niccolini, p. lxi; B. Segni, ii, p. 25; B.N.F. Ginori Conti, 29, 32, insert 3, fo. 21r; *A.S.I.*, i (1842), p. 476.

Strozzi.[140] Filippo was in Rome also in the winter of 1531–2, and both Nerli and Segni record that on his return to Florence in the spring he unfolded Clement's plans to him and to Matteo Strozzi.[141] Segni's account is interesting since it describes both Vettori's relationship with Filippo and his attitude to the pope. He says that on coming to Florence, Filippo 'among the first tested the opinion of Francesco Vettori, being his great friend and one who with him had favoured Duke Lorenzo's greatness'. He found Vettori at first opposed to the idea of Alessandro becoming absolute ruler but eventually persuaded him 'not so much by reasoning as by having informed him in no uncertain terms that this was what the pope wished'. Filippo Strozzi clearly knew of Vettori's respect for Clement. Segni also mentions that Strozzi was the most anxious of all the citizens in Rome to carry out the papal intention of making Alessandro *principe* in both name and fact. It cannot therefore be a coincidence that in Florence Vettori came closest to this point of view, even though, as we have seen, ever since the death of Lorenzo, duke of Urbino, Vettori's realistic attitude to politics had lent itself to a narrowly based type of government, and since 1512 the need to hold the state by force had never been entirely absent from the political thought of either Francesco or Paolo.

Vettori turned the will of the pope, as represented to him by Strozzi, into the reality of the 1532 constitution, for, as Professor Gilbert has pointed out, his third *parere*, of April 1532, must have been the basis on which the 1532 settlement was negotiated.[142] It must have been written before 4 April 1532 since it suggests that the *Balìa* should declare twelve men appointed to reform the government and, according to the ordinance of 27 April 1532, these twelve reformers were appointed by a decree the *Balìa* of 4 April.[143] This was not the only one of Vettori's proposals which was adopted in the final ordinance. As he suggested, the *Signoria* and gonfalonierate were to be abolished by the twelve and the *Balìa* was to be increased to two hundred. From it a smaller council of forty-eight was, as

---

[140] Above, p. 233.   [141] F. Nerli, p. 262; B. Segni, i, p. 343.
[142] 'Alcuni discorsi', p. 13; F. Vettori's third *parere* is printed in *A.S.I.*, i (1842), pp. 442–5.   [143] Printed in L. Cantini, i, p. 5.

CHAPTER XI

Epilogue: Ducal Florence

CLEMENT VII succeeded so well in his aim to strengthen the Medici in Florence that the ruling family was able to survive his death in 1534, the crisis of Alessandro's murder in January 1537, and the rebellion of an influential citizen in the following summer. With these events we come to the close of an epoch in Florentine history, as well as to the end of Vettori's life. Henceforth Florence was to be a duchy, and the struggle of the *ottimati* to retain the political position enjoyed in the fifteenth century drew to a finish with the deaths of its principal representatives. For Francesco Vettori the death of Clement VII and Filippo Strozzi ended respectively a period of papal service and a personal friendship both of which had had a significant influence on his rôle in Florentine politics. The deaths of Vettori himself and of Francesco Guicciardini, Filippo and Matteo Strozzi and Roberto Acciaiuoli helped to deprive the city of aristocratic leadership.[1]

1. THE GOVERNMENT OF ALESSANDRO (1532-7)

From 1532-7 the 'rod of iron' advocated by Vettori was wielded by Duke Alessandro. As long as Clement VII was alive, relations between Rome and Florence seem to have been similar to those before 1527. Segni relates how Alessandro governed with Clement's advice, maintaining in Rome Benedetto Buondelmonti, who wrote continuously concerning even the smallest details which the pope wished to be carried out in Florence.[2] Migliore Cresci writes 'all affairs are con-

---

[1] F. Strozzi died in 1538, F. Vettori in 1539, F. Guicciardini in 1540, Matteo Strozzi in 1541; R. Acciaiuoli died at the age of 80 in 1547; cp. B. Segni, ii, pp. 217-18.

[2] B. Segni, ii, p. 38.

ducted at the behest (*voto*) of Clement'[3] and Varchi states concerning the reform of government that Alessandro did nothing without the pope's prior consent.[4] Within the city control over the citizens became more severe. Various reforms aimed to strengthen the Medici position. The important political reform of April 1532 had established the pyramid-shaped political structure of the Medici government with the Council of Two Hundred at the base, the smaller council of the Forty-eight above, and the four councillors and the duke at the apex; supplementary to this main structure were the *Otto di Guardia* and the Eight. Partisans of the Medici filled these offices,[5] but important posts were held by non-Florentines, and Florentine citizens were little trusted.[6] Already between 1524–7 the cardinal of Cortona, a foreigner, had been the chief adviser of the young Medici, but after 1532 Alessandro made greater and deliberate use in his administration of men from the Florentine dominion or from other Italian states. Segni remarks that, although he came from Colle di Val d'Elsa, the chief secretary, Francesco Campana, was 'in charge of the greater part of the important activities' of the duke.[7] Alessandro's harsh chancellor, ser Maurizio di Romagna, came from the region on Florence's north-eastern border, as his name implies. A citizen from Parma was to be given charge of the new fortress which the pope had decided should be built in Florence;[8] the citadels of Pisa and Livorno were held by pro-imperial castellans from Fabriano and Pisa respectively,[9] and Alessandro Vitelli, the commander of Alessandro's augmented guard was also an outsider.[10] Revolution was to be prevented at all costs: the *Otto di Guardia* were made responsible for disarming the populace who were forbidden to carry any weapons except swords and daggers within an eight-mile radius of the city;[11] the site for the new fortress was discussed;[12] and in 1533 the boundaries of the areas to which the opponents of the regime

---

[3] 'Storia d'Italia', 1525–46, B.N.F. II, III, 65, fo. 121r.
[4] B. Varchi, iii, p. 24.   [5] B. Segni, i, p. 345.
[6] *Ibid.*, ii, pp. 58–9.   [7] *Ibid.*, p. 58.
[8] F. Nerli, p. 282.   [9] G.-B. Niccolini, pp. 231, 217.
[10] J. Hale, 'The End of Florentine Liberty', p. 510.
[11] *Ibid.*, p. 510.
[12] F. Nerli, p. 270; on this fortress, J. Hale, 'The End of Florentine Liberty'.

had been confined were changed.[13] Many of these *confinati*, on finding themselves restricted to even less acceptable places, broke bounds, thus turning themselves technically into 'rebels' whose possessions could be confiscated.[14] Harsh measures were taken against all rebels and those found carrying the prohibited arms.[15]

However, one Florentine, Filippo Strozzi, at first enjoyed considerable power and the confidence of Alessandro.[16] We have seen how in order to ingratiate himself with the pope, he had accepted Clement's plans for Florence and had persuaded Francesco Vettori and Matteo Strozzi to make his nephew absolute ruler,[17] and it seems as if after the establishment of Alessandro, Filippo's position in the city was as much dependent upon the will of the pope as upon his considerable wealth and the large number of his sons. On the entry of the young Margaret, Alessandro's bride-to-be, into Florence in April 1533 on her way from Flanders to Naples,[18] Filippo Strozzi was the leader of the jousts, banquets and other festivities held in her honour; his sons had been among the young companions with whom the duke had passed the previous winter in masquerades and feasting.[19] It was the eldest, Piero, who, as a result of his embassy to Spain on Alessandro's behalf, had caused the emperor to send Margaret to Naples in anticipation of her marriage.[20] Such a seemingly amicable relationship between the Strozzi and the Medici was, however, not to last. Minor disturbances of the peace and amorous intrigues reveal the tensions between the two families. A potion which Alessandro received from his mistress was said to contain poison administered at the instigation of Filippo Strozzi, whose mistress the lady had also been.[21] Piero Strozzi was reported to be one of the three young men who one night attacked and wounded Alessandro's close companion, Giuliano Salviati,[22] in

[13] B. Varchi, iii, p. 75.

[14] F. Nerli, p. 271; cp. J. Hale, 'The End of Florentine Liberty', p. 510, n. 8.

[15] F. Nerli, p. 271.

[16] B. Segni, ii, p. 7.   [17] Above, p. 248.

[18] F. Nerli, p. 269.   [19] B. Segni, ii, p. 20.

[20] *Ibid.*, p. 21; obviously Alessandro feared she would be given in marriage to someone else, and on her arrival in Naples Luigi Ridolfi gave her the ring.

[21] *Ibid.*, pp. 25–6.   [22] *Ibid.*, pp. 20, 39.

revenge for his insulting remarks about Piero's sister.[23] One of Filippo's daughters, Luisa, was said to have been poisoned by Alessandro because she denied him her favours.[24] Segni relates that even before the affair of the potion, the pope was suspicious of Filippo for his part in the revolution of 1527 and wished to separate him from the duke.[25] Seizing the opportunity of the embassy to France for the marriage of Catherine de' Medici to Henry, duke of Orleans, he appointed Filippo papal nuncio to Francis I, giving him the office ostensibly as an honour but in fact as the means of removing him from Florence where he feared the effects of his power.[26]

The embassy to Francis was a turning point in Filippo's relations with the Medici. He was as angry with Clement as with Alessandro[27] because, despite many previous promises to his wife, Clarice, his son had not been made a cardinal.[28] Having consequently no wish to return to Florence, he remained in France as the papal nuncio. Strozzi's sons, too, left the city, either to join their father or to seek the protection in Rome of Cardinal Ippolito de' Medici, who was glad to oppose Alessandro in any way possible.[29] Hence after Clement VII's death in September 1534 and Filippo's subsequent return to Rome,[30] the Strozzi together with Cardinal Ridolfi and Lorenzo his brother, Cardinal Salviati and those other sons of Jacopo who were outside Florence became the leading supporters of Cardinal Ippolito's rebellious moves against Duke Alessandro's government in Florence.[31]

Like Strozzi's, Francesco Vettori's political position during Alessandro's regime owed something to his particular relations with the pope, although Filippo was in a position to lend Clement money on a considerable scale,[32] whereas poverty forced Vettori to accept from him a substantial part of his income. The annual benefice of 200 ducats which he received

---

[23] B. Varchi, iii, pp. 62–7; F. Nerli, p. 272.
[24] B. Segni, ii, p. 65.   [25] Ibid., p. 25.
[26] Ibid., p. 24; F. Nerli, p. 273.
[27] B. Varchi, iii, p. 81; F. Nerli, p. 273.
[28] F. Nerli, p. 272.   [29] F. Nerli, p. 273.
[30] B. Segni, ii, pp. 45–6; F. Nerli, p. 276.
[31] F. Nerli, p. 276.
[32] A. Bardi, 'Filippo Strozzi', p. 68; G.-B. Niccolini, pp. 194, 196, 200.

in 1530 and which was renewed again in 1533 proves that
Vettori both served Clement and was valued by him.[33] In
stating that Alessandro's administration left the citizens little
standing, Segni singles out Francesco Vettori and Roberto
Acciaiuoli as among the few who retained some because they
were trusted by the pope.[34] Certainly Vettori's reputation
would not appear to have derived entirely from the political
offices which he held at this period, for these were few. He had
been one of the twelve Reformers appointed in April 1532 to
alter the constitution,[35] and he was a member of the Council
of Forty-eight.[36] In October 1532 he figures among the third
group of ducal councillors to be drawn for a three months' term
of office since the new constitution began,[37] but he was not
chosen again until April 1535 and July 1538.[38] Unlike
Acciaiuoli and Matteo Strozzi, who were chosen earlier,[39]
Vettori was not appointed lieutenant to take the place of the
duke until 1537.[40] In the election of June 1533 he was appointed
one of the *Dodici Buonuomini*[41] and in September 1535 one of the
Otto di Guardia.[42]

As in 1527, however, Vettori's influence on his city's affairs
was greater than one might suspect from the number of his
offices or the infrequency with which he held them. He was, for
example, one of those who advised Alessandro to choose
Francesco Campana as ducal secretary.[43] External affairs too
provide a clue to Vettori's importance. This he himself reveals
in reporting to Bartolomeo Lanfredini the surprise of certain
Sienese that one so poor could possibly be 'that Francesco
Vettori who had so often been an ambassador and a member of
the Eight'.[44] In March 1532 he had again been appointed to
that office,[45] and five months later his colleagues made use of

---

[33] Above, p. 165; in Oct. 1525 Vettori's income was 130 ducats and he owned
one-third of a house, A. Bardi, 'Filippo Strozzi', p. 44.

[34] B. Segni, ii, p. 7.   [35] L. Cantini, i, p. 5.   [36] Tratte, 85, fo. 192r.

[37] *Ibid.*, fo. 193r, elected 29 Oct. 1532 to take office on 1 Nov. 1532.

[38] *Ibid.*, fos. 193v, 194v.

[39] In April 1535 and October 1536 respectively. Tratte, 85, fos. 193r, 194r.

[40] Tratte, 85, fo. 194r.

[41] B.N.F. Ms. G. Capponi, 102, fo. 118r.   [42] Tratte, 85, fo. 74v.

[43] M. Rastrelli, *Storia d'Alessandro de' Medici*, ii (Firenze, 1781), Bk. iv, p. 5; cp.
R. von Albertini, p. 449.   [44] *Ibid.*, p. 450.

[45] Otto di Pratica epoca del Principato, 30, list preceding fo. 1r.

his knowledge of an area with which he had past official and
present private connections.[46] A dispute had arisen between the
inhabitants of Pietrasanta and of Florence's subject citizens of
Lucca over the course of the river at Camaiore, and as Vettori
was at hand in his villa,[47] the Eight temporarily appointed him
their commissary to settle the matter, notifying Giovanni
Tedaldi, their commissary at Pietrasanta to this effect.[48]
Although the terms of settlement were not drawn up until the
following summer,[49] Vettori must have soon satisfied the Eight
that in accordance with their instructions all he ordered and
commanded had been carried out, for he had returned by the
time they wrote to Tedaldi on 13 September to tell him that
their colleague had reported back to them.[50] Eight months or
so later, as previously in his career, Vettori's help was sought on
papal policy. He had been asked to advise whether Clement
should undertake his contemplated journey to France for the
marriage of his niece or whether it would be wiser first to
consult Charles V.[51] Although evasively declaring himself to be
too old, timid and cautious to discuss such affairs, Vettori's
veiled answer was in fact 'no' to both questions. As Clement
could hardly undertake the journey without running the risk of
offending the emperor, it is not surprising to find that Vettori's
views were shared by Francesco Guicciardini and Jacopo
Salviati, who similarly opposed the projected journey. Although
Strozzi made their opinions known to the pope, Clement
nevertheless persisted in the belief that his expedition could
satisfy France without offending the emperor, and set out from
Rome in September 1533.[52] Vettori's connection with external
affairs continued throughout Alessandro's rule. In January 1535
Niccolò Guicciardini was to observe that he was one of those

---

[46] Above, p. 92. He had a villa in the neighbourhood, see F.V. to Bartolomeo
Lanfredini, 17 Oct. 1532, R. von Albertini, p. 450; Paolo had had connections
both with Pietrasanta and with the area farther south, near Pisa, above, p. 94.

[47] R. von Albertini, p. 450.

[48] Otto di Pratica, epoca del Principato, 30, fo. 33v: 'Trovandosi costì Francesco Vectori nostro Collega et desiderando noi che la differentia nata sopra
il fiume di Camaiore si expedischa ci è parso a proposito dar questa cura a lui e
però l'habbia facto in questo affare nostro Commissario'; cp. Otto, Delib., 9, fo.
127v, Vettori's 'patente' dated 20 Aug. 1532.

[49] Otto, Delib., 9, fos. 288r–293v.   [50] Otto di Pratica, 30, fol. 36v.
[51] R. von Albertini, p. 454.   [52] G.-B. Niccolini, pp. 188, 189.

most frequently consulted on foreign matters. 'Here things go on as usual', he wrote, 'and external business of importance the Duke discusses with Francesco [Guicciardini], Francesco Vettori, Roberto Acciaiuoli and Bartolomeo Valori.'[53] At the end of 1535 Vettori probably accompanied Alessandro to Naples to meet Charles V[54] and in the autumn of the following year travelled with him to greet the emperor at Genoa.[55]

If the pope's confidence in him and his experience in foreign affairs enhanced Vettori's political position, his health and his friendship with Strozzi had a detrimental effect. At the time of the constitutional reform in April 1532 Francesco was in his fifty-eighth year; already in the winters of 1521–2 and 1529–30 he had not been well,[56] and now once again ill health brought its attendant expense and loss of opportunity for service to the Medici. Since the spring Vettori had been 'languishing', with a fever which towards the end of July caused him to decide on medical advice to leave Florence to take the waters, although he could ill afford the outlay.[57] In mid-October he was still not fit and he had not fully recovered by the time he was appointed one of the four ducal councillors at the end of the month.[58] In December he wrote to Lanfredini that if he had felt 'anything like well', he would have liked to go to Rome to kiss the pope's feet, but this desire, like the other to serve Duke Alessandro as he had served his natural father Lorenzo, ill health had caused him to forgo. All he could do was to go each morning to the church of S. Trinita and then return home and read.[59] Such frailty—Vettori described his constitution as of 'glass'[60]—probably meant that, although he was one of the four councillors of the duke when Alessandro had joined Clement and Charles V in Bologna, he was able to take only a limited part in the task of governing Florence in the duke's absence. After his three months' term of office as councillor expired at the end of January 1533, he did not hold political office again until June

[53] C. Strozz., Ser. I, 61, fo. 105r: 'et le faccende di fuori di importanta la Ex.tia del Duca le conferisce con messer Francesco, Francesco Vettori, Roberto Acciaiuoli et Bartolomeo Valori'.

[54] Below, p. 263.

[55] B. Segni, ii, p. 119.

[56] Above, pp. 152, 219.

[57] R. von Albertini, p. 448.

[58] Ibid., p. 449.

[59] Ibid., p. 451.

[60] Ibid., p. 449.

when he became a member of the college of the *Dodici Buonuo-mini*.[61] As the renewal of the pension from Clement VII, of which Vettori received notice in this month, was partly due to the representations he had made to Bartolomeo Lanfredini,[62] and seemingly also to Filippo Strozzi[63] about his heavy medical expenses and consequent poverty, it is at least possible that Vettori's salaried appointment was made for these reasons.

Such energy as Vettori could find during the early years of Alessandro's rule was probably fully taken up by economic and administrative functions. In December 1532 he was elected treasurer of the office responsible for administration of the property belonging to the Florentine wards (*pupilli*).[64] Origin-ally the four officials who constituted this office were elected by lot but because this had not infrequently produced none but inexperienced men, it was decided in 1532 to appoint two by lot and two by election, to ensure the inclusion of at least two qualified men.[65] After seven months Vettori was elected also to the office responsible for provisioning the city (the *Abbun-danzia*)[66] and since two of the seven officials, Filippo Strozzi and Piero Salviati, were absent, an extra burden fell on him; Filippo in fact thanked him for the work which he had done on their behalf, saying that he knew how efficient he was.[67] At the end of this year the duke chose Vettori and Ottaviano de' Medici as officials of the *Monte*,[68] or funded debt, for its annual reform.[69] The choice of Francesco seems at first sight a strange one, as usually the richest citizens were chosen, so that if money was lacking to pay the interest on loans, they could lend from their personal property.[70] But Vettori was poor and himself in debt, and in fact asked Filippo Strozzi for a loan of a thousand ducats to invest in the *Monte* in his own name.[71] His concern for financial order and his administrative ability must have accounted for his election. Already six months before his

---

[61] B.N.F. G. Capponi, 102, fo. 118r.   [62] R. von Albertini, p. 450.
[63] G.-B. Niccolini, p. 189.
[64] Tratte, 85, fo. 137r, 'Rationerius Pupillor.'; *ibid.* fo. 100r for the 4 officers. R. von Albertini, p. 451.
[65] B. Varchi, iii, p. 57.   [66] Tratte, 85, fo. 199r.
[67] G.-B. Niccolini, pp. 192, 195.   [68] Tratte, 85, fo. 56r.
[69] B. Varchi, iii, pp. 29, 30.   [70] *Ibid.*, p. 38.
[71] A. Bardi, 'Filippo Strozzi', p. 66.

appointment Vettori was clearly interested in a reorganization of the *Monte*, and suggested to Filippo Strozzi, for papal approval, the opening of a *Monte di Pietà*. By allowing citizens to invest at 10 per cent on amounts of 25 to 30 ducats at a time, a degree of stability would be introduced, fraudulent practice reduced and the gate barred to the Jews for ever. The pope at first condemned the suggestion but later left it to the Florentines to decide.[72] While Vettori was in office a 'law concerning currency' introduced on 5 March 1534 aimed at restoring confidence in Florentine money after the setbacks of the preceding years and was intended perhaps also to control the export of gold coin. Florence minted a silver piece with a new marking 'which was normally to be the currency for all negotiations and contracts'.[73] Vettori's involvement in the practical working of this new law is revealed by a letter to him from Alessandro thanking him for the advice, which he has adopted, of proceeding with the minting in order to remedy the disorders caused by the change of coinage.[74]

Such was the volume of work that Vettori could not leave Florence in the summer of 1534 to take the waters for his health.[75] On 15 May 1534 a new magistracy—the *maestrato degli ufficiali de' rebelli*—consisting of four officials had been created and on the following day Vettori had been elected one of them.[76] Owing to the boundary alterations made in 1533 many of the *confinati* who wished to avoid confiscations to which as rebels they had then become liable, desired to sell or pawn their possessions and one of the tasks of the new officials was to investigate all contracts made by *confinati* and declare them null and void.[77] Probably to this period belongs a memorandum in Vettori's hand advocating pardon for those in the Florentine dominion who had been condemned for non-political offences.[78] Vettori's reasons are largely economic: owing to the great

[72] G.-B. Niccolini, p. 189.

[73] L. Cantini, i, p. 85; cit. R. Caggese, iii, p. 48.

[74] B.M. Add. Mss. 23,721, fo. 23r, Pisa, 17 March 1534.

[75] G.-B. Niccolini, p. 192.

[76] B. Varchi, iii, p. 75; Tratte, 85, fo. 199v; L. Cantini, pp. 98–100.

[77] B. Varchi, iii, pp. 75–6.

[78] C. Strozz., Ser. II, 86, insert 4. Reference to 'l'Exellentia del Duca et li suoi magnifici consiglieri' dates it to after 1532 rather than to the immediate post-war period.

shortage of men in the dominion brought about by the war and plague, those few who remained ought to be able to carry out their business in peace and free from fear of punishment for past offences. Vettori knew that the money such men paid for their pardons would help the Florentine economy. His recommendation that the captains of the Guelf party should control the amount which those paying for pardons would have to spend on notarial fees is typical of his concern that money should not be squandered or reach the wrong pockets.

An important clue to Vettori's place and activities in Alessandro's government may be found in his friendship with Filippo Strozzi. Evidently the duke regarded him as an intermediary between himself and the Strozzi.[79] Alessandro asked him, for instance, to interrogate Piero to find out if he was responsible for the wounding of Giuliano Salviati. Characteristically in reporting back to the duke Vettori toned down the abusive denial which he had received from Piero.[80] A letter written later by Piero on behalf of his father suggests that Vettori was also employed by Alessandro to write to Filippo asking him to be a member of the ceremonial embassy to the new pope Paul III,[81] an appointment which was interpreted by Filippo's brother Lorenzo as a conciliatory gesture on the part of the duke.[82] As Guicciardini's opinion was sought concerning the number of ambassadors to be sent,[83] and as Vettori apparently wrote to Strozzi about this embassy, probably he was consulted too.

While anxious to avail himself in Florence of Vettori's help as an intermediary with the Strozzi, Alessandro may however have been unwilling to allow Filippo and Francesco to meet away from his control. Although one cannot discount ill health as an explanation, the fact that Vettori was not appointed by the duke to go to France with Catherine de' Medici, although Francesco Guicciardini was, may be an indication of Ales-

---

[79] C. Strozz., Ser. V, 1207, fo. 112v. F. Vettori to F. Strozzi, Florence 19 Feb. 1537: 'a tempo del Duca Alexandro el quale più volte mi volle adoperare a scrivervi et parlarvi'.

[80] B. Segni, ii, pp. 39–40; cp. above, p. 219.

[81] C. Strozz., Ser. III, 108, fo. 138r. Rome, 24 Oct. 1534.

[82] G.-B. Niccolini, p. lxxiii.

[83] G. Canestrini, Op. ined., x (Firenze, 1867), pp. 271–2.

sandro's policy towards Vettori and Strozzi. Vettori would otherwise have been a more likely choice than Guicciardini since it was he who had been in France earlier and had in fact arranged the marriage between Catherine's parents. Moreover Vettori was not appointed one of the ambassadors to Paul III, another obvious choice considering his experience of the Roman court. Filippo remarks to Francesco how much he would have liked him to be one of the ambassadors to Rome so that he could talk with him.[84]

At this period after the death of Clement VII Filippo Strozzi's relations with the duke became further strained, as Alessandro realized that he was joining his rival Ippolito. Lorenzo Strozzi relates that his brother, having told Ippolito of his discontent with the duke, transferred his allegiance.[85] Next he approached Cardinals Salviati and Ridolfi and the jurist Salvestro Aldobrandini.[86] Filippo aimed to prevent the reconciliation between Ippolito and Alessandro desired by Charles V, who on account of the betrothal of his daughter Margaret to Alessandro was concerned with the security of his prospective son-in-law's government in Florence. While deterring Ippolito from accepting the blandishments of the emperor by insisting that with the help of the exiles Florence could be his, Filippo also saw to it that Charles was informed of the iniquities of Alessandro and reminded of the promise made in 1530 that the city should have her liberty; but failing that, the government should at least be transferred to Ippolito.[87] He persuaded Cardinals Salviati and Ridolfi and sent his own son to present to the emperor the views of those nearest in kinship with the Medici; he also caused three exiles—Galeotto Giugni, Paolo Soderini and Antonio Berardi—to put their case to him.[88] Charles, on his way to Africa for the campaign which resulted in the capture of Tunis in May 1535, heard the respective cases but asked the two groups to do nothing until his return, when he promised to take action to their satisfaction.[89] However, before Charles reached Naples on his return from Africa, Ippolito, who had set out to meet him in Sicily, died on 10

[84] G.-B. Niccolini, p. 194.   [85] *Ibid.*, p. lxxiii.   [86] *Ibid.*, pp. lxxiii and lxxiv.
[87] *Ibid.*, pp. lxxiv, lxxvii, lxxix, lxxxi.
[88] *Ibid.*, pp. lxxvi–vii.   [89] *Ibid.*, p. lxxviii.

August at Itri in Apulia,[90] perhaps poisoned by an agent of
Alessandro's, as Strozzi claimed but was prevented from prov-
ing.[91] Although deprived of a figurehead, the exiles under
Filippo's leadership continued in opposition and appeared in
strength at Naples when Duke Alessandro came to meet the
emperor at the end of the year. At the request of Charles'
advisers they put their case in writing and received Francesco
Guicciardini's formal written answer.[92] The threat which they
represented enabled the emperor to demand from Alessandro in
exchange for the hand of his daughter greater obligations than
those previously agreed on, and it was only 'with the utmost
difficulty' that the duke managed to obtain his consent to the
marriage.[93] The exiles' position was considerably weakened by
the loss of Cardinal Ippolito, for the emperor, knowing that
they consisted of two groups—those who like Filippo Strozzi and
Cardinals Ridolfi and Salviati wanted Medici rule but in its
pre-1527 form, and those who desired a return to republican
government—could not be certain that such a disunited body
of citizens would remain faithful to him and not desert to
France.[94] Alessandro thus derived no little advantage from his
rival's death. As Francesco Guicciardini realized, the deciding
factor in Charles' ultimate consent to the marriage was Francis
I's occupation of Piedmont and the emperor's fear that the
duke might defect to him. On the last day of February 1536
Charles' sanction was publicly symbolized by Alessandro's
bestowal of the wedding ring during the pre-Lenten festivities
of Carnival. With the future safety of the Medici house thus
buttressed by a powerful Habsburg alliance, the duke left
Naples for Florence and the disappointed exiles for Rome.[95]

Had he been a member of the Florentine ceremonial embassy
to Rome in November 1534, Vettori might have been tempted
to join or help Strozzi; remaining in Florence, he evidently was
not. Despite the friendship between the two men, it is quite
clear that Vettori now considered it politic to support Alessandro rather than to favour the cause of the exiles. The duke

[90] F. Nerli, p. 278; B. Segni, ii, pp. 83–4.

[91] G.-B. Niccolini, pp. lxxxi–lxxxiii.   [92] B. Segni, ii, pp. 87, 89.

[93] Fra Giuliano Ughi, 'Cronaca di Firenze', in *A.S.I.*, Appendice vii (1849),
p. 180; F. Nerli, p. 282.

[94] F. Nerli, p. 281.   [95] F. Nerli, pp. 282–3; B. Segni, ii, p. 94.

seemed prepared to trust him for he was one of the few whom Alessandro consulted about Filippo Strozzi's suspicious activities in Rome,[96] and Filippo himself appreciated his friend's position.[97] In the spring of 1535 he referred to 'the favour and trust' in which Francesco stood with the duke and he wrote that he had no desire that Vettori's friendship for him should alter his faith in the regime. For his part, Francesco had evidently written to Filippo accusing him of giving financial assistance to the exiles; of supporting Dante da Castiglione, one of the most fervent leaders of the republican party during the siege, who was now seeking the help of Francis I for the exiles; of having incited Ippolito de' Medici to send his secretary to the emperor to request the government of Florence for himself and of having removed his sons from Florence and surrounded himself with exiles.[98] The arrival in Naples of these exiles under Strozzi's leadership made Vettori's political position yet more difficult. Alessandro invited him, together with Francesco Guicciardini, Roberto Acciaiuoli, Matteo Strozzi and Baccio Valori to accompany him south as one of his councillors, but on account of his friendship with Strozzi Vettori at first refused, excusing himself on grounds of ill health. He is in fact not numbered by Segni or Nerli among the four who set out from Florence with the duke, but Segni recounts that Vettori changed his mind later and departed in a litter as befitted the 'great councillor he was at this time'.[99] The chronicler Fra Giuliano Ughi mentions his presence in Naples and so, too, does Varchi.[100] Varchi's reference to Vettori is important because he contrasts his loyalty to the duke with Baccio Valori's desertion. Baccio held secret conversations with Filippo Strozzi and in fact later joined the exiles in Rome.[101] When Alessandro, exasperated by the severe terms which Charles was imposing for his daughter's hand, considered leaving Naples secretly by night, Baccio encouraged his departure but Vettori, together with Guicciardini, Acciaiuoli and Matteo Strozzi, counselled against it. They thus not only saved the duke from dishonour but also enabled him to

---

[96] B. Segni, ii, p. 58.
[97] A. Bardi, 'Filippo Strozzi', p. 77.
[98] *Ibid.*, pp. 74–7.   [99] B. Segni, ii, p. 119.
[100] *A.S.I.*, Appendice vii (1849), p. 180; B. Varchi, iii, p. 203.
[101] B. Varchi, iii, p. 211.

obtain a better contract owing to the situation in Piedmont.[102] In the autumn of 1536 Vettori replaced Valori as a councillor on the journey which Alessandro undertook to greet the emperor at Genoa on his return from an ill-starred summer campaign in Provence.[103] This campaign occasioned in Alessandro's mind fresh hopes of grandeur, for when Antonio de Leyva, the last of the emperor's older generals, died as a result of it, Charles assigned this command to his son-in-law, telling him to prepare for war with France.[104] To help finance future military enterprises, Alessandro proposed on his return to Florence to levy a toll on every bushel of grain milled in the city and the dominion. Even in his despotic government one dissident voice could be heard, though it remained unheeded. True to his past attitude towards the excessive taxation of his compatriots, Francesco Vettori opposed Alessandro's intention on the grounds that the impost was dishonest, harsh and unjust. But his defiance was of no avail. Declaring in anger that he now realized Vettori did not love him, the duke commanded him to be silent and not obstruct the passage of the law; it was passed in secret.[105]

Vettori had accepted Alessandro as prince not because absolutism was his ideal but because, criticize the duke's intentions as he might, he saw no alternative.[106] Just as he had feared the death of Lorenzo, duke of Urbino, he now feared that some danger would befall Alessandro, and he counselled him to be careful. 'What madness is this', he exclaimed, 'that a prince who has conquered Florence by force of arms and is the first ever to have held such dominion should ride forth alone, or with one other, at night with two or three and, what is even more dangerous, entrust one man alone to hold the ladder for climbing a wall.'[107] The wisdom of Vettori's warning became apparent when Alessandro was murdered by his close companion Lorenzo de' Medici in January 1537.

While there is no direct evidence to prove that Lorenzo's

[102] *Ibid.*, pp. 202–3; F. Nerli, pp. 282–3.　　　[103] B. Segni, ii, p. 119.

[104] B. Segni, ii, pp. 117, 120; E. Armstrong, *The Emperor Charles V*, i (London, 1902), p. 287.

[105] B. Segni, ii, p. 120.

[106] B.N.F. Magliab. VIII, 81, fo. 12v; see below, pp. 275, 218.

[107] B. Segni, ii, p. 121.

deed was instigated by Filippo Strozzi, certain facts indicate Lorenzo's sympathy with the exiles' cause. By birth and marriage he had connections with them: his mother was a Soderini[108] and one of his sisters had married Alamanno Salviati,[109] who though himself not in opposition to the duke was nevertheless a brother of the exiled Cardinal Salviati. Lorenzo had been a close friend of Piero Strozzi and the two had exchanged mutual confidences. Piero had complained to him about Alessandro and Lorenzo had confessed to Piero his intention to murder the duke.[110] Later, however, so as to win the duke's confidence and thus facilitate the execution of his crime, Lorenzo had reported Piero's complaints to Alessandro, and Piero in revenge had informed a group of Florentines 'on the side of the Duke' and another 'on that of the exiles' of Lorenzo's intention.[111] Both Vettori and Strozzi were thus fore-warned of what was in Lorenzo's mind, but evidently neither the ducal party nor the exiles took the melancholy young man seriously. Whether they considered them feigned or genuine, Nardi, Segni and Varchi all mention that Lorenzo carried on discussions with the exiles in Rome, which he reported in secret to Alessandro as a means of ingratiating himself with the duke.[112] After Lorenzo had murdered Alessandro, he fled first to Salvestro Aldobrandini in Bologna and then to Strozzi in Venice, who hailed him as Brutus and promised him his sons in marriage to his sisters.[113]

If Lorenzo's motive in murdering Alessandro was really to liberate Florence and not just to avenge some personal affront or to acquire fame, then, as Varchi points out, the crime was badly executed: having performed the deed, he should have made it public and immediately informed the republican citizens in Florence instead of fleeing the city and entrusting the task to his steward.[114] As it was, the courtiers of the dead duke were able to keep the murder secret so that steps could be taken

---

[108] B. Segni, ii, p. 130; B. Varchi, iii, p. 229; G.-B. Niccolini, p. 241.
[109] B. Segni, ii, p. 123.
[110] B. Varchi, iii, pp. 137–8.
[111] B. Varchi, iii, pp. 137–8.
[112] J. Nardi, ii, p. 243; B. Segni, ii, p. 110; B. Varchi, iii, p. 230.
[113] B. Varchi, iii, pp. 236; B. Segni, ii, p. 172–3.
[114] B. Varchi, iii, pp. 237–9.

to prevent a popular rising and to elect a successor before the news had spread.

2. THE ELECTION OF COSIMO

Reactions to the duke's death reveal the diplomatic rivalry between France and Spain and the ever-present fear among the *ottimati* of a popular rising. Outside the city the exiles acted quickly: Cardinals Salviati and Ridolfi, in collusion with the French ambassador, Charles Hémard de Denonville, bishop of Mâcon, hired 1500 infantry and placed them under the command of Gianpaolo da Ceri;[115] Filippo Strozzi, likewise in association with France, moved from Venice to Bologna, where he ordered the levy of a further 3000 troops, these to be placed under the leadership of Count Ieronimo de' Pepoli, a friend of Cardinal Salviati's.[116] Within Florence courtiers of the deceased duke, such as his chief councillor Cardinal Innocenzo Cibo, his principal secretary, Francesco Campana, and Alessandro Vitelli, the commander of his forces, represented the imperial interest.[117] The *ottimati* led by Guicciardini, Vettori, Matteo Strozzi, Acciaiuoli and Niccolini, all of whom had links with their compatriots outside the city, shared the ideal of a limited oligarchical government—'libertas, aut potius ἀριστο-κρατία', as Chiriaco Strozzi expressed it to Filippo[118]—but feared a 'popular' form of government which might lead to their eventual expulsion.[119]

Vettori's reaction to these events provides further proof of that combination of realism and opportunism which had characterized his relations with Lorenzo, Alessandro and Clement VII. Seven years ago he had realized how many were the enemies of the Medici and had seen force as the only solution to the political situation; now he appreciated the incipient danger from the *popolo* and the exiles and in addition the significance of the imperial predominance in Italy. Once again he saw strong government as the only answer and considered the

---

[115] B. Varchi, iii, p. 264.
[116] *Ibid.*; G.-B. Niccolini, p. 223.
[117] G. Adriani, *Istoria de' suoi tempi*, i (Prato, 1822), p. 26.
[118] G.-B. Niccolini, p. 213.
[119] B. Varchi, iii, pp. 241–2 and G.-B. Niccolini, p. xcvii.

election of Cosimo imperative. The choice of Cosimo was, in fact, the outcome of a struggle between foreign, exiled, aristocratic and popular elements, and the particular triumph of the group represented by Vettori and Guicciardini.

Alessandro had been murdered towards midnight on 6 January.[120] The next day, the duke's chamberlains being unable to find him sought out Cardinal Cibo who, although his suspicions were confirmed when he learned of Lorenzo's departure that night for the Mugello, feared, as did Alessandro's secretary Campana, whom he consulted, to open the chamber to discover the truth.[121] The immediate reaction of the court group, of which Cibo was the leading figure, was to conceal the suspected murder from the ducal councillors such as Vettori and Guicciardini and to instruct Alessandro Vitelli to return to Florence immediately.[122] When those 'citizens who by custom came to visit him and do him reverence' arrived at the palace, they were informed that the duke was still sleeping; later, masquerades were enacted in front of the building, insinuating that he was among the masked figures.[123] Rossi assumes that the deceived citizens were Vettori, Guicciardini, Matteo Strozzi, Acciaiuoli and Matteo Niccolini, and this seems likely.[124] Rossi, however, then goes on to dismiss as impossible 'one of the fundamental assertions of Varchi, Segni, Adriani, etc.' that Cardinal Cibo, having learned of the death of Alessandro, immediately took council with those very citizens whom he is reported to have deceived. This is of course unlikely and examination of the sources shows that Varchi at least never said that Cardinal Cibo immediately asked for the opinions of these citizens. His account is interesting; he says that 'il Zeffo', according to his instructions asked certain citizens for their views.[125] 'Zeffo', who was ser Francesco Zeffi, former tutor of Piero Strozzi and steward of Lorenzo's household, had been

[120] B. Varchi, iii, p. 240; accounts of Alessandro's murder and its discovery are given in the contemporary histories. In differences of detail, I have relied to some extent on the reconstruction of A. Rossi, 'La elezione di Cosimo I Medici' in *Atti del R. Istituto Veneto di Scienze, Lettere, ed Arti*, Ser. VII, i (1889–90), pp. 369ff.

[121] B. Varchi, iii, p. 240.

[122] B. Segni, ii, pp. 128–48; B. Varchi, iii, pp. 228–56; S. Ammirato, vi, part ii, pp. 221–6; G. Adriani, i, pp. 19–31.

[123] B. Segni, ii, p. 134; B. Varchi, iii, p. 241.

[124] A. Rossi, 'La elezione', p. 405.   [125] B. Varchi, iii, pp. 237, 241.

ordered by his master to go early in the morning after the murder to Giuliano Capponi and 'many other citizens loving liberty' to inform them of it.[126] Varchi groups the people visited by Zeffi in two sets. This is implied by the words 'they too' which he uses in describing the citizens' reactions. Following his instructions, Zeffi probably went first to Vettori's brother-in-law, Giuliano Capponi, and the 'other citizens loving liberty'. They suspected the news to be a trick either on the part of the duke to find out their reactions or on the part of Lorenzo to do them harm. Consequently they either did not believe it or dared not pass it on. Varchi next relates that Guicciardini, Acciaiuoli, Matteo Strozzi and Vettori were asked what they would do if the duke were not found. They too were suspicious and replied that they would consider the matter only after a search had been made.[127] Even later, Vettori still refused to accept what he had been told until he had actually seen Alessandro dead in S. Lorenzo.[128] In the evening the chamber was opened, revealing the dead duke. The body was wrapped in a carpet, carried to S. Giovannino and thence to the old sacristy of S. Lorenzo. Only at this point did those who by then knew of the murder meet in an upper room of Cardinal Cibo's house and, fearing an uprising, decide to act quickly and call a meeting of the Forty-Eight for the following morning.[129]

The discussions which took place after the discovery of Alessandro's death illustrate the different groups of opinion. According to some sources, the spread of the news had already resulted in a meeting of what may be called the 'popular' group who wanted to restore Florence to her former liberty.[130] Such men as Alamanno Salviati, Alamanno de' Pazzi, Pandolfo Martelli, Filippo Manelli, Antonio Niccolini, Batista Venturi, Bartolomeo Rontini[131] and Bertoldo Corsini (who was in charge of the fortresses) may well have been those 'citizens loving liberty' to whom, besides Giuliano Capponi, Zeffi was particularly commissioned to give news of Alessandro's death. The two meetings of the Forty-Eight on 8 and 9 January respectively

---

[126] *Ibid.*, p. 237. [127] *Ibid.*, pp. 241–2.
[128] B. Segni, ii, p. 135. [129] B. Varchi, iii, p. 242.
[130] *Ibid.*, pp. 246ff.; B. Segni, ii, p. 135.
[131] A doctor, see B. Varchi, ii, p. 34.

show the conflict of opinion between yet two more groups: the so-called 'court' group, consisting principally of Cardinal Cibo and Alessandro Vitelli, and the *ottimati*, among whom Francesco Guicciardini and Francesco Vettori were the most prominent. In these meetings the absent exiles, too, seem to have been represented—Palla Rucellai, for example, wanted to wait for the opinion of Filippo. Very largely owing to the work of Francesco Guicciardini, with whom Francesco Vettori was in close co-operation, all these groups of opinion were persuaded to accept the election of Cosimo de' Medici as duke of Florence.

The attitude of the 'popular' group to Guicciardini and Vettori shows the importance of these two. Alamanno de' Pazzi, one of this group, suggested that they be won over to the cause, for 'if we have them to help us, it will be easier for us to effect the good of the city without either scandal or tumult'. Segni's comment on Vettori's reaction to the group's approach to him is interesting. As he was a 'most astute citizen' he had observed the zeal and political potential of the young men and showed himself 'so graciously disposed towards their wishes' that he was able to check their ardour for revolt and immediately after the meeting hastened to Guicciardini to warn him of the danger of a 'popular' rising.[132]

It was with this fear of insurrection in their minds that the Forty-Eight met on the morning of January 8. Both their records and historical sources agree that the meeting resulted in a temporary offer of the leadership of the state to Cardinal Cibo.[133] Varchi and Vettori provide further information. Varchi is the only historian who reports active steps taken by the 'court' party as well as by a sympathizer of Filippo Strozzi's already during this first meeting.[134] Domenico Canigiani, either at the direct instigation of Cardinal Cibo or in order to win his favour, proposed the election of Signor Giulio, the natural son of the dead duke. As Giulio de' Medici was only six years old, this would have meant that Florence would have been under the control of Cardinal Cibo. The proposition was strongly

---

[132] B. Segni, ii, pp. 135–7.

[133] B. Varchi, iii, p. 246; B. Segni, ii, p. 137; G. Adriani, i, p. 22; Provvisione of 8 Jan. 1537, pub. A. Gelli in J. Nardi, ii, p. 392 Appendix.

[134] B. Varchi, iii, pp. 245–6.

opposed by Palla Rucellai, who, Varchi maintains, was 'without doubt in favour of Filippo Strozzi, to whom he was under an obligation'. Palla's view was that such vital matters should not be discussed while so many important citizens were outside Florence and, as far as he was concerned, nothing would be passed without them. Vettori and Guicciardini had apparently already decided that any delay would be dangerous for they reproved Palla and, since he persisted in his opinion, the meeting resulted in deadlock only resolved by offering temporary power to Cardinal Cibo. In a letter to Filippo Strozzi explaining the election of Cosimo, Vettori wrote that Cardinal Cibo refused the offer, and it would seem that it was then that Vettori and his colleagues turned their energies towards Cosimo.[135]

Rossi thinks that Cardinal Cibo refused the offer because he feared that temporary authority would give the exiles time to unite against him and reform the government of Florence, whereas if he could secure the election of Giulio de' Medici, he would in effect be in control.[136] As the *ottimati* suspected Cardinal Cibo's motives in sponsoring Giulio, and since he had refused their offer to him, Cosimo was probably the only candidate left to them. It was thought, too, that such a choice would be acceptable to the Florentines, as Cosimo was the son of the famous military leader Giovanni delle Bande Nere, and to the exiles since his mother, Maria Salviati, was the sister of Cardinal Salviati. Adriani, who sees the whole episode as part of the struggle between France and the emperor, considered that there was a considerable risk of Florence falling into the hands of the imperialists. Cardinal Cibo, Alessandro Vitelli and the servants of the dead duke were prepared to remain loyal to the emperor, Florence's fortress was in imperial hands, and the Pisans as well as the citizens of Arezzo and Pistoia would seize any opportunity to become the equals of Florence instead of part of her dominion. Fear of insurrection made a quick decision imperative as those in favour of liberty might seek the support of France and this would mean that Tuscany would become the battle ground of the French and the imperialists.[137]

Some of Adriani's reasons for supporting Cosimo are the very

[135] G.-B. Niccolini, p. 217. Florence, 15 Jan. 1537.
[136] A. Rossi, 'La elezione', p. 413.   [137] G. Adriani, i, pp. 26-7.

ones which, according to Segni, Guicciardini put forward in his speech in Cosimo's favour during the second meeting of the Forty-Eight.[138] They are similar to those offered by Vettori to Filippo Strozzi in explanation of his conduct,[139] and, as far as the urgency of the situation is concerned, also similar to the opinion given to Filippo by Matteo Strozzi's son, Alessandro.[140] They show particularly the degree of co-operation and agreement between Vettori and Guicciardini but also that between them and a member of the Strozzi family inside Florence. Guicciardini argued that the city was in great peril from the people who might shout for 'Liberty', from the exiles, and from those holding the fortresses, who could ally with the imperialists. If the government was not organized quickly Florence would fall into the hands of the imperialists who had recently disembarked 2000 Spaniards at Genoa. Cosimo, it was argued, would be acceptable to the emperor and as a nephew of Cardinal Salviati ought also to find favour with the exiles.

Vettori, too, mentioned the position of Florence in relation to the imperialists, pointing out as Adriani does that the new Florentine fortress was in imperial hands, that all the ducal servants were imperial, that the fortresses of Livorno and Pisa were held respectively by a Pisan and another foreigner and that both were pro-imperial. At Lerici there were 2500 Spaniards and at Genoa 4000 Germans, who would soon be in Florence should the imperial agents consider that the city was about to abandon the emperor. Even if the French forces were to help, they would ruin the countryside as the imperialists would the city.

Since Cosimo was acceptable to the emperor, his election must have seemed a way of maintaining the dignity of the city while avoiding the enslavement to the Spaniards or to the French which would follow acceptance either of Cardinal Cibo's candidate or of Filippo Strozzi. But from the terms which the *ottimati* drew up for Cosimo's acceptance it seems clear that they hoped to be able to limit his power and take the place in the government which they always felt was their due.

If, as Vettori wrote to Filippo Strozzi, the *ottimati* turned to Cosimo after Cardinal Cibo's refusal to accept the temporary

[138] B. Segni, ii, pp. 139–41. [139] G.-B. Niccolini, p. 217. [140] *Ibid.*, p. 220.

leadership of Florence, then the important work which Vettori, and above all Guicciardini, undertook behind the scenes to secure the election of Cosimo must have been carried out in the *pratica* which met during the night of 8/9 January between the first and second meeting of the Forty-Eight. After Vettori, Guicciardini, Acciaiuoli and Matteo Strozzi had decided to send for Cosimo and he had appeared without delay, since he was already *en route* for Florence when the messenger met him with the summons,[141] the night was spent secretly discussing a way of making him 'Lord and Head of the Republic'.[142] Guicciardini (who with his colleagues had called the *pratica* 'in order not to give time to the exiles') succeeded in winning over Cardinal Cibo, Alessandro Vitelli and Ottaviano de' Medici from their support of Giulio de' Medici, and also Gino Capponi whose good nature and moderation prevented him, despite his commitment to the 'party of the populace',[143] from starting a revolution. Guicciardini and the other leaders concluded that the Forty-Eight must be called on the following morning and Cosimo elected, even if this meant the use of force.[144] Accordingly, with the way prepared by the secret meeting of the previous night and with Vitelli's troops guarding both the Medici palace and its approaches, the Forty-Eight met for the second time.[145]

Vettori's close co-operation with Guicciardini, shown in the views he expressed in the already-mentioned letter to Filippo Strozzi, is demonstrated during this important meeting of 9 January. He alone, according to one source,[146] together with Guicciardini, according to another,[147] argued the case for the acceptance of Cosimo. He was opposed by Domenico Canigiani and Palla Rucellai. The preparatory work of the previous evening is evident. The terms of the law for acceptance of Cosimo had already been drafted;[148] the Forty-Eight were expected merely to approve. The historians' accounts give the impression that the meeting was a duel, with Guicciardini supported by

---

141 S. Ammirato, vi, p. 224. For the rôle of Guicciardini in the election, R. Ridolfi, *Francesco Guicciardini*, pp. 247–9.

142 B. Varchi, iii, p. 248; B. Segni, ii, p. 138.

143 B. Segni, ii, pp. 138–9.   144 B. Varchi, iii, p. 248.

145 *Ibid.*, p. 249.   146 B. Segni, ii, p. 146.

147 B. Varchi, iii, p. 252.   148 B. Varchi, iii, p. 253; B. Segni, ii, p. 146.

Vettori on one side and Palla Rucellai representing Filippo Strozzi on the other. Vettori's reply to Palla's contention that the opinion of the exiles should be heard before such a momentous decision was taken, is typical of his fears in earlier crises. Almost in anger, he said that Palla had just risen from his sick bed, had recently confessed his sins and was therefore in no fear of death but he himself had already heard the clash of arms in the street and the cries of 'Palle, Palle' and 'Cosimo, Cosimo' and had no wish to die unabsolved. Guicciardini, he urged, should proceed without delay to read the terms of the law. Finding him too slow, Vettori declared realistically that a man of such reputed prudence amazed him by his preoccupation with details in creating the prince for as he proposed to give Cosimo the *guardia*, arms and the fortresses, what was the point of legislation to limit his powers? He himself hoped that Cosimo would be a good prince, but would endure him if he were bad and ignored the terms of the law.[149] Palla Rucellai demonstrated his opposition by taking a white bean, used for voting against a motion, and showing it to all said, 'This is my opinion'.[150] Guicciardini's and Vettori's reply that Palla's bean was not worth more than one vote made plain the understanding reached by Vettori, Guicciardini and the other leading citizens ahead of the meeting of the Forty-Eight, for Palla immediately retorted, 'if you have consulted between you and decided what you want to do, there was no need to call me'; and he rose to leave the room. He was restrained by Cardinal Cibo. Amid this altercation, Vettori, Guicciardini, Matteo Strozzi and Acciaiuoli, together with Niccolini withdrew into another room and there signed the agreement to accept Cosimo.[151]

If Cardinal Cibo had already agreed to support Cosimo, the opposition of Domenico Canigiani cannot by now have presented much difficulty. Segni, in fact, reports Domenico Canigiani's proposal to elect Giulio de' Medici with the comment 'he did not know the secret' as if, not having been at the *pratica*, he were already out of date.[152]

Although it is clear that Vettori was in close co-operation with his colleague, he himself admitted that the greatest effort had been made by Guicciardini. To Filippo Strozzi, Vettori wrote that Guicciardini was 'the most capable man and the best that there is in this city' and that he had worked and was still working incredibly hard; in fact, had it not been for him, he did not know what would have become of the city.[153] Although Vettori gave his support, Guicciardini seems to have been the one responsible for drawing up the terms accepted by Cosimo. They show the old desire of the *ottimati* to limit the power of the ruler, though at the same time they aimed to appeal to the republican element.[154] Cosimo was not to be called duke but 'head and governor of the Florentine republic'; in all letters, proclamations and laws issued by him, his councillors were to be associated in the formula 'the most illustrious Cosimo de' Medici and his magnificent councillors', and in his absence his authority was to be delegated to a lieutenant who, as in the case of other specified magistrates, must be a Florentine and not a foreigner. The income Cosimo was to receive from the city's treasury was limited to 12,000 florins annually which, as Guicciardini remarked at the time of Cosimo's acceptance of the conditions, was nevertheless a 'fine sum'.[155] The names of the citizens appointed during the second meeting of the Forty-Eight to draw up these terms on the following day reveal those who had been most closely associated with the election. They were Matteo Niccolini, Francesco Guicciardini, Roberto Acciaiuoli, Matteo Strozzi, Iacopo Gianfigliazzi, Francesco Vettori, Raphael de' Medici and Giuliano Capponi.[156]

In electing Cosimo both Vettori and Guicciardini were accused of establishing a tyranny. The *ottimati* were cursed for placing the city once more under the yoke of servitude and thus opposing the wishes of the majority of the citizens and the authority of a section of the exiles.[157] Guicciardini especially was blamed, but Vettori too came under censure. During a meeting at which the form of government for Florence was discussed, Cardinal Ridolfi for example, commented angrily on certain remarks made by Vettori that it was 'a very wicked deed'

[153] G.-B. Niccolini, p. 232.
[154] A. Rossi, 'La elezione', p. 432, n. 1.
[155] B. Varchi, iii, p. 253.
[156] See *Provvisioni*, ed. A. Gelli in J. Nardi, ii, pp. 392-6, and L. Cantini, i, p. 116.
[157] B. Segni, ii, p. 150.

to establish a tyranny in their native city.[158] Piero Vettori's eighteenth-century biographer maintains that Vettori's and Guicciardini's 'intrigues' were responsible for creating Cosimo *Signore* instead of restoring the city to liberty.[159] But these accusations seem unfair. Guicciardini had no wish to establish an absolute ruler: he had attempted, however unrealistically, to curtail Cosimo's power by the terms of the agreement, and Segni sees his desire to give his daughter Elisabetta in marriage to Cosimo as part of his intention to bring Cosimo to institute a 'limited and constitutional type of lordship'.[160] Even Vettori expressed hope for a better future. In a letter to Filippo Strozzi dated 30 January he appealed to him not to resort to force, as it might one day be possible to bring the city to 'better habits from which some good may be hoped for'.[161] He would appear also to be expressing the views of the other principal *ottimati* for he follows his remark by greetings from all those to whom Strozzi had wished to be remembered. One was Francesco Guicciardini, and from Strozzi's letter we know that the others were Roberto Acciaiuoli, Matteo Strozzi, Palla Rucellai and Giovanni Corsi.

The political situation in Florence did not develop in accordance with the *ottimati*'s hopes and their period of command was brief. Already during the second meeting of the Forty-Eight Guicciardini's achievement in winning the acceptance of Cosimo owed something to the adroit back-stage management of the imperialist Alessandro Vitelli, and before the end of the following day it was virtually nullified by this ruthless commander's action. During the meeting Vitelli had seen to it that a clash of arms in the courtyard and a shout audible in the council chamber urging haste as the soldiers could no longer be restrained, aroused fears to which the last opponents of Cosimo's election succumbed.[162] By the evening of the following day, the 10th, Vitelli's outrageous sack of the Medici palace and the house of Lorenzino had brought him into possession of a sufficient quantity of jewels and precious objects to enable him, should he wish, to raise the necessary funds for the payment of

[158] *Ibid.*, p. 156; B.N.F. Magliab. VIII, 81, fo. 12v.

[159] B. Segni, ii, pp. 154–6; A. Bandini, *Memorie per servire alla vita del Senator Pier Vettori* (Livorno, 1756), p. 11.

[160] B. Segni, ii, p. 151.

[161] G.-B. Niccolini, p. 232.   [162] B. Varchi, iii, pp. 253–4.

the militia,[163] and he had taken control of the recently-constructed Florentine fortress and was guarding the widowed duchess who had fled to its protection with all her valuables.[164] Henceforth Alessandro Vitelli and the imperial faction, not Francesco Guicciardini or Francesco Vettori and the *ottimati*, dominated the city.

Even the seventeen-year-old Cosimo showed himself a man of action and independence who was not prepared to trust the citizens whose terms he had accepted. On the very day of his election he sent Matteo Strozzi's son, Alessandro, to establish relations with the papacy, Cherubino Buonanni and Bernardo de' Medici, bishop of Forlì, to Spain to report to the emperor, and Alessandro della Caccia with secret instructions to his uncle Cardinal Salviati.[165] When he rode abroad it was noticeable that he was accompanied by the same guard as Alessandro but by fewer of the Medici partisans of whose loyalty he was not yet certain.[166]

Between a well-entrenched imperial faction and a far from compliant ruler, the *ottimati* in Florence did not hold the commanding position they would have liked; they had also to take account of their compatriots outside the city and here too they lost control. Alessandro Strozzi, whom Cosimo had sent to the pope, also received instructions from him to persuade Cardinals Ridolfi and Salviati to come to Florence. Looking back on the sequence of events following on Alessandro's arrival in Rome and his mission to the cardinals, one can see that the suggested visit to Florence was doomed to failure from the beginning. In the first place any opportunity for secret contact or collaboration with the *ottimati* was frustrated by Cosimo's success in finding out what was going on from the very men (for example, Lorenzo del Vigna) to whom the exiles were confiding their intentions.[167] Secondly the exiles realized the strength of the imperial position in Italy. Cardinal Salviati, for instance, hesitated to come to Florence since he knew that the reinforcement of Spanish troops which had just arrived at Lerici had been offered to Cosimo for his protection, and Cosimo not only accepted the offer but gave orders for them to make forced

[163] *Ibid.*, p. 255.   [164] *Ibid.*, p. 260.   [165] *Ibid.*, pp. 256–7.
[166] *Ibid.*, p. 257.   [167] *Ibid.*, p. 270; G.-B. Niccolini, p. 216.

marches in order to arrive on Tuscan soil before the cardinals.[168] Both Filippo Strozzi and the pope appreciated the importance in Florence of the imperial commander. 'Everything is in the power of Alessandro Vitelli', Filippo informed the cardinals and instructed them to try to buy Vitelli's support by offering to give him Borgo San Sepolcro.[169] The pope, either on his own initiative or at the instigation of Cardinals Ridolfi and Salviati, sent Gian Giacomo de' Rossi, bishop of Pavia, to Florence not only with a letter to the Forty-Eight but also with one to Alessandro Vitelli to try to win him from the imperialists.[170] But neither Filippo Strozzi nor Paul III succeeded in making Vitelli change his allegiance. In fact imperial solidarity contrasted strongly with the obvious disunity among the cardinals and the exiles. From the outset Cardinal Salviati was the leader. Intelligent and astute he deceived not only Cardinal Ridolfi who had little to commend him but his good intentions, and Niccolò Gaddi who was prompted by the French ambassador, but also Baccio Valori and Antonfrancesco degli Albizzi.[171] As the brother of Cosimo's determined mother, Maria Salviati, and thus Cosimo's uncle, Cardinal Salviati's views and actions were influenced by family loyalties; in addition he hoped that his family connections with the new ruler of Florence might one day serve his ambition to become pope.[172] In consequence Cardinal Salviati was from the beginning of the mission willing to negotiate peace. Having at the outset left their forces at Montepulciano and agreed to come unarmed to Florence,[173] it was Salviati who was prepared, as we shall see later, to disband them.[174] Cardinal Ridolfi, joined by Baccio Valori, would not consider anything but a republican government for Florence, less broadly-based than before but headed nonetheless by a gonfalonier.[175]

Fear, suspicion and disunity were thus the prelude to the arrival of the three cardinals, Salviati, Ridolfi and Gaddi in Florence on 21 January. Their reception by Cosimo, surrounded by a great concourse of citizens shouting 'Palle, Palle'

---

[168] B. Varchi, iii, p. 269. [169] G.-B. Niccolini, pp. 222, 221.
[170] B. Varchi, iii, p. 271. [171] Ibid., pp. 268–9. [172] Ibid., p. 268.
[173] Ibid., pp. 269–70; G.-B. Niccolini, p. 231: 'lui . . . essere alienissimo dalla guerra'.
[174] See below, p. 279. [175] B. Segni, ii, p. 155.

was hardly reassuring.[176] Cardinals Salviati and Ridolfi lodged in the Salviati residence where in the days that followed many discussions took place.[177]

It is not difficult to establish the subject matter of these meetings, nor the names of some of those present, nor do the various differences of opinion remain hidden. The report of the Sienese ambassador, Girolamo Spannocchi, reveals that at a discussion held on the evening after the cardinals' arrival the imperialists had suggested that the cardinals should let them know whether they were satisfied with 'the greatness of Signor Cosimo under his Imperial Majesty's protection'. According to Spannocchi, the cardinals replied that they were, but at the same time expressed their wish that the exiles be reinstated.[178] Segni, however, insists that the cardinals were dissatisfied with the election of Cosimo;[179] the difference between the two reports illustrates Spannocchi's further remark that the cardinals' wishes were 'ambiguous'.[180] Among those present at the meetings were Cosimo's mother and, Segni says, those leading citizens whom he has frequently mentioned as participating in the government, by which we may take him to mean Francesco Guicciardini, Francesco Vettori, Roberto Acciaiuoli and Matteo Niccolini;[181] among the younger generation would appear to have been Vettori's cousin Piero, apparently regarded by one of Vitelli's soldiers as so republican that he would have liked to cut off his head.[182]

Although Guicciardini made every effort to come to some agreement, no conclusions were reached in the discussions,[183] which is hardly surprising in the tense and suspicious atmosphere. Soldiers watched all who came to visit the cardinals. Alessandro Vitelli with a military escort accompanied Francesco Guicciardini on his frequent journeys to the Salviati house.[184] After some days of this fruitless procedure the cardinals, realizing that the advancing Spanish troops were now very close to Florence, prepared to depart. The court faction,

---

[176] B. Varchi, pp. 273–4. [177] B. Segni, ii, p. 154.
[178] C. Paoli, E. Casanova, 'Cosimo I de' Medici e i fuorusciti del 1537' in *A.S.I.*, Ser. v, xi (1893), p. 286.
[179] B. Segni, ii, p. 154. [180] C. Paoli, E. Casanova, p. 286.
[181] B. Segni, ii, p. 154. [182] B. Varchi, iii, p. 275.
[183] B. Segni, ii, p. 156. [184] B. Varchi, iii, p. 275.

that is to say Francesco Campana and Alessandro Vitelli, as well as Francesco Guicciardini and other leading citizens, however, urged them to stay and it was probably at this point that Cardinal Salviati persuaded Cardinal Ridolfi and Baccio Valori to accept the government's offer to send back the Spaniards to their ships and to reinstate all the exiles on condition that the cardinals would dismiss the forces which they had left assembled at Montepulciano.[185] While Cardinal Salviati was away commanding the dismissal of these troops, on 30 January the assembled Forty-Eight passed a law offering repatriation to the exiles and the restitution of their goods.[186] The imperial troops, however, were not halted[187] so that when Salviati returned having disbanded the cardinals' forces, his, Ridolfi's and Gaddi's position was considerably weakened. None of the leaders outside the city accepted the offer of repatriation; with the removal of the threat of the cardinals' military support Vitelli became insolent and the populace lost hope.[188] At the beginning of February Cardinals Ridolfi and Gaddi left Florence to be followed later by Salviati.[189]

On account of his friendship with Filippo Strozzi, the relationship of Francesco Vettori with the exiles was unique among the *ottimati*. Not only did he write with Cosimo's permission many letters to Filippo beseeching him not to use force against Florence, but he may even have been the official mouthpiece for the duke or at least for the *ottimati* if we accept Varchi's statement that he wrote to Strozzi 'on the order of the government'.[190] The similarity between the content of the letter which Cosimo's envoy, Alessandro Strozzi, wrote to Filippo explaining his commission in Rome and that which Vettori wrote to him a a few days earlier suggests that both represent the views of those responsible for Cosimo's election.[191] Both men explain the necessity for the election, express goodwill towards Filippo and

[185] *Ibid.*, p. 275; B. Segni, p. 156; C. Paoli, E. Casanova, p. 288.
[186] L. Cantini, pp. 125–7.
[187] B. Segni, ii, p. 157 and below, p. 281.
[188] B. Varchi, iii, p. 276.
[189] G.-B. Niccolini, p. 235; B. Varchi, iii, p. 276; B. Segni, pp. 157–8; C. Paoli, E. Casanova, p. 295; the Sienese ambassador Tantucci's account is rather confused.
[190] B. Segni, ii, p. 171; B. Varchi, iii, p. 290.
[191] G.-B. Niccolini, pp. 220–1 and 216–18.

fear of what will befall if he comes armed against the city. In reply Filippo informed Vettori that he had placed himself in the hands of the cardinals, and he wrote to Salviati and Ridolfi that they must reassure those citizens who feared a republican form of government—that is to say Vettori, Guicciardini and the leading *ottimati*—by telling them that the exiles will be content with any form of government they wish, provided it is not tyranny. Clearly had Strozzi co-operated with Guicciardini, Vettori, Acciaiuoli and Matteo Strozzi inside the city, its fate and that of the *ottimati* would have been different. The imperial ambassador, Bernardo Sanzio, considered Vettori, Guicciardini and Matteo Strozzi to be the three leaders in Florence whose authority was of such importance that it was worth obtaining their allegiance by bribery.[192] The pope, too, was aware that the union of the exiles and the leading Florentines would be his best chance of reducing imperial influence in Italy.[193] Hence Vettori's position as one of those most immediately concerned with the problem of the exiles was important not only in the domestic but also in the international context of Franco-Imperial power in Italy, in which, as Paul III realized, the independence of Florence was of the utmost significance.

Vettori may not have attended all the meetings with the cardinals in Florence, for towards the end of January he was ill.[194] He generously acknowledges that the hard work was done by Guicciardini.[195] His presence on one occasion is however established by Segni's report of a verbal exchange between him and Baccio Valori from which we can also appreciate Vettori's fears and views concerning the government of Florence. He is reported to have asked Valori what he meant by his demand for a free government with a gonfalonier. Valori replied that he did not mind what type of government was established so long as it was free, to which Vettori answered that if it were armed it

[192] Misc. Medicea, 39, insert 11, fo. 4r: 'Sono qui in la ciptà tre cittadini molto principali et di gran consiglio messer Francesco Guicciardino, messer Francesco Vettori, messer Matteo Strozzi. Noi intendiamo mantenerli perchè hanno grande autorità nella ciptà et con alcuna lettera generale di pagamenti si confirmano melglio.'

[193] G. Spini, *Cosimo I de' Medici e la indipendenza del principato mediceo* (Firenze, 1945), pp. 54, 58.   [194] G.-B. Niccolini, pp. 231–2.   [195] G.-B. Niccolini, p. 232.

would not be free, and if it were unarmed it would be in danger of expulsion by the populace. Cardinal Ridolfi then intervened to accuse Vettori of wanting to establish a tyranny with no regard to the good of the city and Vettori replied angrily that in these times it was not possible to find a less evil solution.[196] His great fear was war and that if the exiles came armed against Florence, the city would fall into imperialist hands and become another Milan. Even a tyrannical Cosimo would be a preferable fate. Writing to Strozzi on 30 January he said that he was 'so afraid of war' that on learning that Bernardo Salviati and Piero Strozzi, both financed by the French, were moving in the direction of Mirandola *en route* for Florence, he felt he must let him know that any understanding with the French would merely make the Florentines the slaves of the imperialists. Cardinal Salviati had averted the war threatened from Perugia, and Vettori hoped Strozzi would avert the danger from the Romagna and the vicinity of Bologna. To make Florence a republic was impossible, he explained, but if Strozzi refrained from the fatal remedy there was some hope for improved conditions in the future.[197]

The cardinals' departure from Florence did not end the attempts made on both sides to solve the problem of the exiles peacefully. Already on 9 February Cardinal Salviati wrote to Cosimo and to the imperial ambassador Sanzio requesting a safe-conduct for a representative to go to Florence for discussions.[198] Cosimo replied that an agent should be sent for he was prepared to talk.[199] When none came he himself sent an envoy, Jacopo de' Medici,[200] to Bologna, and the instructions written in February by Vettori for an unspecified person going to Bologna to talk to Cardinal Salviati were most probably intended for this envoy.[201] Besides meeting the cardinal's likely complaint that the imperial troops were not only still in the lower Arno valley but had actually been reinforced,[202] Jacopo

[196] B. Segni, ii, pp. 155–6. [197] G.-B. Niccolini, pp. 231–2.
[198] C. Paoli, E. Casanova, p. 296, n. 3.
[199] G. Spini, p. 78. [200] C. Paoli, E. Casanova, p. 298.
[201] Arch. Med. del Principato, 2634, fo. 1r–v.
[202] Cp. C. Paoli, E. Casanova, p. 298, n. 2. The pretext on which Jacopo was sent to Bologna was 'giustificare il non si esser partite le genti imperiali del dominio' as Salviati wrote to Cosimo, Bologna, 24 Feb. 1537.

was to try to ascertain what limitations on Cosimo's power the exiles wanted, bearing in mind that the writer and his associates did not wish to return to 'popular' government, and finally to attempt to persuade them not to use force. 'To those to whom you can speak confidentially', the instructions in Vettori's hand plead, 'you will say that to wage war against us at present would enslave us completely to the imperialists, lose us all our dominions and the peasants their animals and possessions, and those responsible for it will not be any the better. Moreover if they think they are doing the king of France a service, they are mistaken because the city will fall into the hands not of the emperor, which would be less disastrous, but of the imperialists who will treat her as they treated other cities in Italy so that the king of France when he wishes to help her will be unable to do so.'

The only positive result of this approach to the cardinals was the effect Vettori's correspondence with Strozzi had on legislation in favour of the exiles and in deterring Filippo for a while from taking up arms against Florence. Lorenzo Strozzi records that Vettori's appeal to his brother not to use force elicited the reply that it was unjust to expect good behaviour from a citizen who was treated like a bad one and that consequently in an attempt to appease them he and his fellow exiles were reinstated as citizens and their goods returned to them.[203] This remark refers, evidently, to the law of 30 January settling the status of the exiles. Financial considerations apart, it seems, too, as if Vettori's arguments were the decisive factor in his friend's refusal to move his troops from Bologna. At the time of Jacopo de' Medici's departure Vettori wrote to Strozzi[204] stressing French weakness in relation to the Spaniards in Piedmont and reasoning that this was militarily not the best moment to act against Florence: 'I tell you again that if you move while the affairs of France are in this decline you will cause money to be thrown away and you will serve neither the King of France nor yourself.'[205] To Vettori this conclusion was 'as clear as day-

---

[203] G.-B. Niccolini, pp. xcviii–xcix.

[204] Vettori's letter, dated 19 Feb., refers to Jacopo's mission and could have been taken to Bologna by him if he left a day later than expected.

[205] C. Strozz., Ser. V, 1207, fo. 112r.

light'. The outcome of Jacopo's talks with the cardinals reflects the view of Filippo Strozzi, and Vettori's influence on him. Jacopo reported that the cardinals did not want war and that they would try to use their power to prevent the king of France from waging it.[206] As Filippo with some financial support from Francis I would be the paymaster of the expedition, the exiles could not move without him and he incurred the hatred of those who wanted to resort to force in order to see Florence restored to the liberty she had enjoyed before the capitulation of August 1530.[207] But he did not care, he declared to Vettori, for he would be neither French nor Spanish but Florentine in all his actions. He also tried at this time to dissuade his son Piero, in the pay of France, from moving his forces against the city.[208]

Filippo's resistance to the wishes of the more militant and republican exiles was, however, shortlived. Less than two months later the knowledge that an attack against Florence was being planned in earnest and that Strozzi himself had now consented to pay one-third of its cost, hastened the promotion of another attempt to arrive at a peaceful settlement. In order to strengthen his position in Florence Cosimo had from the outset been anxious to obtain imperial recognition and Bernardo de' Medici, Bishop of Forlì, and Cherubino Buonanni, already dispatched to Spain to learn Charles V's views,[209] returned to Florence at the end of March with the information that the emperor would send Count Cifuentes, his ambassador in Rome, to make known his master's mind.[210] In April the news of the exiles' military preparations accelerated Cifuentes' departure.[211] Charles wanted a settlement of the problem of the exiles which offered opportunities for French interference in the city's affairs and immobilized in Tuscany 3000 troops for the protection of the regime.[212] Also to be determined was the exact nature of Cosimo's authority and who was to control the fortresses of the Florentine dominion.

While in Rome, Cifuentes had had discussions with the exiles and after his arrival in Florence on 11 May he wrote to cardinal

[206] C. Paoli, E. Casanova, p. 300.
[207] As indicated above p. 262 there were two sets of views among the exiles.
[208] G.-B. Niccolini, p. 208.
[209] See above, p. 276.   [210] B. Varchi, iii, p. 279.
[211] C. Paoli, E. Casanova, p. 309.   [212] B. Varchi, p. 321.

Salviati that he should send a representative of the exiles' views to the city.[213] Salviati sent his secretary, Giovan Maria Stratigopolo, but in order not to be accused by fellow exiles with whom he was unpopular on account of his pacific policy, of holding secret discussions in favour of his nephew Cosimo, Salviati ordered Donato Giannotti, a former secretary to the Ten who was acceptable to the exiles, to accompany Stratigopolo.[214] The two men entered Florence on 31 May.[215] Donato Giannotti had secret conversations with Vettori and Guicciardini in which he informed them on behalf of Strozzi and the exiles that if Cosimo would be bound by the limitations imposed on him in the law of 10 January, the exiles would be content to return to Florence.[216] Publicly Giannotti proposed that two or three men should be nominated on behalf of the city to discuss with Filippo Strozzi at some place near the confines of the Florentine dominion convenient to both sides. Count Cifuentes, however, refused the suggestion of such an embassy as merely a cover for talks between the principal citizens and the exiles and unlikely to lead to conclusions. Giannotti and Stratigopolo should rather return to Bologna for instructions giving them power to conclude an agreement in the exiles' name.[217] On 3 June they left the city[218] but owing largely to French persuasion they did not return.[219] No conclusion was therefore reached and relations with the exiles remained as before.

As far as Cosimo's title was concerned, Maria Salviati and Francesco Campana would have liked the young Medici to be confirmed in the authority which his predecessor Alessandro had held at his death and to have had possession of the fortresses. But Cifuentes, in accordance with the instructions which he had received from Charles V, did not want Cosimo to be duke but head of the state on the lines of the law of 10 January. To avoid the rupture in negotiations which would have

[213] C. Paoli, E. Casanova, pp. 315, 316.

[214] B. Varchi, iii, pp. 320–1; G.-B. Niccolini, p. civ; B. Segni, ii, pp. 164–5; C. Paoli, E. Casanova, p. 320; G. Spini, p. 108.

[215] C. Paoli, E. Casanova, p. 320.

[216] B. Segni, ii, p. 165; B. Varchi, iii, p. 321.

[217] B. Varchi, iii, p. 321; C. Paoli, E. Casanova, p. 320.

[218] R. Ridolfi, 'Nuovi contributi alla biografia del Giannotti', in *Rivista Storica degli Archivi Toscani*, i (1929), p. 223; C. Paoli, E. Casanova, p. 320.

[219] B. Varchi, iii, pp. 321–2; G. Spini, p. 110.

resulted from this conflict of aims, Cifuentes resorted to a stratagem: subject to the emperor's approval, Cosimo, he declared, would be allowed the same authority in Florence as Alessandro had had. Cifuentes' formula contained, however, an implication not appreciated by Cosimo. In accepting it Cosimo thought of the power which Alessandro was exercising in 1534, not of the more restricted authority granted to him in 1532 in the presence of the imperial representative Muxetula.[220]

Not only did Cifuentes achieve Cosimo's acceptance of this formula but he also obtained his agreement to hold the fortresses of Florence and Livorno in the name of the emperor, leaving only Pisa—of much less strategic importance—to the Medici. On 21 June Cosimo swore allegiance to the emperor, committed himself to the agreement on the fortresses and was recognized as the successor to Alessandro, subject to imperial ratification of Cifuentes' work.[221]

The *ottimati* seem to have been as little able to influence the internal political situation as they were to solve the problem of the exiles. On 23 May Cifuentes addressed the Forty-Eight.[222] In his reply to the Count's speech Matteo Niccolini suggested that since it was difficult to discuss important matters in such a large assembly, a smaller number of citizens should be elected for the purpose. The Forty-Eight then elected Francesco Vettori, Francesco Guicciardini, Roberto Acciaiuoli, Matteo Strozzi, Matteo Niccolini, Ottaviano de' Medici and Giovanni Corsi— all members of the ruler's secret council with the exception of Ottaviano (chosen in any case by Cosimo) and Giovanni Corsi.[223] Vettori may, however, have taken little part in the discussions. In a letter of 25 May Niccolò Guicciardini informed his brother Luigi that Vettori was in bed and that his place had been taken by Giuliano Capponi.[224] In the following month, however, Filippo Strozzi was evidently under the impression that his friend had participated though the fact that he also mentions Giuliano Capponi makes it seem likely that illness caused Vettori to be absent at least on occasions.[225] In any case

[220] G. Spini, pp. 110–11. [221] *Ibid.*, p. 111.
[222] C. Paoli, E. Casanova, p. 318. [223] B. Varchi, iii, p. 322.
[224] C. Strozz., Ser. I, 98, fo. 219r, 25 May 1537.
[225] F. Strozzi to B. Cavalcanti, 15 July 1537 in A. Rossi, *Francesco Guicciardini*, ii, p. 308.

his presence would probably have made little difference to the political outcome of Cifuentes' visit, for the members of the delegation were ignorant of what was going on and unable to control the fate of the fortresses. Niccolò Guicciardini reported to Luigi: [the delegates] 'are dismayed and discontented because they do not know anything and discussions are in progress which will lead to hopeless enslavement to the foreigner'.[226] To Bartolomeo Cavalcanti, the exiles' envoy to France, Filippo Strozzi wrote that Guicciardini, Vettori, Matteo Strozzi and other principal citizens had not wanted to agree to the fortresses coming under the control of the emperor and had vigorously advised Cifuentes against this;[227] indeed there is evidence that the deputies 'protested bitterly' against the handing over of the fortresses.[228] Francesco Guicciardini remarked ruefully that Count Cifuentes 'will leave us as he found us but minus the fortresses and with less reputation and hope'.[229] Regardless of the deputies' opposition, the agreement between Cosimo and Cifuentes was contracted.

After the success of the visit of Cifuentes and the failure of that of the cardinals, the exiles must have realized that little was to be expected from peaceful negotiations with those inside Florence. This fact, combined now with a favourable political-military situation and pressure from Piero, undoubtedly influenced Filippo Strozzi to decide finally to join with France and to seek a solution to their problems by force of arms. On 30 June 1537 Francis I had signed an armistice with Charles V's sister Mary, regent of the Netherlands, which left him free to devote his attention to Italy. An attack by the Turkish fleet on the kingdom of Naples was imminent and would occupy the imperial forces.[230] The *ottimati* in Florence were discontented over the loss of the fortresses and one report states that 'the entire city' supported Cosimo 'unwillingly, being unaccustomed to the yoke of a principality'.[231] Yet on the night of 31 July, twenty-seven days after the departure of Cifuentes, the battle of Montemurlo which might have decided favourably the fate of

[226] C. Strozz., Ser. I, 60, No. 63, Florence, 23 June 1537.
[227] See p. 285, n. 225.
[228] C. Strozz., Ser. I, 60, No. 56, 19 June 1537.
[229] G. Canestrini, *Op. ined.*, x, pp. 304–5; cp. p. 309.
[230] G. Spini, pp. 113–14.   [231] *Ibid.*, p. 115, n. 2

the principal citizens both in and outside Florence in fact pronounced their doom.

The defeat of Filippo Strozzi and his fellow exiles can be explained by the divisions among them and by their own military incompetence compared with the rapid action and able command of Alessandro Vitelli.[232] Francesco Vettori and his colleagues did what they could to save the lives of some of the exiles. Bernardo Sanzio, the emperor's envoy, reported that all of them deserved death but as there were important Florentine citizens among them, he had persuaded Cosimo that they should be imprisoned in the fortresses of Pisa, Livorno or Volterra and not condemned to die without orders from the emperor and his council. He pointed out that Cardinal Cibo, Alessandro Vitelli and Pirro Colonna as well as 'those other gentlemen of the council' (among whom was Vettori) were also of this opinion.[233] On 5 August Niccolò Guicciardini corroborated this report by mentioning to Luigi that Sanzio's view was shared by 'those other citizens of worth'.[234] Filippo Strozzi's life was spared and he was imprisoned in the fortress of Florence whose construction he had advocated. In December of the following year (1538) he committed suicide.

When Strozzi died, Vettori must have felt that he had not much left to live for: Segni reports that thereafter he never left the house,[235] and on 5 March 1539 his life ended. By November 1539 Guicciardini was no longer active in public affairs,[236] and by May of the following year he too was dead. Matteo Strozzi died within the next twelve months, but Roberto Acciaiuoli lived to be an octogenarian, surviving until 1547. An epoch had drawn to a close. The power of the dukes waxed, that of the *ottimati* had waned. Segni observes that the deaths of these leading citizens left the city without counsel,[237] and Varchi considers that the position had already changed with the election of Cosimo. His remarks sum up the new political position: 'And let no one be surprised that I speak always of

---

[232] For a reconstruction of the battle of Montemurlo see G. Spini, pp. 113–22.
[233] A. Rossi, *Francesco Guicciardini*, ii, p. 300, n. 2.
[234] C. Strozz., Ser. I, 60, fo. 132.
[235] B. Segni, ii, p. 217.
[236] G. Canestrini, *Op. ined.*, x, p. 324.   [237] B. Segni, ii, pp. 217–18.

Cosimo and never of the party, the Forty-Eight or the councillors; because neither the government, nor the Forty-Eight nor
the councillors, but Cosimo alone governs everything; nor is
anything said or done, however great or small, to which he does
not give the 'yes' or the 'no'.[238] Varchi was an official historian
of the new ruler and he knew where power lay.[239]

---

[238] B. Varchi, iii, p. 300; cp. 25 March 1537, the opinion of the Sienese ambassador
Girolamo Tantucci, C. Paoli, E. Casanova, p. 306, n. 1.
[239] B. Varchi, i, p. 103.

CHAPTER XII

Conclusion

OVER THIRTY YEARS of European history lay between Vettori's first major mission in the summer of 1507 and his retirement from political life after Filippo Strozzi's death in 1538. They saw such momentous events in the Habsburg-Valois struggle as the victory of the French at Ravenna (1512) and their subsequent expulsion by the policy of Julius II; their recovery and victory at Marignano (1515) and their defeat at Pavia ten years later. They had witnessed, too, the atrocity of the imperial sack of Rome in 1527 and the tragedy of the siege of Florence in 1529–30. For Florence they had brought a change of allegiance, if not of sentiment, from France to the empire and they had seen her sink in association with the papacy into subservience to the victorious Habsburg power in Italy. Internally her aspirations for civic liberty had been crushed and she had become one of the many Italian cities ruled by princes.

On all of these major diplomatic and political events the thought and action of Francesco Vettori has a bearing. A study of his career highlights the problems and contradictory interests with which a Florentine politician was faced. His first major assignment, that of a diplomatic envoy to Germany (1507–9), shows how the alliance with France, so long a cornerstone in Florentine foreign policy, became a stumbling block once the French forces first under Charles VIII and then under Louis XII had actually appeared in Italy. Vettori's reports to the Ten in conjunction with the deliberations resulting from them throw light on Florence's dilemma in being allied with France and yet wishing to gain favour with the emperor. The problem of allegiance taxed Florentine diplomacy even after imperial power had become the dominant factor in Italian affairs, and Vettori's writings often illustrate the clash between personal inclinations and political exigencies experienced by many of his compatriots.

The dispatches and letters of his second important mission, as ambassador to Rome, reveal the complexities of the new situation after a member of the Medici family had become pope. Leo's control over Florence initiates a period in which the city nominally remained independent but in fact was administered from Rome, even the Medici rulers in Florence acting on papal instructions. In this situation an ambassador's task was a delicate one trying to reconcile Florentine aspirations for self-government with those of the imposed rulers both in the city and in Rome. Vettori's pro-papal attitude during his embassy to Leo's court must be seen in perspective: his dual function in having to inform the Florentine foreign committee of papal plans and yet as a trusted papal adviser having to maintain secrecy led to a divided loyalty. Sharing the pope's vision of peace among Christian states, which could not but benefit Florence in the long run, he felt under no obligation to transmit all he knew, as he states in his private letters. This conflict of loyalties continued unresolved in years to come, and, as in the first instance, he reserved the right to decide how best to serve Florence either by supporting the existing government or by co-operating with outside forces. Thus Vettori's support for papal policy should not be overstressed: a guiding factor for him was his desire for the physical safety and interests of his city; it is the key to his many changes of allegiance; it overruled personal friendships and political ideals. One such *volte-face* occurs at the end of his mission to Rome. Once back in his city he supported Lorenzo's aspirations to the captaincy which ran counter to Leo's plans but were an attempt to regain a degree of independence from Roman control.

While Florentine ambassador to France (1515–18) Vettori's repeated complaints of being treated by the papal nuncio Giovanni Staffileo as his inferior are an indication of his city's declining independence. As Lorenzo, duke of Urbino's personal agent, Vettori emerges as distinctly pro-Medici, even to the extent of seeing no need for the time being of a Florentine ambassador in France. Favouring closer links with France which, had Lorenzo succeeded in his plans, might have made

Florence more independent of Leo, Vettori's careful investigations into the prospects of the possible brides for his young patron and favourable reports on the lands, income and parentage of Madeleine de la Tour d'Auvergne were decisive for Lorenzo's marriage to her; the eventual marriage ceremony at Amboise represents one of the peaks of his political career.

Although Vettori had held several offices before his earliest mission abroad, it was between his mission to Germany and that to Rome that he first held high office within Florence, as a prior in the Gonfalonier Piero Soderini's administration. By inclination a moderate he prevented bloodshed at Soderini's deposition. A pattern running through his whole career here emerges: detached judgment, caution and well-timed action rendered him as acceptable to a new regime as to the one he had served before; his intimate knowledge of Florentine affairs and his informed counsel made him indispensable to one regime after another; even the last Florentine Republic made use of his services as ambassador. The many offices he held, which included being one of the *Dodici Buonuomini*, prior three times and gonfalonier once, cannot all be enumerated here, but it is worth mentioning, especially as Vettori himself alludes to the fact, that he was a member of the Eight seven times between 1515 and 1525 and on four further occasions after 1530.[1] He was also frequently called to give advice in the *pratiche* and entrusted with a variety of administrative duties. Together his offices form a mosaic of Florentine internal policy, and not only up to the time of the constitutional reform under Duke Alessandro in 1532, for some were carried over into the new constitution.

To the realm of internal policy also belongs the special position which Vettori held during the rule of Lorenzo, Cardinal Giulio and the cardinal of Cortona. The plans for the government of Florence which Lorenzo had in mind in the year before his death in 1519 are not altogether clear and this is regrettable for a study of Vettori as he was undoubtedly one of the chief counsellors of the young Medici. As at the time of Soderini's fall, he prevented disaster and bloodshed on Lorenzo's death and when Pope Leo died (1521); on both occasions he supported the Medici regime, in which he saw a rôle for the

---

[1] R. von Albertini, p. 450.

principal citizens, against the extreme republicans. But again caution is needed in assessing the extent of his support for the Medici. The stand which he took between the accession of Clement VII and the expulsion of the Medici in 1527 shows him defending Florentine aspirations against the pope's plan to impose direct rule from Rome in the persons of the two young Medici with the cardinal of Cortona in charge. Official and private letters from his several visits to Rome press Florentine financial and diplomatic interests and assert the city's claims to self-determination internally and externally, while an interesting document, a memorandum in Vettori's hand, shows that Clement thought it advisable to consult Florence. Vettori disregarded his close personal ties with Clement VII and those in the past with Lorenzo de' Medici when he took a leading part in the overthrow of the Medici regime in 1527 and in the introduction of the last Florentine Republic. Even so the following years represent the lowest ebb in his political career. His hopes of a Florentine Republic administered by members of his class, the *ottimati*, were dashed when control passed to an extreme republican gonfalonier Francesco Carducci. We gauge from the treatment he received the folly of internal faction at so critical a time, resulting in the tragedy of armed conflict in 1529–30. Again Vettori appears as the indispensable negotiator for his city when the Republic sent him to Clement VII in Rome and Bologna in an eleventh hour attempt to reach agreement.

When Vettori had completed his embassy to the pope but refused to return to Florence, he became Clement's paid counsellor. Consistent with his fears of and bitter attacks on the extreme republicans and thinking as he did that they endangered his city's very existence, he vigorously supported a stern policy towards the besieged town. This period is only scantily documented by some references to him in contemporary letters and there are no letters or dispatches by him after he left Bologna for Rome during the siege of Florence. Again his fate was closely linked to that of his city when he was among the first to return after her surrender. There followed a period of intensive administrative activity and another climax in his career when he was largely responsible for preventing the worst economic consequences of the war and when he paved the way for a new Medicean government based on a revised constitution. Three drafts connected with the political reform are extant and they show the progression towards absolute rule. An analysis of these documents demonstrates how Vettori convinced himself that in a city split by opposing political factions only a government based on force could be expected to produce stability. This is expressed by his proposal in the first memorandum to reduce and in the second and last to eliminate the *Signoria* in which most independent power had so far been vested while the executive rights of some of the remaining offices were reduced. The last draft was logically the most far reaching in its concessions to absolute rule and was incorporated with only minor alterations in the constitution proclaimed in April 1532 with Duke Alessandro at its head.

There can be no doubt that Vettori had been instrumental in restoring law and order but at heavy cost to Florentine liberty. Absolute rule followed almost immediately on the assassination of Alessandro and it was Vettori's fate in association with Francesco Guicciardini to put the final touches to the total submission of his city to Duke Cosimo. The long struggle for a constitutional government with the *ottimati* in control had thus been lost. A chapter in the history of Florence had come to a close.

The *ottimati*, or upper-class citizens, so frequently referred to in this book were mainly wealthy international business men and bankers from whose ranks the majority of renaissance politicians were drawn. While the remarks of Filippo Strozzi about the behaviour expected of a *uomo da bene* and Francesco Guicciardini's references to the political wisdom of his class indicate that the *ottimati* were a definable group, they were not politically homogeneous. Vettori's career shows how often family, commercial and intellectual considerations were the bonds of aristocratic factions and rivalries which split the political structure of the upper class and helped to cause the downfall of the oligarchy. Common humanist interests, shared teachers and school days forged links between the Vettori and some of the members of the politically-conscious, intellectual group meeting in the gardens of the aristocrat Bernardo Rucellai, which was a focus of the opposition to Soderini and of the shift towards the Medici during the gonfalonier's leadership. At the end of his life Vettori confessed partiality towards his schoolmate, Lorenzo Segni,[2] and his association with Niccolò Capponi began in childhood, as may also Capponi's friendship with Segni.[3] The Vettori were also linked to the Capponi in trade. Trade association with the Rucellai and trade disagreements with Soderini could have accounted for Paolo Vettori's alliance with the Medici and opposition to Piero Soderini. The wisdom of Lorenzo the Magnificent's desire to control marriage relationships is demonstrated, as I have indicated, by the marriage connections of the leading political figures in the crisis of 1527. Neither is Francesco Vettori's connection by marriage with Filippo Strozzi to be underrated when considering Vettori's close association with Lorenzo de' Medici, brother of Strozzi's wife Clarice, and his engagement in the affairs of the Medici. The further importance of Strozzi in Vettori's political life I have also tried to show and in addition the political association of Vettori and Guicciardini, likewise signified by matrimonial negotiations. Even Vettori himself, lacking in affection though he seems on the whole to have been, did not neglect the political interests of the members of his immediate family, be they of Paolo, of his son-in-law, Pietro Orlandini, or of the relations to whom he gave diplomatic experience by taking them on an embassy.

Although Vettori's social standing was similar to that of Filippo Strozzi, Francesco Guicciardini, and Jacopo Salviati, with whom he was at various times in office, he was not like them one of the wealthy *ottimati*: financial worries are often echoed in his correspondence[4] and financial considerations frequently weighed with him. Evidently he benefited financially from his association with Lorenzo and this was a reason for his anxiety over the duke's impending death. He accepted a pension from Francis I in recognition of services rendered during the embassy to France but he repudiated it when he associated himself with Cardinal Giulio de' Medici's pro-imperial policy.

[2] R. von Albertini, pp. 434, 429.

[3] B. Segni, iii, p. 327; Lorenzo married Niccolo's sister, Camilla, P. Litta, vol. x, tav. xiv.

[4] F. Machiavelli, *Lettere*, ed. F. Gaeta, p. 245; R. von Albertini, pp. 424, 425, 450.

Perhaps the rejection of this pension coincided with the acceptance of one from Clement VII, but financial dependence on the
pope did not prevent Vettori from turning against him in 1527.
The pension he received from 1530 onwards must be interpreted as a salary from Clement VII when he went into
voluntary exile and joined the papal court during the siege of
Florence. Vettori's attitude to public expenditure was as
stringent as that of the Florentine government: careless of his
own money, he grieved to see his patron's spent unnecessarily.[5]
Consequently, he condemned Leo's extravagance[6] and considered Clement's foreign policy too costly for a pope with
no money;[7] he saved Lorenzo's purse in France and declared
Florence financially unable to join the proposed League against
Charles V in 1525. He proposed reductions in expenditure in
1530 and his poor view of Florence's economy was one of the
considerations which led him to advocate a narrowly-based
government.

Throughout Vettori's career the *ottimati* aimed at preserving
ruling power for themselves; after each political upheaval they
tried to establish a government which would enable them to
occupy an important place. But it is precisely in the type of
government they wanted that the differences can be detected
which led to the fissures in the structure of their class. Thus
Jacopo Salviati consistently favoured a government 'somewhat
more broadly-based' while Benedetto Buondelmonti remained
staunchly pro-Medici. Guicciardini, even at the time of
Alessandro's dukedom, wanted a narrow oligarchy, whereas
Francesco Vettori and Filippo Strozzi were prepared to support
the potential despotism of Lorenzo de' Medici and the actual
despotism of Alessandro's dukedom. After 1534, however,
Filippo Strozzi opposed despotism until his final rebellion and
death whereas in 1537 Guicciardini joined Vettori in establishing what his contemporaries called a tyranny, although Guicciardini at least probably hoped that Cosimo's would be a
limited lordship rather than an absolute one. Although Vettori

[5] B.N.F. G. Capponi, Cassetta 4, I, insert 10, F. Vettori to Lorenzo, 3 March
1518; 'ancora che io sia povero sono molto poco accurato nello spendere el mio ma
quando veggo donare et spendere sanza necessità e denari del patrone mio mene
duole insino all'anima'.

[6] *Sommario*, p. 293, cp., above, p. 78.   [7] *Ibid.*, p. 363.

did not consistently favour a particular type of government certain facts of his career suggest that ideally at least until 1530 he would have liked a narrowly-based oligarchy such as the aristocrats had tried to introduce in the first of the two reforms in December 1494, in which his father had participated, and such as they had attempted to introduce in 1512 and 1527 when Vettori himself had been involved. But in the changed circumstances after 1530 when the Medici in the face of obstinate opposition were reintroduced into Florence with imperial support, Vettori, a realist, saw force and eventually absolute rule as the only way of saving his city and himself from destruction. And he saw more clearly than Guicciardini that in granting Duke Cosimo military protection the aristocrats had defeated themselves. It can, however, be argued that the path pursued by Vettori served his city best, preserving it even though abandoning the aspirations of his class.

Does a study of Vettori as a politician yield an image of him as a person? Many of his private letters exist, as well as letters written to him by friends; judgments on his character of contemporary historians contribute certain facets, yet an intimate picture of him eludes us as a great many personal family letters have probably not been thought worth preserving. That he had the moderation which may stem from lack of passionate convictions, and that he had the flexibility (or, as his enemies might say, the duplicity)[8] required of a successful politician is clear from the fact that he served both the Republic and the Medici and remained so long within the inner circle of power. Careful attention to detail characterizes his investigations into Florentine finance and his political virtue of concern for good administration. No political situation found him unprepared and the many existing memoranda prove the deliberation with which he proceeded at every step. Caution is a key note to his behaviour pattern, stemming from his intelligence and from the timid and easily-cowed personality to which he confesses in his private letters.[9] It is reflected in his passive attitude to the defence of Italian independence from the battle of Pavia to the

---

[8] See Buondelmonti's comment, above, p. 80.
[9] R. von Albertini, p. 440, 444, 446–7; O. Tommasini, ii, p. 1067; cp. N. Machiavelli, *Lettere*, ed. F. Gaeta, p. 476.

sack of Rome, and his not inconsiderable responsibility for his compatriots' loss of civil liberty must be seen in the light of his fears (shared, too, by other Medici *amici*) for the safety of his own position in a vulnerable Medici government which could eventually only be secured by force. But fear must have been strengthened by ambition—not in renaissance eyes a laudable trait[10]—to bring Vettori within the innermost circle of power. 'Ambition follows us even to the grave',[11] he commented some five years before his death and, despite dislike of court life,[12] a disregard for ceremonial and the reluctance he displayed on occasions to accept office, he cannot have been without political appetite. The calculating advice he gave his brother Paolo and the desire he expressed for honour as well as riches do not suggest a man driven to increase his power solely in order to protect himself from the injury of others. One should not, on the other hand, overlook certain Christian and humane principles by which Vettori professed to be guided;[13] such, for example, as the desire which led him in 1512 not to harm Soderini, and the intention reiterated during his last years not to judge or to blame anyone.[14]

Fellow citizens and subsequent historians have frequently wronged Vettori,[15] accusing him of treachery,[16] duplicity and disloyalty[17] and blaming on him a tide of events which no

[10] F. Gilbert, *Machiavelli and Guicciardini*, p. 36.

[11] R. von Albertini, p. 448.

[12] O. Tommasini, ii, p. 1148; N. Machiavelli, *Lettere*, ed. F. Gaeta, p. 270.

[13] R. von Albertini, p. 436; *ibid.*, p. 442; cp. N. Machiavelli, *Lettere*, ed. F. Gaeta, pp. 298, 299.

[14] Above, p. 64; R. von Albertini, p. 449. *Ibid.*, p. 429.

[15] Vettori has not had a good press from modern historians, see A. Reumont, *A.S.I.*, Appendice vi, 1848, p. 263 and the monographs of R. Ridolfi, especially his Life of Niccolò Machiavelli.

[16] Much of the adverse criticism of Vettori relates to his attitude to Florentine liberty especially from 1530 on, see G. Busini, *Lettere*, p. 69; Cardinal Ridolfi's comment, above, p. 274; the eighteenth-century historian, M. Rastrelli (*Storia d'Alessandro de' Medici*, ii, p. 5), however, appreciates Vettori's patriotism and the subtlety of his politics: 'cercava pertanto di indirizzarlo [Alessandro] ove meno ne risultasse il danno della sua Patria . . . e benchè [Vettori] avesse aderito ad imporre il giogo alla Repubblica, erasi accomodato come prudente alle circostanze de' tempi; ed aveva fatta di necessità virtù'.

[17] G. Busini, *Lettere*, p. 69; A. Reumont, *loc. cit.* 'non franco nè leale', and R. Ridolfi's comments on Vettori's relations with Machiavelli, *The Life of Niccolò Machiavelli*, pp. 141ff., 151ff., p. 173, Vettori 'never did anything for Machiavelli'.

politician had the power to stem, overrating his individual
responsibility and doing less than justice to his incessant efforts
to save his city from destruction and to rescue for her as much of
her liberty as he considered compatible with the realities of the
situation. Machiavelli's call for a saviour to redeem Italy from
corruption and to liberate her from the barbarian and Guicciardini's faith in concerted action against the invader were
ideals for which neither renaissance Florence, nor the other
Italian states were either able or prepared to make the necessary
sacrifices. Like many of his less bold and less courageous contemporaries Vettori felt overwhelmed by developments in Italy
after 1494. He saw a divided city with no military forces of her
own facing enemies both within and without. Such was not the
time for playing the lion with tooth and claw but the fox with
cunning and intelligence, reacting to the outcome of events.
This meant the cautious, empirical, opportunist policy which
Vettori personified. It spelt realism not idealism, accepting not
perfecting. Vettori understood the material in which he was
working and he followed the maxim of one of his city's advisers
that 'wise men take what is least bad instead of what is good'.[18]

[18] Cit. F. Gilbert, *Machiavelli and Guicciardini*, p. 33.

ABBREVIATIONS

ARCHIVES, LIBRARIES AND MANUSCRIPT SOURCES

Unless otherwise indicated, all references to archive
material are to the Archivio di Stato, Florence

Arch. Ricasoli	Archivio Ricasoli, Florence
B.M.	British Museum, London
B.N.F.	Biblioteca Nazionale, Florence
B.R.F.	Biblioteca Riccardiana, Florence
B. Cerretani, Dialogo	Dialogo della Mutatione, B.N.F. Ms. Magliab. II, I, 106
Istoria	Istoria Fiorentina, B.N.F. Ms. II, III, 76
Sommario	Sommario e estratto della sua storia scritta in dialogo, B.N.F. Ms. II, IV, 19
C. Strozz.	Carte Strozziane
Cons. e Prat.	Consulte e Pratiche
Dieci, Missive, Legaz. e Comm.	Dieci di Balia, Missive, Legazioni e Commissarie
Otto, Delib.	Otto di Pratica, Deliberazioni, Partiti, Condotte
Otto, Missive, Legaz. e Comm.	Otto di Pratica, Missive, Legazioni e Commissarie
M.A.P.	Mediceo avanti il Principato
Necr. Cirri	Necrologia Cirri, B.N.F.
Parenti, Istorie	Istorie Fiorentine, B.N.F. Ms. II, II, 132, Ms. II, II, 134 and II, IV, 171, have been used.
Signori, Missive, Legaz. e Comm	Signori, Missive, Legazioni e Commissarie
'Vita di Piero Vettori'	Vita di Piero Vettori l'antico scritta di Francesco suo figlio, B.N.F. Ms. Lindau Finaly, 74

PERIODICALS

A.S.I.	Archivio Storico Italiano
E.H.R.	English Historical Review
J.W.C.I.	Journal of the Warburg and Courtauld Institutes

For abbreviations used in referring to Francesco Vettori's published works, see Select Bibliography

SELECT BIBLIOGRAPHY

I. PUBLISHED SOURCES

1. FRANCESCO VETTORI AND HIS FAMILY

(a) *Correspondence and Works*

Albertini, R. von, *Das Florentinische Staatsbewusstsein im Übergang von der Republik zum Prinzipat* (Bern, 1955), pp. 421–54 letters of F. Vettori to Bartolomeo Lanfredini 1527–1533.

Alvisi, E. *Niccolò Machiavelli. Lettere Familiari* (Firenze, 1883).

Gaeta, F. (ed.), *Niccolò Machiavelli. Lettere* (Milano, 1961).

Moretti, A., *Corrispondenza di Niccolò Machiavelli con Francesco Vettori dal 1513 al 1515* (Firenze, 1948).

Ricordo de' Magistrati che io Francesco di Piero di Francesco di Pagolo di Giannozo di Neri di Boccaccio di Vettori ho avuto ed. A. von Reumont in *Archivio Storico Italiano*, Appendice vi (1848), pp. 281–2, cited in text as *Ricordo*.

Vettori, F., *Il Sacco di Roma* in C. Milanesi, *Il Sacco di Roma del MDXXVII. Narrazioni di Contemporanei* (Firenze, 1867), cited in text as *Sacco*.

—, *Sommario della Storia d'Italia dal 1511 al 1527* ed. A. von Reumont in *Archivio Storico Italiano*, Appendice vi (1848), pp. 287–382, cited in text as *Sommario*.

—, *Sommario della Vita di Lorenzo Medici Duca d'Urbino* in O. Tommasini, *La vita e gli scritti di Niccolò Machiavelli*, ii (Rome, 1911), Appendix vi, pp. 1055–63, cited in text as *Vita di Lorenzo*.

—, *Viaggio in Alemagna* (Paris–Florence, 1837), pp. 1–231 cit. in my text as the *Viaggio*; French translation in L. Passy, ii, Appendix i, pp. 45–218.

(b) *Works and Articles relating to Francesco Vettori and his family*

Albertini, R. von, *op. cit.*, pp. 242–60.

Bandini, A., *Memorie per servire alla vita del Senator Pier Vettori* (Livorno, 1756).

Benivieni, A., *Vita di Piero Vettori, l'antico, gentilhuomo fiorentino* (Firenze, 1583).

Croce, B., *Poeti e scrittori del pieno e del tardo Rinascimento*, I (Bari, 1945), Chap. v: Pagine di Francesco Vettori.

Fornaciari, R., 'F. Vettori e la sua legazione in Alemagna' in *Fra il nuovo e l'antico* (Milano, 1908), pp. 165–94.

Gilbert, F., 'Alcuni discorsi di uomini politici fiorentini' in *Archivio Storico Italiano*, ii (1935), pp. 3–24.

—, *Machiavelli and Guicciardini* (Princeton, 1965), Chap. 6, ii.

Guglielmotti, A., *La guerra dei pirati e la marina pontificia*, i (Florence, 1895), lib. iii: Capitano Paolo Vettori, marchese della Gorgona.

Litta, P., *Famiglie Celebri Italiane*, vii (Milano, 1844) Vettori.

Passy, L., *Un ami de Machiavel, François Vettori, sa vie et ses oeuvres* (Paris, 1913-1914), 2 vols. Vol. 2 contains translations of Vettori's dispatches from Germany and the *Viaggio*.

Raccolto delle Azioni di Francesco e di Pagolo Vettori ed. A. von Reumont in *Archivio Storico Italiano*, Appendice vi (1848), pp. 267–80, cited in text as *Raccolto delle Azioni*.

Roth, C., 'I Carteggi volgari di Piero Vettori nel British Museum' in *Rivista storica degli Archivi toscani* (Firenze, 1929).

Verino, U., *De Illustratione Urbis Florentiae* (Paris, 1790).

2. OTHER PUBLISHED SOURCES

Adriani, G., *Istoria de' suoi tempi*, i (Prato, 1822).

Albèri, E., *Relazioni degli ambasciatori veneti al Senato* (Firenze, 1839–63).

Ammirato, S., *Istorie fiorentine*, ed. F. Ranalli, v and vi (Firenze, 1848–49).

Bardi, A., 'Filippo Strozzi' (da nuovi documenti) in *Archivio Storico Italiano*, Series v, xiv (1894) (letters of F. Strozzi).

—, 'Carlo V e l'assedio di Firenze' in *Archivio Storico Italiano*, Series v, xi (1893) (letters of Charles V, etc.).

Buonaccorsi, B., *Diario* (Firenze, 1568).

Busini, G., *Lettere di Giovanni Battista Busini a Benedetto Varchi sugli avvenimenti dell' Assedio di Firenze* (Pisa, 1822).

Brewer, J., *Letters and Papers, foreign and domestic, of the reign of Henry VIII*, iv, part III, 1529–30 (London, 1876).

Calendar of Letters, Despatches and State Papers relating to the Negotiations between England and Spain, ed. G. Bergenroth, ii–iii (London, 1866–77).

Cambi, G., *Istorie fiorentine*, ed. I. di San Luigi in *Delizie degli eruditi toscani*, xxi and xxii (Firenze, 1785–86).

Canestrini, G., Desjardins, A., *Négociations diplomatiques de la France avec la Toscane*, i and ii (Paris, 1859–61).

Cantini, L., *Legislazione Toscana*, i (Firenze, 1800).

Carnesecchi, B., 'L'Assedio di Firenze' in *Studi Storici*, xiv (Pisa, 1905).

Dumont, J., *Corps universel diplomatique*, iv and v (Amsterdam–Hague, 1726–1729).

Giannotti, D., *Opere politiche e letterarie*, ed. F.-L. Polidori (Firenze, 1850), 2 vols.

—, *Della Repubblica fiorentina* (Venezia, 1721).

Glay, A. le, *Correspondance de l'Empereur Maximilien et Marguerite d'Autriche* (Paris, 1839).

Guicciardini, F., *Carteggi*, i–iv, ed. R. Palmarocchi, v ed. P. G. Ricci in *Fonti per la Storia d'Italia* (Bologna, 1938, etc.).

—, *Dialogo del Reggimento di Firenze*, ed. R. Palmarocchi (Bari, 1932).

—, 'Ricordanze' in *Scritti Autobiografici e Rari*, ed. R. Palmarocchi (Bari, 1936).

—, *Scritti Politici e Ricordi*, ed. R. Palmarocchi (Bari, 1933).

—, *Storie fiorentine*, ed. R. Palmarocchi (Bari, 1931).

—, *Opere inedite*, ed. G. Canestrini (Firenze, 1857–67).

—, *La Storia d'Italia*, ed. C. Panigada (Bari, 1967), 5 vols., cited in text as *St. d'It.*

Janssen, J., *Frankfurts Reichscorrespondenz* (Frankfort, 1863–72).

Landucci, L., *Diario Fiorentino dal 1450 al 1516*, ed. I. del Badia (Firenze, 1883).

—, *A Florentine Diary*, trans. A. de Rosen Jervis (London, 1927).

Machiavelli, N., *Niccolò Machiavelli. Lettere* ed. F. Gaeta (Milano, 1961).

—, *Legazioni e commissarie*, ed. S. Bertelli, ii (Milano, 1964).

—, *Il Principe*, ed. A. Burd (Oxford, 1891).

—, *Le Opere*, ed. P. Fanfani and L. Passerini (Firenze, 1873, etc.).

—, *Opere Minore*, ed. F. Polidori (Firenze, 1852).

—, *Tutte le Opere di Niccolò Machiavelli*, ed. G. Mazzoni and M. Casella (Firenze, 1929).

Masi, B., *Ricordanze*, ed. G. Corazzini (Firenze, 1906).

Nardi, J., *Istorie di Firenze*, ed. A. Gelli (Firenze, 1858).

Nerli, F., *Commentari de' fatti civili occorsi dentro la città di Firenze dall' anno 1215 al 1537* (Augusta, 1727).

Pitti, J., 'Istoria Fiorentina' in *Archivio Storico Italiano*, i (1842).

—, 'Apologia de' Cappucci' in *Archivio Storico Italiano*, iv, part 2 (Firenze, 1853).

Romano, G. (ed.), *Cronaca del soggiorno di Carlo V in Italia* (Milano, 1892).

Ruscelli, G., *Lettere di Principi* (Venezia, 1564–7), 3 vols.

Sanuto, M., *Diarii* (Venezia, 1879–1902).

Segni, B., *Storie fiorentine*, ed. Classici Italiani (Milano, 1805), 3 vols.

—, *Vita di Niccolò Capponi, ibid.*, iii.

Spannocchi, G., letters, ed. C. Paoli and E. Casanova in 'Cosimo I de' Medici ed i fuorosciti del 1537', *Archivio Storico Italiano*, Series V, xi (1893).

Varchi, B., *Storia Fiorentina*, ed. L. Arbib (Firenze, 1838–41).

II. SECONDARY AUTHORITIES

Albèri, E., *L'Assedio di Firenze* (Firenze, 1840).

Albertini, R. von, *Das Florentinische Staatsbewusstsein im Übergang von der Republik zum Prinzipat* (Bern, 1955).

Anzilotti, A., *La crisi costituzionale della Repubblica fiorentina* (Firenze, 1912).

Armstrong, E., *The Emperor Charles V* (London, 1902), 2 vols.

Bertelli, S., 'Carteggi Machiavelliani' in *Clio*, April–Sept. 1966.

Bridge, J., *A History of France* (Oxford, 1921–29), 4 vols.

Caggese, R., *Firenze dalla Decadenza di Roma al Risorgimento d'Italia* (Firenze, 1912–21), 3 vols.

Cantimori, D., 'Rhetoric and Politics in Italian Humanism' in *Journal of the Warburg and Courtauld Institutes*, i, 1937–38.

Capponi, G., *Storia della Repubblica di Firenze* (Firenze, 1875), 2 vols.

Cosenza, M., *Biographical and Bibliographical Dictionary of the Italian Humanists and of the World of Classical Scholarship in Italy 1300–1800* (Boston, 1962).

De Leva, G., *Storia documentata di Carlo V* (Venezia, Padova, Bologna, 1863–1894), 5 vols.

Dupré Theseider, E., *Niccolò Machiavelli diplomatico* (Como, 1945).

Falletti-Fossati, P., *L'Assedio di Firenze* (Palermo, 1885), 2 vols.

Ferrai, L., *Cosimo de' Medici, Duca di Firenze* (Bologna, 1882).

—, *Lorenzino de' Medici e la Società Cortigiana del Cinquecento* (Milano, 1891).

Filippi, G., *L'Arte dei Mercanti di Calimala in Firenze* (Torino, 1889).

Francesco Ferruccio e la guerra di Firenze (Firenze, 1889).

Gilbert, F., 'Alcuni discorsi di uomini politici fiorentini', etc. in *Archivio Storico Italiano*, xciii, 2 (1935).

—, 'Bernardo Rucellai and the Orti Oricellari: A study on the origin of modern political thought' in *Journal of the Warburg and Courtauld Institutes*, xii (1949).

—, 'Florentine Political Assumptions in the period of Savonarola and Soderini' in *Journal of the Warburg and Courtauld Institutes*, xx (1957.)

—, *Machiavelli and Guicciardini* (Princeton, N. J., 1965).

—, 'The Venetian Constitution' in N. Rubinstein (ed.), *Florentine Studies* (London, 1968).

Giorgetti, A., 'Lorenzo de' Medici Duca d'Urbino e Jacopo V d'Appiano' in *Archivio Storico Italiano*, Series IV, viii (1881).

—, 'Lorenzo de' Medici, Capitano della Repubblica fiorentina' in *Archivio Storico Italiano*, Series IV, xi (1883).

Hale, J., 'The End of Florentine Liberty: The Fortezza Da Basso' in *Florentine Studies*, ed. N. Rubinstein (London, 1968).

—, *Machiavelli and Renaissance Italy* (London, 1961).

Devonshire Jones, R., 'Francesco Vettori and Niccolò Machiavelli' in *Italian Studies*, xxiii (1968).

Kristeller, P., 'Un uomo di stato e umanista fiorentino, Giovanni Corsi' in *La Bibliofilia*, xxxviii (1936).

Lupo Gentile, M., 'Studi sulla storiografia fiorentina alla corte di Cosimo I de' Medici' in *Annali della R. Scuola Normale Superiore di Pisa*, xix (1906).

Madelin, L., *France et Rome. La Pragmatique Sanction* (Paris, 1913).

Mallett, P., 'Pisa and Florence in the Fifteenth Century: Aspects of the Period of the First Florentine Dominion' in *Florentine Studies*, ed. N. Rubinstein (London, 1968).

Mansfield, M., *A family of decent folk (Lanfredini) 1200–1741* (Florence, 1922).

Mattingly, G., *Renaissance Diplomacy* (London, 1955).

Maulde-La-Clavière, M. de, *La diplomatie au temps de Machiavel* (Paris, 1892).

Mazzoni, G. (ed.), *Le Opere di Giovanni Rucellai* (Bologna, 1887).

Mignet, F., *La Rivalité de François I et de Charles Quint* (Paris, 1875).

Niccolini, G.-B., *Filippo Strozzi, tragedia* (Firenze, 1847), including the *Vita di Filippo Strozzi* by Lorenzo Strozzi.

Nitti, F., *Leone X e la sua politica secondo documenti e carteggi inediti* (Firenze, 1892).

Otetea, A., *Dall'Assedio di Firenze al secondo convegno di Clemente VII e Carlo V* (Aquila, 1927).

—, *François Guichardin, sa vie publique et sa pensée politique* (Paris, 1926).

Paoli, C., *La sconfitta dei fuoroscitti fiorentini a Montemurlo*, notizie, etc. (Firenze, 1876).

Paoli, C., and Casanova, E., 'Cosimo I de' Medici ed i fuorosciti del 1537, da lettere di due oratori senesi' in *Archivio Storico Italiano*, Series V, xi (1893).

Paschini, P., *Roma nel Rinascimento* (Bologna, 1940).

Passerini, L., *Genealogia e Storia della Famiglia Rucellai* (Firenze, 1861).

Pastor, L., *History of the Popes*, v–x (London, 1898–1910).

Picotti, G., *La giovinezza di Leone X* (Milano, 1928).

Rastrelli, M., *Storia d'Alessandro de' Medici* (Firenze, 1781), 2 vols.

Razzi, G., *Vita di P. Soderini gonfaloniere* (Padua, 1737).

Reinhard, H., *Lorenzo von Medici, Herzog von Urbino* (Freiburg, 1935).

Renaudet, A., *Le concile gallican de Pise-Milan* (Paris, 1922).

Repetti, E., *Dizionario Geografico Fisico Storico della Toscana* (Firenze, 1835).

Reumont, A. von, *La diplomazia italiana dal secolo xiii al xvi* (Firenze, 1857).

—, *La jeunesse de Cathérine de Medici*, trans. A. Baschet (Paris, 1866).

Richards, G., *Florentine Merchants in the Age of the Medici* (Cambridge, Mass., 1932).

Ridolfi, R., *Gli archivi delle famiglie fiorentine* (Firenze, 1934).

—, *The Life of Francesco Guicciardini* (London, 1967).

—, *The Life of Niccolò Machiavelli* (London, 1963).

—, 'Nuovi contributi alla biografia del Giannotti' in *Rivista Storica degli Archivi Toscani*, i (1929).

Roover, R. de, *The Rise and Decline of the Medici Bank* (New York, 1966).

Roscoe, W., *Life and Pontificate of Leo X* (London, 1827), 4 vols.

Rossi, A., 'La elezione di Cosimo I Medici' in *Atti del R. Istituto Veneto di Scienze, Lettere ed Arti*, Series VII, i (1889–90).

—, *Francesco Guicciardini e il governo fiorentino dal 1527 al 1540* (Bologna 1896–1899), 2 vols.

Roth, C., *The Last Florentine Republic* (London, 1925).

Rubinstein, N., 'Firenze e il problema della politica imperiale al tempo di Massimiliano I' in *Archivio Storico Italiano*, cxvi (1958), Disp. I and II.

— (ed.), *Florentine Studies* (London, 1968).

—, *The Government of Florence under the Medici* (Oxford, 1966).

Sasso, G., *Niccolò Machiavelli: Storia del suo pensiero politico* (Napoli, 1958).

Spini, G., *Cosimo I de' Medici e la indipendenza del principato mediceo* (Firenze, 1945).

—, *Tra rinascimento e riforma. Antonio Brucioli* (Firenze, 1940).

Starn, R., *Donato Giannotti and his Epistolae* (Travaux d'humanisme et Renaissance, 97 (Geneva, 1968).

Tommasini, O., *La vita e gli scritti di Niccolò Machiavelli*, i (Rome–Turin–Florence, 1883), ii (Roma, 1911).

Tucker, M., 'Gian Matteo Giberti, Papal Politician and Catholic Reformer' in *English Historical Review*, xviii (1903).

Verdi, A., *Gli ultimi anni di Lorenzo de' Medici, Duca d'Urbino* (Este, 1905).

Villari, P., *The Life and Times of Niccolò Machiavelli*, trans. L. Villari (London, sd.).

Wolff, M. von, *Die Beziehungen Kaiser Maximilians I zu Italien, 1495–1508* (Innsbruck, 1909).

Zeffi, F., 'Vita di Lorenzo Strozzi' in *Le vite degli uomini illustri della casa Strozzi* (Firenze, 1892).

Zobi, A., *Delle nozze del Magnifico Giuliano de' Medici con la principessa Filiberta di Savoia* (Firenze, 1868).

INDEX